2303

THE
ROMAN
EMPIRE

John Wacher

BARNES
&NOBLE
BOOKS
NEW YORK

To Sarah

Text copyright © 1987 by John Wacher
Illustrations copyright © 1987 by J. M. Dent & Sons Ltd

This edition published by Barnes & Noble, Inc.,
by arrangement with The Orion Publishing Group Ltd

1997 Barnes & Noble Books

ISBN 0-76070-438-4

Printed and bound in the United States of America

97 98 99 00 01 M 9 8 7 6 5 4 3 2 1

BVG

CONTENTS

LIST OF ILLUSTRATIONS

iii

PREFACE – AN APOLOGIA

The Roman Empire is one of the success stories of history, outlasting all others in time, if not in extent. Consequently, it is worthy of study for many reasons. Most studies have tended to concentrate on what might be called the 'ancient historical' context, with the emphasis on Roman culture, law, society and people; most also tend to view the provinces, especially those most distant from the centre, as not really worth bothering about. By adding a strong archaeological vein to the ancient history and by taking most sources from the provinces and not from Italy, this book has attempted to redress the balance.

The format is simple. An attempt is made to seek the roots of the Empire in the Roman Republic, from which it sprang – not fully armed, but with difficult contortions. The Empire at war, in both success and defeat, leads naturally to a consideration of its frontiers. The basic requirements of law and government in any society next successively introduce urban, rural, economic and religious life. Two chapters on the eastern and western provinces give a compressed sketch of each. Finally, the Empire in all its disarray during its civil wars and barbarian invasions completes the picture. The illustrations are restricted to line drawings which have been prepared specially to advance the text. The cost of plates is now so high and the difficulty of finding illustrations that have not been endlessly used before is so great, that they have been deliberately dispensed with.

The subject is immense; the cover all too inadequate. The writer is well aware of this and that the balance struck is unlikely to please all readers, for which he apologises in advance.

That said, he would like to thank the following for their unstinted help: Professor Peter Wiseman for reading and much improving the original draft of Chapter 1; Mrs Cheryl McCormick for her, as usual, impeccable and speedy typing; Mr Andy Clark for his excellent illustrations.

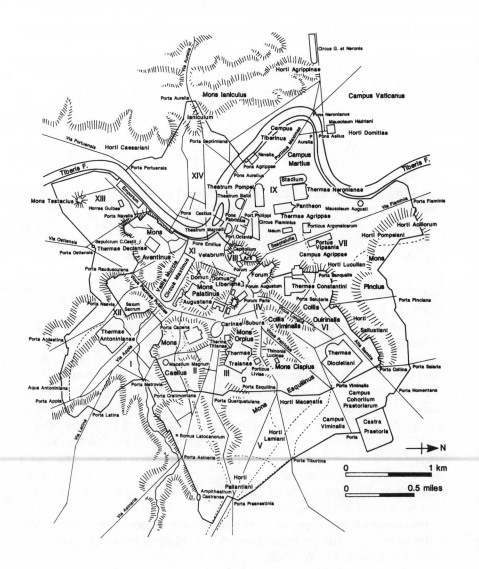

Circus G. et Neronis

Horti Agrippinae

Mons Ianiculus

Porta Aurelia

Campus Vaticanus

Ianiculum

Pons Neronianus
Mausoleum Hadriani

Horti Domitiae

Campus
Tiberinus

Porta Septimiana

P Pons Aelius
Aurelia

Via Portuensis

Horti Caesariani

Navalia
Pons Agrippae

Campus
Martius

Porta Portuensis

Pons Aurelius

Tiberis F.

Tiberis F.

XIV

Theatrum Pompei
Theatrum Balbi

IX

Stadium

Thermae Neronianae

Mons Testaclus

XIII

Horrea Gulbae
Porta Navalis

Pons Cestius

Pantheon

Mausoleum Augusti

Via Flaminia

Porta Flaminia

Pons
Fabricia

Port. Philippi
Circus Flaminius
Iseum

Thermae Agrippae

Porticus Argonaicarum

Horti Aciliorum

Horti Pompeiani

Emporium

Mons

Theatrum Marcelli

Pons Emilius

Port.Octaviae

Saepta Iulia

Portus
Vipsania

VII

Via Ostiensis

Sepulcrum C.Cestii
Thermae Decianae

Aventinus

Pons Aemilius

Capitolium
Velabrum
VIII

Campus Agrippae

Mons

Porta Ostiensis

XI

Ark

Horti Luculliani

Porta Radusculana

Domus
Domus
Liberiana
Mons
Palatinus
Augustana

Forum
Forum Augustum
Forum Pacis

Thermae Constantini

Porta Sanqualis

Pinclus

Porta Naevia

XII

Saxum
Sacrum

Carinae Subura

Collis
Viminalis

Porta Salutaris

Collis
Quirinalis

VI

Horti

Porta Pinciana

Thermae
Antoninianae

Porta Capena

Mons
Orpius

Mons

Thinonis
Lucinae

Horti
Sallustiani

Alta Semita

Porta Ardeatina

Porta Metrovia

Macellum Magnum

Caellus

II

Thermae
Titianae
Thermae

III

Porticus
Livias

Traiana

Thinonis
Lucinae

Mons Cispius

Thermae
Diocletiani

Porta Collina

Porta Salaria

Porta Appia

Aqua Antoniniana

Porta Appia

I

Mons

Porta Crelimontana

Porta Esquilina

Esquilinus

Porta Viminalis
Campus
Cohortium
Praetoriarum

Porta Nomentana

Porta Latina

Porta Latina

Bonus Latocanorum

Porta Querquetulana

Horti Macenatis

Mons

V

Campus
Viminalis

Castra
Praetoria

Porta

Via Asinaria

Porta Asinaria

Horti
Pallantiani
Ampitheatrum
Castrense

Porta Praenestinia

Horti
Lamiani

Porta Tiburtina

N

0   1 km

0   0.5 miles

I

THE END OF THE REPUBLIC

When Tacitus, in his second major work, the *Annals*, related the history of early imperial Rome, he was separated by nearly 150 years from the events which saw the end of the Republic and the establishment of the principate. He was thus able to view the period from a better perspective and with greater detachment than some other earlier authors and in a short and somewhat laconic account he summarises the rise of Augustus in a way so adequate that parts are worth quoting:

> The City of Rome's earliest rulers were kings. Lucius Junius Brutus then formed the consulate and the free republican institutions; dictators took charge in emergencies. Control by the Council of Ten only lasted two years and was followed by an ephemeral arrangement under which senior army officers were given consular authority. Afterwards Cinna and Sulla briefly set up autocracies. Pompey and Crassus soon prevailed, but were outmatched by Caesar. Then the military power which had supported Lepidus and Antony was assimilated by Augustus. He found the whole state worn out by internal strife and established over it his personal rule as princeps. . . .
> With the deaths of Brutus and Cassius, the republican army disintegrated. Sextus Pompeius was defeated in Sicily, Lepidus was deprived of power and Antony was killed; only Octavius Caesar survived to lead the Caesarian faction. He ceased to use the title of triumvir, while at the same time placing greater emphasis on his consular status and also availing himself of the powers of a people's tribune. He ensured the loyalty of the army with extra payments and of civilians with cheap grain; the ensuing peace appealed to everyone, whose support he thus obtained. He then gradually concentrated the functions of the Senate, the magistrates and the law in his own hands. There was no opposition since war

1

and execution had removed those who might have resisted. Surviving patricians found that implicit obedience secured greater political and financial rewards, so that, having profited from the upheaval, they preferred the security which was offered. Moreover, the new dispositions were welcomed in the provinces, where government by the Senate and the people had caused dismay, owing to the quarrels of the powerful and the greed of the officials. Even legal remedies were denied them, as violence, manipulation and, decisively, bribery had flourished.

Tacitus then goes on to note that all was calm in Rome, that officials retained their old titles and that by then practically no one had ever seen a proper republican government in operation, as it had been entirely transformed and nothing was left of the good old days. Stripped of all equality, everyone hung upon the orders of the princeps.

In a few hundred words, Tacitus dismissed the Republic, though he appeared to regret its passing, and he placed his finger neatly on the salient points which caused its demise. But perhaps even in a book to be devoted primarily to the Roman Empire, we should not be so ready to do likewise, for the Republic saw the fashioning of many institutions which, even though they were radically altered under the principate, became an integral part of that Empire. Moreover, it must be remembered that much of the territorial expansion took place under the Republic.

The precise date at which Rome was founded is a matter for argument; tradition has it that it was 21 April 753 BC, but this tradition is unreliable. Even the date of the foundation of the Republic is uncertain, but again tradition says, and we have no strong reasons to disagree, that it came about during the late sixth century BC after the last of the Roman kings, the tyrant Tarquinius Superbus, had been banished. He was replaced by the first consuls, L. Junius Brutus and Tarquinius Collatinus. Its birth was not without difficulties and for some years it was threatened by Etruscans, under whose rule Rome had been. The Republic, however, disposed of the Etruscan threat by making alliances with the cities of Latium, which, according to tradition, had been previously dominated by Rome by which they were now to be treated as equals.

The two consuls were appointed annually from the patrician families who formed a predominantly land-owning aristocracy. The pair had less power than the old-time kings, but they acted as chief magistrates and executive officers of the state. Behind them was the Senate, an advisory council composed primarily of leading members from the same social class. It numbered about a hundred, although it was later enlarged considerably, and it ensured a measure of continuity in the government. Later, also, subsidiary magistrates were appointed, such as praetors, aediles, quaestors and censors, who took over some of the consuls' lesser duties, such as the maintenance of law and order, the upkeep of public buildings and roads, the care of financial matters, and the taking of the census of the population, by which taxes were levied and army service defined. When serious danger threatened the state from any quarter, the consuls could appoint a dictator for a term of six months, who was vested with absolute power.

The common people of Rome also developed various organisations. Basically they were arranged in tribes which by 241 BC had reached 35 in number, with four being urban and the rest rural. Other divisions into classes were introduced for military reasons, each class representing, to a different degree, the quantity and quality of arms that its members carried to war; so were born the centuries of the future imperial army. Later these divisions were related to the tribes. From them developed in turn a new political assembly called the *Comitia Centuriata*, which gradually increased in importance and assumed many of the functions of the older *Comitia Curiata*, which had, presumably until then, been the main political body of the common people, although little is known about it.

Throughout the time of the Republic there was a continuing struggle between the common people who were, when all is said and done, also Roman citizens and the patricians, towards which the formation of some plebeian assemblies forced the issue. Livy referred to 'two states in one'. Even by the early fifth century, soon after the foundation of the Republic, the patricians had been forced to recognise the two tribunes of the people, from which recognition came the formation of the *Consilium Plebis*. This council had restricted authority, but under the lead of the tribunes it could pass resolutions which strictly at first applied only to the plebeians. The subsequent attempts to make these decisions binding on the whole population lay at the centre of the continuing friction between them and the patricians. Originally two tribunes were appointed, and they presided over the council, convened its meetings and carried out its decisions, but by the middle of the fifth century the number appears to have been increased to ten. The most significant power they possessed was the ability to intervene in a dispute between the magistrates and the people, so acting as a buffer and checking possible abuses of the processes of law by the magistrates in the arbitrary execution of their duty. Ultimately their rights were extended to the point where they were able to halt all the processes of government by a simple veto. Consequently, clashes were frequent between consuls and tribunes. One of the results was the suspension of the constitutional order in 451 BC and its replacement by a Council of Ten, all of whom were at first drawn from among the patricians. These *Decemviri* were responsible, among other matters, for beginning the codification of the earliest Roman laws and in the following year, under another Ten, which this time included plebeians, the Law of the Twelve

Tables was completed. Unfortunately the moderation first practised by this new system of government gave way to oppression and by 449 BC the *Decemviri* had been dismissed and the original constitution restored. But an important concession had been gained by the people; the patricians were henceforth compelled to recognise in law what had hitherto been conceded only by custom: the rights of the tribunes.

The remainder of the fifth century BC saw the struggle between patricians and plebeians continuing, in which the former attempted, not without some success, to retain their complete control of the affairs of state. In order to do so, new but lesser magistracies were introduced to carry out some of the duties of the consuls; special censors were appointed to keep the roll of citizens, and quaestors became charged with financial affairs. Plebeians, however, could be candidates for quaestorial office, and by the time of Sulla the position came to be the first step of a career structure leading ultimately to a seat in the Senate and so to the office of consul.

During the formative years of the Republic, and despite the internal frictions, Rome was required to fight a series of wars against her neighbours in Etruria, Latium and beyond. But the partial collapse of Etruscan power together with treaties made with the Latin cities enabled Rome to resist the pressures building up from further afield among the Sabines, the Volsci and the Aequi, and later the Veii. The combined strength of Rome and her Latin allies was sufficient, however, to defeat these enemies, so producing territorial gains. Most of the conquered lands, though, fell at first to the Latins, who founded colonies of citizens in them, and Rome profited little. Consequently when Rome at last acquired territory it was usually closer to the city, whereas the newly-colonised Latin lands were scattered over a considerable area; unified action was therefore difficult for them. Hence in time Rome achieved a greater ascendancy over the alliance, since they were able to provide military assistance more easily and quickly than the widely-dispersed Latin forces. But by the end of the fifth century a greater menace appeared to threaten all alike. Land-hunger in central Europe caused massive and violent migrations of Celts southwards and westwards. A huge tribal army, said to have numbered between 30,000 and 70,000 men, swept down the Italian peninsula. Against it Rome, even with her allies, could only marshall less than half that number. The city was besieged for seven months and partly sacked, although it is recorded that a party on the Capitoline hill held out, thanks to the famous geese.

After this defeat, Rome declined in influence among her allies, but the threat of further Celtic action in Italy brought about a closing of the ranks. Rome herself had gained much good experience in dealing with the opposing army, and, after the Celts had withdrawn, proceeded to rebuild the damaged city and put in hand various reforms. Foremost among the building works, started *c.* 380 BC, was the construction of the first masonry fortifications, a wall 3.66 m thick and 7.32 m high, backed by a massive bank, which enclosed the whole city within a perimeter of 8.86 km. The Celtic attack had also highlighted the weaknesses of the Roman army, hitherto composed entirely of citizens who were called for service when need arose. As we have already seen, the army was originally organised on a tribal basis, each tribe providing its quota of men, every one of whom had to provide equipment and weapons appropriate to his personal wealth and property. Thus the cavalry were composed of *equites*, or knights, who were expected to mount and arm themselves. The duty of calling out the army lay with the consuls, who also called for levies from Rome's allies according to the terms laid down in the treaties. They supervised all the preparations for war and then conducted the campaigns, so that their power was equally divided between civil administration and military government; to the Roman it was as one. Such a citizen army was normally adequate for home defence and it could take some limited action further afield, but it was altogether incapable of dealing with an enemy force of the size gathered by the Celts. Indeed, the first stage of reform towards a full-time professional army, which recognised this shortcoming, had already been introduced during the siege of Veii, before the Celts arrived in Italy, when soldiers were paid in order to retain their services in the field. Further reorganisation followed the Celtic invasion which both increased the number of men under arms and altered the tactical arrangements in battle.

After the Celtic episode there comes a confused period when, once more, Rome's traditional enemies, such as the Etruscans and Aequi, took advantage of the city's weakness. Gradually, however, with the aid of those Latin allies who remained loyal, the situation improved and Rome was able to enjoy a short period of peace. It was but a respite; external warfare was replaced by internal dissent, when the plebeians yet again attempted to increase their power at the expense of the patricians. More concessions followed and these became enshrined in the Licinio-Sextian laws, which created greater social unity and ensured some economic improvement by opening all the magisterial offices to the plebeians. The functions of the civilian administration were also widened and improved by the appointment of additional magistrates: the praetors and aediles. But perhaps the most important of the new institutions was brought about partly by a period of diplomacy and partly by a short and successful war against Rome's former allies, which foreshadowed the relationship that was ultimately to develop with her future provinces. Rome now became the acknowledged leader of the Latin states, and in return extended her own citizenship to their people. Although new treaties were imposed on them, they were allowed to retain their local autonomy; levies of troops had still to be provided but foreign policy became the prerogative of Rome. Among other treaties gained were those with Carthage in 348 BC, the Etruscans in 343 BC and, after further Celtic incursions, with the Gaulish tribe of the Senones in *c.* 330 BC.

The period also saw the expansion of Rome's interests in Campania and the first of the wars against the Samnites in the hills of central Italy. Two further wars against this tribe were necessary before they were finally subdued, so allowing a confederation to take place of all the tribes in central Italy. Rome's influence in the confederation was paramount and was enhanced by the establishment of colonies of citizens at crucial places, as the Latins had done before. Allotments of land were given to the settlers; in return they were expected to defend their area from attack, and in many cases full urban communities developed, so setting the seal on a political institution which was to play a decisive part in the later pacification of a vast Empire. Some of these settlements retained full Roman citizenship, others were given Latin status. The construction of good roads to link the city with its colonies became a necessity, while within Rome itself the processes of both civil and military administration were made more efficient to cope with the increasing demands now placed upon it.

The simultaneous extension of Roman interest into southern Italy, where it conflicted with the established, but embattled Greek colonies, led to the Pyrrhic war in the early third century BC. A clash between the forces of Rome and Tarentum caused the latter to seek the help of King Pyrrhus of Epirus, who arrived in southern Italy with a professional army of some 25,000 men and a troop of elephants. The first engagement ended in a victory for Pyrrhus, causing heavy casualties on both sides, and was then followed by a period of extensive manoeuvring and indecisive battles, during which the king at one point turned towards Sicily with a view to withdrawing from Italy. His intention, however, brought immediate protest from Carthage, who, with strong Sicilian interests, invoked their treaty with Rome and offered ships and money to prevent Rome from making peace with Pyrrhus. On returning from his Sicilian adventure, Pyrrhus was defeated by the Carthaginian fleet, but was nevertheless able to inflict more damage in southern Italy before finally retiring with his army to Greece in the face of superior Roman forces.

The ability of Rome to withstand the attack of a professional army demonstrated to the ancient world the position of military and political strength which she now held and so enabled her to absorb the Hellenistic cities of the south. Tarentum, as a punishment for the Pyrrhic episode, received the first regular outlying garrison of Roman troops, set there partly to guard the south against another Greek invasion. These moves also brought inevitably nearer the time when Roman interests would clash with those of Carthage, for Roman power had replaced the declining Greek influence in the south, and for the first time Italy, from the river Arno southwards, was incorporated as a Roman confederacy.

The Carthaginian empire had expanded considerably in the preceding centuries until by the mid-fourth century BC it embraced much of the north African coast as well as parts of Spain and Sicily. The early treaties which had been made with Rome contained a strong commercial element and in consequence Roman traders were severely restricted in their movements. Later treaties seem to have made greater attempts to define respective spheres of interest but none appears specifically to have anticipated the provision of military aid, so the involvement of Carthage in the Pyrrhic war should be seen as something exceptional. The first clash between the two powers came in 264 BC, in the Straits of Messina, and was followed by the Roman invasion of Sicily. After over twenty years of campaigning with fluctuating fortunes, Rome, so far an essentially land-based nation, was able, by the construction of a massive fleet, to defeat the maritime Carthaginians in their own element. The victory in the first Punic War gained Rome the islands of Sicily, Sardinia and Corsica, the first overseas provinces, and showed her also the benefits of naval power. The first Roman dealings with Sicily illustrate, in addition, the flexibility of approach which later was to be such a marked and successful feature of her provincial government. Although a praetor was ultimately sent to the new province as a governor and a system of tribute enforced on much of the population, some cities, such as Syracuse and Messana, remained exempt from taxes because of the existence of earlier alliances. In Syracuse especially, an alliance with King Hiero survived until his death and fore-shadowed the system whereby client kings, who were to make their appearance in greater number at a later date, were used to rule friendly territories so as to economise on Roman manpower. In fact the system of taxation which was enforced on the tribute part of the population of Sicily was based on that used by Hiero; it was levied as a percentage on agricultural produce, while excise duties were also collected at harbours. Local authorities were made responsible for delivering the assessed amounts. So from these small begin-nings developed the whole system of Roman provincial administration with its military, legal and financial responsibilities.

But Carthage, although defeated, was not vanquished. Deprived of her possessions in the central Mediterranean, she turned with renewed effort to Spain, which increased the risk of a conflict with the ancient Greek colony of Massilia in southern France. Massilia was not only an ally of Rome but also had important trade links with some Spanish towns. Rome was soon ranged on the side of Massilia and when Saguntum, with which there were strong connections, was captured by Hannibal, war became certain. The second Punic War started in 218 BC and lasted for seventeen years, during which time the armies of Hannibal attacked Italy from the north, operations were reopened in Sicily and Philip V of Macedon was induced to enter the war on the side of Carthage. Yet, despite his victories in the field over the

Roman armies, Hannibal was unable, like Pyrrhus before him, to break the solid core of Roman resistance in central Italy. In retaliation, Rome first recaptured cities in northern Italy and in Sicily, and then negotiated a peace with the Macedonians. Next Scipio Africanus defeated a Carthaginian army in southern Spain and, by transferring his operations to Africa, forced Hannibal to break off the war in Italy. Finally he defeated Hannibal at the battle of Zama. Carthage was stripped of all her overseas possessions and interests, but remained an autonomous client state, and Roman control of parts of Spain and of Cisalpine Gaul was consolidated if not finally completed.

There can be little doubt that Rome's forced and successful involvement in an overseas war against Carthage gave her the appetite for further conquests, and the participation of Philip of Macedon was perhaps partly the reason why she next turned her attention to the east, where an alliance existed between Philip and Antiochus, the powerful king of Syria. An element of paranoia can possibly be detected in most of Rome's early conquests and the lurking threat of this eastern alliance, recalling the recent struggles with Carthage, may perhaps have prompted the subsequent action: 'he was going to hit me, so I hit him first'; it was a precept that Rome was to follow increasingly over ensuing years. In the wars that followed, Rome was undoubtedly aided by the petty squabbles of the Greek cities, which she effectively reduced to the status of subject allies. The Macedonian kingdom was destroyed and the Syrians were ejected from both Asia Minor and Egypt. But the settlement in the east was followed, after only a short period of peace, by renewed hostilities in Spain, and indeed, for the next few centuries, Rome was seldom not engaged in warfare in one place or another. Apart from Spain, there were further involvements in Greece, Illyria, Asia and Africa, during which both the cities of Carthage and Corinth were sacked and destroyed. Macedonia and Africa were reduced to the status of provinces.

But this almost unceasing warfare took place against a background of social and political upheaval in Rome itself. The short period of peace after the defeat of Antiochus of Syria was used for the replenishment of the treasury out of the spoils of war. Almost empty at the close of the second Punic War, it was now able to repay the war tax which had been imposed on the people. The wars had also brought much personal wealth to many people as well as providing an almost inexhaustible supply of slaves. The economic expansion which followed was considerable. Large estates grew up, using the copious source of cheap labour, and helped to supply the rapidly increasing urban markets.

Such developments, however, first unsettled and then diminished the free rural peasantry and consequently must have caused something of a social upheaval. An expulsion of non-citizens and then Latins from Rome followed. More importantly, we see in 171 BC, for the first time, two consuls of plebeian origin being voted into office. Yet despite this change, the Roman nobility, recruited from both patrician and plebeian sources, still held power through the Senate, which had in many matters retained direct control of public affairs. But state policy, or the lack of it, could not keep pace with the scale of expansion, either internally or externally. Among the difficulties which had to be faced was the problem of army recruitment. Although by the mid-second century BC Rome was a major colonial power, needing permanent garrisons in the provinces, the army was still only supplied by the levies of men of appropriate age and wealth. It was not until Marius became consul in 107 BC that a reform was introduced by which long-service volunteers without property were accepted as recruits. Land reforms were also needed and carried through against stiff opposition. There was increasing insistence from the growing class of often wealthy *equites*, the class immediately below the senatorial order in the Roman hierarchy, for more involvement in the running of the state.

The fabric of Roman and Italian society could not withstand the pressures being generated. The failure of an attempt to gain full Roman citizenship for the Italian allies led to their revolt and the start of a civil war, which was only decided some years later by a combination of Roman compromise and military success. The war not only brought Marius back into prominence but also introduced Sulla as one of the most successful Roman generals, and what had begun as a conflict with Italian allies now became an internal battle in Rome itself, complicated by the war which broke out with King Mithridates of Pontus. First Sulla was given command of the army in the east, where he reduced Mithridates to impotency and enforced terms favourable to Rome. On his return to Rome at the head of an army composed of twenty-three legions, he defeated the opposition and so found himself sole master of the Roman world. By means of wholesale purges he ensured not only that the opposition would remain unable to strike back, but also that his soldiers would by means of confiscations receive adequate recompense in land as a return for their loyalty.

The object of Sulla's actions was largely to impose and strengthen an oligarchic government. To do so he first revived in 82 BC the old office of dictator for himself, but with important differences; he was to remain in this position until he chose to resign, or died, and he possessed absolute power over all other magistrates. Then he restructured the Senate, much diminished in size by the recent purges, by appointing 300 new senators from the equestrian class so that for some time to come his placemen would hold a majority. This move helped to emasculate the equestrians, while at the same time the tribunes of the people were deprived of all powers of initiative. In the provinces, which now numbered ten (Sicily, Sardinia with Corsica, Farther and Hither Spain, Macedonia, Africa, Asia, Cilicia, Cisalpine and Transalpine

Gaul), he instituted the system whereby the governors were drawn from among men who had already held the praetorship or consulship, thus ensuring that the holders always remained in Rome during their term of office. In 80 BC he became a consul; in 79 BC he gave up his dictatorship and retired to his country home where he died in the following year. But his reforms were not destined to last. His Senate could not survive without the support of the army commanders to carry out its decrees. Such support was largely denied it, and the outbreak of further civil wars, to begin with in Spain, gradually weakened its authority. The powers of the tribunes were restored in the year that Pompey and Crassus became consuls, by the repeal of the law enacted by Sulla, which had made the Senate's approval a prerequisite before any bill could be introduced into the popular assembly. This law had in effect given the Senate full control of all public affairs.

But Pompey and Crassus were essentially rivals and both had maintained their respective armies in the field, by which they were able to force the hand of the Senate. At the end of their consulships both retired to private life, but Pompey was recalled to take charge firstly of suppressing piracy in the Mediterranean and then of the second war against Mithridates in Asia Minor. He succeeded in both ventures and emerged as the victorious leader of the most powerful combined army and fleet in the Empire. Crassus saw his position becoming more difficult and, through his vast wealth, attempted to buy allies in Rome, among whom was a young man named C. Julius Caesar.

The events which led to the rise of Julius Caesar in Roman politics are numerous, devious and complicated. Backed for a short time by both Crassus and Pompey, when their informal but powerful combination is commonly, but wrongly, known as the triumvirate, he was elected consul in 60 BC, having held the propraetorship in Spain. While still consul he was appointed proconsular governor of Cisalpine Gaul, with command of an army of three legions. This ability to recruit an army and hold it outside Rome in readiness for his governorship placed him in a very strong position. Moreover, with the sudden death of the governor of Transalpine Gaul, he found himself appointed to take charge of both provinces.

But with the departure of Caesar, to take up his new duties, the suppressed enmity between Crassus and Pompey once more temporarily flared into the open, only to be subdued again at a joint meeting in Caesar's provinces. Pompey and Crassus received their second joint consulship from the Senate, when it was agreed as well that Caesar should have an extension of time in Gaul, that Pompey should govern Spain by means of legates and that Crassus should take charge in Syria. It was Crassus' last command, for he was killed in battle with the Parthians. In the meantime Caesar completed his conquest of Gaul and also made his expeditions to Britain.

With Crassus removed, the question to be resolved of who was to wield absolute power lay between Caesar and Pompey. Pompey was perhaps more advantageously placed to begin with. He won the support of the nobles and traditionalists and a political struggle for supremacy ensued between him and the supporters of Caesar. Finally, and under much pressure, the Senate resolved that Caesar should relinquish both his provinces and his army, or be declared an outlaw. He responded by crossing the southern boundary of Cisalpine Gaul, the river Rubicon, and invading Italy, so initiating a civil war, for which Pompey was largely unprepared. Despite attempts for a negotiated peace on the part of Caesar, Pompey with many senators fled first from Rome and then from Italy, leaving Caesar in undisputed control. Nevertheless, Pompey still commanded the loyalty of the army in Spain and might also be expected to raise another in the east. Since Caesar could not follow him to the east, for he had no fleet, he placed Mark Antony in charge of Rome as praetor and marched for Spain where he rapidly defeated the Pompeian forces. While returning from his successful expedition, he heard that he had been given the office of dictator. But his first successes were not repeated in Africa, where one of his supporters had been sent with an army to secure the allegiance of the province.

As dictator, Caesar on his return to Rome organised elections in which he was chosen as a consul; he immediately resigned his dictatorship, and made such arrangements as were necessary for his departure from Rome in pursuit of Pompey. The two protagonists, after some indeterminate skirmishes, met in battle near Pharsalus in Thessaly when Pompey was defeated and fled to Egypt, where he was treacherously murdered on the orders of the advisers of the young king Ptolemy.

When the news of Caesar's victory reached Rome, he was given the dictatorship for an indefinite period. But when at length he returned to the City, it was this time to find that the surviving supporters of Pompey had gathered in Africa. Again he was forced to set sail for another province and once more he was victorious. Finally, the crushing of a revolt in Spain, in which the Pompeians who had escaped from Africa joined, led to the end of the civil war. Caesar was now made dictator for life.

But the republican administration was in complete disarray. There was little money in the treasury and the number of unemployed in Rome had arisen to enormous proportions. In addition, his own veterans were seeking settlements of land for their services. He therefore founded a number of colonies in northern Italy, in the Gaulish provinces and in Spain for the veterans, while also increasing the scale of public works in Rome in order to create employment. Some of the new colonies were given full citizenship, others only received Latin rights. His full reorganisation of central government was, however, delayed, for he intended to mount a campaign to defeat Parthia, and he began to make such arrangements as he could to ensure that affairs in Rome would remain under his control in his absence. This delay increased the anger of his many secret enemies and, in March 44 BC, he was assassinated while attending the Senate. The story surrounding his death at the hands of a number of conspirators is sufficiently well-known to require no lengthy repetition here. Suffice it to say that the conspirators saw themselves as restorers of the Republic, whereas their act had doomed it beyond recovery, and emphasised yet again that any good general with an army under his control could take the Senate and the Republic by the throat at any time he wished. Since Pompey's day the army had mistrusted the Senate for its slowness in providing settlements or gratuities for veterans, making peaceful coexistence between them well nigh impossible.

Caesar's mantle fell first on Mark Antony, although Octavian, his adopted son, became his heir. Riots occurred at his funeral, forcing the assassins to flee and leaving behind a thoroughly frightened Senate, which Antony was easily able to subdue. But his plans went wrong when Octavian, taking, as was his right as sole heir, the name of Caesar, returned to Rome to claim his inheritance and proceeded to raise an army from among Caesar's veterans. He first forced Antony's retreat, but then came to terms with him and there was created the second triumvirate in which Octavian and Antony joined forces with Lepidus. But, although they crushed all opposition in Italy, time could not postpone indefinitely the final clash between the main protagonists. First Lepidus was out-manoeuvred and forced into retirement. Antony went to Syria to repel an invasion by the Parthians and suffered a disastrous defeat in which he was fortunate to lose no more than his baggage. Denied reinforcements by Octavian, he extricated himself, but with considerable cost to his reputation, and moved to Egypt where he entered into an alliance with Cleopatra, an act which was to cause his ultimate downfall. There Octavian followed him with a powerful fleet under Marcus Agrippa. Battle was engaged in the Bay of Actium in September, 31 BC, but within a short time most of Antony's fleet had mutinied and broken off the action, to be followed soon after by his army. Antony, following the supposed example of Cleopatra, committed suicide, so leaving Octavian supreme in the Roman Empire. The Battle of Actium, though hardly a great and hard-fought battle, became the watershed between the Republic and the principate, and also brought into the Roman fold the new province of Egypt, of which Octavian personally assumed complete control; thereafter it remained a province of an exceptional nature governed by a prefect on behalf of the emperor.

Octavian lingered in the east for two years after his conquest of Egypt and then returned to Rome to begin the task of reorganising the structure of the government. The Republic had finally failed and almost all of Octavian's energies for some years to come were to be devoted to the construction of an acceptable and workable substitute. Many reasons have been suggested

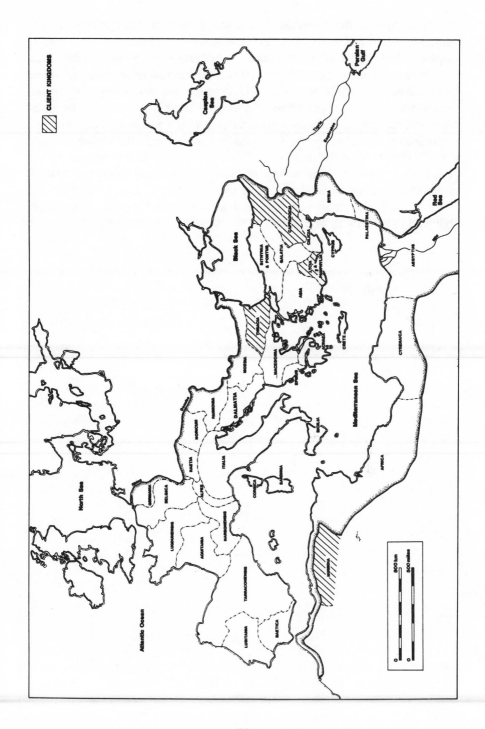

for the demise of the Republic. Some would have it that the political and administrative machine of a city state was not competent to run an extensive empire with overseas territories, since the Romans were unable to adapt their ways to the changing circumstances. Yet it had managed to do so for some time, as had other city states before. But probably the most compelling reason for its decline was the creation of a large standing army which owed its allegiance more to its individual generals than to the Senate and consuls. Any man controlling that army, such as Sulla or Caesar, or finally Octavian, could virtually dictate his own terms to the Senate, which in the circumstances was powerless to prevent him having his way. So we have seen the gradual undermining of the Senate's authority which ended in unrest, civil war and violence, until the right man appeared at the correct time with sufficient ability and authority to say: stop.

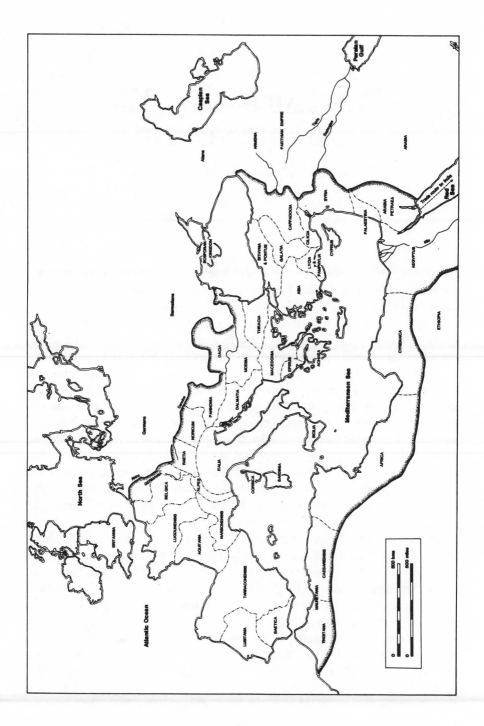

15

II

The Empire at War: Conquest and Consolidation

No empire, either before or since that of Rome, has been created or sustained without warfare. The Roman Empire was no exception and from its beginning to its final rupture at the hands of invading barbarians in the fifth century, it was fighting, almost without intermission, one enemy or another. Consequently its vitality can be directly measured against the strength of its armed forces and the quality of its leaders. As these fluctuated so did the Empire.

Much of the warfare was, as might be expected, contained within the frontier areas, both in the years of expansion and in the years of static defence and sometime contraction which followed. Curiously, much was also accomplished without a central strategic reserve which could be called upon when need arose. If danger threatened any particular sector it could only be reinforced at the expense of another, more peaceful, zone. Consequently great emphasis was placed on the maintenance of good communications and logistics so that large troop movements, sometimes over considerable distances, could be carried out in the most expeditious way. Indeed, the repeated successes of the Roman army under the high Empire were due as much, if not more, to its superb organisation and training as to its fighting ability in action, while its failures frequently stemmed from its inability on occasion to put these assets to the best use. It was an army which might lose battles but, more often than not, would win a war; an army trained to a peak of perfection in conventional warfare, but less effective in dealing with guerrilla activities or impromptu actions.

There are two fundamental types of military training. One method teaches a group of men implicit obedience to orders so that, if commanded to attack or defend a given place, they will do so to the best of their training and ability and probably with considerable courage. Indeed, the more highly disciplined they are in obeying their orders to the letter, the greater is their likely success.

16

But the ultimate triumph will depend heavily on the quality of the orders given by the officers. The second type of training embraces all this but goes further to teach each soldier a degree of personal initiative, so that they can act just as effectively one by one as in a body; detached from, or acting independently of, his section, platoon, century or cohort, each man remains as dangerous to the enemy as he was when banded with his fellows. We might suspect from some of its more resounding failures that the Roman army was not trained in this method of warfare; its strength lay in the mass and not in the individual. Had it been so trained, it would have been virtually invincible. As it was, the absence of this form of individualistic training brought about a lack of flexibility, which from time to time proved the Achilles heel of an otherwise supremely efficient fighting force. It was always at its best when, in either attack or defence, it was able to display its discipline in concert, but its weakness showed when it fought guerrilla attacks in a difficult or hostile environment.

As already indicated in the previous chapter, the Roman army was formed in the early days of the Republic as a body of citizens called to arms when circumstances required. Each Roman tribe furnished a given number of men, who were within the age limits laid down for military service, and who were expected to carry arms and armour appropriate to their personal wealth and status; levies were also expected from neighbouring states in treaty relations with Rome. The consuls were normally expected to provide the generalship, unless a dictator was appointed specifically for the purpose. Later, praetors were sometimes appointed to command armies in the field, while, under the high Empire, command usually devolved upon provincial governors.

Much has been written about the organisation and equipment of the Roman army in both the republican and imperial periods, and it is not the purpose of the present chapter to repeat what is already easily accessible elsewhere. Instead it is the intention to examine the achievements and the failures, the battles won and lost and the effects of victory and defeat on the Roman Empire.

In the late Republic, the fourteen or so provinces then in being contained approximately a legion apiece on a more or less permanent footing. Consequently when major crises arose, recruitment needed to be rapid to reinforce the standing army. Neither was there a permanent general staff, and commanders were appointed by the Senate on a temporary basis, a system which ultimately caused much trouble since it gave power to the ambitious to seek their own advancement. Such private armies had multiplied down to the period of the Civil War and, after the Battle of Actium, Augustus found himself commanding a force of some sixty legions, not all of which were probably at full strength, and some of which had supported his opponents; at full strength, they would have represented over 300,000 men. Augustus immediately reduced the overall number of legions to twenty-eight by a systematic demobilisation which removed disloyal elements and provided a wealth of new veterans to reinforce, or to establish, Roman colonies in the provinces. It is thought that he disposed of well over 100,000 legionaries in this way. In the long term it was a wise move, as the sons and grandsons of these men formed a great reservoir of free-born, Roman citizens from which voluntary recruitment to the legions could be maintained at a satisfactory level, so removing the need for conscription. The term of service was fixed and on discharge a veteran could look forward to a gratuity, or, on occasion when imperial policy felt the need, a grant of land in a new *colonia.*

Augustus retained for himself the *imperium* as commander-in-chief and all appointments to commands in the army were in his gift, to dispose of as he wished. From this factor there arose in time the carefully graded career structures of the imperial service which linked together both military and civil arms. From this system also grew the distinction between imperial and senatorial provinces, the former being those in which garrisons were placed and so technically the responsibility of the emperor, who appointed a man of appropriate rank to act as governor and general officer commanding the garrison. The legionary dispositions made by Augustus were as follows: five or possibly six in Germany, six or seven in Illyricum, five in Spain, three or four in Macedonia, three or four in Syria, three in Egypt and one in Africa, so that we can see at a glance those provinces which the emperor kept under his own control. In order to help towards providing the necessary financial backing for this permanent army, Augustus also created a special military treasury into which were gathered the proceeds from a 5 per cent death duty exacted on citizens and a 1 per cent sales tax on certain transactions.

But many of the provinces inherited by Augustus had been incorporated into the Empire in an unsystematic and piecemeal way, leaving behind unreduced pockets of resistance or breeding grounds for rebellion. There was also the serious and continuing threat of Parthia in the east, which had remained as a disquieting legacy following the defeat of the republican armies of Crassus and Antony and the unfulfilled intentions of Julius Caesar. Coupled with this problem was the need for an effective solution to be found for controlling the peripheral areas in Asia Minor, Syria and Arabia. In terms of outright conquest the theoretical solution to these problems far exceeded Rome's military strength and so Augustus was forced to use diplomacy, at which he was adept, in place of warfare. He introduced a system of client kings, controlling buffer states, whose task it was to secure the frontier regions on behalf of Rome and so enable considerable economies of manpower to be effected; it was a system later tried elsewhere in the empire with varying degrees of success. In many cases, when the time was ripe, and after they had largely outlived their usefulness, these states were incorporated into the provincial system. As an interim solution, however, it had much to commend it, and such kingdoms as Galatia, Cappadocia, Commagene and Judaea duly retained their nominal independence for a space of time. These diplomatic moves in the east were accompanied by limited military action, in which a small expeditionary force commanded by Aelius Gallus is reputed to have reached as far south as Aden.

The southern frontier of Egypt was disputed with the Ethiopians until a mutually acceptable peace treaty enabled it to be defined. The province of Africa, under senatorial jurisdiction, despite the presence of a legionary force, was bounded by mountainous Numidia and Mauretania to the west, Cyrenaica to the east and the desert to the south. With Egypt, the province provided much of the corn required to feed Rome and consequently was of considerable strategic importance. Augustus established a client king, Juba, in Mauretania, an area he deemed too difficult, or unrewarding, for conquest and occupation. But a series of punitive campaigns were required before the tribes of Tripolitania, Cyrenaica and the southern desert could be brought under control, after which a single legion sufficed to keep order.

Spain appears to have presented altogether different problems. Conquest and occupation of the uncontrolled areas, especially in the north-west, were deemed necessary for the benefit of the whole peninsula. The Cantabri of that region proved one of the most unyielding tribes and several years' campaigning in mountainous parts of the country were necessary for their subjugation. By 19 BC, however, occupation was virtually completed. The southern, more romanised part of Spain became the senatorial province of Baetica, while the remainder was divided between the imperial provinces of Lusitania in the south-west and Tarraconensis in the north. The final conquest was impressed more emphatically by the construction of a network of roads splitting up the mountainous regions into areas which could be more easily controlled, a system which anticipated to some extent the methods later adopted to subdue similar terrain in other provinces, such as that in the Alps, Wales and northern Britain. The final conquest of Spain also produced formidable reinforcements for the army, which were recruited as auxiliary cavalry or infantry regiments; they were normally removed to other provinces to circumvent possible mutiny or rebellion.

Equally unpacified were the tribes, such as the Salassi, in the alpine regions north of Italy, who had for long caused trouble to cities in the area. The suppression of these backward peoples had been made even more necessary by the entire annexation of Gaul, which, with the exception of senatorial Narbonensis, was ultimately divided into three imperial provinces, Aquitania, Lugdunensis and Belgica, all, for a brief time, containing garrisons to cope with internal dissension.

The way was now prepared for a solution to be sought to the problem presented by the northern frontiers. Even as early as 298 BC, the Roman army had reached the lower Danube, where by AD 6 the province of Moesia had been formed. But it still remained to find a stable and economical limit to advances in an area which stretched from the North Sea to the Black Sea. Nearly two decades of fierce and continuous fighting and rebellion were to be seen before a reasonable measure of control was enforced. How far north of the Danube and east of the Rhine Augustus intended to advance is arguable. It may be that he contemplated occupying the territories of both the Marcomanni in Bohemia and the Dacians in Transylvania; taken in conjunction with an eastward advance from the Rhine to the Elbe it would have provided a convenient frontier of about half the length of the only real alternative which would have made use of the rivers Rhine and Danube. It also required, if it was to be successful, the pacification of the warlike tribes of the central European uplands.

It has been argued that the early Roman emperors saw no limit to their conquests; frontiers were therefore not necessary. Yet Augustus was essentially a pragmatist, as he frequently demonstrated by his actions and despite the conflicting claims of the *Res Gestae* and sundry court poets. It is difficult to believe, therefore, that he saw no need for a limit to be placed on the advance into central Europe; he was as aware of manpower restrictions as anyone else in Rome. Nevertheless, if it was his intention to advance far beyond the Rhine and Danube in search of a tenable solution, it was a highly ambitious move and would have involved him in a degree of fresh conquest as yet unattempted during his principate, all else so far having been little more than a consolidation of the earlier gains of others. In planning such an advance, Augustus was fortunate in having the services of some excellent generals, his stepsons, Drusus, and the future emperor, Tiberius, and Agrippa, although the last died before the great Danubian conquests had been made.

It is difficult to be precise about the date at which hostilities commenced, as the sources are scanty and contradictory, but it would seem that a revolt in Dalmatia and Pannonia, *c.* 16 BC, precipitated matters. There followed a series of campaigns, led mainly by Tiberius, which were punctuated by further rebellions and attacks from tribes beyond the Danube. By 9 BC resistance in Dalmatia appears to have been broken and the old senatorial province of Illyricum was transferred to imperial control and, coupled with the newly-conquered districts, contained a garrison of some five legions. Subjugation of Pannonia was completed shortly afterwards with an advance that took the Roman army as far as the upper reaches of the river Elbe. Further campaigns between 8 BC and AD 6 were aimed at controlling the Marcomanni and the Dacians and success was near to being grasped when a serious revolt broke out again in Pannonia. It is stated that the rebels numbered over 200,000 and were commanded by men who had seen service as junior officers in Roman auxiliary regiments. Fortunately, the two main strong points at Siscia and Sirmium held, but not without several Roman reverses and the infliction of heavy casualties. It was not until AD 9 that Tiberius, having assembled an army of ten legions and nearly a hundred auxiliary regiments, was, with the utmost difficulty, able finally to force the surviving rebels' surrender.

Meanwhile progress had also been made on the Rhine. As early as 8–7 BC, Tiberius had consolidated positions on the east bank, following expeditions by Drusus into the German interior in the preceding years. Some activity seems to have continued even during the Danubian wars and by AD 9, when P. Quinctilius Varus was appointed to the command, his area of operations was acknowledged to run up to the river Elbe. Scarcely, however, had the glad news of the defeat of the Pannonian rebels reached Rome, when it was quickly followed by information from Germany of a Roman disaster. Varus, temporarily stationed somewhere near Minden, had set out to investigate rumours of a rebellion among the distant Cherusci. With three legions, XVII, XVIII and XIX, he had been lured into the Teutoburger Wald, possibly somewhere near Osnabrück, where ambush awaited him by one of the Cheruscian leaders, Arminius.

Caught in the dense forest, the force was annihilated and its leader committed suicide; it was a classic example of the conditions under which the Roman army were far from invincible. It is also a good illustration of the difficulties facing the Roman high command at that time. Even though Augustus was nominally and factually commander-in-chief, he must have found it well-nigh impossible to coordinate the activities of two major army groups, albeit working towards a common goal, but separated by some four or five hundred miles. It is likely that Varus was not altogether wise in operating so far to the north-east from his base while Pannonia was still unsettled and Bohemia unoccupied. In retrospect, the way to the creation of the Elbe-Carpathian frontier of Augustus can be seen as lying in closely coordinated and simultaneous action in both Rhenish and Danubian sectors, allowing the native tribes no intermission and no opportunity to call on allies, who for their part would have been kept under equal stress from the other quarter.

With no central reserve to draw on, the gap in the Roman army caused by the loss of three legions could not quickly be filled. Tiberius, fresh from his victories in Illyricum, hastened to the Rhine, while reinforcements were brought from Spain, Raetia and Pannonia. His earlier work now proved its value and enabled him to save the river frontier; eight legions were stationed on, or near, its banks, and the command was now divided between two officers, one in Upper, the other in Lower, Germany. But with only twenty-five legions left to him, Augustus could no longer sanction the completion of the Elbe frontier. The idea appears to have been quietly dropped from imperial reckonings and the alternative, much longer, Rhine-Danube frontier was consolidated. Manpower was already beginning to dictate policy.

The foundations of empire laid by Augustus were to remain largely unaltered except for marginal changes. Never again would opportunities arise for the wholesale restructuring of major frontiers. Individual emperors might make plans for major conquests, might gain, or lose, the odd province, but the main lines drawn by Augustus survived the tests of time. He himself realised that the limits had probably been reached and he laid upon Tiberius, his successor, an injunction not to advance the frontiers. But for the *clades Variana* the Empire might have been greatly enlarged, but at what cost to itself no one can say. So, one disgraceful episode for Roman arms dictated ultimate strategy more surely than successes achieved elsewhere; success often breeds a boundless desire to continue, not always healthy for any organisation which may over-reach itself, whereas the infliction of an occasional defeat breeds an awareness of limitations. Perhaps, therefore, the Varus disaster may be viewed in a more advantageous light when the continuing health of the Roman Empire is considered as a whole.

Since the military arrangements of Augustus were to last some time, it is interesting to record them in more detail, to see where the main strength lay and to be able to compare later dispositions with them. The surviving twenty-five legions were distributed between eight provinces, and no one province had more than four legions, so as to remove the means for a mutiny by an over-ambitious commander. They were disposed as follows:

SYRIA: *III Gallica; VI Ferrata; X Fretensis; XII Fulminata;*
UPPER GERMANY: *II Augusta; XIII Gemina; XIV Gemina; XVI;*
LOWER GERMANY: *I Germanica; V Alaudae; XX Valeria; XXI Rapax;*
PANNONIA: *VIII Augusta; IX Hispana; XV Apollinaris;*
SPAIN: *IV Macedonica; VI Victrix; X Gemina;*
DALMATIA: *VII; XI;*
MOESIA: *IV Scythica; V Macedonica;*
EGYPT: *III Cyrenaica; XXII Deiotariana;*
AFRICA: *III Augusta*

It can be seen from this list that by far the greatest strength lay along the Rhine and Danube, with a total of fifteen legions, while the whole of north Africa, including Egypt, mustered only three, with a further four defending Syria; three more in Spain sufficed to protect the western provinces. In every case the legions would have been supported by appropriate auxiliary regiments.

Augustus died in AD 14 and his injunctions to Tiberius concerning the extent of the Empire were strictly obeyed, but events at his accession showed yet another, less healthy aspect of the new Roman army. Tiberius came of the Claudian, not Julian, family and his elevation to princeps caused mutinies among the provincial armies in Lower Germany and Pannonia. Admittedly the legions, after the Pannonian rebellion and Varian disaster, had been diluted by the rapid recruitment of ex-slaves and other undesirables; they were also underpaid and being retained long after their periods of service had expired. But the event serves to demonstrate the extreme volatility of these seasoned troops, and the rightness of the Augustan policy in avoiding an excess of legionary strength in any one province. It was a fatal flaw in the imperial organisation, and was to cause greater trouble in later years.

Despite Tiberius' attempts to maintain the frontiers intact, his reign was not without warfare, although he strove to reduce it to a minimum. Limited offensive action took place on the Rhine and Danube frontiers and there was a lengthy period of hostility in Africa, where the guerilla tactics of the native chief Tacfarinas caused considerable trouble until an extra legion was drafted from Pannonia. There was also a revolt among the Aedui and Treveri of Gaul; its suppression was accomplished by the army of Upper Germany, since by then there were virtually no troops left in the Gallic provinces.

Gaius, the successor of Tiberius, seems ultimately to have thrown aside the Augustan policy concerning frontiers. Late in his principate he accumulated large forces on the Rhine, with the intention presumably of invading free Germany and of perhaps advancing the frontier well beyond the river. The recruitment of two new legions, *XV* and *XXII Primagenia*, is sometimes attributed to this period, although equally they could have been formed slightly later by Claudius. Apart from strengthening the frontier, however, Gaius appears to have taken no further action in that sector and, instead, turned his attention to Britain, for long considered, since Julius Caesar's expeditions, a promising conquest. Again Gaius' plans were thwarted, probably because of the refusal of the army to embark on a campaign across the sea. It was left to Claudius, three years later, to complete what Gaius had attempted, although once more the army had to be induced to cross the Channel.

The reasons behind the invasion and the movements of the Roman army in Britain in the years following are comparatively well-known, although much argument has taken place about the strategy which lay behind them. It has been claimed that, at first, the policy was to proceed no further than the first frontier established along the line of the rivers Severn and Trent, which would have meant the capture of most of what was worth possessing and the defeat of the Catuvellauni, Rome's traditional enemy in Britain. Be that as it may, it was to take several revisions of policy and hard, almost continuous, but not always successful, campaigning over the next four decades before Agricola was able to round off the conquest and organise a properly defended province.

The policy of expansion which Claudius followed neither began nor ended with the annexation of Britain. Almost immediately after his accession, and

23

before the invasion of Britain, a rebellion had broken out in Mauretania, where Gaius had earlier deposed the client king. Military action was necessary and two generals, Suetonius Paullinus and Hosidius Geta, both of whom were later to figure in British campaigns, were dispatched to Africa. With the rebellion suppressed, Mauretania was absorbed into the Empire as two provinces, Caesariensis and Tingitana, each in charge of a procurator. In the east Claudius absorbed a number of client kingdoms, including Judaea, and adopted a firmer attitude towards Parthia by insisting on a Roman nominee for the vacant throne of Armenia. In the west, the most promising general of the day, Corbulo, was sent to the lower Rhine to complete the consolidation of the frontier.

The principate of Nero was chiefly marked by rebellion and culminated in the disastrous civil war of AD 69. In Britain, the revolt of Boudicca at the head of the Iceni and the Trinovantes nearly caused the loss of the new province. Only the steadiness of two legions, under the command of the governor, Suetonius Paullinus, fighting on a carefully chosen battle-ground, saved the day. This crisis in the west was matched by equal and contemporary difficulties in the east, where Parthia had replaced the Roman nominee in Armenia. Moreover, the army in Syria, which always tended to behave differently from the remainder of the legions, was poorly disciplined and had grown soft from being billeted among townspeople. Corbulo, who had already become governor of the nearby provinces of Galatia and Cappadocia, was ordered to take command of three Syrian legions. Reinforcements were also sent out for the governor of Syria from the Danube frontier, where, for once, peace reigned.

Corbulo, so Tacitus tells us, marched his army out into the country, where it was kept under canvas through a severe winter; by such means and by enforcing harsh and rigid discipline, he restored it to the level of an efficient fighting force. That done, he advanced into Armenia where, by excellent tactics pursued over difficult country, he was finally able to capture the capital, Artaxata, which was razed to the ground, and ultimately forced the king, Tiridates, to flee to Parthia. The campaigns included several marches of two to three hundred miles and proved the vindication of the Syrian legions. Unfortunately for Rome, this campaign did not spell the end of eastern difficulties. Corbulo was appointed to the now vacant governorship of Syria, and his place as commander of the army against Parthia was filled by an incompetent general, who not only antagonised the Parthians, but also surrendered to them when under siege in a base camp. Corbulo was able to reach a compromise only after further campaigns of his own.

The Parthian troubles were compounded in the east by a revolt of the Jews which, initiated in AD 62, grew to a major rebellion four years later and which simmered for several years afterwards, in the end requiring a force of no less than three legions, *Legio V Macedonica, X Fretensis* and *XV Apollinaris*, to suppress it. Almost simultaneously there were revolts in Gaul and Spain; in the former the governor of Gallia Lugdunensis, C. Julius Vindex, led the disaffected peoples of the Arverni, Aedui and Sequani until they were crushed by the overwhelming strength of a force, sent from Upper Germany, consisting of *Legio IV Macedonica, XXI Rapax* and *XXII Primagenia.* The revolt by Ser. Sulpicius Galba in Tarraconensis had, however, more serious consequences, for by now Nero had lost the support of almost all segments of Roman society. Galba was hailed emperor by his troops, and by devious means the Praetorian Guard were won to his side. Nero committed suicide in AD 68; there was no obvious heir, and so began a war of succession which is usually termed the year of the four emperors. It was a civil war, of a type already anticipated on the accession of Tiberius, which illuminates all too clearly the principal weakness of the Roman administrative and military machine, while, at the same time it demonstrates, to some degree, the stamina of the system to withstand internal strife. Yet it was not always to be so and, ultimately, civil wars drained away the resources of the Empire at times when it could least afford to lose them.

In AD 69 the army showed quite openly the power which it had to create and destroy emperors; the senatorial provinces, devoid of troops, were almost entirely unable to interfere. As already noted above, Galba, governor of Tarraconensis, was hailed emperor by his garrison and received the vital support of the Praetorian Guard. Failing, however, to pay them the promised bounty, he was quickly unseated and murdered after a reign of only seven months, to be replaced by Otho, at first one of his principal supporters. Almost simultaneously the army in Germany declared for Vitellius and civil war became inevitable. Otho advanced northwards in Italy to meet him and at first won some minor engagements, before being decisively defeated near Bedriacum. He appears to have had little stomach for the fight and was appalled at the idea of civil war, so much so, that he committed suicide. Vitellius survived slightly longer, but the army was by no means unanimously behind him. A vexillation drafted to Italy from Moesia to support Otho decided to put forward their own nominee; their choice fell on Vespasian, who at the time was commanding the army in Syria trying to suppress the revolt of the Jews. Both the prefect of Egypt and the governor of Syria supported him and an offer of help came even from Parthia. Leaving the conduct of the Jewish war in the care of his son, Titus, Vespasian set out for Rome, where his army quickly disposed of Vitellius after a bitterly fought battle at Cremona, in which this ancient *colonia* was almost completely destroyed by Vespasian's troops.

The triumph of the Flavian dynasty marked a turning point in the fortunes of the Empire, despite a troubled start with the unfinished Jewish war still to

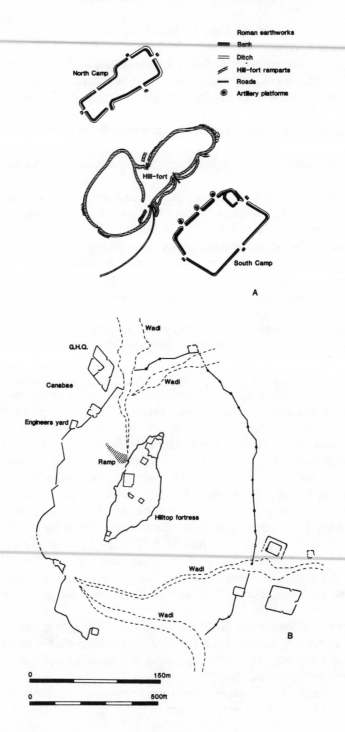

be brought to a successful conclusion; it was achieved only with the sack of Jerusalem and the dispersal of the Jewish people. In addition, a major rebellion had also broken out in Lower Germany. It had been started quite deliberately by Vespasian's supporters in order to keep those German legions, which had adhered to Vitellius, fully occupied; but it rapidly went beyond control. The main protagonist was a chieftain of the Batavi, Civilis, who not only was a Roman citizen, but had also served in the Roman army. Taking advantage of the absence of much of the garrison from the Lower Rhine, he at first declared his support for Vespasian, but, after the battle of Cremona, he refused to lay down his arms. Some German and Gaulish tribes, notably the Treveri, Lingones and Nervii, rapidly joined Civilis and, together with three mutinous legions, succeeded in destroying almost all the fortresses and forts of the Rhine garrisons, with the exception of the legionary fortresses at Moguntiacum (Mainz) and Vindonissa (Windisch). *Legio XV Primagenia*, stationed at Vetera (Xanten), appears to have been annihilated, for it is not heard of again. A very recent discovery, not far from the fortress, seems to have revealed the site of the battlefield; numerous horses had been buried with many of their harness fittings.

Fortunately for Rome, some tribes in the vicinity remained loyal and did not join the rebellion, but the situation was nevertheless tense and could have led to the complete loss of Germany and even parts of Gaul. But Vespasian, once he had disposed of the Vitellian problem, responded with characteristic energy and sent a new commander, Petillius Cerealis, to Lower Germany in charge of four legions, *Legio II Adjutrix*, *Legio XXI Rapax*, *Legio XIV Gemina* from Britain and *Legio VI Victrix* from Spain. Supported by Annius Gallus, commanding four more legions in Upper Germany, Cerealis was able to restore order and receive the surrender of Civilis in person.

The extreme seriousness of the revolt of Civilis to some extent over-shadowed the almost equally unstable position which Vespasian inherited in Britain. Shortly before the civil war had broken out in 69, the governor of the province had been expelled by a mutinous army, while warfare had broken out almost simultaneously on the northern frontier, where a Roman ally and client queen, Cartimandua, had been conducting a personal vendetta with her divorced husband, Venutius. He took the opportunity offered by the disarray of the Roman forces to expel Cartimandua from her native territory in Brigantia. Vespasian was not able to deal with the situation immediately and it is possible that another client king, Cogidubnus of the Regni, helped to hold the province on his behalf until Civilis had been defeated. Then, who better than Petillius Cerealis to send against the Brigantes? Furnished with an additional legion, the newly-recruited but recently tried *Legio II Adjutrix*, he was sent as governor to Britain and, in three years' vigorous campaigning, successfully neutralised the Brigantian menace.

Warfare in the north-west provinces led Vespasian to restore the garrisons of Britain and both Germanies to their original strength, so that each now held four legions. In Upper Germany there were *Legio I Adjutrix* and *XIV Gemina* in a double fortress at Mainz, *XI Claudia* at Windisch and *VIII Augusta* possibly at Strasbourg: in Lower Germany, *Legio X Gemina* at Nijmegen, *XXII Primagenia* at Xanten, *VI Victrix* at Neuss and *XXI Rapax* at Bonn. In Britain there were *Legio IX Hispana* at York, *II Adjutrix* at Lincoln, *II Augusta* possibly at Exeter or Gloucester and *XX Valeria Victrix* probably at Wroxeter. On the Upper Rhine, Vespasian initiated action which resulted in the occupation of the so-called Agri Decumates, lying between the headwaters of the Rhine and the Danube, thereby shortening the frontier and effecting a saving in manpower, although it was left to Domitian to consolidate both this annexation and the German frontier further north.

Vespasian also reorganised the Danube frontier and rebuilt the Claudian fortress at Carnuntum (Deutsch Altenburg) and another at Vindobona (Vienna); the provinces on the Danube remained generally deficient in legionary strength, with *Legio XV Apollinaris* at Carnuntum, *XIII Gemina* at Vindobona in Pannonia, *Legio VII Claudia*, possibly at Viminacium (Koštolac), *V Macedonica* at Oescus (Gigen) and *I Italica* at Novae (Staklen) in Moesia. *Legio V Alaudau* was transferred from Germany to an as yet unknown station somewhere in Moesia. An invasion by the trans-Danubian tribe of Roxolani had succeeded in killing Fonteius Agrippa, governor of Moesia. But again it was largely left to Domitian to consolidate the frontier defences along the Danube after the successful completion of his Dacian and German wars.

In the east, where Vespasian had a personal interest following his command of the army in Syria, the frontier was also reorganised and strengthened by the placing of *Legio XII Fulminata* at Melitene, a crossing of the Euphrates, and *Legio XVI Flavia Firma* at Satala on the Armenian border. But the principal force for the defence of the eastern provinces was still concentrated in Syria, even though the garrison was reduced to three legions, *VI Ferrata* at Samosata, some 80 km, as the crow flies, south of Melitene, and *IV Scythica* and *III Gallica* at as yet unidentified stations; the governor could also call on *Legio X Fretensis* which had garrisoned Jerusalem since its sack. So the entire eastern frontier was divided between six legions, supported by appropriate auxiliaries. The client kingdoms of Lower Armenia and Commagene were also reduced and incorporated into the existing provinces of Galatia and Syria respectively.

The ensuing decade and a half saw considerable military activity: in Britain, where the frontiers were extended to include Wales and the north as far as the Scottish highlands; against the Chatti, dwelling in the Taunus area beyond the central part of the Rhine frontier; and against the Dacians and Germans facing the Danube. All these campaigns had their interlocking features. The conquest and subsequent pacification of large new sectors of Britain under the governors Frontinus and Agricola enabled Domitian to reduce the garrison and thus reinforce in turn the armies of the Rhine and Danube. Having defeated the Chatti, he was able to redraw the frontier from Mainz southwards to enclose much of the Taunus, the Odenwald and the Neckar valley.

But the Dacian kingdom had recently become reunified under a new king, Decebalus, whose capital lay at Sarmizegetusa. A sudden attack late in 85 or early 86 caught the governor of Moesia, Oppius Sabinus, entirely by surprise; he was killed and *Legio V Alaudae* was defeated. Domitian ordered rapid replacement and reinforcement: *Legio IV Flavia* was moved north from Dalmatia, while *I Adjutrix* and *II Adjutrix* were drafted from Upper Germany and Britain respectively, although it is likely that the latter, at its full strength, did not reach Moesia much before 89 or 90. The reinforcement of the frontier was matched by administrative changes made to unite the zone facing Dacia and by the division of Moesia into two separate commands of Superior and Inferior. Two of the newly arrived legions appear to have been stationed near Sirmium, which was now temporarily transferred from Pannonia to the jurisdiction of Moesia Superior; the third is thought to have been brigaded with *VII Claudia* at Viminacium.

In 86, Domitian, who had personally supervised much of the campaign, returned to Rome leaving his praetorian prefect, Cornelius Fuscus, in command. With Moesia now freed of Dacians, Fuscus began another campaign into their territory across the Danube, only to be killed with the entire loss of his army, which included the unfortunate *Legio V Alaudae*. Finally, after Domitian had again returned to the front, victory was gained at the battle of Tapae in AD 88 and Decebalus sued for peace.

Yet even now the Danube frontier was not quiet. The German tribes over the river, opposite the provinces of Pannonia and Noricum, had refused to provide troops for the Dacian war and were now subjected to a punitive expedition. Little is known of the details or outcome, but at least two Roman defeats are recorded, one of which, at the hands of the Sarmatians, was sufficiently disastrous to see the disappearance of yet another legion, possibly *XXI Rapax*, in the early 90s. It was immediately replaced by *XIV Gemina* from Mainz, which once more restored Pannonia to the level of a three-, and by a slightly later addition, four-legion province. Unfortunately, legionary movements and dispositions in this period are nowhere well attested and consequently only tentative suggestions for their whereabouts can be made. Legionary fortresses of the general period, apart from the well-known examples at Carnuntum and Poetovio, probably existed also at Brigetio (Szöny), Aquincum (Obuda), near Sirmium (Mitrovica), possibly at Mursella (Mórich-ida-Kisárpás) in Pannonia; and at Viminacium (Koštolac), Singidunum (Beograd), Ratiaria (Arčer) and possibly Naissus (Niš) in Moesia Superior.

These movements, which withdrew troops from other frontiers, most notably from the Germanies, to strengthen the Danube, underline a significant change in imperial strategy. Henceforth it was to be the Danube which claimed most attention, replacing the military dominance hitherto held by the Rhine garrisons. This is not to say that other frontiers were necessarily weakened to an unacceptable degree; indeed some, such as Britain, had to be considerably reinforced during the second century, but for the next hundred years the Danube was the backdrop to major wars which, erupting periodically, sucked in increasing quantities of Roman arms.

Tension continued to rise along the Danube into the start of Trajan's principate even after peace had formally been made, at a cost by Domitian, with the Dacians and Sarmatians. It was Trajan who, discarding the earlier precepts of Augustus and some of his successors concerning the frontiers, embarked on a series of expansionist campaigns that were to carry the Empire almost to its greatest extent. The first country to be attacked was Dacia, ostensibly to complete the work of Domitian and to prevent alliances being formed which could threaten the Danube frontier. A large army of some ten legions plus auxiliaries was gathered and in 101 a two-pronged attack was launched over the river crossings at Viminacium and Drobeta against the Dacian strongholds in the Carpathians. To aid the advance, Trajan restored Tiberius' road on the right bank of the Danube through the Iron Gates. Yet another hard-fought battle was won at Tapae, but, although defeated, the trans-Danubian tribes were by no means conquered. The following winter saw the Roxolani again in action and it may be that the successful repulsion of their attack resulted in the construction of the war memorial at Adamklissi (Tropaeum Traiani). The summer saw Trajan crossing the Danube again; Decebalus and his Dacians were defeated and numerous garrisons were left in their territory.

That was not, however, the end of Dacian resistance. Three years later, in 105, they launched a sudden attack across the Danube and destroyed many forts. Trajan left Rome, where he had received a triumph for his earlier campaign, and, at the head of a much-increased army, containing all or detachments of thirteen legions, crossed the river at Drobeta and advanced successfully against Decebalus' capital at Sarmizegetusa. Dacia was now incorporated as a province, forming an extension northwards from the Danube as far as the encircling Bihar and Carpathian mountains, so as to include the broad sweep of Transylvania, but excluding a narrow strip of land between the western boundary on the river Theiss and the northward swing of the Danube. It is strange that this projection, over a hundred miles deep and fifty miles wide, into Roman territory was never occupied; it was to prove a source of trouble in later years.

Soon after the occupation of Dacia, probably *c.* 106, the client kingdom of

Arabia Petraea was reduced to provincial status upon the death of its monarch, an action which served to focus attention once more in the direction of the perennial threat to the eastern Empire: Parthia. By the early second century, population growth in central Asia was causing a southward pressure towards the Caucasus and Armenia, hitherto ruled by a king nominated by Rome and an essential buffer between the Roman and Parthian empires. Trajan grasped the problem firmly, as he had already done with Dacia, and annexed Armenia which, however, could not be easily held without the simultaneous occupation of neighbouring Mesopotamia. The conquest of Dacia had shown already how considerable wealth could accrue to the Empire by the creation of new provinces; Arabia, Mesopotamia and Armenia together lay across significant trade routes to the east and Trajan probably believed that their incorporation would similarly bring profits in the form of taxes on merchandise and so pay for their occupation. But he seems to have overlooked the strains which such an expansion would place upon the Empire's manpower and perhaps, as well, did not entirely anticipate correctly the strength of Parthian reaction.

Trajan arrived in the east in 114 to conduct the campaign in person. By the end of the summer Armenia had been reduced with minimal fighting, thus opening the way to Parthia. By 116 the advance had so prospered that Trajan reached the Parthian capital, Ctesiphon, having left a line of garrisons to guard his rear and to keep open the main channels of communication. The Parthian king, Chosroes, fled, but although Trajan gained all the territory that he had set out to do, he had not as yet inflicted a decisive defeat on the Parthian army. Reforming, it mounted successful attacks on the garrisons in his rear, threatening the Roman communications. But, employing the age-old method of dividing the opposition by political means, Trajan was able temporarily to recoup his losses. Nevertheless, early in 117, he was forced to retire with his army to Antioch having failed to overcome Parthia and so extend the Empire to the Persian gulf. The failure was, moreover, again compounded by a widespread revolt of the Jews who, after the sack of Jerusalem in 70, had been dispersed among many provinces in the east and north Africa. Trajan's return to Rome coincided with his attempts to suppress the rebellion. But he died of a stroke on the journey and his supposedly adoptive son, Hadrian, then governor of Syria, became emperor.

Hadrian inherited a troubled Empire torn by internal rifts and threatened from without; not only were the eastern and African provinces involved but also the frontiers on the Danube and in Britain. Hadrian had served with Trajan in the Parthian campaigns and apparently had warned him about placing too great a strain on the Empire by his projected conquests, an estimate that was to prove entirely correct. Consequently one of his first acts was to abandon Mesopotamia. Thereafter he spent much of his principate reviewing and consolidating the provincial frontiers, so setting bounds on the

Empire and creating the first major systems of static defence. He thus instituted an important change in imperial strategy, which did not at first meet with complete approval in Rome; but the opposition was quickly suppressed.

Hadrian largely succeeded in his aims by making an almost continuous succession of tours of the frontier provinces. Within two or three years of his accession he had started for the north-west, taking in parts of Gaul, the Germanies, Noricum, Raetia and Britain. In each he reorganised and strengthened the frontiers, the most remarkable of these being the linear fortifications of Hadrian's Wall in Britain. In some of the provinces he seems also to have encouraged urban life, aided the construction of public buildings and initiated schemes for the reclamation of waste land. From there he travelled to Spain and possibly to Africa where he ended a war in Mauretania: next to the east, through the provinces of Turkey to Syria and then back to Greece, Macedonia and Pannonia. There followed a short stay in Rome in 126 after which he departed again to tour Italy and Africa.

Much of Hadrian's later travels was spent in the eastern provinces, until in 133 he returned to remain more or less permanently in the capital. Apart from the early part of his time as emperor, the frontiers were comparatively peaceful, but his principate was marred by yet another rebellion of the Jews in 132 and a possible war in Britain at about the same time. His chief success in military matters was the transformation of the Roman army from a force, engaged almost continuously on active campaigns, into a mainly static garrison of frontier troops, guarding permanent installations. The change seems to have been achieved by the institution of a series of constant training exercises, drills and building activities which maintained discipline and kept the army employed at a high peak of efficiency despite a lack of combat. What he could not have foreseen, perhaps, was the ultimate demoralisation which ensued among garrisons with little fighting to do and which led to the army assuming, in the later Empire, an entirely different organisation and appearance. The final alteration was not immediate, but the changes, once begun, gathered pace from the end of the second century onwards.

In his declining years, Hadrian suffered severely from a serious and painful illness which seems to have been a combination of tuberculosis and dropsy. He died in 138 and his adoptive son succeeded him. The principate of Antoninus Pius was, like that of Hadrian, comparatively peaceful, although important changes were introduced on some frontiers so as to make the fortifications more effective. In Britain, the weaknesses of the Hadrianic frontier were recognised and the decision was taken almost at once to reoccupy lowland Scotland. The ensuing campaign was successfully completed and a new defensive line, known as the Antonine Wall, was constructed between the Firth of Forth and the Firth of Clyde. This Wall and its installations were mainly constructed of turfwork and timber, and various innovations were made as the result of lessons learned on Hadrian's Wall, which was now evacuated but for some small holding detachments. Considerable changes were also introduced on the frontiers of Upper Germany and Raetia, where new positions were occupied in advance of the earlier lines so as to reduce the overall length. Wood was replaced by masonry in the watch-towers and a series of new forts were constructed for auxiliary regiments along the frontier line from Miltenberg-Ost to Lorch and then eastwards to rejoin the Danube at Eining.

The chief disturbances during the principate of Antoninus Pius were caused more by internal rebellion than by external threat. Reinforcements had to be sent to Numidia and Mauretania in the 140s when an outbreak of brigandage led to an open revolt in the latter province; legionary vexillations were brought from the Rhine and Danube frontiers and from Judaea to quell the uprising. In Britain, a revolt among the northern tribe of Brigantes, *c.* 154, forced the temporary evacuation of the new frontier in Scotland and the partial rehabilitation of Hadrian's Wall. Reinforcements were sent from Germany to help to restore order and repair the damage. An attempt was made early in the 160s to return to the Antonine Wall, but it was short-lived, so that the more southerly line adopted by Hadrian once more became the permanent frontier in Britain. Further rebellions occurred in Egypt and Dacia, but were quickly suppressed. Rumbles of yet another war with Parthia in the east were averted for the time being by diplomacy, but the threat remained. Antoninus' acknowledgement of the importance of the east is perhaps best illustrated by the embassy which he sent to the reigning representative of the Han dynasty in China.

Antoninus Pius died in 161. His efforts to maintain peaceful frontiers were mostly successful, but storms were gathering and war could not long be avoided or delayed indefinitely. To his successor, Marcus Aurelius, probably the least-suited of emperors for prolonged campaigns, fell the lot of almost continuous fighting to defend the boundaries of the Empire from external attack. Additionally his difficulties were made more intractable by the outbreak of an epidemic disease, supposedly bubonic plague, brought back from the east by the army, which was then diffused throughout much of the Empire, exacerbating the shortage of manpower and causing a severe famine in Italy.

One of Marcus Aurelius' first acts was to promote Lucius Verus to the rank of co-Augustus, establishing for the first time a collegiate form of government. It was a wise move, but an unfortunate choice of man, in view of the troubles which were shortly to descend upon the Empire. In Britain the final withdrawal from the new frontier in Scotland took place; the Chatti invaded Germany; in the east, the governor of Cappadocia was defeated and killed by the Parthians, who then invaded Syria. Lucius Verus was sent with reinforcements from the Danube to retrieve the position, while three other legions were diverted to Syria and placed under the supreme command of Statius Priscus. This was fortunate, as Verus showed no great haste to reach Syria. The war was waged on two separate fronts. First Armenia was reduced and pacified, with a new pro-Roman client king being placed on the throne. All the troops were then concentrated in an attack on Parthia; Seleucia and Ctesiphon were captured and peace terms favourable to Rome were imposed on the defeated Parthians. Mesopotamia was made a protectorate and the withdrawal of the army from the area demonstrated the completeness of the victory over Parthia, which remained subdued for some time to come.

But the Parthian war had drained the garrisons of both the Danube and the Rhine. Close on the heels of the good news from the east came tidings of invasions crossing the northern frontiers where external tribes were coming under increasing pressure from the growing populations of central Europe and Asia. Two new legions were raised in Italy and hurriedly moved north. Raetia, Noricum and Pannonia were overrun, and the tribes next crossed the Alps and laid siege to Aquileia in Italy. Only the strong positive action taken by the provincial governors gradually forced back the invaders who sued for peace.

It was not, however, the end of the war. Marcus Aurelius, now sole emperor following the death of Verus, was forced to return to the Danube in 169, where fighting had once more erupted. Several tribes were involved during the confusion of the next few years: Marcomanni, Quadi, Sarmatii, Iazyges, Costoboci. Carnuntum became the imperial centre and headquarters for the campaigns and a new legionary fortress was constructed at Regensburg. Ultimately, after both successes and reverses for the Roman army, peace was restored *c.* 175, although Marcus failed to achieve his avowed objective of promoting two new trans-Danubian provinces of Marcomannia and Sarmatia. Instead a compromise was reached whereby a demilitarised zone was created on the far bank of the Danube and large numbers of tribesmen were settled in depopulated areas of the frontier provinces. This policy was to have far-reaching effects on the constitution of the Empire which gradually with the passage of time reached a climax in later years.

The failure of Marcus to bring the Danubian war to an entirely satisfactory end was partly caused by the arrival of news that Avidius Cassius, commanding the Syrian army, had risen in revolt against the emperor. Marcus immediately planned an expedition to the east, using elements of the Danubian army, but Cassius was murdered before the force could set out. But despite this, no change of plan was made since Marcus wished to satisfy himself that all was well in Syria and Egypt, provinces of great strategic importance. His son, Commodus, now of age, joined the expedition and, by the time the emperor returned to Rome, had been sufficiently initiated into affairs of state to become co-Augustus with his father.

Despite the earlier settlement on the Danube, the war dragged on fitfully and the provincial governors of Upper and Lower Pannonia were unable to bring it to a decisive end. Marcus, together with his son, returned to the area and inflicted a severe defeat on the Marcomanni, but this time his own death deprived him of the ultimate satisfaction of adding two new provinces to the Empire. Commodus thus became emperor in 180 and the period of good government which Rome had enjoyed for nearly a century came to an abrupt end. Instead of completing the Danubian settlement as his father had wished, he reimposed the terms of the earlier arrangements. Coupled with strengthened fortifications, they seem to have been more successful than before, and ensured peace on this frontier throughout his principate. Indeed, Commodus was fortunate in that the extensive wars fought by his father appear to have exhausted Rome's external enemies. Only in Britain was it necessary to wage a major campaign, probably against the northern tribes; there were also minor disturbances in Spain and Gaul.

The intrigue, cruelty and extravagance of Commodus' principate took its toll, and he was murdered towards the close of 192, leaving no heir to succeed him. There followed a vicious war between five contenders, in which an echo of the Year of the Four Emperors, following Nero's suicide, could be plainly heard. Helvius Pertinax was first nominated by the Praetorian Guard in Rome, only to be murdered by them three months later. The Empire was then sold by the Guard to Didius Julianus, even though in the meantime the frontier armies were engaged in making their own nominations. Septimius Severus, governor of Upper Pannonia, was hailed emperor first by his own troops and then by the entire garrison of the Rhine and Danube. In Syria, the governor, Pescennius Niger, was likewise greeted by his troops, while Severus' offer of the title of Caesar to Clodius Albinus, another claimant and governor of Britain, made sure of his becoming enmeshed in the contest. Severus advanced on Rome where he was welcomed by the Senate, which had already deposed Julianus, and quietly executed him. Having stabilised his position there he set out for the east, where, after fighting an extensive series of campaigns ranging through the provinces of Turkey and Syria, he not only defeated Niger, but also punished those people who had sought to profit by the civil war. Only Clodius Albinus now stood between him and the undisputed control of the Empire.

Albinus was first declared an outlaw; in response he was hailed as Augustus by his own troops in Britain. Collecting the garrison together, he crossed to Gaul and made his headquarters at Lyon, hoping perhaps to win the support of some of the German legions to add to that already given by the governor of Tarraconensis. The decisive battle between Albinus and Severus was fought, early in 197, near Lyon, in which Severus was victorious.

The civil war at the end of the second century is a watershed in the affairs

35

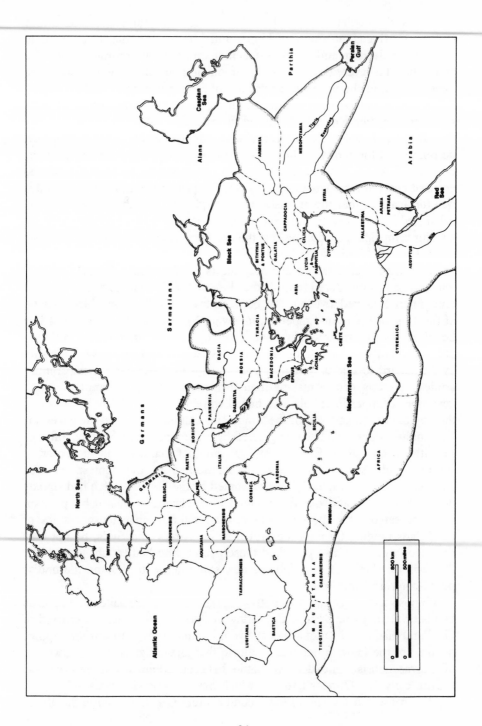

36

of the Roman Empire, and it is possible to see in it the beginning of that long, slow decline, which, with some intermissions, led ultimately to its dissolution. Lack of an acceptable heir to the principate and the army's realisation of its power, both to make and destroy emperors, was a lethal combination which eventually undermined the stability of the state, and never more so than in the troubled years of the third century yet to come.

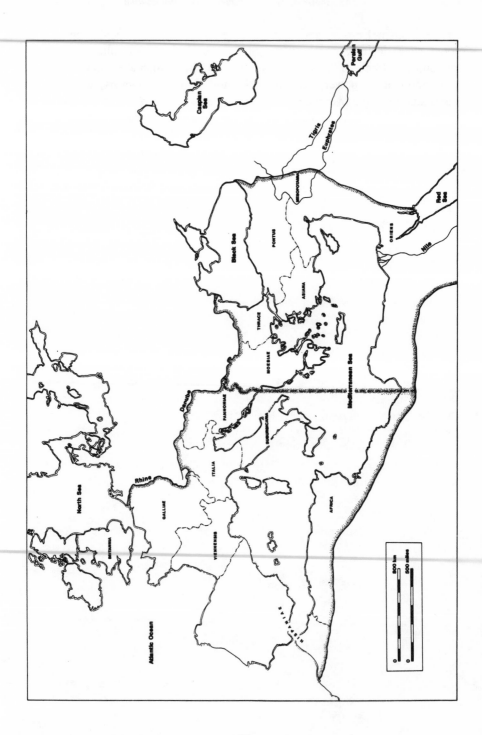

III

THE EMPIRE AT WAR: SURVIVAL AND DEFEAT

Internal strife was to be more destructive to the Roman Empire in the third century than any outside threat. But, although the accession of Severus brought changes, the omens were at first not unpropitious. Severus' immediate concern after the defeat and death of Albinus was once more the Parthian frontier, where the treaty made only two years earlier had been broken and Mesopotamia invaded. Three new legions appear to have been recruited in Dalmatia specifically for this campaign. The Parthian army began to retreat while Severus was still in Syria, and in the pursuit which followed, the Roman army advanced without undue difficulty to capture Babylon, Seleucia and finally Ctesiphon; Mesopotamia was now reduced to provincial status with a garrison of two legions. But an attack made on the isolated desert city of Hatra, whose ruler had supported Pescennius Niger in the civil war, was unsuccessful, partly due to an epidemic of dysentery, partly to a mutiny, in the Roman army, and so Severus' second Parthian war was terminated somewhat unsatisfactorily at the end of the second century.

Yet again the fatal mistake had been committed: the Parthian king, Vologeses, had been allowed to escape, and, despite an impressive total of prisoners, the bulk of the Parthian army seems to have survived to re-form and to fight another day. Hence, although defeated, Parthia once more remained unconquered and a continuing threat to the stability of the eastern frontier. One important consequence, though, was the promotion of the Syrian town of Palmyra to the rank of a *colonia*. Lying across a major trade route to the east, the city was to become one of the richest in the Empire during the third century and was to play a conspicuous role in the later wars.

The next few years of Severus' principate were untroubled by major foreign wars. Some effort was put into rooting out the surviving supporters of Niger and Albinus; considerable benefit accrued in this to the emperor by the

39

sequestration of their estates. But, in Britain attempts by successive governors had entirely failed to expel and defeat the Caledonian tribes which had invaded during the absence of the provincial garrison in the civil war. Consequently the governor, Alfenus Senecio, finally appealed to the emperor, requesting his personal intervention to end the war.

In 209, Severus arrived in York, together with his two sons and the imperial court, and mounted a punitive expedition which penetrated deeply into Scotland. A new legionary base for the operations was established on the river Tay at Carpow, which suggests that reoccupation of parts, or even the whole, of Scotland was perhaps contemplated. Yet, even though Severus' son, Caracalla, was given personal command of the second campaign, the Caledonian forces remained obstinately unbeaten, and in the following year Severus, already a sick man, died at York. Caracalla, now emperor, immediately concluded an advantageous peace treaty with the Scottish tribes and withdrew the frontier of Britain to Hadrian's Wall, which with its outpost forts was repaired and strengthened in many places. It would be interesting to know the terms of the treaty, for it succeeded where others had earlier failed and the most northerly frontier of the Empire appears to have remained peaceful and prosperous for nearly a century thereafter.

Caracalla at first acceded to his father's wishes that he and his brother Geta should control the Empire as joint Augusti, but not for long. On their return to Rome from Britain, Caracalla rapidly laid plans for Geta's murder, after which all mentions of the junior Augustus were erased from inscriptions and his currency was called in.

The scene of major military operations was next switched to the Upper Rhine and Danube frontiers, where the westward migration of the Alamanni was threatening disruption. Caracalla strengthened the fortifications, rebuilding many forts in masonry, and the construction of the Raetian wall has been attributed to him; the latter replaced the earlier palisade between Lorch and Hienheim, but was of comparatively slight proportions although allied with an integrated system of watch-towers. Sometimes also attributed to this emperor was the construction in Upper Germany of the ditch and rampart to the rear of the palisade, which was itself retained, and which had formed the earlier Antonine frontier. The garrison of Raetia was temporarily strengthened for the campaign by the transfer of a legion from Egypt, and by vexillations taken from legions in the lower Danube. A two-pronged attack was launched from Mainz and Raetia across the rivers and was completely successful. This triumph, however, was not matched elsewhere and Caracalla was forced to resort to bribery to keep the peace with the tribes in lower Germany. A brief return to Rome was next followed by a tour of inspection of the Danube frontier defences in AD 214. Satisfied by what he saw, Caracalla was able to turn his attention back to the east where he had for long cherished an alliance with a subdued Parthia, integrated with the Roman Empire.

As usual, an army was mustered by taking vexillations from other frontiers, with the Rhine, the Danube and Africa sending up their quotas. But the initial campaign against Armenia was a complete fiasco and the army had to withdraw precipitately to Syria. Riots in Egypt, whose legion was still apparently absent in Germany, caused a diversion and Caracalla was forced to move in person to reimpose peace. Ultimately in 216 he was able to resume military action against Parthia, although he was not destined to see the results. After some ineffectual campaigning the army advanced into Media, but failed to bring the Parthians to battle; Caracalla was murdered on the orders of Macrinus, prefect of the Praetorian Guard, who was proclaimed emperor in his place.

The accession of Macrinus was a further step in the downward trend which the fortunes of the Roman Empire had taken. He was the first emperor of Rome not to come from the senatorial order, and so set the pattern for his successors, who were mostly soldiers owing their elevation almost entirely to the support of their colleagues. Unfortunately, Macrinus, the first of these soldier-emperors, was neither a good general nor a good administrator. The gains made by Severus and Caracalla in the east were rapidly squandered, with Armenia passing from Roman control and Parthia regaining the ascendancy. The rise of the boy-usurper, Elagabalus, backed by powerful army factions, quickly put an end to the reign of Macrinus, who was executed following his defeat in battle near Antioch.

The reign of Elagabalus was comparatively brief, once the support of the army, which had rapidly seen its error, was withdrawn. Machinations by Julia Mammaea, a cousin of Caracalla, promoted instead the cause of her son, the young boy, Severus Alexander, who became emperor after the timely murder of Elagabalus by the Praetorian Guard.

His reign began peacefully enough and, guided by his mother, he was able to correct some of the excesses of his predecessor. But the arrival of a new and powerful dynasty within the Parthian empire once more created a serious threat to the eastern frontier, a threat that could not be indefinitely ignored. Artaxerxes, of the ancient kingdom of the Achaemenids, overthrew the reigning dynasty of Arsacid kings and was proclaimed the King of Kings. He subdued Parthia, established himself in Media, took much of Mesopotamia and clearly intended to invade Syria and Cappadocia with the intention of restoring the old Persian empire of Darius.

The response of Severus Alexander was to raise an army, partly from new drafts of recruits, partly by withdrawing vexillations from the Danube and the Rhine, but the campaign was from the first beset with troubles. The local garrison in Mesopotamia mutinied; disease was rife. Two of the three columns into which the attack was split entirely failed to achieve their objectives, while one at least suffered disastrous casualties. Only the northernmost advance through Armenia prospered and Media was successfully invaded before the column was withdrawn to Antioch. Again the Roman army had failed to subdue Parthia, although a breathing space had been gained; Artaxerxes for a time abandoned his claims to the territory of Asia Minor.

The reduction in strength of the garrisons on the Rhine and Danube, caused by the eastern war, encouraged the German tribes, in particular the Alamanni, to take offensive action against the frontiers. Several forts were destroyed, including probably that at Pfünz, on the Raetian *limes*, which was not rebuilt. Alexander assembled an army near Mainz with the intention of marching into German territory, but unrest among the troops, caused by his general incompetence both as a soldier and a commander, led to his murder in AD 235 and his replacement by Maximinus, a centurion in charge of a newly-conscripted Pannonian regiment, who became the first emperor to rise from the ranks. It was he who brought this German war to a successful conclusion, but only after suppressing two mutinies in his army.

From now until nearly the end of the third century the Empire was convulsed by a succession of civil wars, internal rebellions and attacks by external enemies. Few provinces or frontiers remained unscathed. From 23ɔ, when Maximinus became emperor, until 284 when Diocletian succeeded to the purple, well over forty men became, or aspired to become, emperor, several for only a matter of months. The period saw the rise and fall of an independent Gallic Empire under the usurper Postumus in 259, who was succeeded in turn by Victorinus. Both were accepted as emperor by the armies of Britain, Germany and Spain and although Gallienus, the 'official' emperor, never recognised that Empire's existence, he was powerless to suppress it. It saw also the spread of plague, probably brought back by soldiers from the east, which caused widepsread depopulation and manpower shortage. There was rapid inflation of the currency which reached its nadir under Gallienus, when coins virtually ceased to have any real value. It saw the degradation and shameful capture of a Roman emperor, Valerian, by Sapor, king of Persia, which had replaced the worn out Parthia.

This was the violent back-drop against which the frontiers were being assailed from many quarters. After Valerian's capture, Parthian forces took Antioch and Tarsus and advanced into Cappadocia, but severe fighting on the northern frontiers prevented reinforcements from being sent to eject them. Goths were invading the Balkan provinces; the Marcomanni, Quadi and Sarmatae were threatening the middle Danube; the Franks broke through the frontier in Lower Germany, overran Gaul and Spain and even raided as far south as the coast of Mauretania; the Alamanni attacked the frontiers of Upper Germany and Raetia, finally penetrating into Northern Italy.

Only Britain and much of Africa remained largely untroubled for the moment, although there was probably a considerable increase in raids on the eastern British coast. But all was not unremitting gloom, black though the scene was. By the early 260s the tide was beginning to turn in Rome's favour, although it was some time before the full effects could be observed. Postumus ejected the Franks and Alamanni from Gaul and Spain, although he was not able to restore the frontier in Lower Germany. In Upper Germany, as in Raetia, most of the land up to the *limes*, and in advance of the Rhine and the Danube, was abandoned, but new fortifications were not immediately built. It was left to Probus (276–282) to initiate the construction of new frontier forts in Raetia, while those on the Rhine were built later still, probably towards the end of the third century.

The Goths, however, continued to raid periodically into the Balkans and Asia Minor; even Athens was attacked by them. Gallienus finally forced a set battle upon them and inflicted a severe defeat, the fruits of which could not at once be fully appreciated by the emperor, as an insurrection in north Italy distracted his attention. In the east, stubborn perseverance had finally forced Sapor and his Persian army out of Cappadocia and back to the Euphrates.

It was at this point that the growing power of Palmyra was tipped into the balance on the side of Rome with decisive results. Odenath, a member of one of the leading families in the city, set himself up as king of Palmyra. Gallienus overlooked this attempt at personal aggrandisement and nominated Odenath as commander-in-chief in the east. In a series of campaigns stretching over several years from 260, Odenath defeated Sapor and forced him to return to his own Sassanid kingdom. Roman arms again appeared in Mesopotamia, and probably Armenia, although ominously they failed to capture Ctesiphon. This series of victories did much to enhance the already considerable prestige of Palmyra, despite Odenath's assassination, and despite the attempts by Gallienus to enforce limits on its expansion. But his involvements elsewhere prevented him from taking action and Palmyra remained supreme in the eastern Empire for some years to come.

The reign of Gallienus represents the lowest trough of the depression into which the Roman Empire fell during the third century. And yet, divided, virtually bankrupt, with an inadequate and poor-quality army and with severe manpower problems, the lowest point, as seen in retrospect, seems to have been passed by the end of his reign. Three following emperors, Claudius Gothicus, Aurelian and Probus, together covering the period 268–282, were able to suppress the independent rulers in the west and east and so reunite the Empire. The remaining barbarian invaders on the northern frontiers were repelled or defeated and a start was made on the construction of new frontier defences, but only after another attempt had been made by the Goths to invade the Balkans in 268 and after a further serious onslaught into Gaul in 276.

Rome itself owed its new and splendid twenty-kilometre circuit of walls to Aurelian, who, not without difficulty, was also responsible for curbing the power of Palmyra in the east. Probus systematically repaired the Rhenish and Raetian frontiers and possibly also strengthened the coastal forts in Britain and northern Gaul; to him perhaps may also be credited the start of the programme of construction of major urban fortifications in Gaul and Germany. Many of the towns were previously undefended and consequently had suffered severely during the invasions. Gradually control of the Empire was reimposed from the centre, although with differences. As already noted, the land between the Rhine, the Danube and the second-century *limes*, the so-called *agri decumates*, was abandoned, while trans-Danubian Dacia, repeatedly assailed in recent years by the Goths, had been evacuated by Aurelian, as its recovery looked to have proved too costly an operation, and unequal to its value as a province.

A brief return to anarchy prevailed after the assassination of Probus in 282, which, however, did not prevent one of his successors, Carus, from recovering the province of Mesopotamia and from capturing Ctesiphon. But the eastern army, returning after its victorious campaigns, once more took matters into its own hands and chose as emperor one of its own officers in the place of Carus' sons; so, in 284, Diocletian emerged as emperor and became one of the best-known and most effective rulers of the Roman state, even though his reign saw the complete alteration of the Empire from what it had been to one of absolute monarchy, and even though, in some of the reforms which he introduced to save it from destruction and to bind it more closely together, there lay the dormant seeds of its final dissolution. But the hour had once more, as at the end of the Republic, produced the man.

Diocletian, like many of his third century predecessors, rose from the ranks to hold the consulship; unlike some of those same predecessors, he seems to have possessed a greater aptitude for administration, diplomacy and statesmanship. His assessment of the Empire's needs was rapidly formulated, some would say in altogether a too hasty manner. But the Empire required instant surgery if it was to survive, so if some of his decisions appear unwise in retrospect, yet, taken as a whole, more good than ill flowed from them. One of his first realisations was that the burden of Empire had become too great for one man to carry; consequently he recruited a friend and colleague of his army days, Maximianus, to help him in his task, and gave to him the title of Caesar, although a year later he was elevated by his troups to Augustus.

The next logical step, which was taken in 293, was the appointment of a Caesar to assist each of the Augusti; and so the Tetrarchy was born with the promotion of Galerius Valerius to assist Diocletian and Valerius Constantius to aid Maximianus. Ultimately it was decided that each Augustus should retire after twenty years in favour of his Caesar, so ensuring a smooth succession and happily the prevention of further civil wars by the rise of usurpers. Moreover, each ruler had territorial responsibilities, with Maximianus and Constantius controlling Italy and the west and Diocletian and Galerius the east. But it is possible to detect in Diocletian's arrangements for the Empire's division the shift in its centre of gravity towards the east; a change which was to be completed in the fourth century.

The early part of Diocletian's reign was not untroubled. Gaul was still unsettled and the weakened frontier was being subjected to further attacks from Germany. Maximianus put down rebellion and once more repulsed the Alamanni, with Diocletian's help from Raetia. Having also defeated the Franks, he acknowledged one of their leaders as a client king, to act as a buffer between the frontier and free Germany. It was probably now, or not much later, that the frontier fortifications of Raetia and Upper Germany were strengthened by the construction of new forts often of a radically different design. The line followed the Rhine from Mainz southwards to Lake Constance and from there across to the valley of the river Iller, by which route it then returned to the Danube. Forts of the period include Burg bei Stein am Rhein at the western tip of the lake and Oberwinterthur a few kilometres south.

Maximianus was, however, less successful in his dealings with Britain. The prefect of the *classis Britannica*, Carausius, given the task of suppressing the many pirates infesting the North Sea and the Channel, *c.* 285, used his position to enrich himself. An order for his capture and execution was issued which caused him to proclaim himself Augustus. Maximianus failed to defeat him in a battle at sea and, with the tacit approval of Diocletian, left him to rule Britain and northern Gaul, which he appears to have done with some measure of popularity and success, until he was murdered by his chief minister, Allectus, probably *c.* 293. Allectus carried far less authority than Carausius and fell to a vigorous campaign mounted by Constantius Caesar; so Britain was once again reunited with the Empire.

Diocletian had in the meantime been active elsewhere. Making his headquarters initially at Sirmium, he inflicted two defeats on the Sarmatians across the Danube. In the east he repelled an invasion of Syria and put down rebellions in Egypt with forces taken from the Danubian army. He was also able to strengthen, for a short while, Rome's claim to Mesopotamia with the replacement of the king of Armenia by his own nominee.

But still the ebb and flow of battle continued on the frontiers, although now, despite individual engagements sometimes being lost, wars were mostly won and Roman authority was, in the closing years of the third century, almost everywhere re-established. In Pannonia renewed attacks by the Sarmatians and Marcomanni were defeated by Galerius, while Constantius repulsed an incursion of Alamanni into Gallia Belgica. Maximianus took the place of Galerius on the Danube, after the latter had been transferred to the east and inflicted a severe defeat on a Carpian force, after which he hastened to Numidia where he successfully repulsed a Moorish invasion from the interior. But Galerius, now commanding the army in Mesopotamia, suffered a severe reverse at the hands of the Persians, and recovered his position only by taking further strong reinforcements from the Danube garrisons.

In 303, Diocletian celebrated his twenty years as Augustus and, in accordance with his proposals for the establishment of a peaceful line of succession, decided to abdicate and, for political reasons, pressed Maximianus to follow his example. Diocletian retired readily in 305 to his palace at Salona; Maximianus was far more reluctant to do so. Constantius and Galerius now became Augusti in their places and Valerius and Maximianus were appointed to replace them as the two new Caesars. The territorial arrangements, which were introduced at the same time, gave Galerius in the east far greater power than Constantius, despite the latter's seniority.

Since the reclamation of Britain in 296, war had broken out on the northern frontier, which ultimately required the presence of Constantius to quell. In 306 he crossed the Channel, taking his son Constantine with him, and defeated the invading tribes, only shortly afterwards to become the second emperor to die at York. The army in Britain immediately proclaimed his son as Augustus, but Galerius refused to confirm the title and, instead, acknowledged him in the lower rank as Caesar, giving the senior post in the west to Severus. There followed six years of extreme confusion in which at one time there were no less than six Augusti in conflict, and which saw the demise of the Tetrarchy and of Diocletian's attempts to ensure smooth successions. This series of civil wars finally ended in 324, after the battles of Adrianople and Chrysopolis, with the Empire again united under the control of one man, Constantine.

Although these internal wars were serious and undoubtedly contributed yet more wastage to Rome's increasingly limited resources, the frontiers fortunately remained comparatively peaceful. There was sporadic raiding which was beaten off without too much difficulty; it would seem that Rome's external enemies were still suffering from exhaustion caused by their earlier rebuffs and defeats. Nevertheless there was one significant change in the direction of attacks. The Goths, instead of running head on into the defences of the Balkans or Asia Minor, had deflected their advance westwards towards the middle Danube, where they were pressing against the Sarmatians; at first they were defeated and made a treaty with Rome, in which they undertook the defence of the frontier and the provision of recruits for the army. War also broke out again in the east just before Constantine's death, in breach of the treaty made earlier with the Persians by Diocletian. Once again their forces invaded Armenia and captured its king; once more they were defeated by the Roman army and once more they were allowed to recover from their defeat. The Roman Empire never possessed the power to conquer and occupy Parthia, later Persia, while similarly Persia could not over-run even the eastern Roman Empire.

The contestants were about evenly matched and, as we have seen, inflicted crippling defeats on each other from time to time, with neither being in a position to capitalise fully on their victories. Consequently, although the fortunes of war swung from side to side, perpetually conflicting interests between the two states ensured its never-ending continuation. Equally, neither side could afford to give up the struggle because at stake was the mastery of the lucrative eastern trade routes overland to India and China. As one of his last tasks, Constantine was preparing to press home his attack on Persia when he died in Nicomedia in 337, and left the Empire divided between his three sons: Constantine II who was at the time responsible for Spain, Gaul and Britain, Constantius for the provinces of Asia, Syria and Egypt, and Constans who commanded Italy, Africa and much of the Danube.

The army fielded by Constantine I differed radically from that of the high Empire. Diocletian was largely responsible for initiating the reforms, although it could be argued that he merely accelerated changes which had begun much earlier. Nevertheless, it was he who made the final separation between the armed forces and civil administration. Increasingly also, barbarians were being recruited into the army, so changing its essential nature. Naturally in time this change caused a down-grading of the legions from their position of eminence, with auxiliaries, more especially cavalry, ranking equal to or above them.

Constantine went further with the reforms by creating a large, mobile field army, the *comitatenses*, drawn mainly from units in Gaul and Germany, with its integral parts commanded respectively by a *magister peditum* and a *magister equitum*. In contrast, and now of lower grade, were the *ripenses*, later *limitanei*, static troops who guarded frontiers, usually under the command of a *dux*. Later the field army was divided between a strategic, central force, renamed *palatini*, an élite which in part assumed the functions of the old praetorian guard, and regional armies commanded, according to their size, by a *magister* or *comes*. Most units of the latter were accommodated in towns on, or near, main lines of communication so as to increase their mobility.

Major field armies were retained in Gaul and in the east, each under a *magister equitum*, while groups of slightly lesser size and each commanded by a *comes* were held ready in Illyricum and Thrace. In many instances also, the old legions were divided into new units, usually a thousand strong, and stationed permanently away from their base fortresses; many new legions of this strength were also formed. In addition, by 365 certain units seem to have been accorded the status of *pseudocomitatenses;* mostly frontier troops, they could if need be reinforce the field armies, although the privileges and pay granted to them were not as great as those of the true *comitatenses.*

The triple reign of Constantine's sons began inauspiciously with a mutiny in the army at Constantinople. In 340 came the first fraternal quarrel between Constantine II and Constans, in which the former was killed, leaving Constans in possession of all the western Empire stretching eastwards to Thrace. Soon after the murder there was apparently serious, but undefined, trouble in Britain, which required the presence of the emperor to quell. Constantius II continued the Persian war bequeathed to him by his father and, although he was able to repulse their army, he was, as with many before him, unable to inflict a decisive defeat.

Less than a decade later, Constans was murdered in a revolt of his senior officers and Magnentius was proclaimed Augustus, only to be defeated in 353 in a pitched battle in Gaul by Constantius II. Casualties were high on both sides and this civil war shows again how the life blood of the Empire was being drained away in self-inflicted injuries just when it was most needed. Constantius II was thus able to assume single-handed control of the Empire, but his path was made more difficult by many new problems which beset him. The rise of Christianity as the state religion had been attended by the growth of numerous schisms in the early Church, which became broadly divided between east and west.

All three sons of Constantine I had been brought up as Christians and the attempted resolution of these religious differences became an important part of their duties. Meanwhile a further rebellion in Gaul was largely the cause of renewed attacks on and behind the Rhine frontier by the Franks and Alamanni, while on the middle Danube the Sarmatians and their immediate neighbours had again to be repulsed. Growing even worse was the position in the east, where Persian forces had renewed their offensive and had recaptured the cities of Amida, Singara and Begabda; so Constantius promoted the young Julian, who was the last male survivor of the Constantinian dynasty, to the rank of Caesar and gave him command of the operations in Gaul, while he returned to Antioch to prepare for a fresh campaign.

Julian proved a popular and successful commander. He restored order in Gaul, but it soon became apparent that this same efficiency would bring him into direct conflict with Constantius. When certain of his army units were ordered to reinforce the east, they mutinied and proclaimed him Augustus. Fortunately for the Empire Constantius died before yet another civil war could deprive it of even more of its resources. But Julian was a pagan and made every effort to reintroduce the old religions; this abrupt transition was

48

itself disruptive and caused open feuds with the Christian communities, who for some time had been in the ascendant.

As many emperors had before him, Julian also had visions of conquests in the east and set about arranging an invasion of Persia, when he was somewhat needlessly killed in a minor engagement, after he had defeated the main Persian army. So ended the Constantinian dynasty, after some sixty years of achievements, which had notably helped in the restoration of the Empire; its end, far more important, broke the direct line of succession and could have induced a return to the anarchy of the third century. Fortunately the Empire was by now altogether more stable and the reforms which Diocletian, Constantine I and others had introduced took the strain and, after Jovian, an officer in the eastern army, had reigned for only eight months, the choice of the officers of state in 364 fell, without conflict, on Valentinian, who in turn nominated his younger brother Valens as a colleague.

The storm clouds were by now gathering on the frontiers and, although the Empire was internally in rather better shape to resist than during the third century, they were but the forerunners of the hurricanes which were to sweep away the western Empire. The Goths were pressing hard on the Lower Danube, while the Alamanni were as troublesome as ever on the Rhine. Moorish tribes were raiding into Tripolitania and a supposed alliance between Picts, Scots, Saxons and Attecotti devastated areas of Britain, killing a senior commander and capturing another. In 367, a section of the field army under Count Theodosius had to be despatched to the diocese to rectify matters. The Persians were again marching against the Empire and thrust aside the pro-Roman king of Armenia from his throne. Slightly later Illyricum was invaded by Sarmatians and Quadi from across the middle Danube and Valentinian died during the campaign to expel them. He had already nominated his elder son, Gratian, to succeed him, who was shortly joined as Augustus, at the instigation of the army in Illyricum, by his younger brother Valentinian II, then aged four.

The next crisis faced Valens, who was then in the east vainly trying to negotiate a settlement with Persia. Tribes migrating westwards from Central Asia, notably the Huns, were pressing upon the Goths and the other peoples living across the Danube frontier. In something approaching panic the latter petitioned Valens to be allowed to cross the river and to settle on deserted lands in Thrace, in return offering almost unlimited recruits for the Roman army. Permission was granted but mismanagement of the huge numbers of refugees resulted in a revolt by the Goths, who defeated an army brought by Valens against them at the second battle of Adrianople in 378; Valens was killed in action. The Goths then allied themselves with their sometime enemies, the Huns and Alans, and turned towards Constantinople where, fortunately, they were beaten back by cavalry before they could attack the city.

Since his brother was far too young to play any part in the imperial administration, Gratian, the surviving Augustus, immediately called upon Theodosius, son of the Count who had restored Britain in 367, to become joint Augustus with him. The frontiers were still far from peaceful, and Theodosius' first task was to liberate Thrace and Macedonia from the Goths and Huns, while Gratian himself faced similar threats to the security of the Rhenish frontier, where the same pressures from the Huns were building up on the local tribes, as had recently happened on the Danube. In addition, part of the Gothic army invaded Pannonia and only resort to bribery restored the situation. Increasingly now also the thinning ranks of the Roman army were being replenished from barbarian sources.

In many cases the conditions of service became so relaxed that desertion and indiscipline were rife, while the loyalty of these new troops could seldom be relied upon. Furthermore, large numbers were being settled in depopulated country, such as Thrace, where, although ostensibly allies of Rome, they were no longer commanded by Roman officers as before, but were allowed to retain their own political and military institutions. The only brightness on the horizon at this time was that, at long last, a settlement with Persia was reached, but it was only achieved at the expense of very considerable concessions on the part of Rome.

There was indeed little else to infuse a sense of optimism, for in 383 Magnus Maximus was hailed Augustus by the army in Britain. Grasping his opportunity he crossed to Gaul, taking much of the garrison with him. Gratian, already much despised by his army, now found himself unsupported and alone; he was taken and put to death. Somewhat surprisingly, Theodosius made no attempt to suppress this new rebellion and at first even acknowledged Maximus as his partner: but not for long. Bowing to requests from the mother of the youthful Valentinian II, he brought Maximus to battle in Italy, finally accepting his surrender at Aquileia. It helped Valentinian II little; still only 23 years old, he was killed by his army commander, after a quarrel, and Eugenius was proclaimed in his place. Again Theodosius had to return to the west to suppress this fresh rebellion; again he was successful, but unfortunately died in Italy shortly afterwards, leaving the Empire divided between his two sons, Arcadius and Honorius. Nevertheless he had succeeded in founding a dynasty which was to rule the Empire for some fifty years, even though it was to see the collapse of the west, the fall of Rome and the irrevocable transfer of the centre of power to Constantinople.

The closing years of the fourth, and the early years of the fifth, century were periods of extreme confusion in which a series of schisms and military disasters overtook the western Empire. Apart from the emperors themselves, one of the principal figures to emerge was Stilicho, the chief *magister militum* of Theodosius I. After the defeat of Eugenius and the death of Theodosius he found himself for a time in command of by far the larger part of the Empire's field armies, both of the east and west. Stilicho was a Vandal by birth and his position shows admirably the way in which even the highest ranks in the imperial service had been infiltrated by men of barbarian origin. But, Vandal or not, he seems to have done his best to reorganise the demoralised army, partly by recalling a large part of the British garrison to the continent and partly by energetic conscription.

Another dominant figure to emerge was Alaric, Visigothic king, who had been settled with his people in the vacant lands of Thrace; for a time he was given the title *magister militum*. But such titles were beginning to have little meaning when given to these men of barbarian origin. They were little concerned with the survival and defence of the Empire and normally would have accepted such positions simply to advance their own prospects; there was little else that the Empire could do in these straightened times but to rely, as expedient, on allies with little loyalty to the state. Such men as Alaric were thus able to profit from the generally unsettled times and cleverly turned the friction which existed between the governments of east and west to their own advantage, usually by playing off one side against the other.

Alaric's first move against the centre of the Empire was the invasion of northern Italy in 401, while Stilicho was away campaigning in Raetia, but he was forced to withdraw since his army, like that of Rome, suffered equally from disease and desertion as well as casualties. Another invasion of the same region took place three years later, but this time by a confederacy of German tribes. Stilicho, by making use of massive reinforcements, which included Goths, Alans and Huns, defeated them the following year, and followed his victory by recruiting much of the vanquished army into the ranks of Rome.

This manoeuvre shows, in turn, the way in which battles fought ostensibly by Rome against her external enemies were, more often than not by now, conflicts between armies in which people of the same ethnic origins were frequently fighting on both sides and against each other. With these new recruits, Stilicho decided that he was strong enough to advance his own career and, by means of an alliance with Alaric, hoped to take the provinces of Dacia and Macedonia, to which he had already laid claim. But a dangerously destructive invasion of Gaul by Vandals and Alans caused the postponement of the campaign, and allowed Alaric to take advantage of the situation by claiming a massive sum for his putative services.

The invasion of Gaul in 406 — 407 also sparked repercussions in Britain, where what remained of the army put forward, in quick succession, three usurper emperors. The last of the three, Constantine III, foreseeing perhaps that Britain would be safe only if Gaul was cleared of invaders, took the remainder of the British garrison across the Channel and attempted to expel them, later laying claim to Spain as part of his dominions. This last move coincided with the death of Arcadius in the east and the decline of Stilicho's influence and popularity with Honorius. His degradation and finally his execution came about as the result of intrigue among officers in the royal household. He was perhaps the one man in the Empire who possessed the competence and authority to have saved the city of Rome and to have controlled Alaric, but his removal from the scene at the critical time almost certainly ensured what was to follow.

Before his death Stilicho had in fact suggested that Alaric and his Visigothic army should be used to suppress Constantine III in Gaul; Honorius refused to entertain the notion. Consequently Alaric was left to pursue his own unfettered course. He first demanded money and land in Pannonia. On this occasion, refused by Honorius, he besieged Rome, finally forcing the senate to agree in part to his terms and obtaining a handsome payment from them. Not fully satisfied, however, he next demanded a further allowance as well as land in Noricum, Dalmatia and northern Italy; again he was refused. He then attempted to win success by nominating his own emperor; strangely he seems to have had no thought of becoming emperor himself. Forcing an unwilling senate to agree, he elevated Attalus, the city prefect. Once more Honorius refused to listen to his requests and retired to the strongly fortified city of Ravenna, where later, after Attalus had been deposed, he grudgingly assented to an audience. The outcome for Alaric was not favourable; he returned to Rome and, without waiting for further negotiations, sacked the city.

Rome had stood triumphant and inviolate for the best part of eight hundred years, the brilliant symbol of the Empire's growth and stability. Not since the Celtic hordes from central Europe had swept down Italy at the end of the fifth century BC and burst upon the city had Rome suffered a barbarian invasion. Even the numerous civil wars had passed by mainly without effect; other cities had been less fortunate. Although it was no longer the real seat of imperial power, the shock to the Empire was stunning. It demonstrated in no uncertain way the depths to which it had sunk, and brought home to every man and woman the true state of affairs which could no longer be concealed. Neither was improvement likely with an Empire relying almost entirely on barbarian soldiers for defence against their fellow invaders; it cannot always have been easy to distinguish between friend and foe.

The west was the most grievously affected and continued for some decades to lurch from crisis to crisis, although some form of government and administration still resembling that devised by Rome was maintained, but it was increasingly applied by foreigners who had no real understanding of the Empire or desire to see its continuation; as one author wrote, it was a time of tyrants. It is indeed difficult in some respects to detect any similarity with the Roman Empire, and although its institutions continued more or less intact in some areas, their survival was only a matter of time. At the passing of every generation that had been reared in the manners and customs of Rome some more was lost, so inevitably bringing the end closer until little other than tradition was left in the west.

The eastern Empire was more fortunate and became the parent of the Byzantine Empire which survived until the Islamic onslaughts of the seventh century removed from its control much of the territory in the east and in Africa. Even then Constantinople lingered on as a centre of culture and Christianity, until captured by the Turks in 1453, and so linked the Roman Empire to medieval Europe.

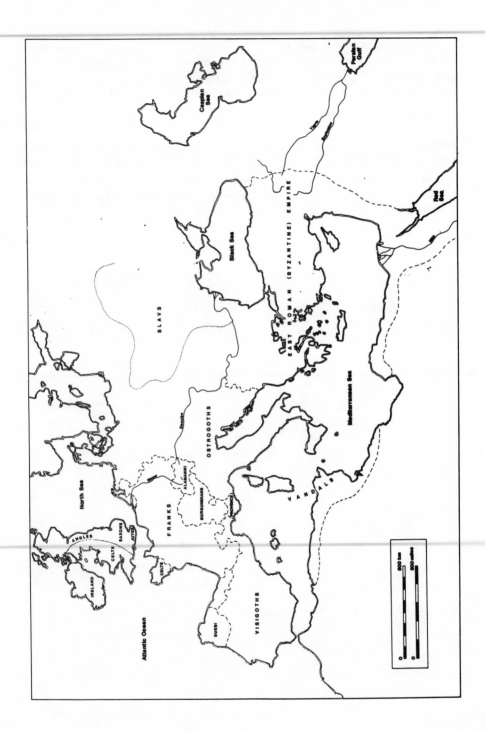

IV

The Changing Frontiers

Something of the Empire's frontiers has been explored in the preceding chapters, in which their growth was placed in historical context. Their strategic importance, however, makes it imperative that they should be considered in greater detail, for they were the protective shield behind which the Empire grew and prospered. Although the frontiers can be divided geographically into four main areas of control, namely the East, Africa, continental Europe and Britain, each with its different and individual problems, often producing solutions unique to each one, all were bound together by a common factor. None, despite the formidable distances involved, was isolated from the others and events on one frontier more often than not caused repercussions on others.

Until the rise of the field armies in the fourth century, the great mass of the Roman army under the high Empire was almost entirely stationed in the frontier provinces. With no central reserve to call upon, a threatened zone could only be reinforced at the expense of more peaceful districts. Mobility was therefore paramount, and the Roman soldier had to be prepared to serve in whichever province he was required. Hence also the need for the extensive network of roads criss-crossing the Empire, the maintenance of which was a matter of the highest strategic priority.

Endless analyses, which have produced a very wide spectrum of opinion, have been made of Roman 'frontier policy'. At one end, it has been argued that Rome possessed no real policy, that unlimited expansion, requiring no frontiers, was the aim. Each halt in the advance was but a temporary interlude to consolidate the gains before it was resumed; once static limits were imposed on this expansion, so the argument runs, inertia set in and the Empire henceforth faced defeat. Some other investigators claim to have detected elements of policies applied to specific frontier areas which owed much to the individual emperors who were operating them. At the other extreme, attempts have been made to recognise limits of expansion to the Empire almost from the first, although such limits were often later advanced, so each time creating a new frontier with another set of problems.

In between these extremes every shade of opinion has been canvassed. It seems to many very unlikely that there was ever in existence a consistent policy towards the frontiers which was applied for any length of time. What finally appears, superficially, to have developed was more a series of pragmatic measures applied to specific problems as and when they arose; in addition each emperor in turn imposed his own inclinations on the proposed solutions. For instance, Tiberius favoured containment, Trajan conquest, while Hadrian defined limits. One emperor's exploits were sometimes reversed by his successor. It is possible, therefore, although perhaps not entirely correct, to refer to a Roman 'frontier policy', when, in fact, no such thing may ever have consciously existed.

Most of the Roman emperors, with only a few exceptions, were realists and possessed a sufficient command of strategic thought for them to have accepted the fact that the Empire could not expand indefinitely, despite the occasional dreams of world conquest and the panegyrics of court poets. The limits were ultimately imposed to a large extent by manpower resources and it is evident that the frontiers of the second century, if not those of the late first, had already stretched the Roman army to the limit of its capabilities. All was well, provided calls were not made upon it on too many frontiers simultaneously, so enabling reinforcements to be detached from peaceful areas and sent where the need was greatest. But when, as happened with increasing regularity in the third, fourth and fifth centuries, conflagrations blazed on several frontiers at once, the army, even when reorganised, could not cope, or could do so only with the greatest difficulty, despite the massive recruitment of barbarian tribes and the formation of mobile field armies.

Almost throughout the Empire, therefore, the frontiers represented lines of stress which could at any time give way under pressure; their peaceful maintenance, consequently, was always something of a gamble. So, it can readily be seen that Rome conquered more than she could strictly control and, ultimately, peace depended on the full cooperation of the occupied peoples and of the tribes beyond the frontiers. Once this was denied, disintegration of the Empire was a foregone conclusion and consequently ensued.

As already indicated in an earlier chapter, it was Augustus who first set about the systematic regulation of the lands which had been conquered under the Republic in a very haphazard manner. In Spain and Gaul the occupation was logically extended to the seas, so, in effect, eliminating the problems caused by an artificial line of demarcation separating Rome from potential enemies. No other areas were so fortunate, although at this stage, imperial thought was not yet considering the fortification of demarcation lines. Probing thrusts aimed at the expansion of the Empire were taking place in Germany as far east as the Elbe and plans were in hand for similar, northward advances from the Danube to unite the two forces. But the great three-year revolt in Pannonia, in *c.* AD 6, followed immediately by the Varan disaster in north-west Germany, caused the cancellation of the whole enterprise. But it is just possible to obtain at this juncture a glimpse into the future of the final frontier arrangements in this quarter, whereby they became linked to the rivers Rhine and Danube.

In the east much reliance was placed on client kings, loyal to Rome, to maintain security and to form a band of neutralised territory between the provinces and the ever-present threat of Parthia. These ranged from Bosporus on the north shore of the Black Sea through Pontus, Cappodocia and Commagene, to Judaea and Nabataea in the south; their strategic importance was great since it enabled the number of legions in the whole of Asia Minor and thence stretching south to the borders of Egypt to be reduced to four, which were at first quartered in Syria.

Equally, the provinces of the whole north African shore were protected by only three legions (one in Africa, two in Egypt) in conjunction with the client state of Mauretania. The remaining legions, plus their attendant auxiliaries, were distributed between Germany (eight), Pannonia (three), Dalmatia (two), Moesia (three) and Spain (three). At this stage, therefore, protection of the Empire depended on the ability of these mobile fighting units to repel or defeat an attack in the field and not from behind some barrier.

The strategy finally adopted by Augustus for control of the borders lasted with only minor changes until towards the end of the first century AD. In the intervening years, some client kingdoms were absorbed; the adequate defence of north-west Gaul led to the invasion of Britain. But there was a growing awareness among successive emperors, perhaps at first barely conscious, for limits of advance to become marked by the establishment of lines that were more permanent, indicated by fortresses, forts, roads and watchtowers; sometimes these coincided with natural boundaries, such as the rivers Trent and Severn in Britain, the Rhine in Germany, or the desert fringe in Africa and Syria.

On the Rhine this had been happening well before the Varus disaster where forts or fortresses were most likely established early on the left bank of the river at such places as Nijmegen, Vetera I (Xanten), Neuss and the double fortress at Mainz, later to be coordinated with fortresses and forts along the river Lippe and in the Wetterau, each of which represented a line of advance into free Germany: among them were the 54 ha fortress at Oberaden on the Lippe and a major supply-base at Rödgen, 3.3 ha, in the Wetterau. Another site of importance on the Lippe was at Haltern, where several enclosures were associated with a fortified harbour. But after the defeat of Varus and the recall of Germanicus, the Roman presence east of the Rhine was very much reduced; in consequence greater emphasis came to be placed on the forts which were retained on the west bank, and their number was increased. New construction appears at Remagen and Koblenz, while the upper Rhine probably received legionary garrisons at Strasbourg and Windisch.

On the upper Danube, however, the forts of Augustan or Tiberian date which had protected the routes through the Alps, such as those at Lorenzberg and Bregenz, remained undisturbed until nearly the middle of the first century AD. Only then were they replaced by others, such as at Hüfingen in Germany; Oberstimm in Raetia; Linz, Enns-Lorch (Lauriacum auxiliary fort) and Zwentendorf in Noricum, the construction of all of which marked an advance towards the river. It was probably no accident that the movement eased the problems of lateral transport along the frontier zone, as well as providing the bureaucratic administration with a firm boundary from which to work; civil and military administrators are never at ease when governing areas possessing no clearly defined limits.

The move probably coincided with, or was perhaps the result of, Claudius' formation of the new provinces of Raetia and Noricum, with capitals at Augsburg and Virunum respectively. The emphasis again, as on the Rhine, was shifting more towards the use of convenient natural boundaries for demarcation and to ensure security. On the middle and lower Danube, as on the lower Rhine, use had been made of the river at an earlier date. At least one legionary fortress had been established at Carnuntum in Pannonia under Augustus, or possibly Tiberius, but the precise whereabouts of the other two Pannonian legions at this time is unknown; they may have been in the fortresses of the interior at Sisak (Siscia) and Mitrovica (Sirmium), although the latter is some 25 km south of the river.

Further east in Moesia one of the two legionary fortresses lay on the river at Ghighen (Oescus) from the time of Tiberius, if not earlier, and he probably also created this new province. The importance of the river for transport was recognised by the forts established at Golubac, Čezava and Donji Milanovac to protect the vulnerable towpath through the Djerdap. Further forts were built to supplement these early arrangements during the middle of the first century AD, as happened also in Noricum and Raetia; in both the latter the garrisons were composed entirely of auxiliary units.

In Britain the earliest limits set to the conquest by Claudius appear to have utilised the rivers Severn and Trent, with the four legions stationed mostly in vexillation fortresses, often no bigger than 12 ha, to the rear of a zone occupied by auxiliary forts; the best-known fortress of this type is at Longthorpe near Peterborough. But the establishment *c.* 49 of a fortress at Gloucester on the Severn, followed later by another at Wroxeter, higher up the same river, would seem to reflect the policy already being adopted on the Rhine and Danube, of moving toward visible boundaries. Consolidation took place under Nero when it appeared that no further major territorial gains were to be contemplated.

The other two frontier zones, in the east where Rome faced Parthia, and in Africa where the desert formed a natural limit to expansion, remained largely unchanged during the first half of the first century AD. Great importance was still placed on the ability of client kings to guard the boundaries in the east and until the accession of Nero the principal Roman force of four legions remained in the hinterland of Syria. Armenia was ultimately the key to the complicated pattern of movements which from time to time took place on this frontier. When Rome controlled Armenia, either directly or by means of suitably disposed monarchs, all was usually well; equally when Parthia attacked, it was almost always Armenia that bore the first brunt of the fighting, and Armenia under Parthian dominance augured ill for Rome. Its importance was great since it lay across the major trade routes from the east, which, because of the precipitous terrain, were funnelled towards the crossings of the Euphrates at Samosata in the south and near those at Melitene and Satala further north. Whoever controlled Armenia, also controlled these lucrative routes.

The last decades of the first century saw fundamental changes in the frontier strategy of the Empire, and for the first time artificial barriers were used to supplement natural features. After the havoc caused by the revolt of Civilis on the lower Rhine and other attendant factors on both the Rhine and Danube frontiers, Vespasian took firm measures to re-establish the defences. A new legionary fortress was constructed at Nijmegen to replace the Augustan foundation which had earlier been evacuated. The double fortress at Vetera I, destroyed during the rebellion, was replaced by another for a single legion. Neuss and Bonn, both on the west bank, were the other fortresses which together made up the complement of four legions in lower Germany. In upper Germany, the number was likewise restored to four, placed at Mainz, which was still a double fortress, and at Strasbourg and Windisch. A limited return was also made to the east bank of the Rhine from the Wetterau southwards, with forts being rebuilt at such places as Hofheim and Heddernheim. Although roads were constructed across the re-entrant angle formed between the headwaters of the Rhine and Danube so as to speed communications between the two frontiers, the governors of the respective provinces were not encouraged to cooperate too freely with each other. The roads were protected by auxiliary forts, especially by those then placed in the Neckar valley. In Raetia a start was made to fill the long gap which had hitherto existed between the forts at Oberstimm and Linz in the neighbouring province of Noricum;

construction at Kösching, Straubing and Eining appears to belong to this period.

It was Domitian, however, who placed the stamp of permanence on Vespasian's arrangements, although some doubts still exist about the apportionment of the work between the two emperors. After the conclusion of Domitian's German war against the Chatti in 83–5 (recent considerations propose a date no earlier than *c.* 90), a series of auxiliary forts, interspersed with some small fortlets, was planted east of the Rhine along a line which departed from the river near Heddesdorf, passed through the Taunus and north of the Wetterau before turning south to join the river Main. From there it extended southwards as far as, and then along, the river Neckar, before turning eastwards some 25 km north of the Danube to converge on that river beyond a new fort at Pfünz. The purpose in this last sector appears to have been to guard the valleys of the tributary rivers flowing southwards to the Danube; it was a system which had recently been introduced successfully in Britain (see below, p. 61). The line was supported by a cleared strip of land which presumably acted as the *limes* as well as a road. Wooden watch-towers were erected along this strip between the forts; although there was no regular distance between them, on average they were set some 500–600 m apart. With the frontier formalised, Domitian was able to create the provinces of Upper and Lower Germany. But the military arrangements here were soon altered to provide troops for the Danube campaigns; each provincial garrison was then reduced to three legions, stationed at Windisch, Strasbourg and Mainz, and Bonn, Neuss and Nijmegen, respectively in the Upper and Lower parts.

The rise of Dacian power under Decebalus, in the last decades of the first century AD, as already anticipated in Chapter II, was the reason why, henceforth, the Danube was to replace the Rhine as the most critical northern frontier. The threat was met at first, and again after the defeat of *Legio V Alaudae* in 85 or 86, by the transfer of further legionary garrisons to the banks of the river, ending, early in the second century, by the removal of yet another legion apiece from each German province, taken from Nijmegen and Windisch respectively; this resulted internally in *Legio VI Victrix* being transferred from Neuss to the unoccupied fortress at Vetera. These moves were coupled with a complete reorganisation of the military commands on the lower Danube, in which Moesia, directly facing Dacia, was divided into two provinces, while that part of Pannonia around Sirmium was temporarily attached to the commander of the army in Moesia Superior. It is unfortunate though that all too little is known about the contemporary troop movements in the area; fortresses were placed at, or near, Sirmium (Mitrovica), at Viminacium (Koštolac), Singidunum (Belgrade), or possibly Ratiaria (Arčer) in Moesia Superior. The dispositions in Moesia Inferior are equally poorly known but appear to have included fortresses at Novae (Staklen), Oescus (Ghighen) and probably at Durostorum (Silistra).

In Pannonia the two fortresses, at Carnuntum and Aquincum, had been increased to four by the end of the first century with additions at Vindobona and Brigetio. The intervals between fortresses were filled, somewhat unevenly, by auxiliary forts connected by a road which kept close to the right bank of the river; comparison between military diplomas of 93 and 100 shows an increase from nine to twenty-one cohorts. It used to be thought that the earthwork constructed in Lower Moesia to cut across the Dobrudja from the Danube to the Black Sea belonged to this period, but a recent reassessment indicates a much later date, probably in the fourth or even fifth century, for its construction. But this frontier remained troubled until the second campaign of Trajan defeated the Dacians and enabled a new line to be drawn well forward of the Danube.

Trajan's new province of Dacia included land bounded by the river Theiss running north from the Danube, thence eastwards along the river Mures into Transylvania, before returning to the Danube along the river Olt. It was defended by a wide arc of forts round the perimeter with others controlling the hinterland, mainly along the lines of transecting river valleys. The auxiliary garrisons were supported by one legion at Apulum and possibly by two others. In parts between Bologa and Teháu a system of watch-towers has been identified, and also some recently identified stretches of artificial barrier.

These dispositions, while making use of the developing linear form of protection on a frontier, were coordinated with block control for the interior, despite the fact that overall strategy was tending to move away from such methods. The boundary between the new province and Moesia Superior, running along the Danube from Viminacium to its confluence with the river Olt, was to a large extent demilitarised, with the evacuation of most of the Flavian forts, including the legionary bases at Oescus and Ratiaria. Two legions were nevertheless still deployed, at Singidunum and Viminacium, along the short stretch of the river to the west of Dacia, where Moesia Superior still confronted potentially hostile territory. Similarly, Lower Moesia continued to be garrisoned by legionary forces placed at Novae and Durosturum, to which was added a third at Troesmis (Igliţa) in the Dobrudja.

The Flavian-Trajanic period also saw considerable changes in Britain. Wales was first conquered and garrisoned by a network of auxiliary forts, placed at tactically suitable points in the valleys, linked by new roads and supported by new legionary fortresses at Caerleon and Chester, in addition to that already established at Wroxeter. A similar arrangement was next employed to subdue the north as far as the Scottish highlands, with legionary bases established at York and Inchtuthil; the construction of the latter prob-

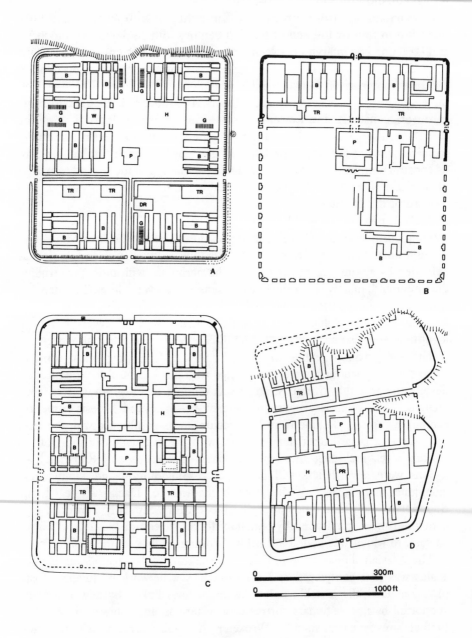

ably led to the temporary evacuation of Wroxeter, while the earlier fortresses at Exeter, Lincoln and Gloucester were totally abandoned.

The frontier system adopted seems to have been highly effective in controlling the turbulent hill-tribes of Wales and north Britain, even if it was somewhat prodigal in its use of troops. As yet there was still no real attempt to supplement their presence with artificial barriers, although it has been claimed that the Cleaven Dyke, situated some 4 km east of Inchtuthil, formed a massive, protective earthwork. There is, nevertheless, a notable contrast in the arrangements in Britain, which still made use of extensive block-control methods, with the developing tendency towards linear fortifications on the Rhine and Danube. The latter were soon to be introduced to Britain with remarkable results.

Britain still contained a garrison of four legions and perhaps as many as ninety auxiliary regiments, which was as large as that possessed by any province on the Rhine or Danube frontiers, down to the middle 80s; thereafter it was reduced to three legions, together with the removal of a number of auxiliary units which were taken to augment the army in Moesia. In consequence, there was a withdrawal from the northernmost outposts, leading to the evacuation of Inchtuthil and its neighbouring forts such as Fendoch. Shortly after the turn of the century most forts in southern Scotland were also abandoned, partly perhaps as the result of enemy action, and the effective boundary in the north became situated on the line of the rivers Solway and Tyne, where some consolidation took place.

The eastern frontier had again come into prominence early in Vespasian's principate, partly because of the Jewish War and partly because of the need to secure the boundary with Parthia, following the annexation of Armenia Minor. The problems of frontier defence here were rendered formidable by the mountainous nature of the terrain. In the north, on the Black Sea coast, lay Trapezus (Trabzon), a useful port for the supply of the frontier garrisons, provided it could be linked to them across the coastal and inland ranges, in places over 3,000 m high; it had already, a few years earlier, become the base for the *classis Pontica*. South of the coastal mountains the natural divide between east and west lay along the sinuous course of the Euphrates, which cuts its way through the precipitous central area of Armenia and Cappodocia in forbidding gorges, often over 1600 m deep.

Vespasian seems early to have established legionary fortresses at Samosata (Samsat) in Commagene and Melitene (Esky Malatya) in Cappadocia, sites of key importance since they controlled not only the two most important east-west crossing points of the Euphrates but also the road north along the frontier. Further north, and away from the river, lies the fortress of Satala (Sadak), also probably a Vespasianic foundation, which, like its companions to the south, guarded the crossing of both east-west and north-south routes.

Its placing was of the greatest strategic importance and it has been described as the most crucially-sited legionary fortress in the whole Empire.

Communications, despite the construction of new roads, must always have remained difficult, especially in winter. Apart from the fortresses, it is unfortunate that little is known of other frontier works in the area. It might be suspected that they were supported by a series of auxiliary forts in the intervals between them. Traces of possible fortlets and signal towers have been observed, but, as a whole, visible evidence is curiously absent. A building inscription of AD 82 found reused in the later defences of Pağnik Öreni mentions an auxiliary cohort, but its fort has still to be located. Drascusa has also yielded information of a fortified site, but it belongs to the fourth century, and may yet be found to conceal an earlier work.

Moving south into Syria, there is surprisingly little evidence for any Flavian frontier controls and for the time being a gap seems to have been left between Cappadocia and Judaea, although further research may yet uncover sites of the period. Nevertheless, Syria still possessed a powerful army group which may have been considered sufficient to repulse attack, without the need for frontier fortifications. The early Flavian period also saw the reduction of Judaea following the Jewish war, and the destruction of Jerusalem, after which *Legio X Fretensis* was placed in the city to watch over the ruins, and presumably to prevent any rehabilitation of the site. Further south a series of *castella*, *burgi* and watch-towers were deployed across the strip of land from the Mediterranean, just south of Gaza, to the southern end of the Dead Sea, to form the frontier facing Nabataea. In many places, and in contrast to the northern frontiers, continued use was made of traditional native fortifications, such as the *castellum* at Tel-Sheba where a series of rooms surrounded a roughly square, central courtyard, the overall dimensions being approximately 31 m square.

Following the absorption of the Nabataean kingdom by Trajan, the whole of the Negev was occupied down to the Gulf of Aqaba, and the gap which had existed between the northern and southern sectors of the eastern frontier was partly plugged by the placing of a legion at Bostra, the Nabataean capital, which now also became the centre of the new province of Arabia. A new road, driven south from Syria to Aqaba on the Red Sea, served to unite the frontier region and also to connect it with the Cappadocian *limes*. It is interesting to compare the two sectors. In the north the Euphrates provided a base line which encouraged, and made comparatively simple, the formation of a linear frontier. Further south, where Syria and Arabia met the desert, there was no other natural barrier to dictate the lay-out; consequently, block control was exercised in places, especially at the northern end where the Roman army took over a number of Nabataean watch-towers. Towards the southern end, the frontier took on a more linear nature with at least two forts placed on the new road at Kithara and Quweira; behind lay the Negev, which, during the second century, gave support to the frontier with its system of fortlets, roads and watch-towers pushed forward from the earlier Flavian *limes*.

Overall, the eastern frontier at this time demonstrates very well the flexible approach of the Roman command towards problems of frontier control when they were inextricably mixed with topographical factors. These variations can also be observed along the longest frontier of all in north Africa, which stretched for well over 4000 km from the Atlantic to the Red Sea. Despite its great length, however, it probably had, for many years, the smallest garrison force of any part of the Empire.

The province of Egypt was what might be called today a 'royal peculiar'. From Augustus onwards it became virtually a private estate belonging to the emperor, entry to which was forbidden to all senators. The task of the Egyptians was mainly to produce taxes and grain, which was shipped from Alexandria to feed the city of Rome. There was little threat to this activity from outside the province, so that the garrison of auxiliary regiments were principally deployed in the Nile valley to maintain internal order, to administer their regions, and to see that nothing interfered with the prime function. This auxiliary force was supported by two legions which, from the principate of Claudius until the early second century, were brigaded together at Nicopolis, near Alexandria; again their prime duty was to prevent internal strife, mainly between the Jews and Gentiles of Alexandria. The neighbouring provinces of Cyrenaica, and Tripolitania to the west, were devoid of troops until at the earliest the early third century and no attempt seems to have been made before then to delimit a frontier; here the desert provided all that was needed for control and, southward beyond its edge, Roman influence gradually waned, before disappearing altogether.

West of Tripolitania was the old republican province of Africa, obtained by Rome's conquest of Carthage. Under Augustus this senatorial province contained exceptionally one legion placed at Ammaedara (Haïdra) until the early Flavian period when it was seemingly transferred to Tebessa (Theveste) for a short time, close to the border with what was by then Mauretania Caesariensis. Early in the second century, and certainly by the first years of Hadrian's principate, it moved again to take up residence at Lambaesis, where its headquarters remained until the third century. It may well have been Trajan who initiated the construction programme of roads and auxiliary forts around and through the Aurès mountains, at the centre of which the legionary fortress was placed. Once, though, the Augustan scheme of defence had been abandoned, a move to block control measures at first ensued.

There is a very close analogy here with the arrangements made slightly earlier in Wales and north Britain and, almost contemporaneously, in Dacia and southern Arabia. In each case one or more legions were held centrally in the rear as a reserve, while actual tactical control of a region was in the hands of auxiliary regiments placed at appropriate points; in such a system the linking roads were crucial for success, enabling a rapid concentration of forces to be brought against both external and internal threats. In essence, the system was permeable but resilient, allowing an enemy to penetrate without doing too much damage to military installations. But once the direction of the thrust had been discerned, forces could be rapidly directed, first to contain it, then to prevent retreat and finally to annihilate it. It was, therefore, an excellent method for controlling frontier areas where no clear division existed between friend and foe. In these conditions a linear barrier, with all the main garrisons concentrated upon it, might have been attacked as easily from the front as from the rear; once it was breached, enemy deployment could have proceeded largely unchecked and the position of the defending forces on the barrier would have hampered pursuit and capture.

There were nevertheless disadvantages in the former method of frontier control; it was expensive in manpower, while a lightning and determined attack on any of the constituent forts might have succeeded before reinforcements could be brought up. On the other hand, where a threat came solely from an external enemy, a linear frontier might be seen to conserve manpower, and it is probably no accident, therefore, that such arrangements had already, by the early second century, been introduced to a large extent in Europe and the east, especially where they were aided by local topography.

Between them, the Flavian emperors and Trajan had together resumed the onward march of the Roman Empire, to bring it, under the latter, to its greatest territorial extent. It is not entirely surprising, therefore, to see why Trajan, the great conqueror, in particular, seemed to favour block control methods of frontier policy, as established in his newly gained territories of Mesopotamia, Dacia, Mauretania and southern Arabia, for it lends itself more readily to further advances, which he might well have been anticipating had he not died when he did. In complete contrast, his successor Hadrian not only brought no new conquests to the Empire, but managed to give the frontiers a solidity which, hitherto, they had lacked; that it also brought inflexibility was not then appreciated.

When Hadrian became emperor he was serving in Syria. Within a short space of time he set out to visit the provinces, especially those near the frontiers, after having quickly abandoned his adoptive father's eastern campaign, together with much of the newly conquered territory. One of his first extended tours was to the provinces of the north and west. In Upper Germany and Raetia he moved many of the Domitianic forts, by now probably rather dilapidated, to more favourable sites, abandoned some altogether and founded others; he also moved up some *numeri* from the rear to new fortlets on the frontier. More important, Hadrian gave a degree of permanence to the frontier by the construction of a continuous palisade along the length where no natural barriers occurred. It consisted of posts about 30 cm thick set a similar distance apart in a massive trench, on average a metre deep; it probably stood to a height of about three metres.

But in Britain an altogether more ambitious project was envisaged, which was to prove the most remarkable of any Roman frontier – Hadrian's Wall. The line between the mouth of the Tyne and the Solway Firth, already partly fortified under Trajan, was adopted, with only minor tactical alterations. The new work was planned to consist of a massive curtain wall, fronted by a ditch, except where the ground did not require it, on which were placed a series of small fortlets (milecastles) interspersed at regular intervals by towers at the rate of two towers between each milecastle, the whole to stretch from Newcastle to Bowness on Solway, where it appears to have linked with the Trajanic defences of the Cumbrian coast. But revisions were introduced during the construction work. The garrison forts, placed at first on the Stanegate road to the rear, were moved forward to the wall, which was itself extended eastwards to Wallsend, but with a narrower gauge. This same reduction in width was also introduced in the middle sector, while westward from the river Irthing the curtain was constructed of turf, with the forts and milecastles built of timber; turrets were, however, still of masonry. This section was not replaced by masonry until a later date, when an intermediate gauge was introduced.

A military road connected the forts and milecastles, while again at a later date an earthwork, known as the *Vallum*, was constructed to the rear with a ditch set between flanking banks. This earthwork has long puzzled archaeologists and many suggestions have been made as to its purpose; it most likely served to mark the boundary of a military zone and to give some protection to the military installations against infiltration from the rear, although this is not an entirely satisfactory suggestion. More important, the garrisons for the new frontier could only be obtained by the evacuation of areas in Brigantia, a decision which was later to have unfortunate results; the grip on Wales, where block-control still remained, was also relaxed in the south.

It is interesting to compare the frontier works which Hadrian instituted in Britain with those in Upper Germany and Raetia. In both cases the frontiers were held entirely by auxiliary regiments, for Hadrian had moved full-sized detachments up to the German *limes*; the legions were held back at Mainz and Strasbourg in Upper Germany, and York, Chester and Caerleon in Britain. No comparable change, however, was made on those frontiers, such as lower Germany and parts of the Danube where legions were already intermixed with other troops. In Britain, though, there was an essential difference from Upper Germany and Raetia, where virtually all auxiliary troops

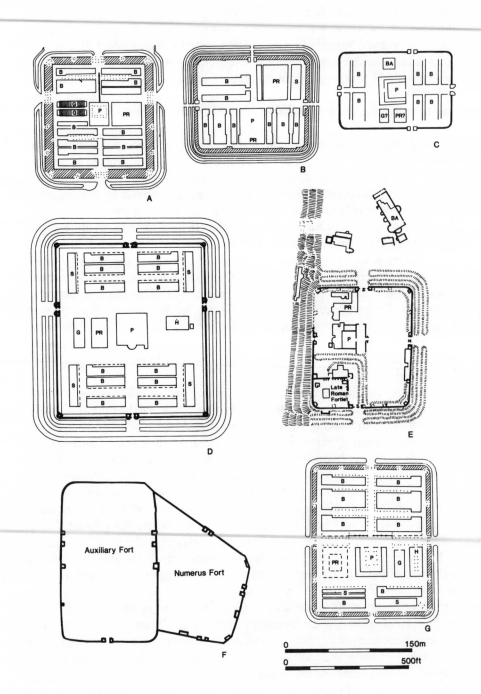

were placed on or very close to the frontier line; in Britain a degree of block-control was still retained by auxiliary forts set to the rear of the Wall, particularly in the north-west, by the outpost forts beyond the Wall, and in parts of Wales. For Wales there was no other solution; as in parts of Brigantia, any trouble could be expected from within. No linear barrier could therefore help them.

The most remarkable differences, though, concern the actual barriers themselves. The contrast could not be greater than between a timber palisade and a stone wall up to three metres thick and perhaps six metres high. It is little use arguing that Germany was then at peace, while Britain had been disturbed by a serious war at the beginning of Hadrian's principate. The war on its own is unlikely to account for the differences. It has been argued variously that Hadrian's Wall was, as with the German palisade, not defensive but only a bureaucratic or police barrier, or that it was but a springboard for offensive actions by its garrisons against an impending attack, attack being the best form of defence. If one accepts either of these proposals, then the Wall, with all its installations, must be seen as a very expensive and unnecessary 'folly' of the emperor Hadrian, who sometimes permitted himself delusions of grandeur, but not normally on the frontiers.

Was this then the exception? It seems unlikely, unless it was deliberately intended to add glamour to the most northerly frontier of the Empire. It has also been claimed that the British frontier required greater strength than that in Germany on account of the more restless nature of its northern inhabitants, but even then, comparing like with like, there appears to be a degree of 'overkill' incorporated in Hadrian's Wall which is difficult to explain.

It is important to remember, though, that a barrier of any kind, whether a timber palisade or a massive wall, is only as effective as the quality and number of its defenders. *No* barrier, no matter of what material, its size or its complexity, is impenetrable if it is left unmanned. The line garrisons of Germany and Britain were not dissimilar; we might argue therefore that, apart from materials of construction, there was no essential difference between the two frontiers. But was that all?

In Germany, by Hadrian's principate as already noted, virtually the entire force of auxiliary regiments was concentrated on the frontier line; both behind and to the front lay peaceful territory. In Britain, the largest concentration was on the frontier, but a considerable number of detachments were placed both to the rear and also in front of the Wall in the four outpost forts, so that it represented a line of strength running through a military zone in what was probably mostly hostile country.

When viewed against this context the German palisade, with its associated forts and watch-towers, but unprotected lateral road, would have been quite inadequate to cope with an attack from behind; but it was probably not intended to do so. Hadrian's Wall would have had considerable advantages in such circumstances, especially with its rear to some extent protected by the *vallum*, as noted, a later addition to the initial works. It is also instructive to compare the so-called 'Pfahlgraben' on the later, Antonine, frontier in Upper Germany; this was a bank and ditch erected *inside*, and between the palisade and its associated road and watch-towers, possibly under Caracalla.

Why this position was adopted for the earthwork is difficult to say. It would have made better sense against an external attack if the ditch had been dug in front of the palisade and the rampart piled conventionally against its rear face. Is there then an approximate resemblance between it and the *vallum?* Admittedly there is a time span between them if the Pfahlgraben does indeed date to the early third century, for the *vallum* had long since ceased even to act as the most rudimentary form of barrier, with numerous crossings built over it during the middle of the second century.

Principally though, comparisons of this nature between the different structures used for frontier defence, which were in being at any given time on any one frontier, might serve simply to emphasise the apparent lack of any common policy for the Empire as a whole, and the pragmatic solutions which seem to have been introduced to meet each case as it arose, were it not for other factors which are outlined below. Superficially, this view might be said to be reinforced by a consideration of the Hadrianic frontier system which was built in the future province of Numidia.

It was probably under Trajan that *Legio III Augusta* was moved to Lambaesis from Theveste and he may also have initiated construction of the frontier defences at the Tunisian end which controlled access from the African interior to the site at Gabes. Hadrian visited Africa in 128, and his review of the troops stationed in and around Lambaesis was recorded on a famous inscription, parts of which have been found near the fortress. He was probably responsible for extending and amplifying the Trajanic frontier defences in this district, normally known as the *fossatum Africae*. Near the fort of Gemellae, these took the form of a wall, ditch and glacis beyond, of varying dimensions and composition, the whole being strengthened by interval towers. A passageway, guarded by a towered gate, provided access through the barrier near Gemellae. Both gate and towers can be matched by structures on Hadrian's Wall, notably the so-called customs gateway at Knag Burn, east of Housesteads, and on the Raetian frontier at Dalkingen. Continuing eastwards there was a long gap in the barrier until the Trajanic fort at Ad Maiores was reached, after which apparently the fortifications continued for about 75 km, although modern opinion has cast doubt on its function. To some extent the gap was blocked by Hadrian with the foundation of new forts at Badias and Thabudeos. North of Gemellae, near the western flank of the Aurès mountains, and again, encircling part of the Hodna mountains, west of Lambaesis, are further discrete lengths of fortification, backed by forts at Djebel Mellah, Thubunae and Zarai. There is, however, argument about the date both of individual parts, and of the whole of the linear fortifications here described, and also about its apparent nature. The orthodox view would ascribe them, as has been done here, to Hadrian, but some have suggested a later, possibly third or even late fourth century date.

The frontier line which developed under Hadrian in Numidia is perhaps the oddest of all in the Empire. In places, it marks, most importantly, the extreme southern edge of the permanent pasture and, moreover, apart from the sections in the Hodna mountains, covers the main caravan routes from the south to the Mediterranean coast. Consequently, it has been interpreted as an administrative, or legal, boundary to control a nomadic, transhuming population. It should not be forgotten that Hadrian's Wall has also been called an administrative, or police, boundary, but the differences between them, in most respects, could not be greater; yet equally there are points of similarity, as we have seen already.

How then are the problems relating to the first artificial, linear boundaries of the Empire to be resolved? Were they, as some maintain, no matter the differences in their appearance, simply administrative or policing lines? Any purely defensive fortification could serve in this capacity, but for an administrative boundary to serve as a defence, it needs something extra. The decisive factor in the ultimate appearance of all these different frontier works would appear to be the strength or weakness of the opposition, and in consequence the nature of any attack which might be delivered against the barrier.

If we look first at Hadrian's Wall, we see a heavily fortified line marking a boundary running through mainly hostile territory, where an attack could come from either front or rear. This was augmented by block control of areas both north and south-west of the Wall, so that it was but part of an extensive system of defence in depth; instead of a strong point, it might well be described as a strong line, made up of a series of strong-points strung together by a massive curtain wall. In Germany there was a threat, not especially serious at the time, of attacks from the front only; behind lay generally peaceful and civilised areas; Hadrian had seen to it that they were.

Along the Danube as far as Dacia, much the same situation could be observed; in Dacia itself, block-control was mainly in use, allied with the local topography, and some recently-recognised linear barriers, which protected the province from external attack, but which could, if needed, be turned inwards against internal insurrection. On the eastern frontier, the menace of Parthia was far greater; although the local topography tended to favour the defender, there were well-attested routes from the east by which an assault could be delivered. It is doubtful, knowing the power of Parthia, whether any form of linear barrier would have been adequate to contain such an attack in the restricted areas where it might have been delivered. In Africa, the only region in which linear barriers were erected was in the comparatively short stretches from the gulf of Gabes to the Atlas mountains, where the discontinuous sections were of no very great strength. The threat here may have had little more than a nuisance value requiring local containment rather than defensive strength.

Looked at as a whole, therefore, the frontiers could, alternatively, be seen as a quite remarkable series of carefully conceived responses, each making use of a variety of controlling methods and with each graded according to the nature of the threat, and developing continuously through the Flavian, Trajanic and Hadrianic periods. If that were so, are we correct in arguing that there was no coherent, Roman 'frontier policy'? The almost total lack of standardisation may, indeed, be the key, even though elements from one area were adopted, seldom totally, in others. Neither must availability of building materials be entirely overlooked; as a critical factor, like topography, it could have dictated the final appearance of a frontier's defensive barrier. Herein, perhaps, in the flexibility of approach which was the hall-mark of so much of the Empire's business, lay the secret of success.

In most cases, the frontiers which received their imprint under Hadrian stood the tests of time. Limited forward advances from them seldom survived for long, while later retirements were largely confined to Upper Germany, Raetia and the Lower Danube. In other places, some were strengthened or enlarged, so showing the excellent strategic thought which had lain behind their conception in the formative years.

Some of the limited advances, and perhaps others, were made soon afterwards and can be attributed to the principate of Antoninus Pius. Among them was the move forward in Britain from Hadrian's Wall to the Antonine Wall, running from the Firth of Forth to the Firth of Clyde, in consequence of which lowland Scotland was once more brought within the Empire. The reason for this advance is not entirely clear and many arguments have developed around the subject. It would seem that the earlier frontier line of Trajan and Hadrian was proving unsatisfactory, partly for political, partly for tactical, reasons, but especially because of the actions of the hostile tribes of Brigantia and south-west Scotland. A reversion, therefore, to earlier policies, whereby an enemy beyond the boundaries of the Empire could best be controlled by conquest and occupation, might be envisaged. This would appear to be an adequate explanation for the advance, until it is compared with that which took place in Upper Germany and Raetia, where similar conditons did not operate; so the new situation in Britain must remain something of an enigma.

The advance into Scotland took the form of a preliminary campaign which culminated in the construction of a new linear barrier running from Bridgness on the Forth to Old Kilpatrick on the Clyde. But unlike the Wall of Hadrian, the new barrier was built of turf on a dry-stone and cobble foundation; in front was a massive ditch. In other respects it also appears dissimilar: the forts, of no regular size, were placed closer together, and there seems to have been a general lack of intervening structures, such as milecastles or turrets. But recent and persuasive arguments have suggested that, as with Hadrian's Wall, changes in plan were incorporated during construction. It has been pointed out that certain forts, notably the largest at Mumrills, were built before, but in anticipation of, the linear bank; set between these major forts were much smaller fortlets not unlike the milecastles of the Turf Wall of Hadrian.

The whole system at this stage could thus have resembled a shortened version of Hadrian's Wall, with approximately the same manpower requirements. To it, however, were then added even smaller, extra forts, which gave the frontier its final, unbalanced look. This view, though, leaves unanswered the question as to whether it was originally intended to include a regular scheme of turrets, as on Hadrian's Wall. None has yet been found, although it has been claimed that the so-called 'expansions' to the rearward thickness of the bank, which have been discovered in pairs in three places, in part fulfilled this function. Insofar as the total garrison was concerned, that deployed on the Antonine Wall was only slightly smaller than that on Hadrian's Wall, even though it was half the length. Moreover, in advance of the Antonine Wall lay the reoccupied outpost forts at Ardoch, Strageath and probably Bertha, while to the rear most of lowland Scotland was clamped once more into the embrace of a block-control system based on a developed version of that originally used by Agricola (p. 61).

It is when comparison is made between the new British frontier of Antoninus Pius and the works which are normally attributed to him in Upper Germany and Raetia that major differences appear. In the first place, this part of the Rhine and Danube frontiers was at the time peaceful; consequently it was not a matter of having to reoccupy hostile territory, as in lowland Scotland. Yet from Miltenberg Ost on the river Main in the north to Lorch in the south the German frontier was advanced by a distance of up to 25 km; along most of its central length it runs in a dead straight line. Its new forts were virtually identical matches in both size and placing as those left behind and it would seem that there was no change in the size or composition of the auxiliary garrison. In at least three places the forts were situated close to the earlier outpost forts of the Hadrianic *limes* at Miltenberg-Altstadt, Osterburken and Öhringen-West.

This close juxtapositioning of successive forts rather than the reuse of existing fortified sites is by no means uncommon and is not confined to these three examples. Frequently there are no obvious tactical reasons for the shift and it may have been due to the slack hygienic arrangements of the earlier garrisons; we might well imagine such a site becoming most unpleasant after a lengthy occupation, perhaps attracting myriads of flies during summer months, which could rapidly spread disease among the occupants, while seepage from latrines, carelessly dug, could possibly contaminate the water supplies.

The corresponding move forward in Raetia was not so marked in its regularity as in Upper Germany. From Lorch to the Danube at Eining several new forts were constructed, sometimes a little in advance of the Hadrianic line, while others were rebuilt. The reformed defences hinged on Aalen where a new fort was constructed for the largest unit in Raetia, the milliary *Ala II Flavia*. Eastwards from Eining, where the frontier coincided with the Danube, forts were mainly rebuilt in their existing positions, such as that at Künzing, although some of the existing longer gaps between them were filled, for instance by the new foundation at Passau-Innstadt, east of Künzing. Finally the new frontier, from the Main at Miltenberg-Ost to the Danube near Eining, was united by the construction of a massive timber palisade along its length a short distance in front of the forts, and supported by numerous watch-towers which were by then built entirely of masonry.

A good deal of discussion has taken place over the date at which the frontier was advanced in Upper Germany and Raetia. Dedications had been set up in the fort at Böckingen, on the earlier *limes*, as late as 148, while the earliest known inscription from the advanced frontier line comes from Jagsthausen and is dated to 161, the year in which Antoninus Pius died. It is usually accepted, therefore, that the advance took place between 140 and 150.

Apart from Britain, Upper Germany and Raetia, little change was made elsewhere in the dispositions of the frontiers under Antoninus Pius, although consolidation of existing lines took place in many areas. It is not impossible though, on present evidence, that this period witnessed the construction of the earth wall on the *limes translutanus* in Dacia, running from the Bran Pass in the Transylvanian Mountains southwards to the Danube, which represents a small advance eastwards from the river Olt. Against this general background of consolidation, it becomes even more difficult to explain the advances which were made.

Strategic and tactical reasons can be put forward for Britain but it is not so easy to account for Germany, Raetia and possible Dacia. Administrative tidiness might be suggested, but is not entirely convincing; neither is it possible to see any real economic benefits being obtained from the generally small areas of territory which were incorporated in the Empire, except perhaps for an increase in recruits for the army. Another reason might be found in a need to exercise a garrison army which was becoming slack and demoralised by inactivity, or which perhaps contained a large number of new recruits.

74

Good examples of the army's practice works are known in Britain and Germany mainly in the form of minor fortifications. What better way to increase the beneficial effect of such military exercises than by adding to their complexity with the construction of a complete new *limes* a short distance forward of the old?

Certainly much of the length of the new frontier in Upper Germany seems to have been laid out with consummate skill and care, suggesting that ample time was allotted for the task, as might well have been expected for the construction of an exhibition piece to the highest standards during manoeuvres. Every professional army down to modern times and including that of Rome has recognised the need to keep troops actively engaged in peace-time, not only to ensure the highest degree of battle readiness for when war comes, but also to prevent idleness and the demoralising effects which can flow from it. The severity of the actions which Corbulo took with the Syrian army group in AD 58 before his Armenian campaign is a salutary reminder in the present context.

A further reason may also be put forward, possibly helping to explain the reorganisation of the German and Raetian frontiers, if the date of the advance is placed after, rather than before, 150. It is known from an inscription from Newcastle-upon-Tyne that large legionary reinforcements were brought to Britain in 154 — 155 from both German provinces. From what precise sources were they obtained? Were they new recruits from the new territories? Did they take with them commensurate auxiliary forces, not mentioned in the inscription? Yet their removal from the Germanies does not appear to have opened any gaps in the new frontier systems, unless these were in turn filled from some other unknown sources.

The transfer of troops from Germany to Britain, c. 155, was carried out so as to reinforce the garrison in the aftermath of a Brigantian insurrection, which had caused the temporary abandonment of the Antonine Wall and a withdrawal from Scotland. Subsequently, at least one brief attempt was made to reoccupy the Scottish frontier, but by the middle 160s all thought of maintaining it seems to have been given up and Hadrian's Wall once more became the most northerly frontier of the Empire, with much of Brigantia also reoccupied by military units.

As with the original advance, it is no easier to account for this retreat. The usual reason given is that it achieved an economy in manpower, but this must be seen against the background of the replacement of the forts in Brigantia and of considerable reinforcements being sent to Britain in the following decades. Certainly the simultaneous occupation of the Antonine Wall, lowland Scotland and Brigantia would have placed stresses on the existing provincial garrison which it could hardly have met without aid from outside. But much of the Empire was at peace and, as before, as well as after, this extra aid could have been immediately found by further detaching units from the peaceful frontiers. That it was not done seems to indicate that lowland Scotland was no longer considered to be worth the cost of occupation and that the Antonine Wall, once tried, was found to be no more effective and no more capable of providing solutions to the military and political problems than the Hadrianic frontier further south.

In the ensuing and final decades of the second century, few changes were incorporated in the frontiers, despite the outbreak of war in several areas. The most serious engagement undertaken by Marcus Aurelius was probably the Marcomannic War on the middle Danube which caused the assembly of a great concentration of troops in all the river provinces from Raetia to Dacia; a new legionary fortress was constructed at Regensburg, so for the first time giving Raetia a legionary garrison, but few radical alterations were otherwise made to the existing frontier fortifications. A secondary line of defence seems to have been constructed near the southern border of Noricum so as to protect north Italy, which had been invaded by the German tribes. Part of this system included a legionary fortress constructed *c.* 171 at Ločica for the newly-formed *Legio II Italica*, so adding weight to the Norican garrison. In central Dacia, then united with Upper Moesia, *Legio V Macedonica* was placed in a new fortress at Potaissa. But when the danger to Italy had passed, the *Legio II Italica* was transferred first to Albing then to Lauriacum on the frontier, to guard the critical junction of the river Enns with the Danube.

The civil war of succession in 192–196 does not appear greatly to have affected the frontier dispositions, since the Roman army was preoccupied with internal affairs. It is true that the absence of the British garrison in Gaul may have allowed Hadrian's Wall and much of Brigantia to have been overrun, but it was subsequently restored and brought up to date tactically by Severus and, after him, by his son Caracalla; despite its restoration it is not impossible that Severus again contemplated the reoccupation of lowland Scotland. Apart, though, from this incident in Britain, these two emperors were equally active on several other frontiers, strengthening and modernising existing fortifications in a series of movements which, by returning to the offensive, restored the initiative to the Empire as an aggressor: something which had not been seen since Trajan.

After two major campaigns against Parthia, partial capture of Mesopotamia followed, which required the Hadrianic *limes* to be reorganised in a major way, although few details of its arrangements are known beyond the massive reconstruction of the Chabina bridge over the river Cendere Su on the road from Melitene to Samosata; a garrison consisting of two legions taken from Syria, plus auxiliaries, was planted in the new province to guard the main lines of communication and in its placing carried a permanent threat pointed at Parthia, the apex of which was the legionary base at Singara. Further south in Arabia extra forts were constructed and others rebuilt at such places as Qasr el Hallabat and Qasr el 'Uweinid, to guard the mouth of the Wadi Sirhan, one of the principal routes leading up from the Arabian peninsula, while another new fort appeared at Jurf-ed-Darawish on Trajan's Via Nova which runs south towards the Gulf of Aqaba; renewed penetration into the Negev served to protect the western flank of the Arabian *limes*.

These moves indicate that pressure was growing from the nomadic tribes in the deserts of central Arabia, perhaps casting covetous eyes on the well-cultivated land behind the frontier, in apparently much the same way as the desert tribes in the interior of Africa were simultaneously threatening the richer agricultural areas of the Roman provinces, where for the first time genuine forts appear on the Tripolitanian frontier, deep in the desert. Three, at Bu-Ngem, Gheria el-Garbia and Gadames, manned by detachments of *Legio III Augusta* from Lambaesis, controlled and channelled access respectively from the south-east, south and south-west. In addition, farms were fortified in the interior of the province, presumably to protect the rich, irrigated agricultural areas; they do not appear to have been garrisoned by units of the regular army, but by a local militia, the forerunners of the ubiquitous *limitanei*.

West of Tripolitania, in Numidia, the existing arrangements, set up by Trajan and Hadrian, were amplified by the construction of a series of new forts from Castellum Dimmidi in the west to Gemellae and el Kantara in the east, all occupied by regular army units. Equally, in Mauretania Caesariensis, the military posts of the garrison, still consisting entirely of auxiliary regiments, were pushed south of the coastal mountain range, seemingly to mark a new frontier, with a milliary *ala* occupying the western, and presumably most critical, extremity of the line. In Mauretania Tingitana, still further west, an army again consisting of auxiliary units continued its block-control of this small province with a garrison not dissimilar in size to that of its eastern neighbour, although, under Severus, there are firm indications of a forward movement possibly to establish a delimitation of the southern boundary of the province beyond Volubilis.

On mainland Europe, very similar activities can be observed. A general consolidation took place in Dacia with forts in some instances being moved to better positions. But little change can be detected in Pannonia or Noricum, despite the rise to power of the Alamanni facing the latter province across the Danube. Improvements seem to have been restricted to the creation of a better road system. It is also usually assumed with some caution that this period saw the construction of the Pfahlgraben, the rampart and ditch set behind the palisade in Upper Germany, giving rise to an unusual sequence of barriers. It is normally argued that both palisade and earthwork were in use together, but the former would have been by then some 50–60 years old and was perhaps showing signs of decay, and certainly it was found necessary to replace it in Raetia. Was it still an effective barrier? Behind the bank ran the frontier road, to the rear of which was the line of watchtowers. Their placing on this stretch of frontier is therefore in contrast to those on the refurbished Raetian *limes* where the palisade was actually replaced by a narrow-gauge wall, which, running from watchtower to watchtower, incorporated them into a united system; it may, however, be earlier in date.

The frontier reforms of Severus and Caracalla, while in part arising from a renewed aggressive instinct, also demonstrate the accelerating change towards a stronger defensive capacity in permanent fortifications. Almost all forts and fortresses were by then enclosed within massive masonry walls, sometimes with added *ballistaria* and external towers. With most internal buildings also constructed of masonry with, presumably, tile or slate roofs, the risk of fire during an attack was considerably reduced. In those areas, such as lowland Scotland, north Africa, Mesopotamia and Dacia, where outpost forts were manned even further than before in advance of conventional boundaries, one can perhaps detect the beginnings of a radical change in strategy incorporating a desire to keep an attacking enemy at arm's length, thereby ensuring his defeat before critical areas were reached. Such new arrangements required careful placing of garrisons, and a high level of mobility. To some extent, although including modifications, this is the beginning of the return to the block-control methods, the defence in depth and the buffer zones of the early Empire. Linear frontiers might be said to have reached their state of maximum evolution under Antoninus Pius; corrections were required now that their weaknesses were becoming apparent.

Soon after the death of Caracalla, invasions by the Alamanni across the linear frontiers of Noricum, Raetia and Upper Germany showed all too obviously the fragility of this form of defence. Forts were destroyed in the attack, but nevertheless rebuilt, until the continuous warfare and internal rebellions of the mid-third century culminated in the great barbarian invasions across the Rhine and Danube, and ultimately in the total abandonment of the *limes* over the rivers. In Upper Germany this evacuation appears to have come under Gallienus, although some disagreement still surrounds the date of the end of the Raetian frontier; current opinion, however, seems now to favour a similar date for both. There are indications, though, in the absence of rebuilding in some ravaged forts, that both frontiers were allowed to run down before the final retreat was ordered.

The declining years of the third century after the invasions, saw efforts being made to re-fortify the river lines. Probus may be said to have initiated the work, especially along the river Iller, at sites such as Betmauer, which connected the Danube frontier to lake Constance and thence to the Rhine in Raetia. The work was continued under Diocletian and Constantine I; the former was largely responsible for new forts in the upper Rhine area, such as the legionary fortress at Kaiseraugst and forts at Burg bei Stein am Rhein and Oberwinterthur.

Constantine was the builder of Köln-Deutz, a bridgehead fort across the river from Cologne and probably at nearby Haus Bürgel. He also was primarily responsible for the complete reorganisation of the army and the redistribution of units which this caused. To him as well can probably be attributed many of the fortified road stations, *burgi*, along the arterial routes of the north-west Empire. They were no part of the *limites*, but they were nevertheless an important element in the new system of imperial defence and served to protect the tax-gathering and local administrative centres and to provide guards for the transport of essential supplies, as well as adding by their support to the depth of the linear frontiers. The system once more harks back to the defensive measures of the earlier Empire, only this time incorporating civilian areas as well as military zones.

Along the middle and lower reaches of the Danube the evacuation of the trans-riverine province of Dacia had also thrown the frontier back to the river, yet the name of the province survived, partly we might suspect for propaganda reasons, partly to accommodate its evacuees, in a strip of land south of the river taken from the Moesias. Strengthening of fortifications occurred along much of this stretch as well as in neighbouring sectors, although specific construction dated to Diocletian is difficult to find in Pannonia.

One notable feature though is to be observed in the development of special fortified beach-heads on the far shore of the Danube in Sarmatian territory, probably indicating much greater naval activity. Some were also built along the Rhine, while another much later example occurs at Caer Gybi on the Island of Anglesey in Britain. These forts were only walled on three sides, with the fourth open to the river, and their presence in Sarmatia, such as those at Nógrádveröce and Horány, implies some formal Roman connection with the tribe. It has been suggested that the so-called Devil's Dyke, which surrounds the Sarmatian lowlands, acted as a perimeter for the area which the tribe then occupied, although it is unlikely to have served as a defensive frontier.

In the east, the repercussions from the Empire's civil wars in the third century had far-reaching effects. A series of ineffective campaigns was mounted against the Sasanid successors of Parthian power. Control of Armenia was lost and with it the Severan province of Mesopotamia. The appearance of the Goths in the Black Sea and Mediterranean also added to the turmoil. Antioch fell; Trapezus was sacked; Samosata was evacuated, and much of Asia Minor was invaded. The frontier ceased to exist. At first, the vacuum left by the retreat of Rome was filled by the growing strength of

Palmyra. Much of the lost ground was, however, recovered before Diocletian became emperor, although the Roman hold remained precarious until he brought massive reinforcements to the area, placing new legionary forces at the terminal points on the frontier at Trapezus on the Black Sea in the north and at Aqaba on the Red Sea in the south, as well as at such intermediate places as Udhruh and Lejjūn in Arabia. Many auxiliary regiments were also brought in to help cover this long line between the Black and Red Seas.

Special attention was paid, as before, usually in the form of restored legionary garrisons, to the points where the main east-west trade routes crossed the frontier. This system may have been additionally reinforced by groups of towers watching over critical areas along roads or rivers, although some difficulty has been experienced in dating these structures. But the new fortifications no longer clung to the linear frontier and overall they give the same impression, already noted elsewhere, of the abandonment of such schemes and a reversion to defence in depth or block-control arrangements.

The return to similar policies can also be seen clearly, if somewhat earlier, in Africa, where a continued increase in the size of provincial garrisons is indicated by the construction of new forts. One major factor affecting the troop distributions in Numidia and Tripolitania was the apparent removal during the third century of *Legio III Augusta*, following its involvement in the civil wars. Then either the three legionary outpost garrisons in Tripolitania would have been replaced by auxiliaries, or the forts evacuated entirely, as might have been the case. No agreement seems yet to have been reached as to whether the legion returned to Africa after its rehabilitation. But Tripolitania saw a considerable increase in the number of fortlets, and of fortified farms of a type almost unique to this province: the fortlet at Mselletin or the nearby fortified farmhouse at Gasr Ghifa, both in the Wadi Merdum.

Forts, similarly planned but usually rather larger than that at Mselletin, are highly characteristic of the late African and eastern frontiers. Most are squarish in shape with square, or occasionally rectangular, projecting towers at corners and at intervals along the walls. In the smallest forts, a single gate usually gives access to a central courtyard around which are clustered the internal buildings, which in turn back on to the inner faces of the perimeter wall. In the larger examples, such as that at Bourada, a Constantinian construction on the Numidian frontier, the gate is flanked, as is more normal, by towers and the fort contains a central official building with baths, while the rest of the accommodation is built against the inside face of the wall. In Tripolitania small units of local militia under the command of *centenarii* seem to have been created to guard strong points within a system otherwise largely made up of farmer-soldiers (*limitanei*) working from the fortified farms.

The provincial frontier was also divided into a series of decentralised defence zones, each under its own commander. So evolved the *Limes Tripoli-*

tanus in the period between Severus and Diocletian, in a way almost unknown elsewhere in the Empire at the time, to become a series of fortified zones, in its later stages occupied entirely by local troops. It is interesting that the *Notitia Dignitatum* makes no reference to regular units even of a field army in the province, which might well be said to have set the pattern, at a comparatively early date, for the establishment of static frontier troops – the *limitanei* – who, together with their families, lived off the land but who were expected to defend it if it was attacked. Only in Tripolitania does the system seem to have been developed to the point where no back-up was required from regular units or a mobile field army.

The contrast with its immediate neighbour, Numidia, is considerable; the *fossatum* seems to have been maintained, if somewhat slackly, as a linear barrier, although greater emphasis was placed on support garrisons situated behind it, with new building construction in the region around Gemellae and at such places as Aqua Viva and Aquae Herculis. Despite, therefore, a sometime close connection with the defence of Tripolitania, the *limes* in Numidia still relied to an extent on elements of a strategy which was becoming rapidly outdated.

Much the same can be said of Britain, where complete reliance continued to be placed on Hadrian's Wall and its forts. The collapse of the Carausian empire at the end of the third century had caused the breakdown of the frontier defences, which had then to be restored early in the fourth century. Although some tactical changes were introduced, the Wall and its installations continued to function much as before, in conjunction with the four outpost forts and those to the rear in Brigantia; only the outposts were abandoned after the invasion of 367.

In Wales some control was still kept on the centre and north-west, while a new form of frontier defence, allied to that in Gaul, came into its own along the south and east coasts to combat the growing menace from sea raiders. This consisted of a system of coastal forts, the first of which were built early in the third century, on the three major estuaries on the east coast, and which contained army units probably intended to cooperate with the *classis Britannica*. The number of forts was later greatly increased. Although much less well-known, an associated series of forts probably existed on the northern coast of Gaul.

The rehabilitation of the frontiers by Diocletian and Constantine, after the upheavals of the third century, owed much to their imaginative reforms of the Roman army, which was then put in far better shape to face threats entirely different from those faced by the old imperial army. Fortunately, most of these changes were recorded in the *Notitia Dignitatum*, a documentary source which has provided, and will continue to provide, material for discussion for many years to come. Basically it shows that the army was broadly divided between infantry and cavalry, with quite new internal divisions, entirely different from those which had once existed between the old legionaries and auxiliaries. The new units of infantry and cavalry were further distinguished between static frontier troops, the *limitanei*, and the mobile field armies, the *comitatenses;* there were, though, some minor gradations, such as that between these forces and the palatine troops who formed the imperial bodyguards. The removal of military duties from provincial governors meant also that a new chain of command had to be formed in a system which sometimes transcended provincial and diocesan boundaries.

The frontiers of the Empire which evolved in the late third and early fourth centuries changed little in their positions until events caused their final abandonment. In the turmoil of the late fourth and early fifth centuries repeated efforts were made to keep them in working order, notably by the emperor Valentinian. By then most urban centres of any importance were also fortified and, although the linear barriers, both natural and artificial, were maintained intact as far as possible by their garrisons of *limitanei*, the overall effect of the changes had been to turn the whole Empire into one great fortified citadel, relying on stage upon stage of defence in depth, right back to its centres in Rome, Ravenna and Constantinople. Meanwhile mobile field armies worked within this system to reinforce any sector that came under threat, or to defeat enemies which had penetrated the perimeter. The reversion to the frontier strategy of the early Empire was, with modifications, complete.

MERCER BOOKS
206 MERCER ST
NEW YORK NY 10012
212-505-8615

Terminal ID: *****645
                                    ***4
8/6/23
                            4:58 PM
CAPITAL ONE VISA - INSERT
AID: A0000000031010
ACCT #: ************5036

CREDIT SALE
UID: 321810991609   REF #: 8820
BATCH #: 280   AUTH #: 04629C

DESCRIPTION : _____

AMOUNT
                            $8.66
        APPROVED

ARQC - DBB4C9FB86ABA5DC

        CUSTOMER COPY

f, a city state. It is hardly city state can come to extended outwards from he spread of urbanisation ents had been unknown. t not only for those who country and who farmed he eastern Mediterranean gyptian and Carthaginian urban communities; but it nean littoral, had to be

argely the inability of the ment, from those required creasing territorial empire about its downfall and the nsummate statecraft, who ollection of territories onto could have taken on this only to possess the flair for picking men of genuine ability to help him, but also to have such men as Agrippa, Drusus and the young Tiberius available at the right time. In all his earlier acts, Augustus had made a great show of restoring the Republic by, among other things, reforming the Senate, thereby appealing to the continuing republican instincts of a large section of the Roman population. In return, and over a period of time, the Senate voted him extraordinary powers, by which, although still within the revised constitution, he obtained undisputed control of the army, and consequently of many provinces. These same powers were gradually, if unobtrusively, extended and increased as the Senate came to realise that Rome could not do without him. Strictly, therefore, Augustus and most later emperors owed all their powers to the Senate; once these powers were given, though, the Senate became virtually impotent, and unable to retract them even if it had desired to do so. But no emperor, no matter how powerless the Senate became, ever dared even to try to abolish it.

Although much argument has taken place as to the nature of the powers which Augustus obtained, they would seem to depend on three main constitutional elements: *imperium*, coupled, to an unknown degree, with *auctoritas:* the tribunician power, ultimately bestowed on him for life even though renewed each year: and his eventual accession as *pontifex maximus*, which gave him charge of all state religion. The last presents little difficulty of definition and it enabled Augustus to manage the state religion in a way which was of maximum political use in supporting his position. This was especially important in the provinces, where civil and military administration became inextricably mixed with religious practices, embracing both formal oaths of loyalty to the emperor, sometimes coupled with Rome, and informal dedications by individuals or groups to the *numen* or *genius* or some other spiritual attribute. The power conferred by the tribuneship, although but a shadow of the former office under the Republic and little more than an honorary appointment, was nevertheless still politically useful in its appeal to the plebeians in Roman society and to the holder's ability to call assemblies and meetings of Senate.

The definition of *imperium* and *auctoritas* and their inter-relationship is much more difficult to define, implying as both do, certain concepts of Roman government. *Imperium* was the highest administrative power awarded to an individual and ultimately wielded by a number of officials, including generals and certain classes of magistrates, which enabled them to interpret and to execute the law, within strictly-defined limits. Consuls among others possessed it, but as an addition to their *auctoritas*, which was the authority and esteem gained by elder statesmen who had been foremost in public activities, both in peace and war. When Augustus resigned his last consulship in 23 BC, he lost this *auctoritas*, but the Senate in compensation awarded *imperium maius*, so enabling him to exercise exceptional powers in areas which until then had been forbidden to him; he would though have retained his *imperium* from his status as a proconsul. Yet he seems, if a disputed passage in the *Res Gestae* is accepted at its face value, to have retained in his own eyes some *auctoritas*. His position as an accredited senior statesman also attracted the old republican title of *princeps*. Lesser, and minor, offices accrued as well, some only for short, specific periods or occasions. But, in the end, all these powers, obtained by one means or another became consolidated into a form in which the individual elements could be scarcely distinguished, so that, with power greater than that normally accorded to a constitutional monarch, Augustus became in effect an absolute ruler and supreme commander of the army, who was in addition worshipped as a god, sometimes in conjunction with Rome, in many parts of the Empire. His successors inherited these powers, although in practice the Senate usually ratified them for each new emperor.

What then of the Senate? It was perhaps one of the most perceptive moves of Augustus to retain it in being as the outward and visible sign of his avowed 'intention' to restore the Republic; yet, in the end, although it retained much of its prestige and a little of its independent authority, it only functioned by permission of the reigning emperor. The extent of the authority which it wielded was normally determined by his whim. Equally, though, most emperors continued to realise their need of it, since their *imperium* and legitimacy on accession was derived from the Senate's approval of their nominations. Hence arose the dichotomy which was such a distinguishing feature of Roman government, with the growth of two closely interrelated, yet theoretically independent, authorities. Under the Republic the Senate had acted mainly as an advisory body and as a place for debate on affairs of state. Under the principate, when most of the Senate's actions ultimately came to be controlled by successive emperors, its deliberations received the force of law; hence emperors achieved their aims by its manipulation. But the Senate still ostensibly retained some inalienable rights as a political forum, which included theoretically the selection and approval of a new emperor, of greatest importance when there was no heir-apparent, although in fact the choice was more often than not imposed upon them, frequently by the army. It also included the government of Italy and, through proconsular governors, certain of the older provinces which contained few or no troops such as Asia, Africa, Cyprus, Baetica and Gallia Narbonensis; the pronouncement of deification or *damnatio memoriae* on emperors after death; and the minting of certain coinage. The emperor controlled silver and gold currency, since it was principally used to pay the army. Equally important in its mainstay was continued recruitment, from among its ranks, of all the highest officers of state, such as the consuls, most provincial governors, legionary commanders and certain priestly offices.

So, although the Senate and its membership may have been controlled by the emperors, its powers of influence behind the throne remained both real and considerable, and the wise emperor listened to its advice. In its revised capacities a new judicial role was also created for it, though again this function was largely manipulated by the emperor. Perhaps most important of all, it ensured the survival of a reservoir of legal, military and administrative excellence, and provided a degree of stability and continuity in the government in the sometimes stormy succession of one emperor by another. It was a system, therefore, that worked well when moderation and cooperation existed between emperor and Senate, but the balance was critical and the Senate had little means of recompense if it was upset by a despotic and wilful *princeps:* when all was said and done, he controlled the army, to which there could be no reply. In this respect also governors of senatorial provinces were at a distinct disadvantage to their brethren in the imperial provinces when wars of succession erupted, since they had no real garrisons at their disposal.

The principal consequence of the reforms of Augustus was that executive control was left firmly in the hands of the emperors, who, if they felt so inclined, made an appearance of deferring to senatorial opinions and lived in harmony with it, but who, equally, could ignore it entirely, with little ill effect to themselves. Similarly, with the emasculation of the powers of the Senate, so the ancient and supreme office of consul became little more than a sinecure, with a residue of judicial action and with most nominations being made by the emperor; nevertheless, as was the case with lower offices as well, it remained a door through which holders could pass to more important and remunerative positions in the imperial service, such as certain provincial governorships, or curator of the aqueducts or public works and religious offices in Rome.

The creation of an administrative system for the Empire, especially for the provinces, evolved slowly from the foundations laid by Augustus. At the centre, the Senate was still ostensibly responsible for controlling Rome and all Italy, which it did through a series of officials and lesser magistrates, for the Senate itself lacked administrative facilities. The need to make good this lack and the growing complexity of matters of state caused first Augustus, then other emperors such as Claudius and Hadrian, to recruit freedmen and equestrians into the imperial service. Foremost of the public officers were those connected with finance. Under the Republic the *aerarium*, controlled by the quaestors was the depository of documents, laws, state treasures and bullion. Charge was later given to praetors or prefects served by the officers and clerks in the emperor's treasury, *a rationibus;* both Senate and the emperor appear to have had access to it and, from the time of Augustus onwards, were able to authorise payments.

To ease Augustus' growing associations with the army, however, he established in AD 6 a separate fund known as the *aerarium militare* from which payments and pensions for retiring soldiers were financed; he provided the capital from his own resources. A further complication was introduced with the founding of the *fiscus*, since its origins and functions are both disputed and somewhat obscure. Strictly it was a fund containing the emperor's private wealth, and the office was clearly in full operation by the end of the first century. Increasingly, however, along with the growth and consolidation of the provinces, it came to be more associated with their financial affairs through the emperor's position as supreme governor, and became the imperial equivalent of the senatorial *aerarium*. In it the emperor held public money, mainly derived from the imperial provinces, which had been effectively removed from public (i.e. senatorial) control and was, technically at least, earmarked for their upkeep. Within the general framework of the office, though, it is possible to detect a little of its organisation, with different controllers managing the revenue and accounts from a variety of sources and activities, such as that which received payments from manumitted slaves. Moreover it had authority to appear in a special court before a praetor or procurator for the settlement of disputes; Hadrian was the first to appoint a lawyer to the office to prepare and present the cases. In addition to the *fiscus*, the emperor's private wealth was also represented by the twin offices of the *patrimonium* and the *res privata*. Little is known of the division which separated them or of their precise areas of competence, except that their importance seems to have grown with the acquisition either by inheritance, confiscation or reclamation, of imperially owned property in the provinces; local officials attached to one or other are known from several provinces, including Gallia Belgica and Narbonensis.

In sum, therefore, the *aerarium* remained the Senate's source of public funds, even if they were primarily controlled by the emperor, who possessed his equivalent financial office in the *fiscus*, while at the same time controlling the private income represented by the *patrimonium* and *res privata*. The extent to which these sources of income were either intermingled or kept separate is virtually unknown, but since financial policy, in the form of accounting, estimating and budgeting, lacked all means of sophistication, it would be surprising if confusion between them did not sometimes occur. Neither is it entirely surprising that corruption and fraud were often rife among the officers. How far difficulties in accounting were compounded by the Roman system of numerals is difficult to judge, although it is generally accepted that it was only the introduction of Arabic numerals which enabled mathematics, and all that flowed from it, to evolve.

Yet considering the importance of revenue to the survival of the Roman Empire, we cannot but wonder how the primitive methods of recording, assessing, collection and accounting achieved so much since it can only have been the product of largely empirical applications.

The revenue for these financial offices of the Empire came from a variety of taxes, the two most important of which were levied on all citizens and non-citizens of the provinces: the *tributum soli*, a land tax, and the *tributum capitis*, a poll tax. There were, nevertheless, exemptions, such as the inhabitants of some *coloniae* and of Italy, while the special case of Egypt gave rise to a complicated system, the object of which was partly intended to produce grain for Rome. The levels of taxation exacted are uncertain, although they would have been based on the census valuations, possibly varying by as much as one to ten per cent. Augustus was again responsible for organising the census of the imperial provinces, though often at irregular intervals. It was carried out probably by the provincial governors assisted by local magistrates and officials; full details of land, property and other possessions were recorded, and this information was kept up to date by periodic revisions. By the second century revenue was collected by local magistrates for forwarding to the *procurator*, or financial officer, of each province, or sometimes a group of provinces, in both cash and kind; the latter tax was applied specially to provide essential supplies of food, such as grain, and other materials to Rome and later to provincial garrisons. At first this tax was organised as a system of compulsory purchases at an artificially fixed price; by the third century it had become yet another element in the general system of revenue extraction and was applied not only to the provinces but also to Italy.

Other revenue was obtained from a tax on inheritance, payable by all, including citizens, and by customs duty exacted on goods passing, not only the frontiers of the Empire, but also across some internal boundaries; the latter were created by organising together blocks of provinces, such as those in Africa and Gaul, into joint customs areas. Levels of duty seem to have varied from as low as two and a half per cent up to the almost penal rate of twenty-five per cent, with the higher rate applying most often to imperial frontiers. Duty in the early Empire was still collected by tax-farmers working under contract, although it is probable that the task of collection, as with other taxes, was ultimately transferred to the *procuratores*.

As the number of provinces grew and they were incorporated into the Empire, so a system of provincial government came to be developed. As already noted, the older republican provinces of Africa, Asia, Gallia Narbonensis and others had been governed by proconsuls appointed by lot in the Senate. Under the principate this custom remained in force and some of these governorships became much sought after as rewards for a lifetime of loyal imperial service. In general, the senatorial provinces had no garrisons, except for a small body of troops acting as a bodyguard for the governor. The only exception was Africa, where, until Gaius, the proconsular governor also commanded *Legio III Augusta*; elsewhere when garrisons were implanted in senatorial provinces they remained under the control of the army commander. In the imperial provinces the status of the governor usually depended on the quantity and type of troops at his disposal. Those with more than one legion and auxiliaries in garrison, such as Britain or the Germanies, were normally commanded by a man of proconsular rank, although to avoid difficulties of precedence with the emperor they normally took the lower title of propraetor: *legatus Augusti propraetore*. Provinces with only one legion and auxiliaries, such as late second-century Noricum, were governed by a man of propraetorian rank while those with only auxiliaries, such as Raetia before the Marcomannic wars, were most frequently in the hands of a man of only equestrian rank, a procurator or prefect; Tiberian Judaea is the best-known example of a province governed by a procurator, Pontius Pilate, while Egypt was ruled by a prefect; the position was usually considered as the peak of the equestrian career structure. All were appointed by the emperor.

In the early Empire, there was some variation in the length of the term of office of a governor, some being appointed, especially under Tiberius, for life. But by the end of the first century AD, the normal term had been reduced to about three years. Each governor was allowed to recruit a small personal staff to take with him on his tour of duty; they were normally selected from among his friends or even his family. He was also provided with funds to meet the costs of his governorship. Some authorities, both ancient and modern, have credited governors with various philanthropic motives, but it must be remembered that the primary duty of a governor was to maintain his province in a peaceful condition for the benefit of Rome. Any benefits which accrued to the provincials would mainly only arise from the satisfaction of this need, although it was not unknown for some governors to provide them with various forms of aid, but even then, usually in pursuit of the primary aim. As far as non-Roman citizens were concerned, the governor was the final arbiter in military and in both civil and criminal matters of law, although for the Roman citizen there was always, in theory, the right to appeal to the emperor, if he could afford it. In imperial provinces a separate officer, the procurator, was in charge of most financial matters such as tax and revenue collection and management of imperial estates. Procurators were likewise appointed by the emperor and came from the lower social class of the equestrians. Strictly therefore they occupied lower positions than most provincial governors, but in fact they were answerable only to the emperor and, as Tacitus comments, he was a wise governor who refrained from interfering in the affairs of the procurator; they were therefore able to check or prohibit the activities of a dishonest governor. Some procurators were responsible for more than one province, such as Petronius Honoratus who served Gallia Belgica and both Germanies. Procurators were usually provided with clerks and a small body of troops and could preside over their own courts concerned with revenue matters.

It is worth remembering that in most provinces, Rome relied on government by consent. In imperial provinces, the very small number of men allocated for civilian administration could never have enforced law and order on their own but could always be reinforced by the military garrison when an emergency arose. But even when a garrison was present, governors did not always succeed in imposing their authority, as happened in Sardinia, where, in the later first century AD, a sequence of boundary disputes between two municipalities was scarcely resolved even by the threat of the severest punishment; how much more difficult then would have been the task of a senatorial governor with virtually no forces at his disposal. As time passed, the legal duties of some provincial governors grew to unmanageable proportions, especially where military activities were equally heavy. To ease the burden from Flavian times on, a law officer of propraetorian rank, a *legatus iuridicus*, was sometimes appointed to help. His duties would be mainly confined to the law courts, although he did not carry the full powers of the governor and could not impose the death penalty. He might also be involved in settling major legal disputes between, and drawing up treaties with, provincials. The work was often complex, requiring knowledge of local as well as Roman law, and it is not surprising that some holders of the office, such as Iavolenus Priscus in Britain, towards the end of the first century AD, were eminent jurists, who often rose to the highest legal positions in the Empire.

The laws by which the Empire was governed began in a comparatively simple way under the Republic and gained in complexity, as the size of the Empire and the volume of legislation increased, to a point where further simplification became necessary by codification. It is usually recognised that the code known as the Twelve Tables was the first attempt made, in the middle period of the Republic, to summarise existing law. The tablets on which the laws were inscribed were erected in the Forum, but were destroyed when Rome was sacked by the Gauls. They seem to have been a summary of the basic rules by which Roman society regulated itself, and were exclusive to Roman citizens. Although never repealed, many became superseded or obsolete with the passage of time, particularly during the principate, and mainly because expanding contacts with a growing Empire demanded more far-reaching laws which could embrace both the new conditions and non-Roman citizens.

Rome recognised a distinction between public and private law in both the civil and criminal spheres. The first regulated the powers and structure of public bodies and their relations to the private citizen, while the second, as might be expected, was concerned with the actions of citizens one with another, but this is not to say that a considerable body of law was not enacted by the state to regulate the latter, and so became part of public law. Within this structure it is possible to detect three kinds of relationship. There was that of a citizen to the state, an absolute condition which came within the realm of public law; for major crimes expiation could only be obtained by the death of the offender. There was that of the members of a family to its head, which was again absolute in its condition, but where excesses were guarded against by further applications of public law; and there was that of one family against another which was the sphere of all private law.

In the later Republic the administration of the law was in the hands of certain magistrates, who eventually acquired the power to develop it according to previous decisions: hence the introduction of a system akin to modern case law, whereby earlier decisions of the courts were binding in subsequent similar cases, unless upset by a superior court. But gradually, also, from Augustus onwards statute law increasingly played a greater part in the legislative processes, first through decrees of the Senate which were intended to advise the magistrates; then, by the second century AD and with the emperor more and more controlling the Senate, by imperial edicts and constitutions which received the force of law. Woven through and through this legal system were the writings of independent jurists such as Gaius, Ulpianus and Papinianus. Sometimes employed in the imperial chancery, they were in an unique position to influence the law both publicly and privately. Many of their opinions were epitomised in the *Digest* of Justinian, the last great attempt at simplifying the law by codification. Areas of private law with prolific sources were, for example, contract, marriage, guardianship, inheritance, tenancy and slavery.

In criminal law the dividing line between public and private facets was always diffuse, since the state began gradually to assume responsibility for crimes committed outside the supreme categories which threatened its structure or safety. It became the norm in the principate and by the time Justinian's *Digest* was published, that the punishment of almost all criminals was the state's prerogative and obligation. There is far less systematic treatment of the criminal law by the jurists and in most cases classification is by penalties rather than by offences. Treason and some forms of murder normally attracted the death sentence, which could be executed in a variety of ways, ranging from the most severe – being mauled by wild beasts – to crucifixion, decapitation – for the military – or burning, or simply being drowned in a sack. Condemnation to the mines was considered almost as bad as the death penalty, while lesser offences were punished by banishment, flagellation or confiscation of property. Imprisonment was only used to secure or coerce felons and never as a punishment. But it should also be remembered that many offences, in these days now deemed to be criminal in their content, such as theft or assault against a person, were then considered no more than civil offences. Apart from offences against the state, where the state apprehended and tried the malefactor, it was otherwise left to the wronged person to bring an action against him. If he was met in the street, he could be forcibly taken before a magistrate, who then had to hear the case, taking statements from any witnesses which might be needed, and pronouncing the penalty, usually in the form of some sort of reparation. On occasion a magistrate could issue an injunction, without full investigations, to protect the plaintiff's interests before a full trial.

The above system, before the early third century, only applied strictly to Roman citizens, but after the conferment of the citizenship on all free-born members of the Empire by Caracalla, it was naturally extended to all provincials. Until then, provinces had been permitted to organise their own legal affairs based on local laws. But, since each province possessed a growing body of citizens, either immigrants, army veterans, or those on whom citizenship had been conferred, dual legal systems were usually operating side by side. Misunderstandings and confusions not infrequently occurred, especially where suits arose between citizen and non-citizen; when a governor was unable or unwilling to give a ruling, the cases were usually referred to the emperor. He did not always favour the Roman law and consequently provincial law had a tendency to creep into the system, where it was to have a decided effect in the late Empire.

The gaining of Roman citizenship by a provincial was a valuable prize, carrying with it rights and privileges as well as duties. Latin citizenship had first been extended to the allies and subjects of the neighbouring cities of Rome and next to all Italy under the Republic, with ultimate promotion to full citizenship. With the growth of the provinces, notably at first under Caesar and later under Augustus, colonies, usually of retired veterans, were founded, providing reservoirs of citizens; this was often followed by the grant of Latin rights to provincials themselves and the foundation of appropriate cities. Augustus conferred citizenship virtually on the whole of Spain through the medium of twenty-one chartered cities. A number of the wealthier members of this new citizen body achieved aristocratic rank and were enrolled in the Senate, although there was some resistance to the measure. Claudius adopted an even more liberal policy, particularly towards Gaul, and his address to the Senate is not only paraphrased by Tacitus, but also partly recorded on a remarkable archaeological find from Lyon; it consisted of thick bronze plates on which is inscribed in fine calligraphy the text of his speech, by which he gained acceptance for the adlection of Aeduans to the Senate. Other of the commoner ways in which provincials could enter the citizenship were by recruitment to the curial class of a chartered town and to one or more of the local magistracies, for which there were additionally property qualifications, or by joining the army. Most auxiliaries under the principate were granted citizenship on retirement, if not before for distinguished service by the whole regiment. Increasingly also, the widening of the recruiting net of the legions to the provinces gained this privilege for those on enlistment. On receiving the citizenship it was customary to take, as part of the *tria nomina* required by all citizens, the appropriate names of the emperor under whom the grant had been made. Hence it is usually possible to trace the origins of these citizens back to the approximate date of the grant.

The number of provincial Roman citizens would have increased only gradually, but nevertheless at an accelerating rate, until AD 212. Before that, though, there was a far larger number of non-citizens abiding by their local laws, be it in Britain, Greece or Judaea, and enjoying more or less of the benefits of self-governing communities. Local government tended to be enshrined in some sort of council, but based on different types of unit, according to the province; although the pretence that most councils were democratically elected was retained throughout the early Empire, they more resembled self-perpetuating oligarchies. In Asia Minor, Greece, Syria, parts of north Africa and Spain the main unit tended to be the city or the town, in many cases chartered after Roman usage (*colonia, municipium*), with a council and two or three pairs of magistrates. These came nearest to the Roman ideal of urban settlement, even though their urban origins may have predated their Roman 'foundation' by hundreds of years. Cities and towns also grew gradually in the Danube and north-western provinces. But there, with chartered cities fewer and further apart, the concept of 'city' adminis-tration was widened in scope to include whole areas as units of local adminis-tration (*civitates*), as often as not based on Iron Age tribal communities. In the Greek east the local councils tended to be called a *boule*, which was originally a body formed to advise a king of a city state (*polis*), but equally it could act in an oligarchy or democracy and approximated to the citizen assembly of the Roman world. The chief magistrates were called *archontes*. Egypt, though, was a special case and unique in the rest of the Empire; the existing Hellenistic administrative apparatus was carefully preserved by Augustus and adapted to its new functions. The term nome (*nomos*) was used to describe the administrative areas, of which by the third century AD there were nearly sixty. Each was governed by a *strategos*, equivalent to the Roman *praetor*, and subdivided again into country units and villages. There is a great deal of surviving information about the administration of the province, mainly from papyri, but it can only be applied with the greatest caution elsewhere. Egypt was vital to Rome as the principal granary of the City, and was run accordingly; senators were forbidden to enter the province without the permission of the emperor. It is worth noting that a similar form of local administration is to be found in some parts of neighbouring provinces. But about AD 300 the nomes were replaced by the more orthodox Roman system whereby the territories were attributed to cities.

In the Danube provinces and elsewhere in the west outside Spain the traditions and customs, bred and fostered by urban settlement, had barely begun by the time the Roman armies arrived. Consequently the new cities which emerged took on a much greater similarity to Rome and were only rarely influenced, as in the east, by existing urban foundations. The idea of the town was a new concept here and Rome could begin with a blank sheet. It is hardly surprising, therefore, that the idea took longer to develop the further the area was away from Rome. Encouragement was again given by the establishment of veteran colonies in some of the more newly acquired provinces, as had earlier occurred under Caesar and Augustus in northern Italy, Gallia Narbonensis and Spain. Otherwise administrative communities (*civitates*) were set up in the meantime to take account of the more widely dispersed populations in a multitude of small villages and farms. But even these communities needed centres of government formed on the Roman model, and there emerged throughout the three Gauls, the two Germanies, Britain and parts of the Danube basin, a series of newly-founded towns (civitas capitals) intended to act as administrative centres, and, perhaps more importantly, as tax-collection points.

As before also, the accelerated promotion of some of the larger and more prosperous civitas capitals to municipal status, with Latin rights, rewarded those who were prepared to adopt romanisation as a way of life; some cities were ultimately promoted to *coloniae*. The populations of the veteran *coloniae* would have been predominantly Roman citizens, although, in many, room was found for native inhabitants. Administration was by a council (*ordo*) of decurions and two or three pairs of magistrates: the *duoviri iuridicundo*, responsible for the law courts and most legal matters, the *aediles*, responsible for public works and land, and sometimes *quaestores*, responsible for finance. The charter of constitution would have been based closely on Roman ideals, although local requirements may also have been recognised. In the native *coloniae* or *municipia*, the proportion of non-Roman inhabitants would have been much greater, a factor probably reflected more in the foundation charter, which could have included native laws and customs. Usually, though, the evidence points towards similar administrative machinery as in the *coloniae*, with the magistrates and sometimes the decurions receiving citizenship.

In the native *civitates*, as well as in their capitals, where most of the resident population would have been non-Roman, a form of administration resembling that of the chartered cities seems to have been the norm; the first magistrates and decurions appointed on constitution presumably were those tribal leaders acceptable to the governor. In time, though, native laws may have become moderated by Roman. There was also more room for flexibility and variation, so that in the *civitas* of the Aedui in Gallia Lugdunensis there is some evidence to show that an alternative name for the *duoviri* was *vergobreti*. But since this tribe was the first in Gaul to return senators to Rome, it is unlikely that the name was for long retained in the face of such determined romanisation. Legally the civitas capitals, no matter their size or wealth, ranked as villages (*vici*) unless promotion to chartered status occurred.

Vici were the smallest units of built-up land to receive any degree of legal status and a measure of autonomy. They could be districts of a city or large town, small urban centres, villages, or even settlements on large private or imperial estates. They were therefore probably the most numerous and ubiquitous nucleated settlements in the Empire, occurring from Scotland to the Euphrates and from the Danube to the Sahara. Whether or not they possessed assemblies or councils of the villagers is unlikely but dedications by *vicani*, presumably as a corporate body, are known. They were administered by a magistrate, either a *magister* or *aedile*, elected by the villagers in the countryside, or by *vicomagistri* in cities or towns; some also possessed official priests. In many cases they formed the centre for a country district (*pagus*), to which they were subordinate.

Beginning with the three imperial provinces of Gaul in 12 BC, Augustus also established councils in other provinces. These *Concilia Provinciarum* were composed of delegates from all the self-governing constituents of the provinces. They had no legislative competence, but from the time of Tiberius they were empowered to communicate directly with the emperor over the governor's head. Theoretically therefore they could act as a check on his performance, but there is little evidence to show that this power was much used, and their chief duty appears to have been connected with the fostering of the imperial cult; the president of a provincial council was also its chief priest.

In many areas of the Empire, but more especially in frontier provinces, a military administration was maintained. This, however, did not prevent self-governing communities from developing within the zones, often from the *vici* or *tabernae* founded adjacent to fortresses and forts. Such sites as Budapest (Aquincum) and Petronell (Carnuntum), right on the Danube frontier in Pannonia, started as military bases and then became legionary fortresses. The development of civilian settlements alongside them was in both cases ultimately acknowledged by promotion to colonial status. Both were well placed for capitalising on the large volume of trans-Danubian trade. In Britain, York is a somewhat similar example, although further removed from the actual frontier line. In the east, however, where from the early Empire, army units were often billeted in or near cities and towns, such as the legionary fortresses at Jerusalem and Alexandria, there was little need for the development of associated civil settlements. Despite the growth of self-governing communities in this way, there were still many other civil settlements in these military areas which were probably administered directly by the army, represented usually by the commander on the spot, so that he might find himself having to play the part of local policeman, magistrate and arbitrator as well as commanding the local garrison.

There were also areas which lay outside military zones but in which the inhabitants were considered not to be advanced enough to be capable of any degree of self-government. In the early Empire some tribes in the Alps, such as the Salassi, and upper Danube were in this category. In the circumstances either a local or neighbouring tribal leader would be appointed as *princeps civitatis*, or else an army officer, usually a centurion, would be seconded for duty as a *praefectus civitatis;* both would resemble a district commissioner and would mainly be responsible for the tribe's good behaviour, see that taxes were paid and administer justice. In time too, they might inculcate a knowledge of administrative processes, so that ultimately the tribe could advance to self-government.

No imperial administration, at any level, would have been possible without a reasonable system of communications between major centres and outlying areas. Rome, as a city state, had originally never possessed much desire, need or ability to become a naval power. Only when faced with the fleets of Carthage was she forced to do so – and made a considerable success of it. The sea-power established then remained to clear the Mediterranean of pirates and to initiate peaceful trade routes between Rome and her outlying possessions. In the same way on land, a series of strategic roads linked provincial centres with the capital and became part of a unified communications system which held the Empire together. Armies could be moved wherever they were needed with the minimum of delay; the emperor could visit his provinces in person without undue discomfort, and his officers could send dispatches to him with no great difficulty. Probably within a matter of weeks, the emperor would know what was happening on even the most distant frontier. News of Nelson's victory at Trafalgar took as long to reach the Admiralty in London and travelled no faster than it would have done in the Roman period; not until the invention of wireless-telegraphy would there be any real improvement.

Augustus appreciated that speedy and precise information on distant events was of crucial importance in the conduct of affairs of state. He therefore created a regular system of couriers, the *cursus publicus*, to carry dispatches and other official property between Rome and the provinces. Special stations were established along routes and at ports where the couriers could obtain accommodation and changes of horse. But the burden of upkeep of the system generally fell on the local communities through which the routes passed. Since all roads led to Rome this was especially heavy in Italy until Nerva relieved them of the charges. The system was also open to abuse, and from time to time emperors issued edicts regulating its use by private individuals.

The government and administration of the Roman Empire was a complex business which was constantly evolving and developing with the passage of time, but not always for the better. It had in the early Empire a fairly high measure of success, mainly because a degree of local autonomy was conferred on peoples who were willing to accept the rights and duties that went with it; apart from that, Rome did not then have the military strength or manpower to create the full apparatus of a police state. It did not always work; rebellions, even full-scale civil wars were not unknown. Increasing state intervention in municipal affairs, especially in financial matters, led to greater direct control and a gradual erosion of self-government. Legal standards also deteriorated from the middle of the third century AD, while the formation of a demilitarised civil service by Hadrian eventually led to a stifling bureaucracy. By the fourth century almost all local autonomy, except in the most trivial matters, had been suppressed and superseded by virtually total state control.

VI

CITY AND TOWN LIFE

Many cities and towns in the Empire were already old by the time the city of Rome was traditionally founded; she thus inherited a strong tradition of urbanism which was derived from the east, Africa and Greece. In contrast, there were extensive areas in the north and west of the Empire where the idea of urbanism had barely penetrated before the arrival of Rome. Yet by the time of the high Empire a recognisably uniform basic image had been stamped on all examples from the Clyde to the Euphrates; no matter the scale or the localised style of architecture, or variations in materials of construction, a man passing from one end of the Empire to the other would not have failed to mark the similarity, and felt a welcoming familiarity in all. Hence Barates, a native of Palmyra in Syria, could settle comfortably at Corbridge, having married a British wife, and could enjoy very much the same order of basic amenities as he would have done in his native city.

This common end was achieved by a wide variety of means, amongst which, as probably the widest spread and most popular, was the establishment, from the later days of the Republic, of new towns (*coloniae*), primarily for retired legionary veterans or for communities of Italian merchants. In some cases they were grafted on to cities of long standing, such as Heliopolis in Syria, Salona in Dalmatia or Arles (Arelate) in Gallia Narbonensis, where *coloniae* were established by Augustus and Julius Caesar respectively for flourishing communities of Roman traders and settlers or demobilised drafts of legionary veterans.

Often the new foundations assumed a dominance over the old. In other cases they might be established on largely virgin sites, such as Timgad (Thamugadi) in Mauretania under Trajan for veterans of *Legio III Augusta*, Aosta (Augusta Praetoria) in north Italy under Augustus for a demobilised group of Praetorian Guards, or Xanten (colonia Ulpia Traiana) on the lower

Rhine under Trajan, where the earlier civilian settlement seems to have been completely demolished during the Civilis revolt, and so made way for the new city. In these the regularity of the orthogonal planning and the use, following the Hellenistic model, of the Hippodamian grid, clearly indicates virgin sites, unencumbered by existing streets or buildings. In a number of rarer cases the sites of evacuated legionary fortresses were converted to colonial foundations, such as Lincoln (Lindum) or Gloucester (Glevum) in Britain, or Ptuj (Poetovio) in Pannonia and Arčer (Ratiaria) in Moesia.

In all instances, though, no matter the manner of foundation, every new colonial city would be constituted as a self-governing community on the Roman model, with senate and magistrates of varying names, degrees and duties. An area of surrounding land would also be attributed to the new foundation to provide farms, pasture and arable for the inhabitants. Although provision was often made for native residents, by far the larger proportion of the inhabitants would have been Roman citizens. So each city would become a small reservoir of romanisation, exporting to the surrounding native population the new trading links, new technology, new religions, culture and the whole range of ideas which lay behind Roman urbanisation; scattered as they were through many parts of the Empire, they had enormous power of influence. Consequently, although many of the ancient cities retained an unchanged core derived from Hellenistic, Carthaginian or eastern origins, a veneer of romanisation, varying in thickness in each case, was overlaid, leading them, at least outwardly, to resemble in time the new foundations.

At any one time, therefore, there was in the Empire an immense variety of urban settlements representing all of its heterogeneous and cosmopolitan nature and ranging from the newly founded and brashly Roman at one end of the spectrum to the almost unaltered native at the other; absorption, amalgamation and fusion was the key to success.

The laying out of a new city on a virgin site was the job of fully-trained land surveyors, the *agrimensores*. Although at times both fragmentary and corrupt, a collection of surveyors' manuals has survived which provides important information about the instrumentation, surveying, recording and allocation of land in the Empire. Also important for reference are the *Ten Books on Architecture* by the Augustan architect Vitruvius, in which we are treated not only to a discourse on the education of an architect, but also to sections on town-planning and the materials of construction. Further commentaries on boundaries and land regulations have been provided by the Trajanic author, Hyginus Gromaticus. As with most things Roman, these literary sources tend to show just how heavily the surveyors and architects depended on Greek or Hellenistic models.

Although many Greek cities retained their traditional irregular layout, some, such as Miletus, set the fashion for orthogonal planning, which was later to

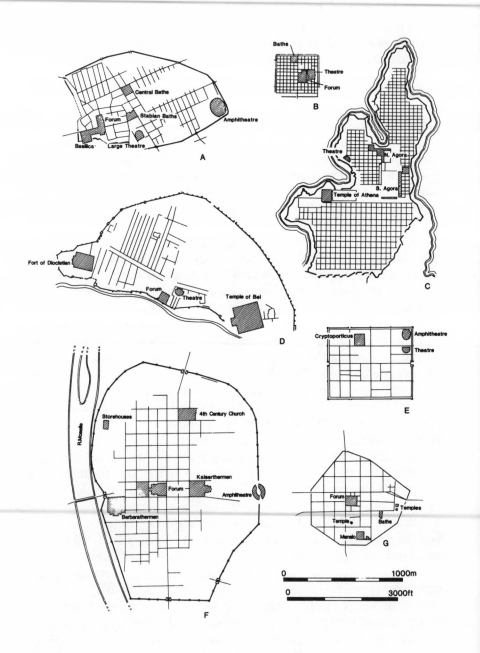

A — Central Baths, Stabian Baths, Forum, Basilica, Large Theatre, Amphitheatre

B — Baths, Theatre, Forum

C — Theatre, N. Agora, S. Agora, Temple of Athena

D — Fort of Diocletian, Forum, Theatre, Temple of Bel

E — Cryptoporticus, Amphitheatre, Theatre

F — Storehouses, 4th Century Church, R.Mosele, Kaiserthermen, Forum, Amphitheatre, Barbarathermen

G — Forum, Temples, Temple, Baths, Macelo

0 — 1000m
0 — 3000ft

100

be freely adopted by the Romans. Hippodamus, after whom the system is sometimes named, was a native of Miletus, and it was he who was responsible for introducing the regular grid pattern of streets during the reconstruction of the city in the fifth century BC, although it is likely that the system had been used before (fig. 9).

Other contemporary evidence for town planning comes in the form of maps, inscribed on marble, of Rome and of the centuriated territory of Orange (Arausio) in Gallia Narbonensis; the former probably dates to the early third century AD and the latter mainly to the principate of Vespasian, although there are also elements of two apparently later land allotments. Such maps would have been fixed to the wall in the forum or one of its associated offices. Tombstones of surveyors also provide evidence of the practitioners, such as that of L. Aebutius Faustus from Ivrea (Eporedia) in north Italy, while the contents of the workshop of a surveyor named Verus, which were buried in the ashes of Pompeii, contained fragments of a groma, one of the principal instruments for laying out lines and right-angles.

The basic Roman measurement, with which almost all surveys and laying-out operations were conducted, was the *actus*, equivalent to 120 Roman feet or 35.5 m (116.4 ft). Two *actus quadratus* (240 Roman feet square) were equivalent to the *iugerum*, an area probably equivalent originally to what could be ploughed in one day by a man and a team of oxen. Two hundred *iugera* made up an area of one *centuria*, which was the unit measure of the system known as centuriation; consequently each centuriated plot measured 20 *actus* (706 m, 776 yd) square. Although the *actus* was subdivided into Roman feet, it is unfortunate that two versions of the foot are known: the *pes monetalis*, the standard for which was kept in the Temple of Juno Moneta in Rome, and which measured 296 mm (11.65 in), and the *pes Drusianus* which measured 332 mm (13.1 in). The origin of the *pes Drusianus* is somewhat obscure. It is mentioned by Hyginus as having been in use among the Tungri, a tribe in Gallia Belgica where it may possibly have become related to the campaigns of Drusus in Germany. It has also been pointed out that it closely resembles some Greek measurements, such as the Pergamene foot (330 mm) and the Aeginetic foot (333 mm). It could therefore be either a Gaulish measurement adopted by the Roman army, or a customary one used by a Greek or Greek-trained surveyor, perhaps serving in the army of Drusus. The measurement certainly reached Britain, either by kinship with Gallic tribes or by transfer through the agency of the Roman army.

The use of the *pes Drusianus* has been satisfactorily demonstrated in the initial planning of some towns in Britain, Gaul and Germany. It has been claimed that the masonry forum at Silchester is based on a measurement of three *actus*, *pes Drusianus*, while the small central *insulae*, representing presumably the original core of the town, at Amiens (Samarobriva) measure 4 x 4

101

actus, pes Drusianus. Elsewhere its use has been observed in the earliest timber buildings at Augst (Augusta Rauricum) and in the first shops of Insula XIV at Verulamium. But by the middle of the second century AD, measurements appear to have reverted to *pes monetalis* whenever rebuilding took place. It must be admitted, though, that such comparisons often create impossibly high standards, not only in the measurements of the original surveyors, but also in those of modern excavators, where differences of centimetres and millimetres become critically significant. It has consequently been argued that it is only safe to attempt to identify these measuring units when the original surveyor was working in whole numbers or even in round figures.

In the laying-out of towns on virgin sites, much attention was paid to the definition of the boundary, a process which was linked with religious observances. Within the boundary the surveyor would first set up his *groma* at a central point and site off two principal lines at right-angles to each other which would become the two main streets. These were often related to the points of the compass, and termed *cardo maximus* (east-west) and *decumanus maximus* (north-south). The remaining streets within the city boundary, parallel to the *cardo* and *decumanus*, would then be laid off to form the *insulae*, and, where the surrounding *territorium* was to be centuriated, this would follow, allowance being made for the *limites*, or accommodation paths and roads serving the *centuria*. In many cases, though, even when there is evidence for the regular lay-out described above, many unorthodox systems were used, particularly with regard to measurements. At Xanten (colonia Ulpia Traiana) there were considerable variations in the sizes of different *insulae*, where, from the *groma* point in the centre, the *decumanus* measures 11 *actus* (388 m, 1273 ft) to the south end of Insula XX but only 10.5 *actus* to the north end of Insula XXII. In addition the most southerly row of *insulae* does not conform to the earlier lay-out and appears to have been added at a later date, probably when the walls were constructed to include the amphitheatre in the south-east corner. But apart from the measurements quoted above, there were otherwise few at Xanten related to the *actus*.

In contrast, at Timgad most of the *insulae* were of a standard size, but, except for those containing the principal public buildings of forum, basilica, capitolium, theatre and baths, they were much smaller and more compact than those at Xanten, each enclosing only 12.6 ha (20 acres). Again, though, there is at the west end a departure from the initial, rigid demarcation of *insulae*, but the extreme regularity of the remainder would argue for the employment of a surveyor who was given a precise brief for a *colonia* to house a specified number of veterans. It is worth noting also that the overall size of the planned city approximated to a quarter of a *centuria*, although the western irregularity caused a marginal reduction.

Planning a regular layout on a virgin site was not always so easy, as in the case of Lyon (Lugdunum). Here the first settlement of Roman traders, fleeing northwards from Vienne during a revolt of 62 BC, occupied an *oppidum* on a narrow ridge west of the confluence of the rivers Saône and Rhône and on this same ridge the *colonia* was founded some forty years later. The site defied any sort of regularity, although some magnificent buildings were provided, including a theatre, and unusually for Gaul a smaller *odeum*, two fora and several colossal temples. The ground on the summit of the hill on which the principal forum stood seems to have been partly levelled to receive it, although massive foundations were also called for. Moreover, with no natural water supply on the hill-top, considerable cost and ingenuity had to be expended in the construction of syphon aqueducts to remedy the deficiency. There were, though, subsidiary reasons for the development of the city. The spur of land contained between the two rivers may well have been a religious site of some antiquity for the Celtic tribes of the region; be that as it may, it was developed under Augustus and Tiberius to become the principal sanctuary of the three provinces of Gallia Belgica, Lugdunensis and Aquitania. The site was early equipped with an altar dedicated to Rome and Augustus; later an amphitheatre and temple were added.

But far more common throughout the Empire were newly-founded cities and towns built on inhabited sites; in the provinces and frontier regions these were more often than not the sites of military installations such as fortresses and forts which had been evacuated. Often also fortresses and forts generated adjacent civilian settlements which, in the course of time, were promoted through the various grades to the rank of *coloniae;* in the same way a village formed in other contexts could be developed or amalgamated, often by an initiative starting from within the community, which sought to emulate its greater and more prosperous neighbours. Moreover, in the Balkans and the east and in parts of Africa sites of some antiquity were frequently modified by the construction of new buildings in the Roman manner; this tended to be a continuous process and was sometimes aided by natural disasters such as fire, as in Rome itself, or earthquake, or by donations from prominent men, even including emperors. Equally though, the architects and surveyors did not have quite such a freedom when planning cities and towns on such sites and their work was circumscribed by the existence of buildings which needed to be preserved and to some extent by the lines of streets, aqueducts and pipe-lines, sewers and possibly fortifications.

The march of urbanisation in the late Republic and early principate can often be traced by the adoption, or conferment, of names associated with the rulers: Juliopolis in Galatia, Caesarea in Judaea, Caesaromagus in Britain, Juliomagus in Gaul, Augusta Emerita in Spain, or Augustodunum in Gaul. It was a tradition which had begun in the east under such rulers as Alexander the Great and it continued throughout the duration of the Empire. Jerusalem was renamed Aelia Capitolina by Hadrian after its destruction and refounding following the second Jewish rebellion in AD 135, and Byzantium became Constantinopolis when Constantine created the new capital of the eastern Empire, *c.* AD 325; usually such name-changes were accompanied by massive demolition and reconstruction of public buildings. Equally, though, major refurbishments could be carried out without a change of name. Lepcis Magna in Tripolitania was the birth-place of Septimius Severus. It had begun as a Punic settlement possessing a small, natural harbour, expanded rapidly under Augustus and reached the peak of its prosperity during the early third century when it benefited from major reconstructions and extensions begun during the principate of its imperial son.

The concept of urbanisation for the Romans embraced local autonomy as well as several established functions, which were extended through a hierarchy of different grades. Most major cities ultimately reached colonial status and some became, by virtue of their geographical position and prosperity, provincial capitals and the seats of the governors or assize centres. Some larger cities in the latter category had jurisdiction over subsidiary towns and villages and even smaller cities, such as Apameia in Phrygia, as well as over their surrounding territories which often extended for several hundreds of square kilometres. In most of the older provinces with a tradition of urbanisation, almost the entire area would be so apportioned.

In the hellenised east, the *polis* continued as the administrative unit; elsewhere *coloniae* and *municipia*, promoted by the central government with the conferment of relevant status and privilege, acted in the same way, leaving only a residue, mainly in parts of the north and west where the traditions of urbanisation were less strongly developed, to be organised on the basis of tribal communities. Even these communities were nevertheless properly constituted and received the title of *civitas*, although this term, in a looser sense, could also be used to describe cities and towns of all degrees. All *civitates* had administrative capitals, which in the course of time might well develop and be promoted from their original village (*vicus*) status through the municipal grade to that of a full *colonia*, such as Vienne (Vienna) in Gallia Narbonensis.

The administrative function of all cities and most *civitates* was concentrated in the hands of an autonomous council or senate which was recruited from among its inhabitants and not from elsewhere; its members were usually required to have a certain level of wealth, be freeborn and above a set age. These were the *decuriones* or *curiales*. Originally elected by the assemblies of citizens, they became in time almost self-perpetuating oligarchies. Annual magistrates were either appointed or elected, usually in pairs, and tradition sometimes decreed that they retained their old names: *stephanephorus, strategus, demiurge, prytaneis, archon*, whereas *duumvir iuridicundo, aedilis, quaestor* and later *curator* were the normal Roman equivalents.

The duties of these bodies and their officers were to maintain peace by local policing, administer justice and the law within defined limits, oversee the upkeep of public buildings and works and, probably more important than any other function, assess, collect and forward to the provincial government the correct amount of tax. There is no doubt that the spread of urbanisation greatly facilitated these duties, and was one of the prime reasons for the encouragement given by Rome to backward communities so to organise themselves. Full delegation of these responsibilities to the local communities would not otherwise have been possible.

But cities and towns developed other functions, foremost amongst which would have been an economic value, since they helped to generate the wealth from which taxes were paid. Even a comparatively small nucleated settlement could become a market and service centre for the land around it, so providing the country dwellers in the area with goods and facilities which they could not provide themselves. The larger the settlement the greater the diversity of goods and facilities which it could supply, so that a great city might serve not only a large number of rural inhabitants, but also those living in small cities, towns and villages which came within its ambit.

All nucleated settlements also exhibited a protective function, whether fortified or not, simply by virtue of the agglomeration of a number of people in one place: the larger the number the greater the degree of protection afforded. In Roman eyes too cities and towns had an educational function by which the ideas of Roman language, culture, religion and technology could be more easily transmitted; the concept of *aemulatio* was strong and in time aided the maintenance of peace and the collection of taxes, and even civilised sometime barbarian tribes within the empire.

But perhaps the most important function of all, by which genuine cities and towns could be distinguished from lesser settlements, was the level of amenities which they provided. These could range from the monumental, landscaped architecture of Pergamum to the great colonnades of Palmyra or Jerash, from the wide and commodious streets of Lepcis Magna to the massive arched aqueducts which carried water to Nîmes or Segovia and, associated with them, the sophisticated systems for its distribution, and for the disposal of sewerage. The theatres, amphitheatres, circuses and gymnasia provided a wide variety of entertainments or leisure activities which catered for all tastes ranging from religious festivals to classical drama, from racing and blood sports to physical exercise. In major cities, several bath-houses, both public and privately owned, not only established a minimum level of hygiene but also provided a place for strenuous exercise and the meeting of friends and acquaintances, where a light snack might be taken while the daily news and gossip was exchanged. So great was the spread in the Empire of these vehicles of romanised life that even a very minor town might possess a bath-house or an amphitheatre.

Yet another urban amenity was the provision of quality domestic housing, at least for the well-to-do, while even trusted slaves probably benefited to some degree. These might range from flats or maisonettes in apartment blocks mainly to be found in Rome or Ostia, where the richer occupied the more convenient and better-serviced lower floors, to sumptuous dwellings, ornamented with mosaics and wall-paintings, equipped with water supply and drainage and often provided with enclosed gardens, such as those which have survived so well at Pompeii and Herculaneum. Some owners of houses, even on this scale of luxury, were not always against letting those parts of them facing on to streets to shopkeepers or artisans with an eye to an ·extra profit. Otherwise this latter class of city worker would normally own, rent or manage a strip-like building, often in a block, in which he could combine business and residential functions.

Although some minor settlements might contain one, or even two or three of these amenities, only very seldom did they contain all, and it was the full range possessed by cities and major towns which set them apart as the real vehicles of romanisation and the settlers of civilised standards. But it would be a mistake to overlook the significance of the minor settlements in this process and they are given some attention below. These differences were recognised by Pausanias, a Greek topographer writing in the second century AD, in describing Panopeus as a *polis* of the Phocians:

> ... if one can give the name of city to those who possess no government offices, no gymnasium, no theatre, no market-place, no water descending from a fountain, but live in base shelters just like mountain cabins, right on a ravine.

Yet this 'city' possessed an organised administration and sent delegates to the Phocian assembly, so contradicting its lack of amenities.

The anatomy of the romanised city developed mainly along easily recognisable lines, as has been briefly noted above. Many cities which were first established as Greek colonies or under Hellenistic or other influences frequently developed around a fortified acropolis which formed the core of the settlement, and which was often situated on an eminence above it. In Italy and some western provinces similar early nuclei can sometimes be identified in the irregularities which appear in the street grids, or else appear as an outside limb of the later and usually more extensive development, as at Pompeii, where the south-west quarter is the obvious candidate. Even the small civitas capital of Caister-by-Norwich (Venta Icenorum) in Britain shows evidence for an early, pre-urban centre in the north-eastern corner, where a haphazard arrangement of streets extends beyond the later circuit of fortifications.

The acropolis of Balkan and eastern cities usually represented originally a military power base, but, as time passed and Roman influence increased, its importance would wane as the new forms of democracy were introduced. Hence the source of political power, often coupled with an economic function, shifted to the *agora*, situated in or near the centre of the expanded settlement, and often rebuilt after the manner of a *forum*. In Italy, parts of Africa and the north and west, the forum was from the first the political, economic and usually the religious centre of the urban community. As with the *agora*, it consisted of a squarish or rectangular paved, or gravelled, open space, more often than not embellished with colonnades. In early examples the related buildings were disposed about it in a somewhat haphazard manner, with little or no attempt at organised planning (fig. 10).

Often the most prominent position was occupied by the principal temple, dedicated to the Capitoline Triad, Jupiter, Juno and Minerva, and lifted, as it were, straight from Rome itself; temples dedicated to other major deities, or to the imperial cult, might also be placed within its boundaries. Other buildings found in association with the forum were the *curia* (council chamber), a hall of justice, equipped with tribunals, and usually a basilica; the two latter were sometimes combined, and, occasionally in some major cities, more than one basilica is to be found.

At Sabratha in Tripolitania, for instance, a complex sequence can be detected. The first forum, thought to have been laid out in the early imperial period, was several times altered, or had other buildings added to it. It consisted of a rectangular open space, at first flanked by rows of shops on its north and south sides. These were soon demolished and replaced by colonnades. A major temple, dedicated to Liber Pater, closed the east end; opposite, at the west end was another temple, thought to be the Capitolium. The basilica, probably of mid-first century date, was placed asymmetrically behind the southern portico, and contained at first a single tribunal, although another was added in the second century. The *curia* lay almost centrally behind the north portico and although the currently visible building dates to the late fourth century, it almost certainly conceals the foundations of an earlier version.

Probably the oldest temple in the city, dedicated to Serapis, and almost certainly ante-dating the forum, was situated west of the *curia*. Of two later temples, added during the second century, one, south of the Temple of Liber Pater, was dedicated to the Antonine emperors; the dedication of the other, situated south of the basilica, is not known. Not far away, Lepcis Magna provides both a resemblance and a contrast to Sabratha. The old forum there

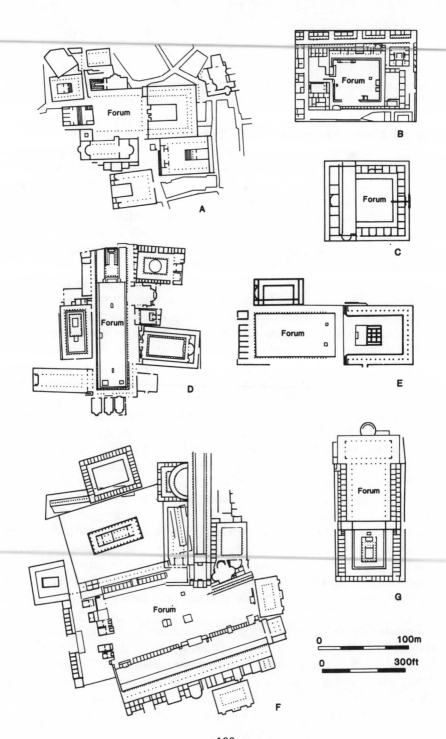

A

B

C

D

E

F

G

0   100m

0   300ft

108

displays the same haphazard arrangements and probably dates also from the early imperial period. In contrast is the later, Severan forum, planned on a separate site as a unitary, if asymmetric, complex of forum, basilica and capitolium, the temple of which projects eastwards into the piazza from the west end.

By the middle of the first century AD this unified planning of the forum and basilica complex was becoming more common. One of the most interesting recent discoveries has been the evidence that the masonry forum and basilica at Silchester (Calleva Atrebatum) was preceded by a wooden-framed building, almost certainly a timber equivalent, probably of mid– to late-first century date, and so far unique in the Empire. But the date of the very first complex to be planned in this manner is not known. The forum and its associated buildings at Iader in Dalmatia is thought to date from the Augustan period, although it appears to be of the double-courtyard type; the forum at Asseria, in the same province, seems to make use of a unitary plan, probably of mid-first century date, but its interpretation is difficult. In Britain it has been argued that the complex at Verulamium, dated to the principate of Titus, is the prototype of the great tripartite Gallic fora of the late-first to mid-second century. Certainly its lay-out is sufficiently different from most other fora in Britain to justify such a suggestion.

Perhaps the apogee of the Roman ideal of a provincial administrative centre developed in the so-called Gallic forum, although fora planned in this way were not entirely restricted to Gaul, being found also in Germany and at Iader and Salona in Dalmatia. But in Gaul itself the plans of several examples are well known, as at Paris (Lutetia Parisorum), St Bertrand (Lugdunum Convenarum), Bavay (Bagacum Nerviorum), and Augst (Augusta Raurica). In all these complexes the basilica usually lay across one end of the forum, which itself consisted of an open piazza flanked on at least two, and sometimes more, sides with colonnades and shops or offices. On the side opposite the basilica a street usually separated the forum from the temple in its own enclosed courtyard. Most fora of this type, therefore, occupied at least two and sometimes more *insulae*.

Although most fora were situated at or near the centre of the city, it was not always so, even in the most obviously planned examples; the forum at Timgad is noticeably off centre, and the capitolium is separated from it. Considering also the architectural grandeur of these buildings and the obvious care and cost which went into the construction of what was the centre-piece of municipal pride, it is surprising that so little opportunity was taken to place the forum on an axis of symmetry and in a position where it would be part of an architectural scheme by creating a perspective vista along the approach roads. Some such arrangement may have existed at Trier, London and Gloucester where the fora exceptionally interrupted the line of the *cardo* and would have provided an architectural perspective of some grandeur to anyone approaching from a distance.

This lack of foresight seems to show that contemporary architects planned more for convenience and regularity than for visual effect. But it must be remembered that many basilicas, and some major temples raised on *podia*, were exceedingly large buildings, often constructed on the scale of medieval cathedrals; consequently they would have dominated their surroundings in much the same way that the cathedrals did in medieval cities, and so achieved an architectural impact.

A number of provincial towns and cities possessed more than one forum. These were also usually situated in the centres and not too distant from the main forum. Their function was entirely connected with trade, whereas the principal forum would have also been used for political and other assemblies. The presence of a second forum, probably better called a *macellum*, therefore denotes a thriving commercial community. They were planned in a similar way to a forum, with an open piazza surrounded on two or more sides by rows of shops or offices; some as at Leicester (Ratae Corieltauvorum) even possessed a covered market hall (fig. 11).

The *municipium* established near the legionary fortress at Budapest (Aquincum) contained a small market, consisting of a rectangular peristyle surrounded by shops; the centre of the courtyard contained a circular structure not unlike the two *tholoi* in the similar building at Lepcis Magna, which shows perhaps an influence possibly derived from the Balkans. The trade at Aquincum would have benefited greatly from the proximity of a major route across the frontier and the river Danube. As indicated above, the fine early market at Lepcis Magna also contained two circular *tholoi* within octagonal colonnades. On one of the surviving counters standard measures of length, area and volume are marked, while the names of various *aediles* are inscribed on some of the columns; part of the duties of the *aediles* was the supervision of the markets. Rome itself had markets with specialised functions, such as a cattle-market, but it is not known if all provincial towns were likewise equipped.

No Roman town or city of any pretension was complete without at least one public bath-house, and many possessed several. Corinth, after its destruction by the Roman army in 146 BC, was provided with at least seven; one was constructed in the late-first or early-second century AD by a public benefactor, Eurykles, while another great building, probably covering more than ten thousand square metres, was dedicated to Hadrian and is mentioned by Pausanias in his description of Grecian topography. Hadrian was also invoked in the construction of a bath-house of almost equal size at Lepcis Magna where it was attached asymmetrically to the south side of the *palaestra*. It is worth noting in this context that Hadrian was attracted by major building

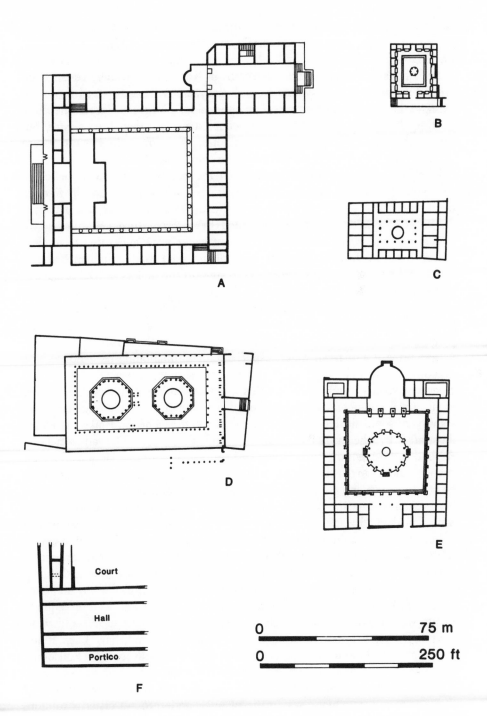

A

B

C

D

E

Court

Hall

Portico

F

0   75 m

0   250 ft

schemes and exhorted many of the communities, through which he passed on his extensive travels, to undertake such works, possibly also providing financial assistance.

Bath-houses, including the great baths in Rome, were usually constructed around a central line of symmetry, with the major rooms disposed about the axis and the minor ones leading off on either side. The great 'Barbarathermen' in Trier is equally symmetrical and occupied no less than four *insulae*, but the north baths in Paris lack this symmetry, as do many in Britain, where generally smaller establishments are to be found (fig. 12).

The basic provision of all baths, even the humblest, was a sequence of rooms of varying heat, ranging from very hot to cold, with additionally a series of plunge baths, rooms of wet and dry heat, changing-rooms and usually a public lavatory. The heat was provided by external furnaces attached to hypocausts and wall-ducts; steam and hot water were generated by boilers placed over the furnace flues, as can still be seen in the Stabian baths at Pompeii. Large iron beams were used to support the boilers of lead or copper and have been found as far distant in the provinces as in a small bath-house at Catterick. The siting of bath-houses within a town or city was usually related to the provision of water and drainage. Consequently there is no one place in which they may be sought, as in the case of the forum.

The provision of fresh water, especially for a functioning bath-house, was one of the principal amenities of an urban settlement, as were the drains and sewers necessary to take away surplus water and effluent. A very high degree of technical competence was developed by Roman hydraulic engineers and some very sophisticated systems were constructed. The care taken is amply illustrated by the works of Vitruvius and Frontinus. The aqueducts at Aspendus, Pergamum, Aosta, Lyon and Lincoln all required siphons for their proper functioning, whereby water from a source higher than the city could be led to it over intervening low-lying ground; closed systems of pipes were here required. But the more normal aqueduct consisted of a channel, sometimes cut through rock, sometimes carried on arched bridges, or else dug in the ground surface, in which water flowed by gravity to the distribution centre in the town. From this centre it was transmitted by pipes of lead, ceramic or wood, or by channels cut in stone blocks, to the points of use. Public drinking fountains were deemed the most important of the latter, followed by the bath-houses and lastly private use; both private domestic and industrial requirements were served. A water rate was charged to private users, and well-engineered pipes and stopcocks, in both bronze and lead, have been found at Pompeii and Herculaneum, whereby the quantities delivered to a household could be measured.

In the drier parts of the Empire where there was no regular rain-fall all the year round, much use was made of huge underground cisterns to store

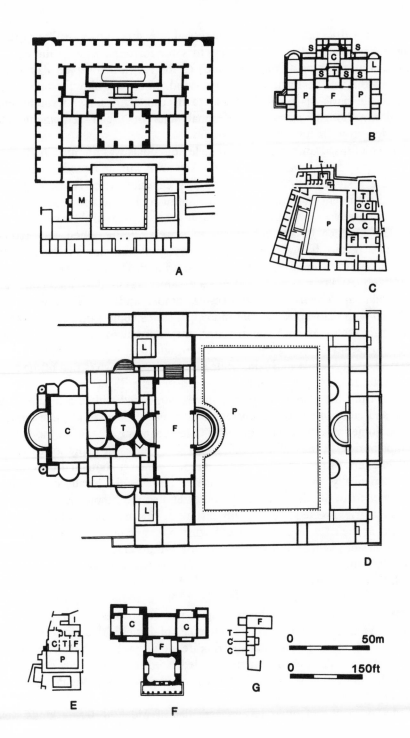

water for the dry seasons. Corinth possessed one, dug in rock, with a capacity of nearly a quarter of a million litres. In some fortunate sites in the eastern provinces, use was made of oases, such as the two which served Palmyra in Syria, or that of the Fayum which provided water, not only for one of the most fertile parts of Egypt, but also to its capital, Arsinoë. Despite such provisions, though, many of the inhabitants of urban settlements still depended on wells for their water supply.

The chief disadvantage of Roman-style aqueducts was the inability to turn off the supply once it had been started. Any town with an aqueduct therefore needed a system of drains with a similar capacity, to carry away surplus water, the effluent from the bath-houses, industrial waste and sewerage from domestic premises. A strange lacuna in much modern literature is the complete absence of any references to sewers, despite their importance; aqueducts receive frequent mentions but not so the sewers. Yet main drains were of considerable size, high and wide enough for a man to pass along them freely. At Trier, Lincoln and Aosta masonry was used for their construction, while at Amiens and Cirencester, timber sufficed. They were also equipped with man-holes, so that municipal slaves could gain access to clean and repair them. As with water mains, they normally ran under or beside streets to facilitate this access. Outlets through town walls can still often be observed, as at Merida in Spain, while perhaps best known is that of the huge *cloaca maxima* in Rome where it discharged into the Tiber.

Apart from the principal urban temples connected with the forum, most towns and cities of any worth possessed a variety of other religious establishments. Sometimes these were grouped together in one area, as in the famous 'Tempelbezirk' in the Altbach valley at Trier. But as in many towns of the north-western provinces, most of the temples which it contained were of the characteristically Romano-Celtic form. The same localised religious phenomena can be identified at the other end of the Empire in the temples and sanctuaries erected to essentially eastern deities in Palmyra and Heliopolis in Syria; at the latter even the great Augustan temple of Jupiter was endowed with an eastern veneer and gave rise to the variant cult of Jupiter Heliopolitanus. Yet such was the power of some of these deities, and their ability to travel, that they crossed the Empire to Corbridge on the north-west frontier, where there are dedications to Herakles of Tyre and Astarte, while a dedication to Bel, one of whose main temples was at Apamea in Syria, has been found at Vienne in Gaul. Apart from temples of deities with a local or esoteric flavour, most towns throughout the Empire would probably have contained a representative collection of sanctuaries dedicated to the imperial cult and to the gods and goddesses of the classical pantheon: Mars, Venus, Bacchus, Mercury, Diana, and so on (fig. 26).

Entertainment and other leisure activities of widely differing kinds were

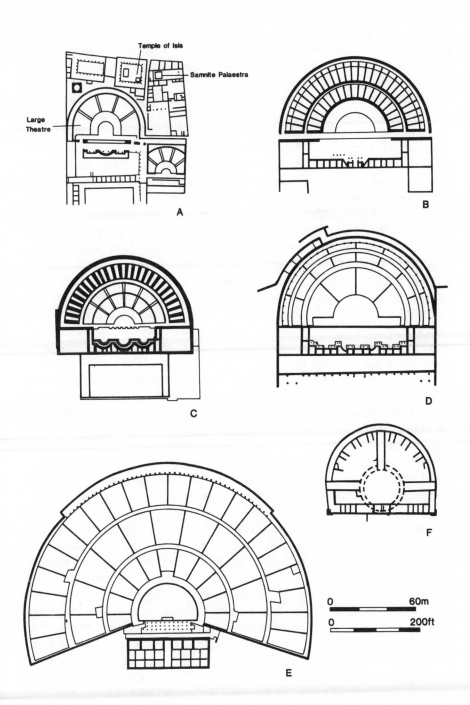

Temple of Isis

Samnite Palaestra

Large
Theatre

A

B

C

D

F

E

0   60m

0   200ft

provided for the populace in theatres, amphitheatres, circuses and gymnasia. Theatres and amphitheatres are not infrequently closely linked with temples, a juxtaposition which was clearly not accidental and which indicates that they were most often, if not invariably, used for performances or other activities connected with the festivals of the associated deities. One of the best-preserved theatres is that built under Augustus at Orange where the seating banks are backed into a hillside, on top of which was situated a major temple. When local topography suited, both theatres and amphitheatres made use, in this way, of convenient slopes, sometimes even disused quarries, as an economy in construction. Perhaps one of the most remarkably placed is the original Greek, but later romanised, theatre set in a hillside at Taormina in Sicily, where a distant view of the eastern flanks of Mount Etna sloping gently down to the Mediterranean provides one of the finest backdrops for which any theatre could wish. At Arles both theatre and amphitheatre are situated quite close together, but on flat ground, which would have required more construction work. A similar propinquity can be observed at Merida (fig. 13).

The amphitheatre was conceived entirely by the Romans, the earliest known example having been built in the Sullan colony at Pompeii, *c.* 80 BC, and the first to be constructed in Rome was in 29 BC, by which time many had also been constructed in the provinces. Architecturally they are simple buildings with the tiers of seats being constructed round an elliptical space – the arena. Some make use of earth excavated from the arena and revetted by walls to form the seating banks, a process used not only at Pompeii, but also in the remoter provinces such as Britain. In others the seats were carried on masonry vaults, as at Merida, or on massive stone lintels, as at Nîmes. Entrances into the arena were situated at the ends of the long axis and access to the seats was by external stairs, as at Pompeii, or by internal staircases in most all-masonry examples. Provision for elaborate stage effects was sometimes made under the floor of the arena, as in the greatest amphitheatre of all, the Colosseum in Rome, while in some, the arena could be flooded for naval displays (fig. 14).

Unlike the amphitheatre, the origin of the theatre dates back at least to fifty-century BC Greece, if not earlier. The simplest form consisted of a circular, or near-circular, orchestra surrounded, usually in part, by an auditorium; behind the orchestra was a simple tent, or hut, for the convenience of the performers. The Roman theatre developed from these simple beginnings into a great, basically semi-circular building, with a large stage area backed by an architecturally ornamented wall, the *scaena frons*, which rose as high as the top of the seating banks. The orchestra was reduced to a semi-circle, and the stage was probably covered. This type of unified structure became common even in Greece during the Roman period, although there were local variants, of which the so-called 'Romano-Gallic' theatre of Britain,

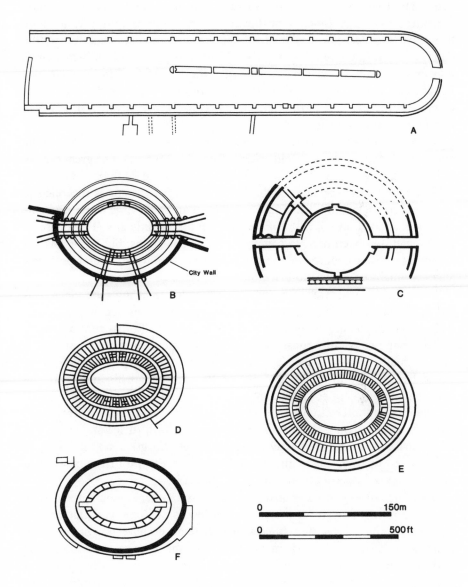

A

B

City Wall

C

D

E

F

0   150m

0   500ft

north Gaul and Germany is one. In these the orchestra is once more expanded almost to a full circle, as at Verulamium, or even to an ellipse, as in Les Arènes, Paris, while the stage is reduced in size and is usually little more than a short chord across the orchestra. It has often been argued that these structures had a dual function of theatre and amphitheatre, but it is far more likely that they were so designed to suit the performances required by the cults of the characteristically planned Romano-Celtic temples, with which they are most often associated. Diminutive theatres of Roman form are also known, and are usually called *odea:* they were used primarily for recitations or musical recitals, and were often roofed, as in the *odeum* which lies next to the main theatre at Lyon.

Theatres and amphitheatres were large structures which could, even in the smallest, accommodate large gatherings of several thousand. The great theatre at Ephesus, in which St Paul was shouted down, seated 24,000, while that at Orange could accommodate 7,000. The Colosseum in Rome is reckoned to have held nearly 50,000, while most provincial amphitheatres could probably have held about a fifth of that number without undue difficulty. These figures have sometimes been used to compute urban populations, but since it is not known how many country-folk might have gone to town to attend performances, it might be unwise to place too much reliance on them.

The circus in which chariot and sometimes horse racing took place, was less common outside Italy. It was not unlike a greatly elongated amphitheatre, with the arena containing an axial barrier for about half of its central length, so providing two parallel runs. The stables were situated at the open end. A race normally covered seven laps, which in the Circus Maximus in Rome would have meant an overall distance of 10.5 km (about 6½ miles). In the east, the hippodromes at Constantinople, Alexandria and Antioch were noted for their races; other circuses are known in Spain, at Merida, Tarraco and Urso, in Gaul at Lyon, Vienne and Arles, and in north Africa at Cyrene and Lepcis Magna, to mention only some examples. So great was the love of gambling on these events by the inhabitants of the Empire that decrees were made by some emperors to enforce limits (fig. 14).

Domestic housing of a reasonable quality was another amenity provided by cities and towns. Except for the apartment blocks of Rome and Ostia and a handful of other places, few houses elsewhere rose above one storey. The basic house-style, to be seen in most parts of the Empire, was completely enclosed and inward looking, partly one suspects for security, and was constructed round a peristyled courtyard or garden; not infrequently houses fronting streets had shops or workshops built into their ground floors. Naturally, also, there were many variations from the norm. In the north-western provinces, where pressure on land was perhaps less severe, a more sprawling style was developed with sometimes only two or three wings. Some richer dwellings also possessed their own private bath wings.

Many examples of the standard house style are known from such places as Vaison, St Remy, Ostia, Herculaneum, Tipasa, Volubilis, Ephesus, Palmyra, and Dura, but it is unfortunate that in many of the larger and more important cities, such as Jerash and sites in Spain, little attention has been paid to domestic dwellings and work has been mostly concentrated on public buildings. Nevertheless there is sufficient evidence to deduce that many houses of the richer classes all over the Empire were elaborately decorated with mosaics, painted frescoes, statuary and architectural features; they were also amply supplied with top-quality ceramics and glass, as well as silver and copper-alloy metalwork. The finest mosaics usually incorporated a pictorial scene, often taken from mythology, hunting or the amphitheatre, or else they made do with geometrical patterns and formal devices of flowers and animals. One popular scene depicts Orpheus charming the beasts, birds and trees; it occurs at several urban sites in north Africa, such as Volubilis, Sabratha and Thaena, in Germany at Trier and in Britain at Cirencester. This demonstrates very adequately the wide dispersal of artistic ideas and representations, either in the form of pattern books, or at the hands of itinerant craftsmen. The same was probably true for wall-paintings, which frequently made use of similar mythological designs, although a good deal of architectural perspective work was also incorporated. The House of the Mysteries at Pompeii illustrates as a continuous theme on two walls what is usually interpreted as a Bacchic initiation ceremony. Pictures of harbour scenes or gardens, viewed as though through a window, were also popular; a recently-excavated private house at Ephesus depicts Socrates with an appropriate painted inscription and also scenes from the theatre, which was another common form of illustration, even reaching Britain (fig. 15).

The rooms of a dwelling house would be divided between the owner's living and sleeping quarters and the domestic offices. The principal room would have been the dining-room, which can usually be identified by its size and the lavish manner of its ornamentation. It would have been equipped with tables and couches or perhaps, in some less-romanised provinces, with chairs; lamps and possibly braziers would also have been required, since only few rooms, even in the northern provinces, were heated by hypocausts. Bedrooms would have also contained couches and probably some cupboards or chests for storing clothes. Most rooms would have appeared sparsely furnished to modern eyes, and a lady's bed-chamber depicted on the inside of a stone sarcophagus from Simpelveld in Holland is probably over-furnished, showing as it does a whole range of closets, receptacles, tables, chairs and washing apparatus. The kitchen would contain an oven and probably a grid-iron over a raised, open fire, as well as tables, shelves, cupboards and cooking

119

utensils of different kinds: colanders, saucepans, strainers, skillets, frying-pans, knives, choppers and spoons, as well as a pair of millstones for grinding corn. Spits for roasting large animals were also used and in some northern provinces large cauldrons would have been suspended over open fires on long triple chains. Large storage jars and amphorae would contain grain, oil and wine or even beer.

Much of the commercial activity was concentrated in town centres, usually near the forum and the markets. In some quarters lines of narrow, strip-like buildings jostle each other for space along the streets. They were often open-fronted, with shutters to close the entrances and covered by an arcade or colonnade, sometimes more than one storey high. These were the true shops and workshops of the trading and artisan classes, in which not only was the business carried on, but also the trader and his family lived, either behind the shop or in an upper storey. In a number of towns, different trades were sometimes gathered together in one street (fig. 15).

As in many eastern bazaars today, the goods would be manufactured on the premises, usually to a specific order, while the general merchandise would be displayed in the open front, in the colonnade, or overflowing into the street. A relief in Dresden Museum shows a trestle-table carrying merchandise and probably set up in a colonnade. All manner of metal-working, carpentry, cloth and clothing manufacturers, purveyors of food and drink were represented, although trades which required more space or gave rise to noxious effluents were usually segregated on the outskirts of the town, or even outside it; hence the tanners were so placed, while the manufacture of brick and pottery was normally prohibited inside the boundaries. Inns and brothels would not have been uncommon and the well-known brothel at Pompeii was decorated with appropriate frescoes. It has proved possible in some places to suggest several types of possible relationship between those who worked or owned shops. The simplest was, of course, the owner-occupier, who had either inherited or bought himself into the business, perhaps with the proceeds of his *peculium* while a slave and after his manumission. Both tenants and managers are also attested and freedmen, slaves and clients can be identified in these capacities.

The protection which towns and cities provided for their inhabitants was frequently amplified by the construction of fortifications, although many towns in the Empire remained open for long periods of time. Even Rome was not provided with fully comprehensive defences until the late third century under the emperor Aurelian. Much depended on a town's situation and its distance from the frontiers as to when it received fortifications. Aosta, being near the troublesome tribe of the Salassi, was provided from the first with a free-standing masonry wall, as were many of the early *coloniae* in Spain, Gaul and Germany, such as Merida, Narbo and Cologne. In some cases, though, especially where defences were provided for civitas capitals, such as Autun

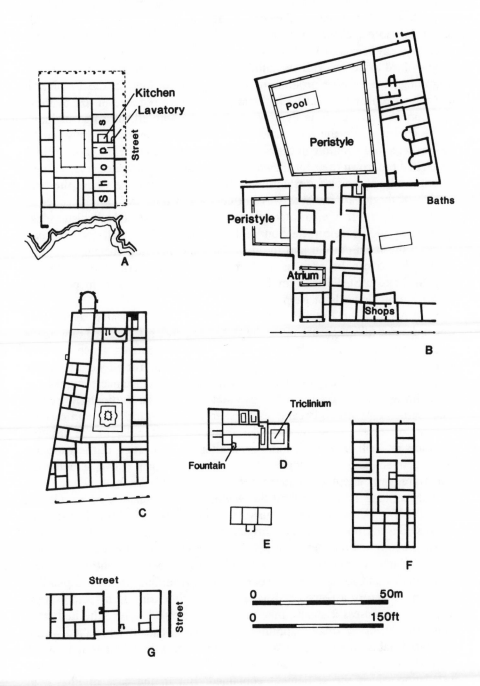

Kitchen

Lavatory

Shops

Street

A

Pool

Peristyle

Baths

Peristyle

Atrium

Shops

B

Triclinium

Fountain

D

C

E

F

Street

Street

G

0   50m

0   150ft

121

(Augustodunum), there is more than a suspicion that pride and status were the motivating forces behind the construction, although this reason can hardly be invoked to explain the anomalous second century earthwork fortifications given to many towns in Britain.

The third century, with its upheavals and barbarian invasions, saw the beginning of a massive programme of urban fortification in the Empire. It had some peculiar effects. In Gaul many towns were reduced in size by these new curtain walls, such as Périgueux where the amphitheatre was included in the circuit, while the late enclosure of Paris was centred entirely on the Île-de-Paris in the middle of the Seine. By contrast, a number of eastern cities which had outgrown their fortifications in the preceding decades received new curtain walls, of which Constantinople is the prime example where the final version of the great land wall was not completed until the early decades of the fifth century. It is also interesting to see the revival of Hellenistic ideas of defence in the reintroduction of both the low fore wall (*proteichisma*) between the main curtain and the ditch, and the galleried curtain wall. The former device can be seen as well at Singara in modern Iraq, at Nicaea (Bithynia) and at St Blaise in southern Gaul, while galleries were incorporated in the Aurelianic walls of Rome.

In all parts of the Empire there were many, small, nucleated settlements which did not fully measure up to the status or standards required of a major town or city; there were also even more, lesser settlements which are best treated as villages (*vicus* in the west; *komé* in the east). Yet all were towns or cities in embryo and any of them, given the right circumstances, might have risen through the ranks to true urban status. This was particularly true of those settlements which became established as *vici* outside forts and *canabae* outside fortresses. Most of these lay, somewhat naturally, in the frontier provinces and either remained and grew after the evacuation of the garrison, or burgeoned beside it. Others started as pre-Roman native settlements, which gradually adopted Roman ways and changed with them, while some grew up as road stations around the *mansiones* of the *cursus publicus*. Others grew to serve specialised needs: major religious shrines, industrial or mining centres. But all, no matter their origin, would have had a primary function for their continued prosperity, in which they resembled in a more limited way the major towns: they would have acted as minor service centres for their communities and for an area of countryside surrounding them and possibly providing in return a reservoir of labour for neighbouring farms and estates. Some might possess a small range of amenities: piped water inherited from an evacuated fort, a small amphitheatre or theatre, usually connected with a religious establishment. Many were also fortified, although it is not always clear whether it was for the benefit of the community or for some government installation which the settlement contained. But in the case of Phasis, in

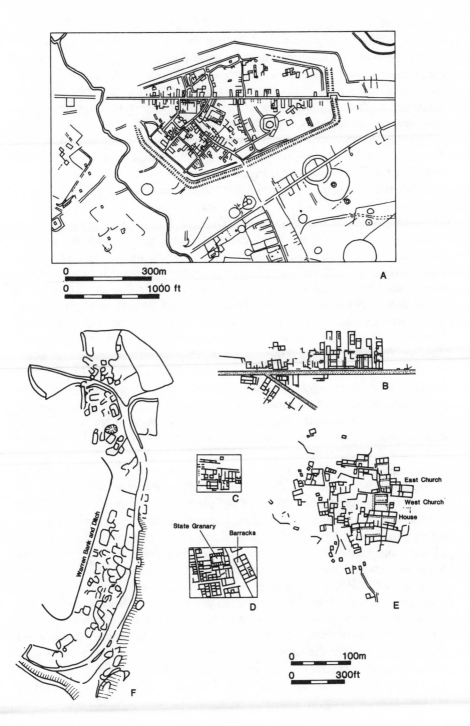

0   300m

0   1000 ft

A

B

C

State Granary

Barracks

D

East Church

West Church

House

E

Warren Bank and Ditch

F

0   100m

0   300ft

123

Cappadocia, it is known that the governor ordered walls to be built around the *vicus* to protect it from invading Alans in the mid-second century, although it must be admitted that this might be exceptional. But none could provide the whole range of amenities of a major town, a factor which helps to distinguish them from their more prosperous relatives, and, because most developed haphazardly, following the needs of spontaneous economic expansion, they seldom possessed regular street systems (fig. 16).

Naturally those settlements associated with a major military garrison had most chance of increasing their prosperity, with a captive market of several thousand men. It is not surprising, therefore, that many of them made the grade to full municipal or colonial status. The settlements which began as the *canabae* of the fortresses at York (Eboracum), Xanten (Vetera), Nijmegen (Noviomagus), Budapest (Aquincum), Deutsch-Altenburg (Carnuntum) and Lambaesis among many others, all eventually achieved that rank. Some, such as York, show evidence for major replanning when the coveted award was made, but since most received only honorary titles it is unlikely that a territory would have been attributed to them. It is also clear that other subsidiary settlements could occur on the land attributed to a fortress in addition to the extramural *canabae*, such as the two *vici* of Verecunda and Lamiggiga near Lambaesis. Such *vici* can also be found on imperial and private estates. Auxiliary forts, too, attracted their quota of artisans and tradesmen who would be settled in a *vicus* outside the fort. In Britain, those at Carlisle (Luguvalium) and Corbridge (Corstopitum) grew to considerable size and may even have been promoted to municipal status. More normal was the *vicus* at Housesteads (Vercovicium), while that which grew outside the Saxon shore fort of Brancaster (Branodunum) has a degree of regularity about it which suggests a more formal foundation.

The speed with which such settlements could spring up is demonstrated by those attached to forts on the Antonine Wall, where little more than fifteen to twenty years saw the establishment and presumably the demise of an official *vicus* at Carriden (Veluniate). Similar *vici* can be seen growing round most forts on the imperial frontiers, such as those on the edge of the Sahara at Ad Maiores and Gemellae in Mauretania. It is evident also that they sometimes acted as administrative centres of rural districts (*pagi*) such as Chesterholm (Vindolanda) in Britain or Veţel (Micia) in Dacia, where inscriptions refer to a *curia*, or council, of the Textoverdorum and the *pagus Miciensis* respectively.

The importance of road-stations acting as magnets for village settlements cannot be under-estimated, since there were a very large number strung along the main highways of the Empire and indicated by the various route lists such as the Antonine Itinerary. In these the principal building was the *mansio* or inn for members of the *cursus publicus*. The well-explored *vicus* at Saalburg on the Taunus *limes* in Germany contained a *mansio* which would have

124

provided for the locals an additional attraction to that already created by the fort. At Catterick (Cataractonium), a *mansio* replaced an early fort situated on the main road north to the frontier, while a small military detachment stationed at Aïn Wif (Thenadassa), on the main road running along the Gebel watershed in Tripolitania, gave reason to a settlement around the nearby oasis.

Many pre-Roman native settlements also survived to become villages in the Empire, although the way in which they were administered varied from province to province and even within a province. Villages, for instance, remained the centres of local administration in Egypt, where cities had little importance until the reforms of the fourth century; the local *strategos* represented the provincial administration, while a council of elders, a policeman and a scribe governed the village. On the Syrian frontiers centurions were seconded to oversee some villages, as happened also in other parts of the Empire, where a variety of government officials, such as *regionarii*, *beneficiarii*, were also detached from military service to supervise the state's involvement in local affairs. Eastern native villages tended to be more compact than those in the west, where sprawling Iron Age settlements had often been the precursors, such as at Braughing in Britain. Of the sites where continuity can be observed in the west, that at Titelberg in Luxembourg is one of the most interesting, having begun as a Celtic *oppidum* and prospered under Roman rule, developing a strong industrial base with the manufacture of glass and pottery.

There were many minor settlements also which had some special reason for their existence. Godmanchester in Britain may have been the headquarters of an imperial estate, while nearby Chesterton (Durobrivae) owed most of its prosperity to its flourishing pottery industry. At Aljustrel (Vipasca) in Lusitania, an important settlement grew in conjunction with the rich copper, gold and silver mines. Inscriptions show that it was under the control of the local procurator and, therefore, part of an imperial estate, with almost all trades and buildings leased out and not privately owned. Baden (Aquae Helveticae) in Germany, Bath (Aquae Sulis) and Sidi Moulay Yakoub (Aquae Dacicae) in Mauretania Tingitana were some of a number of settlements related to mineral or hot springs, which had acquired reputations as health resorts, some, so it is suggested, even being used as convalescent stations by the Roman army. These springs were frequently associated with deities and, in a number of cases, large religious establishments were developed around them. Other minor settlements grew up because of the presence of simply a religious sanctuary, although they were not always unconnected with water; indeed the sources of rivers were popular places, as the establishment founded at the source of the Seine in Gaul shows. Other great Gallic sanctuaries existed at Ribemont-sur-Ancre, Sanxay and Champlieu. In all, generous accommodation was provided for visitors, in addition probably to a range of services.

Many of these minor settlements and villages were fortified, although not normally before the later Empire. Where walls were built much smaller areas than the whole settlement were often enclosed, but it is not always possible to deduce whether this was because either the settlements had shrunk, or the population was compressed within the enclosure, or whether it was deliberate policy only to protect some significant government activity, such as the collection of taxes and the maintenance of safe records. As an extension to the problems relating to the fortification of these small settlements, there is also that of the *burgi*, small, late, walled enclosures usually standing astride a major road. These are not uncommon in Gallia Belgica and midland Britain, but whether they can be truly distinguished in a separate category from other minor fortified sites is not so easy to decide. It may be that they contained small detachments of the army to provide a more effective defence in depth than could be given by the linear frontiers. If so then the troops would probably also have had duties to maintain law and order in their respective areas. In style and intent, therefore, they may not be very dissimilar to the small forts that are so characteristic of parts of the late frontier regions of Tripolitania and Arabia.

It can be seen from the foregoing that urbanisation was a continuous process of organic growth throughout the Empire, which was as applicable to the ancient cities, towns and villages of the eastern provinces as it was to the newly promoted growths of the west. All had something to learn and to gain from Rome.

VII

RURAL LIFE

The entire economy of the Roman Empire, as with most pre-industrial societies, was based on the produce of the land: either crops or stock from the surface or minerals and building materials from beneath. Even one of the largest and best-known of industrial activities, the manufacturer of ceramics, was to some extent secondary, providing mainly building materials or containers, and cooking and serving vessels, for food and other agricultural products, while the comparatively sophisticated currency system simply made marketing transactions easier.

Although contemporary society could support a considerable number of specialist manufacturers, who were agriculturally unproductive, they had to be fed, as did the vast mass of urban dwellers and the army. In this the city of Rome represented a unique example, which was mirrored in a smaller way in most other urban communities elsewhere, no matter their size. Since, though, the large population of Rome itself was close to the source of the Empire's power structure, most emperors took great care that it should always be well supplied with cereals. Hence the sarcastic reference of Juvenal to *panem et circenses*. Hence also the importance which Augustus originally attached to Egypt during his principate, the source of much of the city's grain; his successors were equally careful over that province's viability and security. Later, other areas of Africa, and also Gaul, contributed to the Roman dole. Elsewhere, the frontier provinces had the burden of supplying the army. The shadow of the tax collector therefore brought about pronounced changes in the more primitive provinces, where, before the arrival of Rome, most production had been little above subsistence level; there had been no need to produce more. But the necessity to placate the tax collector, or starve, introduced the idea of a permanent surplus of production, which could be expanded further to provide a saleable asset, leading to real profits and the creation of wealth, and which in turn could be invested in buildings, land or luxuries. In Italy and some other parts of the Empire there was little fresh in this concept, even by the time of the late Republic, but in the newer and more distant provinces its introduction must have produced some far-reaching reforms in land-ownership and the development of land-use.

Basically, therefore, there were these two over-riding criteria which governed most aspects of rural life: land-ownership and land-use. By far the largest landowner in the Roman Empire was the emperor, possessing estates in many parts. Some came by inheritance, some by confiscation; most were agricultural, although others were concerned with the extraction of minerals, including salt. All were administered by procurators, sometimes through *conductores*, but as time passed encouragement was given to tenants (*coloni*) to establish personal interests in the land they farmed, so making up for the growing shortage of slaves and agricultural labourers. Evidence for this happening can be seen on inscriptions from an estate in the Medjerda district of Tunisia in Africa. There, under Trajan and later under Hadrian, the tenants were given particularly favourable treatment if they recovered waste land, provided they were prepared to live on it, which could amount to rent-free occupation for as much as five to ten years. Moreover, such land holdings, although not saleable, could be inherited by the tenants' decendants, so giving each a more than lifelong interest. Once established, the tenant was required to surrender a certain share of the crops, and possibly provide a number of days labour to the procurator or agent, or pay a set rental in kind, as occurred in Egypt. Intended as a liberalising measure, it had an end result that could not have been foreseen. With rising taxes in the later Empire, many tenants found themselves in debt to the procurators, and so could not leave their land. In consequence, most became bound to it, sons inheriting from fathers; although ostensibly 'free', they were little better than serfs.

But the emperor was not the only landowner. There were many others, not only in Italy, but also in the provinces. Pliny claimed that half of the province of Africa was divided between only six men at the time of Nero, but then he also reckoned that the growth of *latifundia*, excessively large estates, had ruined Italy and was threatening to ruin the provinces in the same way. It may be that he overstated the case as far as most of the provinces were concerned, for it can be demonstrated in a large number that a very wide range of estates existed and that the land-holding in most provincial contexts was of a highly complex pattern. There were estates large, medium and small: estates which were managed by a bailiff for an absentee landlord or tenant; large estates split between a number of tenants; land owned by municipalities or tribal communities; land owned singly or communally by small free-holders. Moreover, land was being bought and sold, leased, abandoned and recovered; neighbouring estates might be amalgamated, or large estates broken up;

plough might revert to pasture, or vice versa; new vineyards or olive or fruit orchards might be planted while the older were grubbed out. As with so many aspects of the Roman Empire, the picture often gained by the modern viewer is of a largely static rural life, which it was far from being; the ever-changing pattern which it most likely resembled was further complicated by an overlay of local customs, traditions and laws that varied from province to province.

A good deal was written about estate management and agricultural practices by contemporary Roman authors, such as Pliny, Cato, Varro, Virgil and Columella. But much of it was written from the viewpoint of the Roman country gentleman. Fortunately archaeology can now supplement their information, although it must be admitted that it is still seldom possible to identify precise arrangements of ownership and tenancy. Columella wrote at length on the lay-out and management of a large estate, recommending tenancies rather than direct slave labour; but where an overseer was appointed for the latter, he advised that he should be given a woman companion to keep him within bounds! He also perceived that the farm houses should be divided between the *villa urbana*, the residence of the owner, and the *villa rustica*, the residence of the bailiff or manager. The chief difficulty lies in trying to distinguish between the two, since there are many instances, which, one suspects, were not visualised by Columella, where there was little difference between them. Only in some of the most obvious cases in Italy and the provinces is it possible to distinguish the former from the latter.

If one excludes those lands which were farmed from towns, then it is true to say that at the centre of every farm in the Empire, no matter where it was or what its status, was a domestic residence for the actual farmer and his family and any number of subsidiary buildings relating to the farm. The residential quarters could range from the primitive and totally-unromanised round houses of the northern fringes of the Empire to the huge, palatial villas of north Africa, Spain or Italy, such as the great villa attributed to Catullus at Sirmione on the shores of Lake Garda. Villas in the latter class were exemplified by Martial in an epigram as *rus in urbe:* country in town. Although deeply influenced by urban standards and consequently to some extent insulated from the countryside, they were nevertheless the product of a successful agricultural regime and were largely maintained and developed by its profits, even if capital from other sources was sunk in them to begin with. The creation of wealth both needed, and was a result of, their existence; it also required accessible markets. It is not surprising, therefore, that there was a close affinity between urban settlements and villas, since the former, at all levels, provided most of the essential markets. Equally, it comes as no surprise that, where urbanisation weakens and runs out either inside or on the fringes of the Empire, there are few, if any, villas.

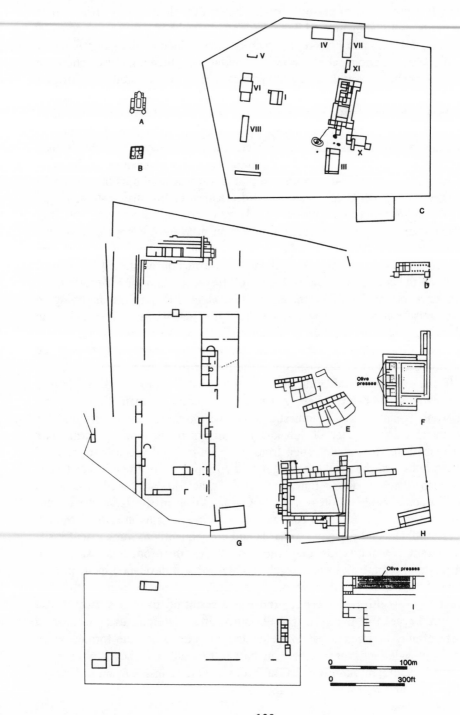

What then was a villa? The definition has been the subject of some dispute and even now not all authorities are agreed, while even the Romans were not always consistent in the use of the word. But there are some properties which all seem to possess. They should, for instance, be connected with farming, even though some appear to have an industrial base as well; they should also be connected to the Roman social and economic systems. The visible display of a degree of romanisation in their planning and architecture is also required, although here there is no firm agreement on the dividing line between what is acceptable as a villa and what is not. Strictly in Roman law, a villa could not exist in a town, even though the term may permissibly be used to describe a suburban building (*villa suburbana*). But this restriction excludes a number of what were demonstrably urban farms, and leads us inevitably to the nonsensical conclusion that a farmhouse is a villa if it is in the countryside, but not if it is in a town. In the circumstances, while making due acknowledgement of the opinions of Roman jurists, it might be best to accept that the word villa has now become so totally anglicised (the normal plural 'villas', as opposed to the correct *villae* is a token of it) that it could be redefined so as to take in all types of romanised farmhouses wherever they may be found.

One further factor has to be taken into account when considering villas. Although many had features in common, each was the product of an individual: owner, tenant or bailiff. Each will, therefore, display the individual needs, and express the individual habits, of the occupier, which will vary between all the villas in the Empire; the figure has never been calculated. Considering the number of possible variables, it is perhaps surprising that there is so much similarity in the basic types; fashion presumably decreed what was or was not acceptable. As a rough-and-ready rule, a villa represents private or rented ownership of land, and its size and luxuriousness is a measure of its profitability, and hence of the wealth of its occupier. But a rich man does not need to live in a palace; a cottage will suffice if he feels that way inclined. Equally, the dweller in a palace, who squandered his money in all directions, might live virtually on the verge of bankruptcy (fig. 17).

The chronological development of villas around the Empire was, of course, influenced by what had gone before. In Italy they had respectable republican origins, both in the great landed estates of eminent aristocrats like Cicero, and in the smaller and simpler farmhouses, or *villa rustica*, such as those recently investigated in the Campania. At Posto near Francolise, the small, first villa was constructed around 120 – 80 BC. It was essentially a simple house, although it was attached to a large farmyard. During the succeeding century it was enlarged and a bath-wing was added in the middle of the first century AD. At nearby San Rocco a more sophisticated house was built from the first, *c.* 75 BC. Its subsequent development, *c.* 30 BC, though, was very different from Posto. Part was restructured as a peristyled villa of characteristic type, while beside it was built a standard *villa rustica*, with slave quarters, two courtyards and a garden plot. The latter was later equipped with oil-extraction equipment and two tile-kilns. Some early villas in Italy were constructed on an open-ended U-plan, which was clearly shown at the third century BC site at Via Praenestina, near Rome, to have been converted into a conventional, closed, peristyled villa at a later date.

From Italy, the simple basic form of the compact, peristyled villa spread outwards into the provinces, reaching its zenith in houses like those of Tác-Förenypuszta, or Hosszúhetény in Pannonia, although the latter also incorporated a north-western feature in the two towers which flanked the front elevation. In Africa the tradition of intensive farming, developed by the Carthaginians, proved fertile ground for the introduction and spread of the villa system. In Spain and southern Gaul the arrival of the villa followed closely on the heels of the Augustan and Julio-Claudian urban promotions, while the system had been generally introduced into the rest of Gaul, Germany and the Danubian provinces during the first century AD. Unfortunately, less is known in the east, where much land was farmed from the cities, and established chronologies are more difficult to arrive at. Britain, befitting its position as one of the last provinces to be added to the Empire, saw only modest rural development in the first century AD, and, apart from isolated examples, it was not until well into the second century that villas became common and also developed a recognisable form.

The simplest villa is probably that which is usually referred to as the cottage type, consisting of a single rectangular block divided usually into several rooms, as at Frocester in Britain, but not all authorities accept these in the general category of 'villa'. There are one or two examples, such as Welwyn in Britain, or Mareuil-Caubert in the Somme valley, where the building is accompanied by a verandah, which provides a clue to the next stage of development. Projecting wings were added at the ends of the verandah block, giving rise to one of the commonest provincial types: the winged-corridor villa. In the simplest of forms, like the earliest villa at Mayen in Germany, there appear to be no internal divisions in the central range, although an arrangement of posts might suggest a roof spanning the whole area. This has prompted arguments that it, together with large central rooms in similar, but partitioned villas, were either left open as internal courtyards, or were roofed as large halls. The growth of villas of this type from the simple rectangular block implies the introduction also of social change. In the cottage plan, access to some rooms could only be gained through others, creating an almost complete lack of privacy for the occupants. But a verandah gave covered access to most rooms individually, so enabling the first separations to be introduced between master and man. The introduction or development of the provincial peristyled, or courtyard, villa meant that this distinction could be made still more positive, setting apart the domestic and farm servants in separate wings away from the main residential quarters of the family.

It is difficult to judge whether the courtyard villas of the provinces were a genuine export from Italy, where, as already indicated, the prototypes lay in the clusters of farm buildings, as at San Rocco, out of which grew, through sheer convenience of plan, the enclosed peristyled houses of the later periods, or whether they represent an independent line of development. It is perhaps best to see them as the latter, since there are distinguishing features, but they cannot have been totally uninfluenced by Italian models. However they were formed, it must be considered that the central courtyards, where there were no secondary yards, would have been more farmyard than garden, although there may have been some space set aside for herbs, fruit and vegetables. But the dwelling was still inextricably in contact with the farm. It is not surprising, therefore, that some very large and wealthy villas spawned a second courtyard, surrounded by farm buildings, the presence of which enabled the residential quarters to be distanced from the farm activities and where the inner courtyard could be treated wholly as an amenity. The ultimate in such development, especially in the north-western provinces, came with the construction of sumptuous houses, such as some of those recently surveyed in the Somme Valley in northern Gaul, at Grivesnes and Cavillon, in an area around Amiens, which was densely populated with villas; at Cuevas de Soria, near Numantia in Tarraconensis; and at Woodchester and Bignor in Britain. These villas, though, still tended to have a compact, integrated feel about their plans.

Altogether different, although probably sharing a common origin, and often incorporating large winged-corridor villas, are a series of huge establishments containing many different-sized buildings. These are usually detached, but nevertheless grouped around a central, rectangular space, and sometimes enclosed within an external boundary wall. A number have been found in the Somme Valley survey, and one of the largest is at Estrées-sur-Noye, where, to some extent, the principal residence is separated from the other buildings by a private court, as can also be seen at Warfusée-Abancourt and Athies. But at Béhencourt-Lahoussoye and some others no such internal division appears to exist. The type is also known outside the Somme Valley, and perhaps the best example is that at Anthée, near Namur, where the entire complex covered an area about 550 m (600 yd) by 200 m (220 yd).

Yet even these are outshone by the huge residential houses at Montmaurin in the Haute-Garonne, or at Haccourt, near Liège in Belgium. It is possible that the heavily-walled site at Gatcombe, near Bath in Britain, is an example of the same type, although here the subsidary buildings were arranged less formally; indeed there is a strong resemblance to the fortified villa at Keszthely-Fenékpuszta in Pannonia. Similar loose conglomerations of buildings can also be seen at Baláca and Parndorf in the same province. Perhaps the strangest feature about the establishments of this type is that they also occur with comparatively modest residential quarters, such as that at Vaux-sur-Somme, in the Somme Valley, where a simple cottage dwelling sufficed, although even here there are indications that it was separated from the farmyard by a fence. It is difficult to envisage the circumstances which brought about these various developments with both their contrasts and comparisons. The sheer scale of many of these villas would imply huge estates running to perhaps a thousand hectares or more each, but the simple, unsophisticated residences which many possessed would suggest the presence, not of the owners, but of tenants or even bailiffs.

There is one further aspect of villa development which is worth consideration: the aisled farmhouse, largely restricted to the late-Roman period in Britain and possibly to some other north-western areas such as Holland and Germany. In their simplest form they consisted of rectangular buildings with two lines of posts or piers, parallel with the long axis, which divided the interior into a central nave flanked by aisles, such as that at Castlefield (Hampshire). In the more developed forms, internal partitions, usually but not always reflecting the main divisions, were provided to make rooms, such as at Clanville. In other cases, such as Stroud, two projecting corner rooms at each end of one of the long sides must have given the external elevation the appearance of a winged-corridor villa; as a variant these two rooms could be placed at the corners of one of the short sides, as at Norton Disney. A degree of sophistication was sometimes incorporated in the developed forms with painted wall-plaster and even mosaics. Several attempts have been made to relate these houses to prototypes in Holland or West Germany, where similarly planned structures are known. But there are differences, and, although all are probably derived from a common origin, developments obviously took place during the diffusion of the plan over a comparatively wide area. It is interesting that some occur as subsidiary buildings in larger villas, as at Brading in the Isle of Wight and Ickleton (Cambs), and at Crouy in the Somme Valley. This may, indeed, help interpretation; either, when isolated, they were the combined dwellings and byres of small-holders or tenants, or, when associated with a large house, the house and byre used by the agricultural labourers. It has been suggested that these buildings were also the prototypes of medieval halls.

The identification of the main residential quarters of a villa is seldom in doubt. In those of better quality there is normally one or sometimes more attached bath-suites, and hypocausts, mosaics and painted walls heated and decorated the principal rooms. The functions of the subsidiary farm buildings, though, are frequently more difficult to assess. A square structure with massive, sometimes buttressed, walls suggests a tower granary, as at Köln-Mungersdorf in Germany, or in the village of Karanis in Egypt, while a barn with a raised floor normally indicates the same use, as at Lullingstone in Britain; oil-mills and presses and their associated apparatus can be used for little else other than olives, as in so many of the farms around the Mediterranean, such as Henscir Sidi Hamdam and Henscir Salamat in Tripolitania, Bir Sgaoun in Numidia, Boscoreale near Pompeii, even in urban buildings in Volubilis, to mention but a handful of examples chosen at random. The same is true for the production of wine, with the presses and storage jars and vats for fermentation easily identifiable. Not only did Boscoreale possess vats for storing some 18,000 lit (4,000 gal) of olive oil, but also over 100,000 lit (23,000 gal) of wine, all produced on the estate.

Recently, in the Rhône valley a site has been excavated at Donzère, just south of Montelimar, which could produce even greater quantities of wine that was contained in large ceramic vessels set in the ground. Each could hold about 1,250 lit (260 gal), making the total capacity of the establishment some 2,500 hl (550,000 gal). Also identified were the presses as well as the vats where the grapes were trampled; in Lyon Museum there is a fragmentary mosaic showing the trampling of the grapes, so stressing in a visual way the importance of viticulture in the local Rhône valley economy.

But, unfortunately, not all agricultural activities leave such characteristic evidence; to distinguish a byre for oxen from a stable for horses, or a pigsty from a sheep pen, is not easy, although a number of attempts have been made, some more successful than others. It is even more difficult to relate the size of buildings to the areas of productive land. Among several attempts which have been made, two are worth considering: Köln-Mungersdorf and Bignor.

Köln-Mungersdorf was a farm with a winged-corridor villa, measuring some 70 m (77 yd) by 40 m (44 yd) overall. It stood in the centre of an irregular, walled enclosure, about 300 m (330 yd) by 200 m (220 yd) maximum dimensions; it faced west and there were no buildings in front to obscure an uninterrupted view of the surrounding countryside. Behind, though, and to each side, were a series of unconnected buildings arranged roughly in a rectangle within the boundary wall; the only exception was Building I, interpreted as a dwelling for the servants. Other buildings were interpreted as a granary (III), a large barn (IV), an open-sided shed, perhaps a shelter for lambing (V), a tower building interpreted as a silo, but probably more a granary, as already indicated above (VI), a stable for horses (VII), a sheep fold (VIII), a pigsty (IX), a cold store (X), an underground cellar (XI) and a base raised on posts probably for a haystack (XII) (fig. 17).

Bignor lay at the foot of the north-facing scarp of the South Downs, not far from the civitas capital of Chichester. Unlike Köln-Mungersdorf it was a very large double-courtyard villa, measuring approximately 180 m (200 yd) by 105 m (120 yd). The residential end consisted of three main wings

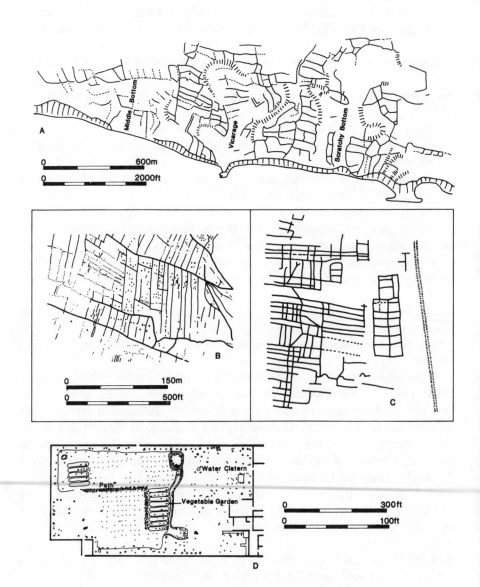

A

0 ——————— 600m
0 ——————— 2000ft

B

0 ——————— 150m
0 ——————— 500ft

C

D

Water Cistern
Path
Vegetable Garden

0 ——————— 300ft
0 ——————— 100ft

surrounding a central courtyard, with the fourth side closed by a double colonnade; it faced south-east. In the outer, and far larger, courtyard were four buildings, one of which was situated in the south-east corner and resembled an aisled house or barn. Applebaum has argued that a barn of this size, separated as it was into a central nave with side aisles, would have accommodated a herd of about fifty-five cattle, stalled in the latter, with the centre being used for hay and fodder. Similarly, a smaller rectangular building in the eastern corner of the yard is of a width appropriate for the stalling of twenty-four oxen, the plough-teams of the villa. The third building, set slightly off-centre in the yard, measures approximately 37 m (40 yd) by 6 m (7 yd) and is divided into three unequal parts, with the smallest at the east end. By comparison with Köln-Mungersdorf, it has been argued that this would have accommo-dated about 200 sheep, representing the winter stock figure, with living quarters for the shepherds in the east end. Likewise the apparently unroofed enclosure just to the west of the sheepfold has been interpreted as the lambing pen (fig. 17).

Although the farm may also have kept other stock, there is unfortunately no evidence for them. Neither is it possible to estimate stock which may have been kept permanently at pasture, or with shelter provided elsewhere on the estate. It is inconceivable that the estate did not possess woodlands, in which pigs could forage, while chickens and geese could have inhabited the farmyard, and been let into the stubble fields after harvest. It would also be surprising if there were no horses, mules or donkeys. The storage capacity of the central part of the barn has been put at about 22,000 bushels, implying a total arable of some 320 ha (800 acres), but it cannot be certain that this was the sole production of the 'home' farm, or whether it also included tithes yielded by tenants; moreover, the above figure does not allow for fodder, although this could have been stored in ricks in the farmyard, as seems to have occurred at least in part at Köln-Mungersdorf.

While it is both necessary and instructive to quote figures like those above in order to see how a 'total' farm operated in the Empire, it is also imperative that the greatest caution should be displayed in using them. The calculations themselves can only supply, in the most general way, figures which might deviate considerably from reality, perhaps by as much as fifty per cent or more.

Although very large areas of land in the Empire can be attributed either to imperial or municipal ownership, or to private ownership as represented by villa estates, it would be misleading to conclude that there were no other ways in which land could be owned or managed. In the east, there were vast tracts in between the *territoria* of cities which seem to have been left to the native, and possibly partly nomadic, farmers of the regions. The same certainly applies to parts of Africa, in particular to the more mountainous regions of

137

modern Algeria and Morocco, where the transhumance of stock between the winter pastures of the south and those of the summer in the north provided a viable way of life to the stock-breeders of the interior. In both areas there is also ample evidence of farming being carried on by village communities, sometimes, but not always, as adjuncts of the dominant cities and towns. A recent survey of an area in southern Syria, near the border with Jordan, has revealed extensive traces of both regular and irregular land divisions on a fertile, volcanic plain.

It is more than likely that the regular allotments belong to the official *territorium* of a settlement – possibly nearby Salkhad – but there are also a number of villages which could have provided the sources for the local exploitation of the land. A somewhat similar arrangement of intermingled villages and isolated farms (it is difficult to call them villas) also occurs in parts of Tripolitania, as again shown by recent surveys. They were often situated in or near the numerous wadis of that part of the world, from which they would derive a periodic water supply, supplemented by large cisterns. The village of Wadi Mimoun contained a number of conglomerated buildings and yards on the edge of the wadi, which suggested stock as well as cultivation, while at Wadi Merdum it was possible to distinguish the residential cores of the buildings from those parts devoted to agriculture.

Numidia has also been the subject of some recent surveys. Inscriptions show the presence of both imperial estates and veteran settlements with a rich, rural economy, in which the olive played a major part. But there is also evidence for pastoralism in the southern part of the province bordering the desert, and it is interesting that the discrete lengths of linear barriers constructed possibly by Trajan or more probably by Hadrian tend to lie on the boundaries between permanent pastures and the desert. This might suggest nomadic transhumance on quite a large scale, with the barriers designed to control – and tax – such traffic. It has been observed that the mountainous areas, notably the Aurès mountains, were mostly tree-clad, that the foot-hills provided arable, while the salt-marshes and their surroundings, such as Chott Zana or Chott Djerid, because of the high salinity of the soil, provided adequate pasture; the Hodna basin, too, seems to have provided a quota of this type of pasture.

Equally there were parts of Spain, Gaul and Britain where pastoralism and primitive cultivation at native peasant level continued during the Roman period. They were sometimes based on individual farms or on small villages or hamlets. The Vosges area of Gallia Belgica is noted for its large number, such as those at Wasserwald and Wahlscheid, or Landschied further north; these sites are very similar to Chisenbury Warren on the edge of Salisbury Plain in Britain. All are rambling, uncoordinated settlements, with meandering roads, rectangular (they are romanised to that extent) buildings or hut platforms and are invariably linked with field-systems. But great care must be taken in believing that all such settlements belong to the free, independent native population. In some places, such as the Vosges area mentioned above, or in the Cranbourne Chase-Salisbury Plain, or the Fen areas of Britain, the existence of imperial estates has been argued, in which case the communities represented by these low-grade settlements were probably tenants, or even slaves, of the emperors. On the other hand, there are definite areas where no such imperial connection can be demonstrated. The purely local development of the courtyard-house in West Cornwall, in Britain, led to the foundation of small villages, some combined with round-houses. Ewe Close was a village, or large farmstead, in Northumberland, while the reuse of the north Wales hill-fort at Dinorben in the late-Roman period saw both round and rectangular buildings being constructed. Yet the farmer who continued to live there, in the traditional Iron Age manner, was not so backward as to eschew the use of modern technology; he seems to have possessed the heavy, mouldboard plough with asymmetric share. This demonstrates admirably the concept put forward above, that a farmer in the Empire did not have to build himself a villa, and its lack need not be taken to mean that he was not thoroughly up to date in his agricultural practices, or for that matter necessarily poor. All these sites are connected to demonstrable field-systems. Likewise in the middle Danube area, mixtures of round and rectangular houses, built of wood and clay, have been noted in Pannonia at Halimba, in the Hadrianic period; similar buildings of the same date occur across the frontier of the Danube.

Estimates of the amount of land which would be attached to each farm or estate have sometimes been attempted, as indicated above, by relating granaries or stock buildings to the areas of land needed to fill the granary or run the animals in pasture. As with the identification of farm buildings, such figures must be taken with caution, as overlaps could occur. Stock could be fattened on stubble after the harvest, or in cultivated fields left temporarily fallow. Some land is not suitable for grazing sheep, but might be perfectly suitable for cattle. Not all land was necessarily cultivable. An estate, therefore, which possessed parcels of different land types, such as downland, woodland, water meadows, on the appropriate clays, gravels, chalks, limestones, schists or granites, would be at a distinct advantage over one which had only one or two variants. It also explains why the distribution of villas is invariably related to soil types. Villas are seldom to be found in areas where soils are so poor, thin or sour that cultivation is not possible. Some soils, though, such as the salt marshes of Numidia, sometimes support a rough pasture suitable for grazing, but it is seldom sufficient to support the more broadly based and varied economy of a villa. From this it may be concluded that most villas practised mixed farming, with the requirements of stock being judiciously balanced with cultivation, so making the maximum use of the different soil types which it might possess.

But land use in the Empire was not only governed by soil type. In parts, the rainfall was also critical in husbandry, and, if not sufficient for all-the-year-round maintenance of crops and pasture, might sometimes be supplemented by irrigation. Probably of almost equal importance, but less predictable, was the incidence of frost and sunlight. In Egypt especially, the annual cultivation depended on the Nile flood, or artificial irrigation, and a sharp demarcation line existed between the bordering desert and this watered area; use was also made of oases, of which the Fayum was perhaps the largest and best. Inscriptions also mention systems of irrigation in Numidia.

The two interacting factors of climate and soil type led to the division of the Empire into a number of different parts, according to what crops could be grown. In Italy itself, the level alluvial plains of the Po valley – heavily centuriated – and the coastal strips were ideal for pasture, cereals and other fruit and vegetables, although cereal cultivation suffered a serious decline during the principate. Columella noted that, even by the end of the first century AD, production had fallen to four to one, as against around ten to one elsewhere. The lower reaches of the central spine of the Apennines proved excellent for the cultivation of olives and vines, possibly interplanted with annual crops before the trees and vine-stocks reached maturity, or even afterwards, if enough room was left between rows. The wine of Falernia in the Campania was particularly noted. The higher hills provided forests, containing various nut species, useful for man and beast alike, especially pigs, or, if cleared of woodland, summer pastures for stock wintered in the lowlands.

With some variations the pattern in Italy was repeated around most of the provinces bordering the northern shores of the Mediterranean, as well as some of its islands. Sicily was early noted for its cereals, while the littorals of southern Gaul and eastern Spain, particularly Baetica, were very similar to those of Italy, producing an abundance of wine and olive oil, which was exported to many northern provinces. The Rhône valley itself must have produced cereals, including millet, as attested by the remarkable double sequence of fourth century, water-driven mills running down a hillside at Barbegal near Arles. In the Adriatic, and more especially in Greece and the provinces of Asia Minor, long-standing traditions of husbandry were handed down from past cultures, in which different systems of land tenure played their part; much of the land seems to have been worked directly from the towns and villages. In the Asiatic provinces, as also in Greece and Italy, in addition to wine, oil and cereals, figs were of considerable commercial value, being easy to dry and store for winter use.

In Africa, much of the area inherited from Carthage, which ultimately became the senatorial province of Africa Proconsularis, was heavily cultivated already. In many parts of modern Tunis, there is evidence for large areas of centuriation on several different alignments, suggesting that cultivation was continued into the Roman period, concentrating mainly on producing cereals, and a significant number of grain stores have been identified in this province. The coastal areas of Tripolitania and Cyrenaica probably received more rainfall during the Empire, possibly induced by a greater abundance of trees than there are now; the arrival of the Arab, with his herds of peripatetic and omnivorous goats, is reputed to have effected the change. But even today Cyrenaica enjoys a higher rainfall than its neighbouring areas. Certainly olives flourished. Moreover, there is a great deal of evidence to show that their growing was greatly expanded throughout Africa during the Roman period; almost every farm contains equipment for the extraction of the oil. Even as early as Caesar, Lepcis Magna could pay a fine of three million pounds of olive oil.

In the eastern provinces, grain and sometimes rice, which required irrigation, were cultivated, usually on the coastal strips, as in Italy, and probably intermixed with vines and olives on the lower slopes of the hills; dates were also grown, as were cotton and flax. In marshy areas on the edges of rivers grew the rushes from which papyrus was made. Famous also were the great forests of cedars in Lebanon, which supplied excellent and fragrant timber for building.

In the more temperate areas of the northern provinces of Gaul, Britain, Germany and the Danube basin, there was obviously more emphasis on cereals, wheat, barley, rye and oats, although the hillier regions may have supported limited vine-growing, as today. But it is generally argued that it was not until Probus, in the third century, that viticulture was permitted outside the traditional areas around the Mediterranean. Ample pasture, well-watered for most of the year, was also an asset not possessed by all the southern and eastern provinces.

All areas of the Empire where cultivation was possible and the climate suitable also grew a wide variety of other vegetables, of which perhaps the most important were legumes, providing winter fodder for stock and, when dried, nutritious food for man; several different kinds were known. Legumes also had the additional advantage of putting back into the soil some of the nitrogen used by other crops. Rotation of crops is attested in Egypt and probably became accepted practice elsewhere, as an alternative to leaving fields fallow. Legumes, especially lupins, were also used as green manures; they were sown in the spring, and the young growth was ploughed or dug in to rot down before the normal autumn sowing of cereals. Needless to say, farmyard manure was accumulated in stacks and spread on the fields, together with the residue from wine-making and olive-pressing, where it was available. Running stock in the stubble after harvest, or when the fields were fallow, also effected some degree of manuring. It is generally acknowledged, though, that there was never enough manure for all requirements. Both liming and marling of fields were also practised to correct acidity or to create a richer loam on poor, thin soils.

Other crops included beans, cabbages, carrots, lettuce, parsnip, peas, radishes and turnip, which could be used as fodder as well as food. A large number of herbs were also cultivated; some were used for medicinal purposes, others for flavourings or as vegetables. Apart from grapes and figs, fruits, such as cherries, peaches, apples, pears and plums, and nuts, such as hazels, walnuts, chestnuts and almonds, were grown in places with appropriate climates or else harvested from the wild. Stands of hazel and willow, once pollarded, would also yield valuable wood and bark for hurdle-making, basketry and vine props and ties. Other trees, in particular beech and chestnut, when pollarded, provided a crop of excellent wood for charcoal-burning every dozen years or so.

The fields in which these crops were grown varied according to the nature of the soil and terrain, the climate, the crop and the size of the estate; secondary factors were the types of implement used for cultivation and harvest. In principle, field size was dictated in antiquity by the area one man, with a plough and team of oxen, could plough in a day, even though Columella states that four days were required to plough a *iugerum*. Naturally, this factor could not always be observed, especially on hillside terraces. But on moderate slopes or level ground, fields would be set out with boundaries formed either by ditches, for drainage or irrigation, or by dry-stone walls, fences or perhaps hedges. In areas where centuriation had been introduced, such as the Rhône and Po valleys or in Africa, the boundaries would have been supplemented by access roads. The upkeep of the boundaries was always considered an important duty of both tenants and owners. The commonest implement of cultivation, again throughout the Empire, was the simple ard, a type of plough without mouldboard or coulter and drawn by one or two draft animals, which mainly shuffled the soil. Although it was ideal on light soils, the fields often needed cross-ploughing for full effect, and also to cover the seed after broadcast sowing. But it was useless on heavy clays and also failed to bury weed growth, so that seed crops tended to be contaminated (fig. 18).

The development, therefore, of the heavy plough with mouldboard and coulter in the north-west during the Roman period not only enabled heavy soils to be brought into cultivation, but was also beneficial on lighter soils. What is not known is how widely spread these implements were, or in what numbers, although it is generally agreed that it was never much used in the lands surrounding the Mediterranean. Cultivation could also be carried out by spade or hoe; the latter was also used in a number of different forms for weeding. The spade, made of iron-bound wood, was essential for harvesting

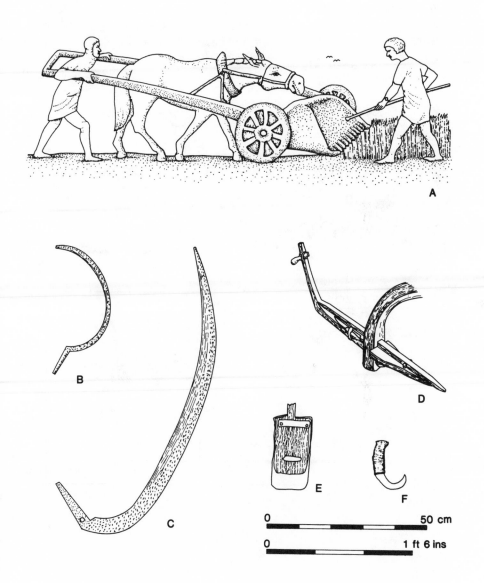

A

B

C

D

E

F

| 0 | | | | | | | 50 cm |
| 0 | | | | | | | 1 ft 6 ins |

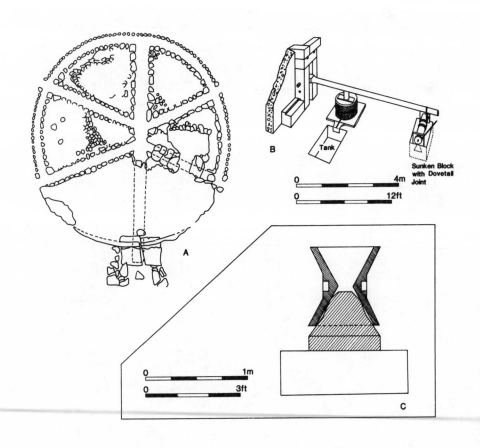

B

Tank

Sunken Block
with Dovetail
Joint

0   4m

0   12ft

A

0   1m

0   3ft

C

root crops, digging and clearing ditches and for planting vines, olives and fruit trees, which were usually inserted into trenches partly filled with compost or other rotting organic matter. Pruning hooks, knives and small saws were also important to the viticulturalists and fruit growers.

The main cereals grown were spelt, a wheat suitable for autumn sowing even in central and north-west Europe, a six-row barley, used mainly as fodder or for making beer – Gallic beer was quoted in Diocletian's list of fixed prices – rye, millet in Gaul and the eastern parts of the Empire, and possibly oats in more northern parts. Harvesting was carried out commonly by a form of short reaping hook, although the balanced sickle and scythe were introduced. Of interest are some monster scythe blades, from Britain, over 1.5 m (5 ft) long. They appear extremely unwieldy, although similar scythes are still used in the lower Danube regions today. A form of harvesting machine, known as the *vallus*, is attested in northern Europe and also mentioned in the literature. It consisted of a hopper-like receiver with broad, pointed blades projecting forwards from the front, lower edge. As it was pushed through the crop by a donkey or mule, the blades would pluck or strip the ears of grain which would then fall back into the hopper. In some of the northern provinces the grain seems to have been harvested almost green and then dried artificially in kilns. The ripe, or artificially dried, grain was threshed on special floors, either with flails or being trodden by animals, after which it would have been winnowed and stored in granaries, large jars, or sometimes even pits, following the traditions of the Iron Age in north-western Europe. When flour was required, the grain was either milled in large, donkey-driven, hour-glass shaped querns, or in small, domestic, hand-turned stones. Water-power was sometimes used to turn the millstones, as at the Barbegal in the Rhône Valley and on Hadrian's Wall in Britain, but it is surprising that so little use was made of it (fig. 19).

The care of vines, olive and fruit trees is extensively dealt with in contemporary literature, as is also the choice of variety for a particular climate and situation. Vines appear to have been grown as standards or on trellises, being pruned either in the autumn or in the early spring according to the danger from frost. After the grapes had been harvested they were trodden and pressed, the liquid being contained in jars, barrels or vats for fermentation. The must was often used as a manure, while the lees of wine barrels provided a useful pigment. Olive trees needed careful nurturing; since some time elapsed between planting and fruiting, they tended to be an investment for the future, and, as with young vines, could be underplanted with annual crops. The ripe olives would be picked if accessible, or brought down by beating or shaking the upper branches. The fruit would be macerated in one of a variety of mills and the oil then expelled by pressing; it would be stored in vats or jars. As with the must from wine-making, the solid matter left after pressing was deemed a good manure (fig. 20).

The growing of vegetables was frequently carried out on a domestic scale in the courtyards or gardens of villas. Some spectacular archaeological evidence of gardens has come from Pompeii, which although not strictly rural, must have been frequently repeated in the countryside. The positions of trees and vines and potted plants have been pinpointed with some precision from the voids created by their decay in the surrounding volcanic ash, while evidence for vegetables and flowers is provided by wall-paintings and, most recently, by pollen analyses. The painting in the garden room of the Villa of Livia shows a mixture of formality and informality in the lay-out. This mixture of formal and informal has also been demonstrated in the great palace-villa at Fishbourne in Britain, where a jar of carbonised seeds of *Lathyrus sp.* indicated one of the plants grown; even the small villa at Frocester in the same province has produced evidence for flower, herb and vegetable borders against the house. It is unlikely to have been the only example. Elsewhere, though, vegetables seem to have been grown on a commercial scale on irrigated plots in Syria and Egypt, in market gardens on the outskirts of Pompeii and possibly in some Fenland settlements in Britain, where there are series of unusual fields divided up into narrow strips, not unlike modern large asparagus beds.

As already stressed above, most farms in the Roman world were mixed, raising stock as well as crops, and often using stubble or fallow land, which might have amounted to as much as a half of the area of cultivation at any one time, to fatten cattle or other herbivores. That is not to say, though, that there were no areas of permanent pasture which could be used for all, or part, of the year, depending on the climate; there is a considerable amount of evidence for cattle and sheep ranching on a large scale in some provinces. In some places, notably Egypt, pasture was actually sown the previous year for cattle grazing. Transhumance was also practised widely throughout the Empire; it involved the movement of stock, sometimes considerable distances, from summer to winter pastures, according to the climate in each.

Stock, including birds, can be divided broadly into two categories, according to whether they provided primarily a commodity, such as meat, wool, hides, or a service, such as traction or hunting; in some instances the categories overlapped. The animals, birds and insects which provided a commodity were cattle, sheep, goats, pigs, chicken, geese, pigeons and bees, all of which were reared in captivity. The ability to raise and maintain domestic herds or flocks throughout the year came about, either by the provision of harvested fodder, or by transhumance, and by the recognised need for some kind of shelter during winter months in the less clement areas of the Empire.

Cattle were probably the most important stock, and were grazed extensively on large ranches in Sicily, parts of Italy, Asia Minor, north Africa and Syria, Gaul, Britain and the upper Danube. Milk was an important product, from which some butter and cheese was made, and a breed of cattle in Greece was noted for its high milk yield; hides and meat were equally important, since leather was required in vast quantities for the clothing and equipment of the Roman army. Size and glue and other artefacts from the bones, and horn, were also valuable commodities; manure was a useful by-product. There is evidence from a number of provinces, especially Egypt, that improvements in breeds were made during the Empire, leading to larger and more productive beasts. The importance of cattle to the Roman economy is shown by the recognition of a bull, a boar and a ram in the *suovataurilium*, one of the earliest religious manifestations of Rome.

Next to cattle, sheep were probably the most valuable livestock, not only yielding the commonest textile fibre in the Empire – wool – but also, in and around the Mediterranean, milk and cheese; the price for sheep's milk was fixed in Diocletian's Edict, but cows' milk is not mentioned and seems to have occupied a secondary position. Indeed, there were sheep in the Empire wherever there was appropriate pasture. But probably the finest wool was derived from the sheep of Miletus in Asia Minor, which were later imported into southern Italy; the sheep were wrapped in winter to protect their fleeces. Sheep and goats also provided skins suitable for the manufacturer of parchment, which was first made at Pergamum in Asia. Numidia was noted for its woollen goods and it is interesting, as already mentioned above, that the so-called '*fossatum Africae*' (p. 70), a discontinuous series of linear barriers in and around the Aurés mountains, tends to mark the southern borders of the permanent pastures. So important was the wool industry that, in the fourth century, if not before, a number of imperial weaving mills existed to provide cloth for the army and the ever-increasing band of imperial officials. One such mill was at Carthage, no doubt served by the Numidian flocks. Numerous woollen garments are also listed in Diocletian's Edict, including cloaks from Africa and rugs and hooded capes from Britain. As with cattle, some cross-breeding was successful in producing larger animals with better-quality fleeces.

Goats furnished products similar to those of sheep, although perhaps in the Empire they were less valued, even if as widely distributed. Their principal advantage over sheep was their ability, at times destructive, to eat and digest almost any vegetables no matter how woody, but they were probably more susceptible to disease. Goat-hair, although strong, is less curly and elastic and therefore more suited to making felted materials and ropes than is wool; Cilicia was noted for its goats'-hair products. Pigs were equally widely distributed and provided meat, skin, bristle, and lard which was an essential part of army rations. Both pork and ham were considered excellent food, especially in the Celtic areas of the Empire, such as Spain, Gaul and Britain, where no doubt they were supplemented by hunted wild pigs, as attested by an inscription from northern Britain, referring to a hunt in which a 'wild boar of remarkable fineness' was killed. Although pigs could often be left to forage for roots and other matter in woods, there is also a good deal of evidence to show that pigsties existed on many farms, and that both protection for farrowing, and for artificial fattening, was often provided.

Poultry, pigeons, ducks and geese were bred for food, while they also provided eggs, quills, feathers and down, as well as manure; bird manure is more concentrated than farmyard muck and therefore can be used with greater economy. Northern Gaul was famous for its geese, which were even sent to Rome, often alive and on foot, as was done in medieval times, when geese were often herded from Norfolk to London; then, a coating of pitch was normally applied to the feet before the journey. Chickens were reared for the table and Columella refers to three varieties, of which the Gallic species was well known. Pigeons and doves were also fattened for food in pigeon lofts, which much resembled the medieval dovecot; although they were common in most Mediterranean provinces, the principal varieties originated in Egypt and the east, Pergamum being a noted breeding centre.

The animals which provided a service were oxen, donkeys, mules, horses, camels and dogs, although sometimes cows might be used in place of oxen to draw the plough. But oxen were the principal draft animals of the farm and it was reckoned that an estate of 60 ha (150 acres) required three teams, which would be brought into stalls at night and carefully tended. The next most important beasts of burden were the donkey and the mule, obtained by crossing an ass with a mare. Mules, when well bred and trained, have an intelligence, ability and strength that make them superior to donkeys. Their importance even warranted special mule vets, *muliomedici*, one of whom is known from the Thames Valley in Britain. Apart from being used as pack animals, mules were also used harnessed to vehicles; these, of which a number of different styles are illustrated on monumental reliefs, ranged from light, two-wheeled curricles to heavy, four-wheeled wagons capable of carrying large loads and probably drawn by teams of four or six animals. But the donkey was probably the universal beast of burden in the Empire, being used as pack animal, draft animal and indispensable for driving millstones, treadwheels, olive-macerators and operating water-wheels for irrigation; they were harnessed to carts and even to the plough. They were reasonably hardy and could withstand shortages of food and water and considerable ill-treatment, as indicated in the *Metamorphoses* of Apuleius.

Horses, on the other hand, although sometimes used for drawing light vehicles and carts, figured little in the agricultural system. They were used for riding and as pack animals, and obviously played an important part in serving the cavalry regiments of the army. They were also foremost in horse and chariot racing, for which selective breeding was important; most inhabitants of the Empire delighted in gambling on the results. Camels, though, were used for both man and merchandise and not only in Africa and the eastern provinces; they could also be yoked to the plough. The army seems to have used them as transport animals, even in north-west Europe, while the *Ala I dromedarii milliaria* was recruited under Trajan and served in Arabia. Dogs were used both as watchdogs and for herding and hunting; there is the delightful wall painting of a pet dog, something between an Airedale and a collie, illustrated on the wall of the House of the Epigrams at Pompeii. At the same city, the volcanic ash from Vesuvius had also buried alive a chained watchdog. Several provinces had specific breeds with their own characteristics. Britain was noted for a mastiff and a form of lurcher, as well as types of terriers; southern Italy produced herding dogs.

But during the Empire, dogs, among other animals, were also kept as pets. There is a charming terracotta group from Bordeaux which shows a double couch occupied by a man and a woman; across their feet lies the household dog, fast asleep and obviously relishing the comfort. A recent find at Stanwick (Northants) in Britain was that of a burial of a young girl; close nearby, carefully enclosed in a small cyst, were the bones of her pet dog, a miniature breed only 15 cm high. Bones of the Barbary ape have been found as far north as Catterick in Britain; it was clearly a pet, or perhaps even a performing monkey. Peacocks presumably fulfilled a dual function, providing both ornament and food. Tame herds are depicted on some mosaics and reliefs, while the bones of cats are not unknown from excavations; one is also illustrated on a painting at Pompeii, sitting on a low cushioned stool. In Egypt it was a sacred animal; elsewhere it would have been used to keep down vermin. In parts of the Empire, dormice were reared and fattened as a delicacy, but they can equally make delightful pets, as can linnets and other species of songbirds.

As already indicated, the domestic diet of the Roman Empire was frequently supplemented by hunting, and on pots, walls and floors there are numerous illustrations of hunting and fishing scenes. Exotic animals like lions and leopards for the lucrative trade for the amphitheatres can be seen being hunted on paintings in the cold room of the hunting baths at Lepcis Magna, while the eastern entrance hall showed scenes of hunters and animal pelts. Normally hunting was carried out on foot with the aid of dogs and nets, which enable the animal either to be captured alive or dispatched with a spear or club.

Wild pig, deer, hares, wild geese and duck and other smaller birds are all listed in culinary texts; it is claimed that the pheasant was a Roman introduction to north-west Europe. Both sea- and fresh-water fish were caught and eaten in appropriate places, together with shellfish, notably oysters, which were traded widely in barrels of seawater, but it seems unlikely that any fish were 'farmed' in the modern manner, although fish ponds and lakes could have been kept stocked by transferring fry. A house in the city of Utica, not far from Carthage in Africa, contained a mosaic with the head of a sea god, numerous types of fish and two fishermen in a boat. Fish was most valuable when transformed into *garum*, a type of sauce which was extensively used throughout the Mediterranean region and beyond as a popular condiment. Much was produced in Spain, especially at Cartagena, from where it was exported in large *amphorae*. Both Lixus and Thamusida on the Atlantic coast of Mauretania Tingitana possessed factories for its production. The honey from wild bees was also important, since it was the only concentrated sweetening agent known to the ancient world; indeed so necessary was it that bees were domesticated at a very early date in Greece and Egypt. Different breeds and methods of keeping were recognised, and became recorded in the standard agricultural texts of the day. It was reckoned that one hive could yield from 3 to 82 l (6–18 pints) of honey. Even then the honey from Mount Hymetus in Greece was noted for its quality.

What then was life like for the country-dweller? For the really rich, a retreat from the rigours and demands of the city; for those comfortably off, both landowners and tenants, a not unpleasant way of life with ample and varied food, drink, clothing and some amenities, such as the bath-house, attractive flower and herb gardens and hunting if so inclined. But for the poor tenant, especially in the later Empire, the peasant, even the free smallholder, and the agricultural labourers, whether slaves or free, it was a life of unremitting and continuous hardship and toil, governed solely by the changes of seasons and the local climate; there could be no relief from heat or cold; food and accommodation at best adequate, at worst primitive. Yet it was the way of life for by far the largest proportion of the Empire's people.

VIII

THE EMPIRE AT WORK: ECONOMY AND INDUSTRY

Probably the two factors which contributed most to the growth of trade and industry in the Roman Empire were the introduction of a reasonably stable, and usable, common currency, and a well-organised system of communications. Add to that the growth of primary markets in the army, the cities and the towns, and the *pax Romana* which enabled merchants to travel mostly unthreatened by piracy or brigandage, and the result was the growth of a vigorous economic community of a size then hitherto unseen in the lands of the Mediterranean and Europe. It may be that this is an over-simplificaton, even an over-statement, for there are those who argue strongly that the Empire's economy was in no sense unified and completely integrated with the community. But it must not be forgotten that its origins were not so peaceful; trade follows war as much as war is often provoked by over-competitive trade, and the ultimate capture by republican Rome of the valuable commercial links belonging to Carthage, Asia Minor, Syria and central Europe, contributed greatly to her eventually successful economic dominance of the known ancient world.

In theory, the Roman monetary system of the early principate appears deceptively simple, being based on that generated in the late Republic, when issues of gold and silver coinage were struck mainly to pay the armies then in contest for the Roman world. To some extent this coinage conflicted with the standards of the eastern Empire which were still related to the Greek tetradrachm, but incorporated as *denarii*, and there still was lacking an Empire-wide, acceptable small change; many local issues of low-value copper-alloy coinage sufficed until replaced by more standard forms in the first century AD. The only exception was the gold *aureus*, which, from the first issues, was uncompromisingly Roman. Any trimetallic system of coinage, as it became, suffers from inbuilt weaknesses caused by fluctuations in intrinsic

151

value of the three metals, which could upset a true comparability; thus, in the Roman world, gold tended to command a premium over silver and silver over copper alloys, which pleased the money-changers, but was not good for the stability of the currency. With the emperor retaining the sole right to coin in gold and silver, there was also inbuilt the temptation for a profligate emperor to devalue the coinage and so make a profit. Consequently there was an accelerating debasement, so causing a creeping inflation which culminated in the appalling devaluations of the later third century, when the money market virtually collapsed. Theoretically, though, the formal rate of exchange was based at first on 1 *aureus* = 25 *denarii* = 400 *asses*, although significant changes were to take place later.

The principate of Augustus saw a greater degree of standardisation in the copper coinage, with lesser values than the *as* coming into circulation from mints in Rome. Many bore the superscription SC in bold letters, designating senatorial control. Such issues circulated widely in the western Empire, but local issues tended to remain supreme in the east, where a number of provincial mints were operating. The whereabouts of mints producing gold and silver are not entirely certain in this period, although for a time one was situated at Lyon, and so accounts for the presence of an urban cohort in that city, one of only two outside Rome; later this mint was transferred to Rome, possibly under Nero.

The later first century AD saw the beginning of inflation, when Nero reduced the weight and fineness of gold and silver, although ostensibly maintaining the same face value. Copper-alloy coinage was also reformed with the standardisation of the lesser values of *sestertius*, *dupondius*, *semis* and *quadrans*. The value of individual coins continued to decline at an accelerating rate throughout the remaining first century and on into the second, until under Commodus the amount of silver in the *denarius* had sunk to 70 per cent. The early third century saw an even greater and more rapid decline; under Severus the *denarius* fell to 50 per cent silver, although the standard of the *aureus* was maintained, a change which seriously upset their inter-relationship. In consequence a new, larger silver coin, the 'antoninianus', was introduced by Caracalla to restore the parity with the *aureus*; it has been variously argued as representing one, one and a half or two *denarii*. Although for a time the *denarius* continued in circulation alongside the new coin, its ultimate demise came before the middle of the third century. By then the 'antoninianus' had decreased in both weight and fineness, together with the *aureus*. Under Gallienus it reached its nadir, containing little more than 5 per cent silver even though a silver wash on the surface suggested a higher content; large numbers were minted to make up for its declining value, while forgery was rife. This inflation had far-reaching effects on the economy and contributed to the general malaise which then struck the Empire.

The need for monetary reforms became an absolute priority. Partial restoration was made by Aurelian, who founded two new Italian mints and standardised a heavier 'antoninianus' containing 5 per cent silver. Simultaneously a reduction of about 20 per cent in weight was made in the Alexandrine tetradrachm. These reforms were completed by Diocletian, who was the first emperor successfully to dispose of locally minted coinage, and who returned the system to the gold standard, creating a new *aureus* of standard weight. Although again reduced in weight by Constantine I and renamed the *solidus*, it remained the basic coin until well beyond the end of the Empire in the west. For a brief period a return was also made to the finer silver *denarius* during the late-third and early-fourth century; beyond that the issues of copper-based coinage were many and varied and continued so throughout the fourth century, matched by a proliferation of provincial mints. Many had an inflated value, so encouraging forgery on a large scale.

If the inflationary cycles of the Roman Empire are considered, it must be immediately apparent that they seriously affected its economy, although it is not yet fully understood how precisely this came about. Although emperors might well have wanted to control the economy by juggling with the coinage, in practice they were almost impotent to interfere in what was basically a free market economy. The one great attempt to do so by Diocletian in his Edict of Prices and Wages, despite the savage penalties for any breach of the Code, was as disastrous as most attempts by modern governments have been, and soon became unenforceable, simply because market forces were more powerful. Nevertheless the seriousness of the situation can be gauged by the imperial reactions of Severus, Diocletian, Constantine I and others, and it is likely that the thoughts which were uppermost in their minds were concerned with payments to the army and to the expanding corps of civil servants, and with the collection of taxes to meet these payments. It is hardly surprising, therefore, that a return was made to the payment of taxes with goods rather than money.

A citizen army, such as that of the early and middle Republic, might be prepared to fight for nothing or, if paid, wait for its remuneration. But a 'mercenary' army, as it largely became in the late Empire, with little loyalty to those it protected, would either mutiny or desert if no pay arrived. Indeed it is likely that this was one of the factors which contributed to the fall of the western Empire; it certainly happened in Pannonia. When it is also remembered that army payments were one of the principal ways of distributing new coinage around the provinces, the non-arrival of the pay-chests would have had an immediate effect on the local economies. Although it is unlikely that barter was ever completely ousted by currency in the Empire, it was a form of exchange which would have been most unwieldly in the comparatively more sophisticated economy then prevailing; yet, with a scarcity of coin, there would have been no alternative. Most of the social and economic ills of the late Empire can probably be laid to this cause; in a modern political idiom, the rich got richer and the poor became poorer.

The second major factor to influence the economy was the system of communications which grew in the Empire. Sea-routes there had been from time immemorial and unmetalled tracks since the invention of the wheel; some were guarded against brigandage by the people who lived along their ways, and who often extorted tolls for doing so. Most tracks, though, would have followed sinuous courses to avoid major obstacles. In Italy roads were pioneered by both Etruscans and Greeks, and from an early age they were improved and extended by the Republic to connect Rome to her allies' territories and beyond; the names given to the gates of the city record those of the roads which led to them: Appia, Flaminia, Latina, Salaria, for example. It was natural, therefore, that as the march of Rome progressed around the Mediterranean, the roads followed in the wake of the army. It was not unnatural either that they came to be surveyed and constructed by the army, usually helped by native labour, which rapidly became skilled in such work.

The roads were primarily essential for the rapid movement of troops, so that strategic road-building became a feature of all new conquests. Unlike their predecessors, they were engineered to provide wherever possible the shortest route between two points, even if this meant surmounting major obstacles; wherever possible also they were constructed in straight sections. Locally-available materials were normally used for the metalling, and careful attention was paid to drainage by raising the carriageway on a low mound, the agger, cambering the surface, and digging lateral ditches, not only to carry off surface water, but also to increase stability by draining the subsoil.

It must be remembered though that the road surfaces, however well paved or compacted, were not waterproof; consequently, wherever there was a risk from frost, winter disruption of the surface would take place, so that annual repairs would be called for each spring. If these were not carried out, the roads would have been rapidly reduced to muddy potholes. It was not until the invention of tarmacadam that this difficulty was resolved, and although bitumen was used in building construction by the Babylonians as early as the fourth millenium BC, and despite the fact that bituminous asphalt occurs naturally in parts of Africa, south-east France and Switzerland, it was never used during the Empire for this purpose. If the subsoil was inherently unstable, great efforts were often made to correct it; peat would be stripped to bare rock as at Craik Cross in northern Britain; a corduroy of brushwood or heavier timbers would be laid, as at Hautes-Fagne on the *via Mansuerisca* in northern Gaul. This was not a new technique and corduroy tracks of the late Bronze Age have been found in the peat-bogs of Somerset in Britain. The cambered running surfaces were sometimes embellished with a central ridge, presumably to separate the opposing streams of traffic, and with raised kerb stones, such as the roads in Syria which connected Apamea with Theleda, and Bostra with Damascus and Palmyra; both were also paved and were some 6 m (20 ft) wide, giving ample room both for two traffic streams and for overtaking. It is curious that no one has yet discovered if there was a rule of the road!

The way in which roads were laid out in the Empire has caused a good deal of argument. For short sections, intervisible sighting positions could have been used, but the methods employed for long-distance direction-finding are not so easy to establish, especially in view of the accuracy often to be observed despite the absence of the compass. A recent suggestion envisages the employment of homing pigeons to indicate the direction by their line of flight; it would also be possible to work out directions by noting the position of the sun at midday, when it lay on the southerly point of the compass.

The construction of a good road system also required subsidiary engineering work on bridges, cuttings and fords. Many Roman bridges are still in use today, such as Tiberius' bridge over the river Rubicon at Rimini, the bridge at Alcantara over the Tagus in Spain, for which a Syrian architect was employed. These were built entirely of stone, but equally common were those constructed of timber on stone piers such as the great bridges which crossed the Moselle at Trier and the Tees at Piercebridge. Most minor bridges, though, were constructed entirely of timber, and have since perished, although occasionally traces survive in waterlogged soil, as at Aldwinkle in Britain. In one or two places, also, roads were cut out of vertical rock faces, as can be seen in the Aosta valley of north Italy on the route of the *Via Flaminia*. Similarly the road through the Danube gorge at Djerdap, intended to act as a tow-path for shipping, was at first constructed by cantilevering a timber way from the sheer rock face, although Trajan rebuilt it by cutting back into the face for some 2 – 3 m (6½ – 10 ft), at the same time renewing the timber extension. A minor aspect of road building in the Empire was the provision of milestones on the arterial routes measured out with hodometers; normally they were inscribed with a dedication to the reigning emperor and may, or may not, have mentioned the distance they marked and the town from which it was measured. Many examples are known from all over the Empire, and especially in parts of north Africa, where several often occur together in their original positions, probably representing different periods of repair.

The construction of the road system in the Empire for military purposes would have benefited those communities which lay along its sections, even if eventually these local communities became responsible for the upkeep of the roads in their territories. In time the network expanded with the addition of minor roads and tracks linking small settlements and outlying farms and villages with the greater towns and cities; it has been argued that the peasantry were the chief beneficiaries. Indeed, there was only one drawback to the full use of this enormous asset by merchants and travellers: the cost. The figure most often quoted as an illustration relates to the cartage of 500 kg (½ ton) of wheat over 500 km (300 miles): the price would have doubled during the journey. Water transport therefore always remained an integral, and cheaper, part of the system. The cost of shipping the same 500 kg of wheat from one end of the Mediterranean to the other would have cost less than the land carriage over 120 km (75 miles).

Shipping in the Empire was typologically of three kinds, inland, coastwise and ocean-going. Supreme among the inland waterways were the three great rivers of the Empire, the Nile, the Rhine and the Danube. Almost the entire production of that narrow strip of fertile, irrigated land flanking the banks of the Nile could have been shipped directly to Alexandria by the river which provided it. The adherence of the northern frontier in mainland Europe to two of its greatest waterways may not be wholly unconnected with the ease and cheapness of the lateral transport of men and supplies which they provided. Certainly the huge barges, up to 40 m (130 ft) long, which plied the lower reaches of the Rhine would have carried very large quantities of material. To facilitate passage on the Danube a canal was cut in the Iron Gates by Trajan. Other rivers, like the Tiber, Euphrates, the Rhône, Seine, Garonne and Thames, played proportionally important parts. Riverside quays, sometimes in quiet backwaters off the main stream, have been identified at London and Xanten, and of course at Rome on the banks of the Tiber, while the use of floating jetties has been proposed at some ports on the Danube.

Pliny suggested to Trajan that a canal system should be built from Lake Sophon to the nearby port at Nicomedia on the Sea of Marmara in Bithynia, but it was never constructed. The wharves along the Tiber at Rome linked the city with its sea-going port at Ostia, whence came, among many other vessels, the great grain ships from Egypt and Africa; some were capable of carrying up to 1000 tonnes of grain, together with supercargo of glass, metal or pottery. The original harbour at Ostia was greatly extended in turn by Claudius, Nero and Trajan, although the famous shipping offices were constructed under Augustus. Ostia, though, despite its growth and eminently suitable position, never entirely replaced Puteoli on the Bay of Naples, which had been the first port of Rome. Other harbours for both coastwise and ocean-going vessels were liberally dotted about the shores of the Empire. In Africa, Cherchel, Lepcis Magna and Carthage still display harbour works, the latter having been adapted from the Punic naval base; Alexandria was equipped with two famous lighthouses. Fréjus on the south coast of Gaul possessed a harbour which was land-locked and entered from the sea by a canal. On the southern shore of the Black Sea Trabzon not only accommodated the numerous traders from Armenia who crossed the Zigana Pass, but

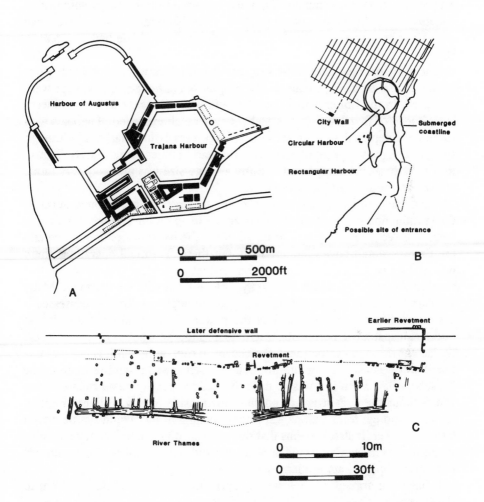

Harbour of Augustus

Trajans Harbour

0   500m

0   2000ft

A

City Wall

Circular Harbour

Rectangular Harbour

Submerged coastline

Possible site of entrance

B

Earlier Revetment

Later defensive wall

Revetment

River Thames

0   10m

0   30ft

C

157

was also the chief supply port for the Euphrates frontier forces and the base of the *classis Pontica;* Hadrian constructed the harbour where previously there had been only an open roadstead (fig. 21).

Taken together, the main trade routes of the Black Sea, Mediterranean and north-west Europe, as well as most of the navigable waterways, must have been congested with shipping. They were serviced by the many shipowners (*navicularii*) in the Empire, such as those from Narbonne who had an office at Ostia, while their near neighbours at Arles on the Rhône had an agent in Beirut.

The principal merchant ships were heavy, wide-beamed and probably slow, relying at first on a single mainsail for propulsion, although large sweeps were also used. In the Empire ancillary masts and triangular sails were introduced, but a speed of four knots was probably never much exceeded. Tugboats with rowers are depicted sometimes, towing large vessels into harbour. Although very large vessels capable of carrying a thousand tonnes or more were known, they were probably exceptional and the average size was probably very much smaller at about fifty tonnes capacity.

If currency and transport were the key to large-scale economic success, then production was the lock. The movement of agricultural goods has already been referred to in Chapter VII; they formed the backbone of commerce and the Empire would have foundered without them. Yet in all operations there was a distinct attitude of *laissez-faire*, so that in the middle of the fourth century Antioch starved, with plenty only 80 km (50 miles) away. Many scholars have commented on the fact that although the Empire possessed a basic scientific knowledge, such as the power of the wind or steam, it was utterly incapable of harnessing them to productive ends. One mechanical device appeared to escape them, the eccentric cam, although it is not impossible that it was used to operate the water-driven saws for cutting stone in the Moselle valley. Even if it was so used, it would appear to be an isolated case. But without the cam it is not possible to translate rotary to linear motion. Hence, although force pumps were not uncommon, they could not be driven by water power. It almost seems that there was a complete lack of any incentive to improve even by what would appear to us today the simplest of observations and their empirical applications.

It has been argued, not necessarily correctly, that an abundance of cheap slave, or semi-slave, labour made inventiveness unnecessary; yet there were manpower shortages in the late Empire. Neither was there an inhibiting factor, like the all-powerful Church in the Middle Ages, to hold back progress, except perhaps for some Roman equivalents of the Luddites, to which sect Tiberius would apparently have belonged; the story concerning him and the unbreakable glass would have been worthy of an Ealing Comedy on the lines of *The Man in the White Suit*. Perhaps it was that the Romans lacked a latter-

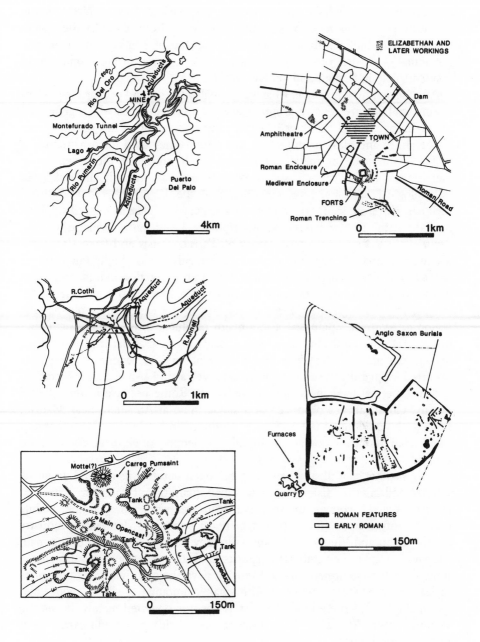

day Archimedes, a Galileo or a Leonardo to give a lead, especially when it is remembered just how few men were responsible for the birth, in the Renaissance, of our modern scientific era. Apart from aids like the water-wheel or treadmill, both of which were capable of being used to provide horizontal or vertical motion by systems of gears, power in the Roman world resided solely in human and animal muscle.

After agricultural produce, what was probably the second principal source of commercial activity centred around the extractive industries which generated mainly minerals and building materials, but also included the raw materials for ceramics and glass manufacture and some stones used for ornament.

The occurrence of metallic minerals which produced the seven or so metals used in the Empire was uneven. Spain was probably the richest in mineralogical deposits, producing much of the Empire's gold and silver, together with iron, lead, tin, copper and mercury – the last as the red sulphide used to paint in the letters on inscriptions. Gold came principally from Asturias, in the north-western corner of Tarraconensis and from Baetica; it also occurred in the alluvium of some rivers. Silver was chiefly found in the area around Cartagena, but also from Rio Tinto in Baetica and, in conjuction with lead, at Minas de Mouras in Lusitania; Rio Tinto also produced copper in quantity, although the richest source was to the east of the gold-bearing region of Asturias. Spain was also a major producer of tin, which was found not only at Rio Tinto, but also more abundantly in Galicia; lead was mined in Baetica, and in Cantabria and Cartagena in Tarraconensis. Iron ores occurred in quantity in southern Baetica as well as in Lusitania and Cantabria, and in time replaced those sources nearer to Rome because of their better quality. Cinnabar was produced at a single mine at Almaden, near Madrid. Indeed, the only metal not seemingly produced in Spain was zinc; otherwise the Iberian peninsula possessed virtually a monopoly of all metals used in the Empire.

Gaul was not so well supplied and it has been said that its mineral desposits were something of a disappointment. Small quantities of gold were extracted as well as silver, copper, tin and lead. Iron ores were more prolific, mainly in the central area, and were sufficient to support a flourishing industry around Lyon and Vienne. Gaul and Germany, though, were two of the main suppliers of zinc. The mineral desposits of Britain were perhaps also something of a disappointment to the Romans; nevertheless, significant quantities of lead were extracted, together with smaller amounts of silver, copper and tin. A single gold-mine in south-west Wales was operated mainly during the second century. But as in Gaul, iron was more widespread and extracted in quantity in a number of places.

In central Europe and the Balkans there were also several sources of useful minerals. Gold occurred in Dalmatia as well as Dacia, where it was the principal metal found in northern Transylvania. Although gold is frequently mentioned in the pre-Roman period as coming from Macedonia and Thrace, and also some of the islands of Pelopenese, there is little to show that mining was carried on into the principate, and it may be that the deposits were exhausted, as seems to have happened to the region's silver mines, although an attempt was made to reopen Laurion in the fourth century. The other metal of importance was iron, found in Macedonia, Dacia, Dalmatia, Moesia and Noricum. The mines in the last province lay mainly in Carinthia and Upper Styria and their products achieved some fame, being known as *ferrum Noricum*, a metal, which when treated by a special process, apparently invented in Noricum, was almost the equivalent of steel; Hadrian issued coins with the legend *met(ella), Nor(ica)* as an eloquent testimony to the industry's importance. It is worth noting that the island of Elba also had important deposits of iron ore and it has been estimated that 11,000,000 tons were mined.

Silver, copper and iron were all extracted in lesser amounts in Asia Minor and the other eastern provinces. Silver came from the area south of Trabzon, while deposits of copper ores were worked near Pergamum in Asia, in the Sinai peninsula and on Cyprus. Iron ores were mined near Nicomedia in Bithynia. On the whole, though, the resources did not measure up to those in other provinces. Africa was equally poorly represented, and the only really worthwhile deposits were at Meroë in Egypt, where gold, copper and iron were worked, together with some gem-stones. Sardinia and Sicily produced iron ores and also argentiferous lead, while the volcanic nature of the latter island provided supplies of sulphur, which was used for bleaching cloth; sulphur was also found around the base of Vesuvius and apparently exported from Puteoli (fig. 22).

In order to extract minerals the Romans employed a remarkably diverse series of mining techniques which depended on the nature of the ground rock and its position. Some techniques were surprisingly sophisticated, although again we are brought up hard by their almost complete ignorance of even the simplest geological methodology. If a vein was broken by a fault, they had no means of knowing whether it would resume above or below their existing level. Yet they could follow even narrow veins with great accuracy, and their methods of de-watering wet mines, although primitive by modern standards, were comparatively effective, making use of water-wheels or Archimedean screws; a single wheel of appropriate diameter could raise nearly 100 1 (20 gal) of water per minute over a height exceeding 3.5 m (4 yd). Several screw pumps and fragments of water-wheels have been found in Spanish and Gaulish mines, while a fragment of wheel has come from the sole gold-mine in Britain. It was customary to arrange these machines in ascending series, and at Rio Tinto sixteen such wheels were so arranged giving an overall lift of nearly 30 m (32 yd). The other implements and tools related to mining in the Roman world were remarkably standardised and remained so throughout the middle ages. Wood, stone and metal were all used to make a variety of picks, shovels, gads, wedges, chisels and panning cradles; the mined ore was carried in baskets or buckets made of copper or esparto grass.

As noted above, mining operations depended on the nature and position of the ore. Most alluvial deposits were unsuitable for shafts or adits, so that surface working was normal and was often characterised by huge open-cast areas, from which the material containing the ore was extracted by straightforward digging, sometimes assisted by releasing a rapid flow of water to loosen the ground; after crushing, the dross would be separated from the ore by flotation in running water. Most of these deposits would have been originally created by the weathering of outcrops of the primary ore veins in geological times.

When, however, it was necessary to mine unweathered veins, underground workings had to be made in which shafts, adits and galleries all played their part. A great variety of shapes and sizes have been recorded, ranging from square to trapezoidal and often little more than a metre (40 in) high. Where necessary, props and shores were inserted and a regulation at Vipasca stipulates that it was an offence to interfere with them. Lighting was by ceramic or metal oil lamps, and ventilation shafts were sometimes dug in parallel to the main shaft. Even then the air was probably foul, although no methane would normally have been present to cause explosions. Both Lucretius and Pliny refer to the bad atmosphere in deep mines, which would not have been improved if fire-setting was employed to split the rock. Apart from the roasting of sulphide ores which would have released sulphur dioxide, vinegar was sometimes used to quench the fire so as to shatter the rock, since it has a higher latent heat than water and therefore cools more quickly. Chemical reaction between the vinegar and hot sulphides might also have released hydrogen sulphide. The combined odour of sulphur dioxide, vinegar, hydrogen sulphide, not forgetting also possible vaporised heavy metals, such as lead, would hardly have provided a healthy atmosphere. It is little surprise, therefore, to find that most miners were either slaves or criminals, condemned *ad metallum*, a punishment which was little better than the death penalty.

As already indicated in Chapter V, most mines in the Roman Empire were the property of the emperor and constituted as imperial estates, to secure their valuable products for the state, especially gold, silver and copper which were required in large quantities for coinage. As such they were usually administered by a procuratorial assistant (*procurator metallorum*), or leased out to tenants-in-chief (*conductores*) who might be single operators or companies (*socii*). In the Noricum iron mines the *procuratores ferrariarum* assigned licences to *conductores ferrariarum*. Some small lessees worked their own concessions

162

on a percentage basis under the procurators, not unlike one of the systems in force during early tin-mining days in Cornwall. Some surviving Hadrianic inscriptions from Portugal relate to the administration of the silver mines at Aljustrel (Vipasca). The regulations were extremely detailed and relate not only to the working of the mines, but also to the associated settlement. Nevertheless, there are some areas where ores, mainly of iron, were so widespread and easily extracted that working seems to have been carried on without any formal control.

The smelting of metal ores was most often carried out at the mines. Those ores known to the Romans did not present much difficulty in smelting: gold was normally in its natural metallic state; silver and lead yielded to a charcoal fire, after, if sulphides were present, a preliminary roasting in air. Separation of the two metals was achieved by cupelling the resulting alloy. Copper and tin were subjected to the same processes, although a higher temperature was required for the former. Zinc, though, vaporises and does not melt, so that a cooled object had to be placed over the fire, on which the metal condensed. Only iron required more sophisticated techniques, due to its higher smelting temperature and to the fact that if melted it forms on cooling hard, brittle, and to the Romans, unusable cast iron. Two types of furnace were known: the bowl and the shaft. The latter was more efficient, but both in the end produced a spongy mass of metal, usually called a bloom, which had to be heated and beaten to squeeze out slaggy impurities. The bright malleable iron left could then, if necessary, be carburised and quenched to provide a material not greatly different from mild steel.

The winning of metal ores was not the only extractive industry in the Empire. Salt was a very important commodity, not simply as a condiment, but as the only preservative treatment for various foodstuffs including meat, so allowing surplus stock to be killed in the autumn, in order to save fodder, while at the same time a continuous supply of meat was provided for the winter months. It was also used, in certain conditions, for making leather. Its importance in the ancient economy is attested by several roads and tracks throughout the Empire called 'saltway' or *via salaria*, chief of which was the road of that name which fed Rome. The mineral was normally obtained by the careful evaporation of sea-water, in order to remove harmful potassium chloride, before the sodium chloride was concentrated. Many estuarine and coastal regions were used for its production, either, when the climate was suitable, by evaporation in the sun, or in pans over fires. Some inland places with salt springs were also used, and the name Salinae usually indicates such a site. There are reasons to believe that the salt-making industry was also under imperial control.

Of other non-metallic minerals, building stone was obviously important, and huge quarries operated in the areas where the best occurred; the products often travelled long distances, as did the massive, monolithic columns of pink Egyptian granite, each weighing 84 tonnes, which adorn the portico of the Pantheon in Rome. Although it no longer survives, the column of Antoninus Pius, of the same material, was even larger. It must be admitted, though, that great architectural pieces like these were transported comparatively infrequently and only for very special structures. More common, since they weighed less, were statuary and the thin wall veneers cut from ornamental stone, which travelled all over the Empire where they embellished mainly public, but also some private, buildings. Grey and white marbles came from the Greek Islands; Carrara marble from Luna was extensively used by Augustus when he rebuilt Rome; a green-veined stone, cipollino, came from Euboea; a red-veined, yellow stone was quarried in Algeria and Tunis, and the famous deep red, rosso antico, came from Cape Matapan in Greece. In Rome a storehouse for imported marbles existed on the bank of the Tiber. These stones represented the upper end of the market and must have commanded premium prices.

More normal were the quarries all over the Empire which provided stone for local buildings. In the quarry near Baalbek in Syria there still lies a monolithic block, weighing 1,500 tonnes, which, it is thought, was intended for one of the great temples. The quarries, which provided Rome with the travertine and Gabine rock from which much of the city was built, can still be seen upstream on the Tiber; unfortunately travertine was decomposed by fire and was little used after AD 64, a major exception being the Colosseum which is said to contain nearly a quarter of a million tons. The late-Roman poet Ausonius mentions the noise of the saws cutting local 'marble' in the Moselle valley, which must have provided Trier with its building stone. Indeed, wherever suitable building stone was found, it was used. Some noted examples, in which the names of the work parties were carved on the quarry face, have been recorded in the region of Hadrian's Wall in Britain.

Stone, however, was not only employed for building. Some stones and minerals, such as the different-coloured varieties of iron and copper ores, cinnabar and red lead, were finely ground to provide pigments for wall-paintings. Shale and jet were used to make furniture and trinkets in the north-western provinces; jet from Whitby (Yorks) in Britain was exported to Cologne for working. Precious, and semi-precious stones like garnet, agate, cornelian and jasper, were carved, frequently with religious or mythological scenes, and set in signet rings. The *gemmarii* who cut intaglios and cameos were often highly skilled, wealthy and important people. Dioscurides was summoned from the east by Augustus, solely to make an imperial seal, and his artistic ability must have been widely recognised.

As stone was not only required for building, so buildings need other materials. Large quantities of limestone and chalk were burnt for lime; sand

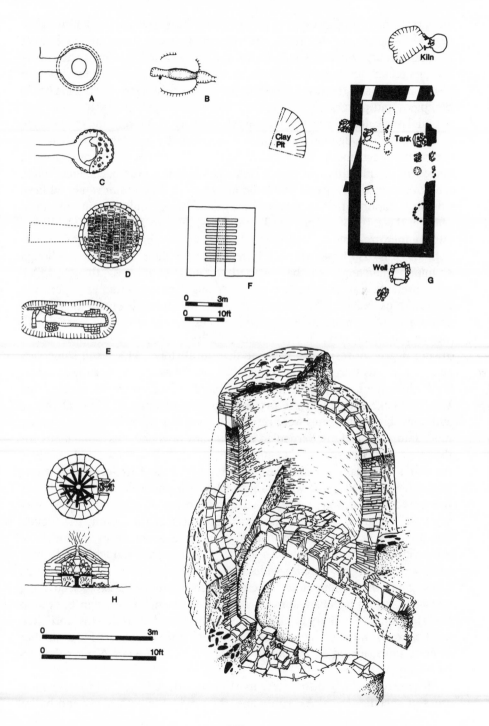

and gravel had to be excavated for aggregate in mortar and concrete, while gravel was also used for road construction. In many areas of the Empire ranging through Britain, Gaul, Africa and the east much construction work for vernacular buildings was carried out using clay, either as mud brick or pisé. Clay was also the raw material of the ceramics industry, producing brick, tile, pipes and pottery.

Our knowledge of the Empire's brick industry is uneven, mainly because of a lack of investigation. The most well-attested examples lie in Italy and the western provinces. Fired brick was used in the eastern provinces in considerable quantities, but no systematic study has ever been undertaken; moreover the abundance of fine building stones in Asia Minor rendered fired brick less important. Pliny refers to a 'Lydian' brick, while inscriptions, most often in the form of stamps on the products, refer to a brickyard at Miletus and another probably at Pergamum. Apart from the ubiquitous military products, there is also little evidence from Africa for their production, although an import trade appears to have existed; the number of bricks, though, which carry overseas stamps is so few that they might be explained as supercargo or even ships' ballast. The city of Rome itself was probably one of the greatest consumers of ceramic building materials, especially after the great fire in Nero's principate when it was found that brick-faced concrete possessed a greater degree of resistance to flame than local stone. As a result some very large brickyards were developed; many lay on the estates of wealthy Romans.

Much of the brick production was stamped, usually with the name of the kiln foreman, although in the provinces private companies, imperial estates and municipal magistrates were referred to, and it is possible to extract rather more information. One particular Roman yard provided the foundations for the family fortunes of Cn. Domitius Afer; through inheritance and marriage the works eventually became the property of Marcus Aurelius, and it is one of the few attested cases where the wealth of a politically important family was based on industry, normally anathema to the Roman nobility. A very large slave element seems to have provided most of the labour. Production was probably seasonal, but even then a small yard was perhaps capable of producing about a million bricks a year. Undoubtedly, though, the Roman army was the largest, Empire-wide manufacturer and user of brick in all its forms. Since most units stamped their products, there is a massive list covering almost all known legions and many auxiliary regiments. For instance, even in the late Empire a military brick and tile works existed at Andiesen-Holzleiten on the river Inn in Noricum, where it manufactured products for a number of army units, including a *numerus* and several *alae*; *Legio I Noricum* had its own tilery at Ybbs.

Since clay is widely distributed, most brickyards only needed to serve local areas or specific towns. As with stone, the product is both heavy and bulky,

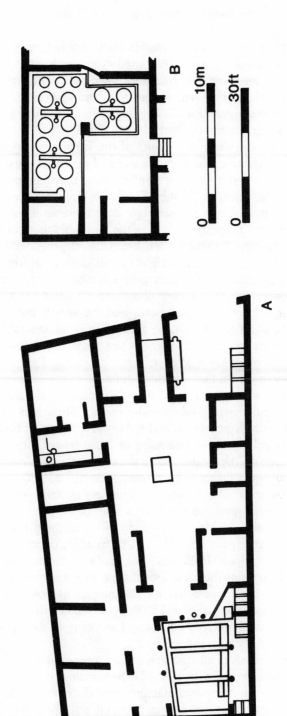

making water-transport the only economic form of travel; consequently large quantities never moved very far. Admittedly the yards of Rome provided much of the brick for Ostia, but transport down the Tiber made it feasible. Another famous Italian brickyard, owned by Tiberius, seems to have been on the northern Adriatic coast near Rimini; its products travelled not only along the coast but also across the sea to Dalmatia (fig. 23).

The other important ceramic product of the Empire was pottery; all was then made of earthenware, although for some of the better-quality wares the clay was refined. As with brick, we suffer from the unevenness of pottery studies. That great work by Tenney Frank, *An Economic Survey of Ancient Rome*, admittedly published fifty years ago, does not even mention pottery in the index for Greece. Yet pottery is one of the most ubiquitous of all industrial products in the Empire. Although it was breakable, the fragments are virtually indestructible in the soil. It often exhibits rapid changes in form and fabric, while quite a large number of vessels were stamped with the makers' or the estates' names, so making for easy classification. Most production in the Empire was carried out on a local basis, and the vessels normally followed the pre-Roman, traditional forms, so giving rise to innumerable variations. The large quantities produced made the potter one of the commonest artisans in the Empire; whole villages of potters are attested in Palestine, while the great Syrian city of Jerash had a potters' guild.

Much pottery was made solely to provide containers for the storage and carriage of foodstuffs: wine, oil, cereals, *garum*. These jars and *amphorae* were sometimes very large indeed and held over a thousand litres (220 gal); Pliny refers particularly to the huge size of those from Chios. Most appear to have been made on the estates where their contents were produced. Spain in particular was noted for its *amphorae* which carried oil and wine over large areas of Italy and the western provinces; most are stamped with the name of the factory or estate, and are sometimes marked in paint to indicate the contents and quantity. At Monte Testaccio in Rome there is a heap, 900 m (3,000 ft) in circumference and 43 m (140 ft) high, composed of *amphora* fragments from the Spanish oil and wine trade to the capital; it has been estimated that it contains the remnants of over forty million vessels. Not only do they provide vital information on the origins of both containers and commodities, but also the names of 150 shippers who carried on this lucrative trade and which, until Severus confiscated so many of the Spanish estates, severely threatened Italian production.

Other ceramic vessels of all sizes and shapes were used for table or culinary purposes. Worthy of mention were the kitchen mixing bowls, *mortaria*, which had a wide range of both manufacture and distribution. As with many *amphorae*, these vessels too were often stamped with the name of the potter or factory, making it comparatively easy to trace their origins. Cheap earthen tableware, referred to by Pliny as *vasa Samia* and not to be confused with the Samian ware or *terra sigillata* of the west, was highly regarded in the east; also mentioned are the 'Pergamene' and 'Trallian' wares which were produced widely in a series of different regional fabrics in Asia Minor, and traded as far as the southern Balkans and Palestine. In Italy and the west, the commonest quality-ware was Samian or *terra sigillata*. At first made in Italy, mainly at Arezzo, it was traded over the whole Empire. Its bright red, glossy surface and decorative features rendered it attractive. One of the earliest known and most prolific producers was M. Perennius Tigranus, who may have migrated thither from Alexandria. From Arezzo potters migrated to Gaul and ultimately Germany to set up factories at a number of places, where the production virtually excluded Aretine wares from the west; it was also traded as far as Italy and Greece. It too was often stamped with the maker's or factory's name. One workshop at La Graufesenque, probably owned by Castus, employed thirty-eight workmen and had a recorded production of half a milllion vessels. Other fine table wares are known and include a white clay, very thin 'eggshell' ware, colour-coated cups and beakers, and green and brown lead-glazed vessels. In the early Empire, many of these were made at Lyon.

Other products of the ceramics industry were terracotta figures, normally made in moulds. Tarsus in Cilicia and Myrina near Pergamum possessed noted workshops. During the principate a number of workshops developed in Alexandria, Italy, Sicily, Germany and Gaul, as well as other places. Production tended to follow the original Hellenistic patterns, but the designs were often adapted to suit local cults. Not all, though, were restricted to religious subjects, and a number of secular models became popular.

The making of glass, as with ceramics, involves both the extractive and manufacturing industries. The principal raw material required is sand, preferably of a high degree of purity and containing little iron. The latter gives a natural green or brown colour to the metal, although it can be removed by adding traces of manganese salts, a fact known to the Romans, even though they did not always use it. The manufacture of glass was far older than the principate; then the main centres of production lay in Egypt, Syria and Asia Minor. The vessels made at that time were technically quite advanced; elaborate polychrome bowls were made by fusing bundles of different-coloured rods together. Trails and threads could be applied for decoration in the same way, but using single rods; cutting and engraving was of high quality. Moreover, in its cheapest forms, it rivalled pottery in everyday use. As a result the vessels were traded over long distances, and, as in other industries, the manufacturers followed the traders, eventually setting up glasshouses in Italy, Gaul and Germany, among other provinces. Production, though, was revolutionised, probably in the first century BC, when free-blowing was invented; it is usually attributed to the Syrian glass-houses. In the late Empire Cologne became a major manufacturing centre in the west, and the products were widely distributed. Window glass was produced in Britain, as in most provinces. Among the more esoteric objects made of glass were primitive magnifying lenses, and paste was used to replace gemstones in signet rings.

The making of ceramics and glass, as already indicated, has implications for both extractive and manufacturing industries, and leads us on logically to the consideration of the latter.

Among the many manufacturing industries which existed, that related to metals was probably the most important. Blacksmiths and coppersmiths must have been almost as common in the Empire as they were in Britain during the early part of this century; most settlements of any size would have had their resident practitioners, while towns and cities often had whole streets or quarters devoted to them. Numerous relics of their existence, ranging from hoards of scrap metal to their workshops and tombstones – often elaborately carved with references to their trades – have been found all over the Empire. Specialists in cutlery also existed and some may have made use of the wickedly expensive Seric iron, which was in reality a steel imported from India. Among this general distribution of small-time artisans, there were one or two places, which, because of the nearness to the source of metal, or to the excellence of manufacture, exceptionally became major production centres. Aquileia, a port at the head of the Adriatic, was ideally suited for the development of a centre which used the high-quality iron from nearby Noricum; Capua, near the important harbour of Puteoli, was noted for its copper-alloy vessels. But it must be remembered that, no matter how successful such centres were in making and trading their products, they tended to be in a minority. They could, though, perhaps be matched by the work of the army, which had its own smiths and must have consumed very large quantities of iron and copper for the manufacture and repair of equipment. Military workshops of considerable size have been identified in some fortresses, like that at Inchtuthil in Scotland, where the entire legionary stock of nails, weighing 11 tonnes, was buried at the time of the evacuation.

Goldsmiths and silversmiths are, as might be thought, not so commonly attested. Yet even the small town of Norton in northern Britain possessed a goldsmith's workshop, managed by a slave, possibly catering for nearby military demands. In Rome the Via Sacra seems to have been the jewellers' street, and among a number of inscriptions are mentioned two goldsmiths, an engraver and a maker of silver. It is possible that factories existed for the manufacture of silver plate, in view of the large number of pieces of excellent ornamental workmanship which have been found singly or in hoards, such as those from Boscoreale, the Esquiline in Rome, and Mildenhall in Britain. As with most industries in the Empire, much of our knowledge comes from the records of artisan guilds – associations of workers in the same industry (see below, p 173). Smyrna possessed a guild of both goldsmiths and silversmiths, as did Palmyra. Indeed, it is generally thought that Syria and Egypt possessed the best workshops in precious metals.

In contrast it is likely that plumbers were almost as common as blacksmiths. Lead was used extensively for water-pipes, linings of baths, roofs and coffins, and, when alloyed with tin to make pewter, it was used as a substitute for expensive silverware in the late Empire. What is surprising here is that, despite the complexity of the work, no large factories emerged, even in Rome, where the demand for water-pipes was considerable, and where the state water service often had to employ private contractors. Yet it is difficult to conceive how the large, multiple pipes of the Gier aqueduct which served Lyon were manufactured, without appreciable organisation. Otherwise it seems likely that only the army worked on a more efficient scale, since most fortresses, and often forts, had water-distribution networks.

Apart from metal industries, the Empire needed and employed all manner of other artisans and craftsmen: carpenters, wheelwrights, coopers, locksmiths, spinners, weavers, dyers, fullers, tanners, bootmakers, button-makers, painters, mosaicists, architects, besides others. As already indicated, much of our knowledge of these trades comes from literary and epigraphic sources, often relating to guilds, especially since the products of those who worked in perishable, organic materials has often not survived, save in exceptional circumstances. Consequently Pompeii and Herculaneum are supremely important if, for instance, we are to find out anything about furniture, while the workshops of dyers and fullers have also survived there with much of their equipment intact (fig. 24).

In many ways the use of the word 'industry' to describe what was mostly going on in the Empire is an anachronism, implying, as it does today, large-scale manufacture in specially designed factories. Apart perhaps from the production of some ceramics, notably bricks, there is very little evidence for such organisations, and the reverse is almost always the case. Most artisans and craftsmen in the ancient world worked in small premises, combining both shop, workshop and probably domestic accommodation. Some might be freeholders, perhaps manumitted slaves, or free tenants; others might be slave managers, hoping possibly one day to gain their freedom and to buy the shop wherein they worked. Although some shops might display a stock of goods for sale, most articles would probably be manufactured to specific customers' requirements, and it was not unknown for the customer to provide his own raw material, especially in the jewellery trade.

The guilds which these practitioners formed were carefully regulated by

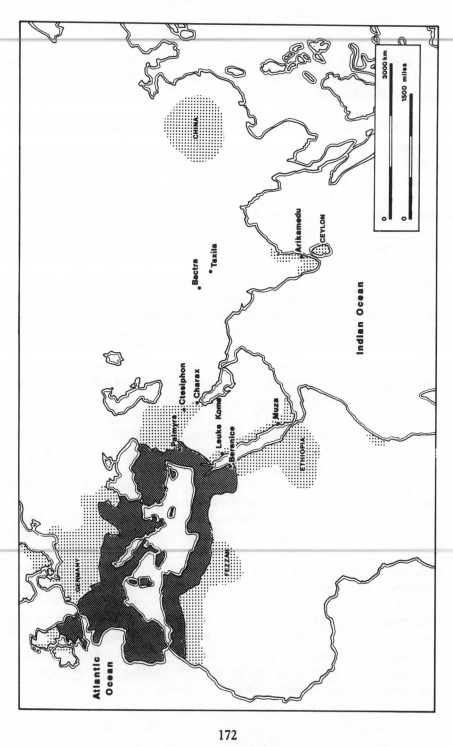

Atlantic
Ocean

GERMANY

FEZZAN

Palmyra
Ctesiphon
Charax
Leuke Kome
Berenice

Muza

ETHIOPIA

Bactra
Taxila

CHINA

Arikamedu
CEYLON

Indian Ocean

3000 km
1500 miles
0

the state. They were in no sense trade unions or professional bodies as we know them today. It was not their duty to protect or foster either the trade or the workers, but to encourage friendliness and good social relations among the members. They also acted as burial clubs, by which, for a small subscription, a member was ensured a decent burial and adequate memorial after his death. It is not surprising, therefore, that a very large number of appropriately ornamented tombstones are found all over the Empire. They are clear evidence that this function of the guilds was carried out punctiliously and we owe them a great debt for the amount of recoverable information which they have made available to us today.

The Empire, in addition to its manufacturing industries, also needed what, in modern terms, would be described as 'service' industries, which would have included cooked-food shops, money-changers and leaders, bankers, teachers, lawyers, priests, interpreters, musicians, actors and actresses, brothels, taverns and bath-houses. Again their nature makes it likely that all would have been widely distributed throughout the Empire; even small towns and some villages boasted a bath-house, while major cities would probably have had several privately run establishments in addition to the public baths; Pompeii possessed the baths of M. Crassus Frugus which advertised both fresh-and sea-water bathing, while the well-known brothel, with its illustrations of erotic paintings, would probably be repeated in most large and many small towns, and, in less expensive ways, military *vici* in the frontier provinces.

No treatment of the Roman economy would be complete without some comments on prices and wages. It is nevertheless a subject in which a great deal of caution must be exercised for a number of reasons. Although there is a fair amount of evidence of one kind or another, mainly from Italy and Africa, but to a lesser extent from some other provinces, much of it is of a highly specific nature and related to narrow dates. Any extrapolation of the data is therefore extremely dangerous since, as in all societies, wages and prices could fluctuate with remarkable rapidity. Some attempts have been made to compile statistical information, not always successfully; qualitative treatments are perhaps more acceptable. But in general it is only safe to acknowledge certain fundamental facts relating to the economy of the Empire.

In a slave-owning society, labour was a capital investment, but, once bought, cheap to run. The wages of freemen and prices would have been linked, but not necessarily as closely as they are today. Political or other crises would have had an effect on both, but they are not always easy to gauge. The abundance or scarcity of slaves on the market at any given time was often a reflection of the Empire's successful wars and conquests. Indeed it has been argued that, after most of the systematic conquests under Augustus had been completed, the supply of slaves from external sources dwindled badly. Crises and shortages tended to inflate prices but not necessarily wages. Yet wars could be beneficial in stimulating trade, especially when they resulted in the acquisition of new territory. There is no doubt also that, in times of scarcity, people in the Empire hoarded goods deliberately, for release on to the market only after the price had risen. In consequence, some of the better-known famines, such as that in Antioch in the mid-fourth century, were artificially stimulated. The Empire has been described as a 'free market economy', which by and large it was, in which both prices and wages settled to their natural levels, and despite spasmodic imperial efforts to control the economy; but it is important to remember that there were restraints on trade, although it is difficult to assess their effectiveness, and most were so clumsy as to be capable of circumvention, as even happened to that most famous attempt at control introduced by Diocletian's Edict.

Lastly, it is important to look at the trade connections which the Empire enjoyed with its neighbours. Extensive links were built up from the earliest days of the principate with the near East, India, central and eastern Africa and with the trans-Danubian and trans-Rhenian peoples of central and northern Europe, which in the east stretched round the northern shores of the Black Sea. The overland silk-route had early been pioneered to China and Marcus Aurelius is recorded as having sent an embassy to the court of the Han Dynasty. The natural origin of silk was not known in the Empire and China jealously guarded the secret. Silk, either as yarn or cloth, was imported overland through north India and modern Iran and Afghanistan, or by sea through the intermediate ports of southern India and thence to the Persian Gulf or Red Sea ports. The passage was aided by the monsoons. But silk was by no means the only commodity traded with the near and middle east; an Indian ivory statuette has been found at Pompeii. But the list of spices which reached the Empire as a result of this trade was long and included many familiar to us today: cinnamon, coriander, nutmeg, cardamom, myrrh and ginger, to mention but a few of the commoner species. There was also pepper, perhaps the most renowned of all. In Rome a special spice quarter existed, in which Domitian constructed new pepper warehouses, *horrea piperatoria*. When Alaric laid siege to Rome, he demanded and obtained as part of the price for raising the siege three thousand pounds of pepper. Many of these products were used for medicinal purposes as well as for flavouring food; none can have been cheap, and some carried an import duty of 25 per cent which made them even more costly (fig. 25).

In India itself there were a number of important trading stations frequented by merchants plying between the Empire and the east. The ancient city of Taxila in the modern Punjab lay astride the route to Peshawar and thence by the Khyber Pass to Kabul and on to Bactra where it joined the Silk Road. In southern India, coastal sites like that discovered by Wheeler at Arikamedu, near Pondicherry, or Barbaricon at the mouth of the Indus, and others on the Coromandel and Malabar coasts, acted as staging posts on the sea routes from China and south-east Asia. These routes seem to have been most active in the early Empire, particularly under Augustus, which was an age of initiative and discovery; by the fourth century many had declined in importance and activity. In return for imports Rome exported pottery – Aretine ware has been found at Arikamedu – trinkets, metalwork including vessels and small statuettes and, from *amphora* fragments, possibly wine or oil. Roman gold and silver, and later bronze, coinage was at a premium in these trading centres, so much so that fears were expressed in Rome that it represented too heavy a drain on imperial resources, since it was money lost to the Empire which would not be recycled. Further afield Roman coins have been found in the Mekong delta and it has been argued that, since glass was not apparently made in China until the early fifth century AD, vessels of an earlier date, which have been found there and in South Korea, originated in the Empire.

This trade from the east benefited those cities just within or on the boundaries of the Empire, and was largely the cause of the occasional outbreaks of war between Rome and Parthia/Persia. Trabzon, Samosata, Palmyra, Damascus, Petra, and the Red Sea ports such as Myos Hormos, Leukos Limen and Berenice, waxed rich on the dues charged. Palmyra in particular profited and · became one of the most powerful cities in the east during the third century. To a lesser extent, the Mediterranean ports of Africa gained equally from trade with the interior, although it is likely that the volume was never so great as that from the east. The principal area of trade seems to have been the Fezzan, 700 km (430 miles) south of Lepcis Magna and peopled by nomads, for whom the Garamantes appear to have acted as middlemen. In exchange for pottery, glass, wine and cloth, Rome received gold-dust, ostrich eggs and feathers, ivory, precious stones and woods, probably slaves from Aethiopia and wild animals, among which were elephants and lions. The ports of the Red Sea also operated ships down the east African coast, possibly as far as Dar-es-Salaam, whence came tortoiseshell, ivory, rhinoceros horn, palm-oil and spices and also slaves, while the usual manufactured knick-knacks and weapons went from the Empire in return. Perhaps the most surprising thing about African trade is that although the east coast was penetrated so far south, on the west there is little information of comparable measures, even though the most southerly city, Rabat (Sala), is 200 km (120 miles) south of the Straits of Gibraltar. As already indicated above (p. 151) the area was noted for its fish and fish-sauce, but there is little evidence of wider and more far-reaching contracts further south.

By contrast with west Africa, trade into central Europe was noted not only for the quantity but also for the distance travelled. One of the oldest and most important routes was the Amber Road, which stretched from the shores of the Baltic, where much amber was found, southwards along the Vistula to Lake Goplo and thence to the river Prosna and the Glatz Pass through Upper Silesia, ending at Carnuntum on the Danube. Apart from amber a very wide spectrum of traded goods must have passed this way and by other, nearly parallel routes to the east: metal vessels of copper alloy, gold and silver, Samian pottery, statuary and glass all travelled outwards into 'free' Germany and beyond; it was backed by thousands of Roman coins, and at least four hundred hoards have been found beyond the frontiers in this region. Apart from amber, it is likely that furs and skins formed part of the return trade, together with dried fish and possibly even cattle. It is also known that there was trade northwards from Britain, reaching to the Outer Isles and possibly to the Orkneys and Hebrides. Trade to Ireland is more difficult to estimate. Roman coins and other objects have been found, but they are largely restricted to a narrow band along the east coast.

The Empire's trading connections were wide and varied, encompassing the then known world, but it is almost impossible now to quantify it, or to decide just how important it was to the Empire. One suspects that it was largely a trade in luxury goods, and that it represented the gilt on the gingerbread to many of the Empire's inhabitants; the large mass of the population, outside those actually engaged in it, probably never came into contact with it.

IX

THE EMPIRE AT PRAYER: RELIGION AND BURIAL

It is probably true to say that there was no such thing as a purely Roman religion, since the Empire absorbed and adapted to its own ends a multitude of pagan cults derived from all its parts. The concept of religion to the Romans was perhaps best summed up by Hadrian, in the words put into his mouth by Marguerite Yourcenar, when he rebuilt Marcus Agrippa's Pantheon in Rome: 'My intention had been that this sanctuary of All Gods should produce the likeness of the terrestrial globe and of the stellar sphere that globe wherein are enclosed the seeds of eternal fire, that hollow sphere containing all.' But for the fact that it contains a vivid anachronism, since it was then believed that the world was flat, it is probably a good expression of Hadrian's beliefs. The fact that the Pantheon was dedicated deliberately to All Gods of the Empire and elsewhere, both known and unknown, also illustrates the basic, underlying superstitions of the Roman world.

Ancient, and even primitive modern, pagan religious ideas and practices were and still are founded on a strong vein of superstition. Most are born of ignorance, and a lack of understanding of the many natural phenomena which impinge on everyday life. Primitive man observed many of these phenomena, such as the regularity of the movements of the sun, the stars and the planets which gave rise to the four seasons and the changing weather; he observed that crops germinated, grew, matured and were, in due course, harvested before starting another cycle; he observed that after sexual intercourse between animals – and man – the product was often a new life. He may have observed all these things and many more, but he did not understand fully why they happened, so he came to believe that there were unseen powers which controlled them, and over which he himself had little control. Even now, although we know a good deal about the physical acts of procreation, we know very little about the enigma we call the human soul, which is meant to set mankind above the animals. It is therefore easy to understand why people who did not even possess our knowledge developed all kinds of imaginable forces which controlled all actions of their everyday lives and all things around them. It also accounts for the fact that the Romans showed considerable respect to deities which were not strictly their own and even incorporated them into their pantheon under the *interpretatio Romana;* there they were often equated with the classical gods and goddesses, which had themselves mainly been imported from the Greek and Hellenistic worlds. But there was one major addition which Rome made, largely under the guiding hand of Augustus: the imperial cult. It was a politically rather than a religiously inspired act, intended to provide a centre of loyalty for an outwardly hetero-geneous collection of peoples, who nevertheless shared common fundamental superstitious beliefs. As conceived, it was probably more appropriate to the eastern Empire, where the tradition of god-kings was firmly established, even though Augustus was reluctant to follow the same pattern; indeed he was more concerned that the spirit of Rome should be invoked, and seldom appeared himself in a dedication unless it was coupled with Dea Roma.

As in many other spheres, the Empire saw a great upheaval in its religious affairs during the fourth century, with the large-scale arrival and ultimate ascendancy of Christianity. It was the last act in a long history of religious development; it was also a creed which was so fundamentally different from all its predecessors that it could not but cause sweeping changes. There were attempts to turn the clock back, but none achieved much. Christianity partly succeeded by fulfilling a psychological need which the pagan religions had entirely failed to do, since they required no real personal commitment. People were more easily able to identify with the tenets of the Christian Church, as represented by a Man who had actually lived on earth with them, than with a series of shady, mythological figures that had largely outlived their usefulness.

Much of the classical religion of Rome was inherited almost without change from the Greeks and Etruscans but for the names of the deities who were in due course romanised. The three chief deities, Jupiter, Juno and Minerva, were known from their temple on the Capitoline Hill in Rome as the Capito-line Triad, and together with Saturn, Mars, Neptune, Apollo, Ceres, Venus, Mercury, Bacchus, Diana and some lesser figures embodied the state religion.

The temple of Jupiter in republican Rome was, in fact, the largest of the early temples and is thought to have been dedicated in 509 BC. It contained three *cellae*, one for each of the deities enshrined. He was sometimes known as Jupiter Optimus Maximus – best and greatest of Jupiters – a name whose form is normally attributed to the Etruscans, an interpretation borne out by the Etruscan style of architecture employed in the Capitoline temple; often abbreviated on inscriptions to IOM, it became a popular form of Jupiter

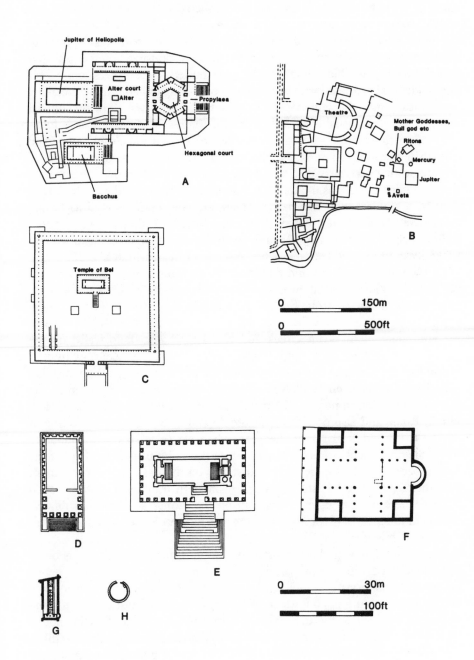

A

Jupiter of Heliopolis

Alter court
☐Alter

Propylaea

Hexagonal court

Bacchus

B

Theatre

Mother Goddesses,
Bull god etc

Ritona

Mercury

Jupiter

S.Aveta

0 ——————— 150m

0 ——————— 500ft

C

Temple of Bel

D

E

F

0 ——————— 30m

0 ——————— 100ft

G

H

worship in the provinces. Jupiter was also equated with Zeus, the Greek god with a proven Indo-European origin, and as such he was rated the Father of the Gods and protector and ruler of his family. His particular sphere of influence was the sky and hence he was held responsible for the weather; thunderstorms, in which thunderbolts were hurled, were expressions of his anger. He was associated with war and also the taking of oaths and the making of treaties. Juno, the equivalent of the Greek Hera, was Jupiter's official consort and was probably of Italian origin. Represented usually as a fully-draped, matronly figure, she was the goddess of women and closely connected with their sexual lives; in Rome she was known as Juno Regina, a form of attribution that was carried to a number of provinces. The third member of the Capitoline Triad was the Italian goddess Minerva, equated with the Greek Athena, a goddess who was patron of the arts and crafts as well as having certain warlike attributes; indeed it was she who, in mythology, was reputed to have helped Perseus slay Medusa. In return he donated the head with its snake locks to the goddess and it became one of her attributes.

Of the other main gods and goddesses in the Roman pantheon, Saturn is perhaps the most difficult to comprehend. Reputedly of Greek origin, or alternatively imported from Etruria, he was the only Roman god to whom sacrifices were made bare-headed. There are also suggestions that he was the equivalent of the grim Greek god Kronos, who mythologically, on the advice of his mother, castrated his father. If this is so, then Zeus, or Jupiter, was in fact the youngest and only surviving son of the marriage, the remaining male issue having been swallowed and later regurgitated by their father. Be that as it may, Saturn possessed a major temple on the slope of the Capitoline Hill in Rome and also presided over the festival of Saturnalia. It was one of the most relaxed festivals of the year, when slaves were given temporary freedom and presents were exchanged. It remains with us today as Christmas, having been adapted by the early Christians, on the basis that if you cannot beat them, join them! It still gives rise to modern traditional customs, such as that where officers in the Navy wait on the ratings at Christmas dinner, the appointment of boy bishops and the various ceremonies connected with the lord of misrule.

Mars was the next god in importance to Jupiter; most festivals in his name were concerned with the preparation of equipment and men for war; hence his name became synonymous with a war-god. Yet, he seems also to have had an agricultural function, which often comes through most clearly in some provincial versions of the cult. Neptune was an Italian god of water, not to be confused with Poseidon or Oceanus as god of the sea, although sometimes confusion between them does arise. Apollo, of almost pure Greek origin, was a god of art, music and beauty, and of all high ideals; he was also connected with healing in republican Rome. Augustus erected a very fine temple to him on the Palatine, and some consider that he was almost as important as Jupiter. Ceres was the ancient Italian goddess of corn, and therefore might be said to have some affinity with Saturn. But Saturn looked after the seed; Ceres produced an abundant crop. Venus was an obscure goddess of Italian origin and usually equated with the Greek Aphrodite, goddess of love, beauty and fertility. She was the patron deity of prostitutes and her cult at Corinth involved sacred prostitution.

Mercury, the Roman equivalent of the Greek Hermes, was primarily a god of traders; consequently his cult was popular and widely disseminated throughout the provinces. In ancient mythology he was also the messenger of the gods. Bacchus, the Greek Dionysus, seems to have originated in Thrace; although often associated with wine, and often depicted in a drunken stupor, he also had a wider emotional appeal which gave vent to the wild *orgia* of his cult. There was, though, a more mystical side which is depicted in the continuous sequence of wall-paintings in the Villa of the Mysteries at Pompeii. Diana, although equated with the Greek Artemis, was a goddess of ancient Italian origin; she was sometimes identified with the moon. Although sometimes associated with hunting and often worshipped in woodland settings, she was far more a goddess of women and especially of human fertility, children and child-birth.

There were several lesser deities, such as Silvanus and Priapus and also the immortals – offspring of the mythical coupling of a god with a mortal – such as Hercules, the equivalent of the Greek Heracles.

The sanctuaries and temples dedicated to these deities were often shared, as in the case of Capitoline Jupiter. Throughout the Empire, most temples which were dedicated to classical deities were built in the classical style with a *cella*, or shrine, in which the cult statues were housed, a front portico, approached by a flight of steps, with the number, arrangement and style of the columns set according to the size of the temple and order of architecture employed. Sometimes the columns were continued round the sides and back of the temple, as a peristyle or alternatively as half-engaged. The portico was spanned by the architrave and frieze, on which the dedicatory inscription was cut, and which supported in turn the triangular *tympanum*, on which illustrations were sometimes carved to show some aspect of the deity concerned. In front of the steps leading up to the portico, the main altar would be placed, and the temple, altar and courtyard, constituting the sanctuary, would be enclosed, usually by colonnades or subsidiary buildings. Nevertheless, some surprising compromises occurred in which the classical style was merged with that of the provinces, giving rise in some examples to quite distinct architectural forms (fig. 26).

One of the greatest temples of the Roman world was that dedicated to Diana, or Artemis, at Ephesus, rated one of the seven ancient wonders of the world. The building which survived into the Empire had been constructed after the fire of 356 BC and was destroyed again by the Goths in AD 263. Although some architectural pieces are in museums, little is known of the actual site, except for the altar, which has been identified. Better known is the sanctuary and temple to Jupiter/Baal, with the attendant so-called temple of Bacchus at Baalbek (Heliopolis) in Syria. Here the main temple lay on an east-west axis in the sanctuary which was nearly 400 m (440 yd) long, and which included many other monumental buildings; although the architectural concept is largely Roman, the lay-out and planning owes much to eastern traditions. It is thought that Augustus was the originator of the scheme, although many alterations took place in subsequent principates. The main temple was constructed on a peristyle plan, 10 columns by 19; each column was 19 m (62 ft) high and of the Corinthian order.

Another major provincial temple lay at Lyon, the religious centre of the three imperial Gaulish provinces of Aquitania, Lugdunensis and Belgica. There was first founded, on a sacred site of suspected Celtic origin at the confluence of the rivers Rhône and Saône, a sanctuary and altar to Rome and Augustus for the imperial cult (see below, p. 184). The site was later embellished with a temple to the same cult, while under Tiberius a huge amphitheatre was constructed to seat the delegates from all the Gaulish civitates when they attended festivals. Not all that far from Lyon, there survives at Nîmes today one of the best-preserved Roman temples anywhere in the Empire, known now as the Maison Carré. It is likely that it was constructed under Augustus, although there are arguments which favour an original foundation by Agrippa. It lay in the forum, and may have been the *capitolium*, although the dedication is uncertain. It was built using the Corinthian order with a hexastyle portico, three columns deep, and with half-engaged columns surrounding the *cella*. The ceiling of the portico is ornamented with elaborately carved coffering.

It is not possible to consider in detail any other of the numerous fine temples which so often dominated the urban scene in the Empire, but a general comment about the associations with their respective deities might be in order. A temple in the ancient, pagan world was the physical residence of the god or goddess. This is borne out most clearly by the passage in I Kings, chapter 18, where the conflict between the priests of Baal and Elijah took place. Elijah mocked the priests when their incantations had no effect: ' . . . cry aloud: for he is a god; either he is talking, or he is pursuing, or he is on a journey, or peradventure he sleepeth and must be awaked.' The implication is clear. The priests of Baal considered that the temple was the residence of their god and that for some reason, as elaborated by Elijah, he was not answering their invocations. This concept, when taken in conjunction with the very large number of temples to any particular deity scattered about the

Empire, obviously gave rise to some theological difficulties since the deity could not be in residence in all the temples at the same time. Hence local variants tended to grow up in certain cult centres, with their own, and often specific, attributes and areas of influence, which served to distinguish them from their fellows: Jupiter Capitolinus of the Capitoline Hill in Rome, Jupiter Heliopolitanus of Baalbek; Jupiter Dolichenus of Doliche in the district of Commagene in Syria are examples already touched upon above, and there were many more throughout the Empire. Secondly, again as already mentioned above, it was often common that, especially in the provinces, the *interpretatio Romana* was invoked to create temples jointly dedicated to a classical god and a provincial deity. Bath, in Britain, is an excellent example, where the tetrastyle classical temple, dedicated both to classical Minerva and Celtic Sul, or Sulis, lay in a large and splendid sanctuary enclosing the hot springs.

Central in this proliferation, and among the many varied couplings which resulted, lay the imperial cult. The divinity of a ruler was not new to the Egyptians and other eastern peoples; yet the Romans both feared and hated the idea, perhaps because of their early history. Caesar himself put aside the offer of kingship, realising that it would not be popular with the great mass of the Roman people. Nevertheless, he was deified sometime after his murder, ultimately receiving the title Divus Julius. But as with many things in the governing of the Empire, it was Augustus who eventually regularised and gave order to the concept of the cult, partly because he saw it as necessary to maintain his power, and partly to provide a religious focus for the Empire as a whole, and it is probably true to say that its observances were mostly strongest in the provinces. But he moved with caution, knowing full well the opposition that might arise from the traditional republican element in Rome. He may have desired divinity after his death, like Caesar, but he was more hesitant in adopting it during his lifetime; he was only mortal, and like Caesar could also be murdered. One of his first steps was to take the title of *divus filius* and Augustus, which title Livy translated as superhuman.

Gradually, opinion strengthened, guided skilfully, one suspects, by Augustus himself. In the east, the name Sebastos, the Grecian equivalent of Augustus, was incorporated in other dedications, such as that at Mytilene, where it appears in the form Sebastos Zeus, Caesar Olympios. Other centres followed, as at Pergamum (Asia) and Ancyra (Galatia). In the western Empire, where the tradition of divine rulers had been hitherto unknown, the first signs occur at Tarraco in Spain, possibly in emulation of the Mytileneans, where an altar was erected to Augustus *c.* 26 BC, or somewhat later, apparently in the lower forum of the city. This was followed in 12 BC by the erection of the altar to Rome and Augustus at Lyon on behalf of the sixty *civitates* of the three Gauls; probably slightly later the *ara Romae et Augusti* was dedicated at

Cologne, to which it gave its name as *ara Ubiorum*, while by AD 11 Gallia Narbonensis possessed another dedicated to the *numen Augusti* in the provincial capital at Narbo. After Augustus, in the newly conquered province of Britain was founded the main cult temple at Colchester, which, although there has been some argument, was almost certainly dedicated to Claudius from its completion; it was a massive affair with probably an octastyle portico, two columns deep, and its size and grandeur even excited unwelcome criticism in Rome.

Later still, under Vespasian, the Arae Flaviae was founded at Rottweil in south-western Germany, possibly to serve as a provincial centre for the about-to-be-formed province of Germania Superior. At Tác (Gorsium) in Pannonia an impressive shrine has been identified called the Templum Provinciae, which was probably intended to be the imperial cult centre for Pannonia Inferior. Indeed, in time the imperial cult became widely venerated throughout the provinces, but again, as with other cults, variations crept in. One section of it was theologically correct in worshipping past, deified members of the imperial household. Few major dedicatory inscriptions, even of secular buildings, fail to mention the reigning emperor's deified ancestors; reference is also sometimes made to the whole *Domus Divinae*, sometimes on its own or sometimes coupled with the *numen Augusti* or another deity. The titles *numen*, or *genius*, *Augusti* were the titles most commonly used by living emperors and denoted their spiritual or physical powers respectively.

The sum of the provinces of the Empire represented as remarkable a diversity of religious cults and observances as has probably been seen either before or since in any community of peoples, ranging from eastern mystery cults at one end of the Empire to Celtic veneration of natural phenomena at the other. Since people, especially traders and army personnel, travelled widely, it is not surprising that some of these cults travelled with them and became diffused throughout the provinces. In doing so, the cults often picked up as well a classical outlook through the *interpretatio Romana*. It would be quite impossible to give any more than a most general account of a highly complex subject in the present work, and it is only possible to take some characteristic, but entirely random examples from different parts of the Empire and see to what extent they were assimilated into the Roman pantheon. It is important to remember, though, that many of the deities of illiterate cultures are known to us solely through the form of romanised inscriptions and sculptures. To what extent, therefore, they represent the 'pure' strain of the original cult, uncontaminated by Roman thoughts or ideas, cannot be estimated. Occasionally some nameless deity appears in a native context, which has clearly not been so influenced to any great extent, but it is seldom possible to make much of it, because of the lack of associated evidence, usually in the form of inscriptions.

In Syria and Arabia the most important of the local deities were the variants of Baal and Bel, like Jupiter both sky-gods and lords of the heavens; their eventual conjunction was therefore only a matter of time, especially since the area had been heavily influenced by Hellenism before the arrival of the Romans. As already indicated, the great sanctuary at Baalbek was the product of one of these fusions. At Palmyra there were splendid temples to both Baal and Bel. Chief, though, among the Syrian deities, and extending through to Arabia, was the Dea Syriae, essentially a fertility figure, possibly linked with Baal. She appears to have had different names in different places, such as Allat in Nabatea, and even reached Hadrian's Wall in Britain, where dedications to the goddess by a cohort of Syrian origin have been found at Carvoran. One of the great gods to come out of the east was Mithras, of Indo-Iranian origin. He was lord of light, of the truth, and of the sacred oath. His nature differed in many ways from the general run of classical and provincial deities in that it demanded a definite commitment on the part of his followers to maintain a reasonably high standard of personal conduct. He also held out the hope of immortality and happiness after death. Mithras' appeal, therefore, became especially significant to soldiers and merchants, but others were also attracted at a time when it was beginning to be felt that the ancient deities no longer fulfilled personal, psychological needs.

In the Mediterranean region, the earliest *mithraeum*, which was usually a fully-enclosed structure, partly underground, or a 'cave', is recorded in southeast Asia Minor during the first century BC. From the first century AD onwards the cult spread widely, if thinly, throughout the Empire. Ostia possessed a fine example with the central aisle floored with a mosaic which depicted the seven, ascending grades of initiation. But probably the densest areas of distribution are those along the frontier zones of the Danube and Germany, also eastern Gaul, Spain, Britain and the western half of the north African frontier. Since these were the areas with the biggest troop concentrations, many men having served in the east at one time or another, the connection between the cult and the army becomes immediately apparent. Large centres of commerce were likewise popular and Rome, Dura-Europus, Aquileia, Carthage and London all possessed one or more *mithraea*. But the cult was secret and did not admit women, which meant that it never enjoyed the popularity of that other great cult which originated in the east in Judaea: Christianity (see below, p. 191).

Egypt had possessed a well-established religious repertoire long before it fell to the Romans, even though much of it had been thoroughly hellenised by the Ptolemies. Isis, Osiris, Ammon and Serapis were widely venerated and in time equated first with Hellenistic, then with Roman deities, so that Ammon became Zeus and Jupiter, Isis became Aphrodite/Venus. One of the most notable religious centres was on the island of Philae in the Nile, near the first cataract, where the main sanctuary was dedicated to Isis and Harpocrates. In the rest of north Africa much of the indigenous religion was based on that of the Carthaginians, with the goddess Tanit and god Baal Hammon being two of the principal deities. In Spain many of the local deities seem to have been obliterated by the strength of the introduced Roman cults. Bearing in mind the origins of pre-Roman Spain with its Carthaginian colonies and essentially Celtic, Iberian peoples, one would expect to find at least traces of evidence for their cults. There are few signs of the former, but the odd Celtic cult appears from time to time, usually in a specific locality: Suleae Nantugiacae at Condado, Tameobrigus where the rivers Támega and Douro met, Tongoenabiagus, Durbedicus, Bormanicus and Endovelicus all have names with Celtic stems, even though they are latinised versions, and carry an echo of some similar deities in Gaul, Germany and Britain.

The central religious themes of the northern and north-western Empire were based on those of the Celtic Iron Age. They tended to be related to the natural phenomena of earth, air, fire, water and light. Many conceal fertility symbols, since the procreation of humans, animals and crops was vital to the continued existence of the communities. There were a number of cults which seem to have had universal importance: the head, a horse-goddess Epona (the great mare), various forms of mother-goddesses and hooded figures – both normally in triplicate; a hammer god, usually known as Sucellus. In addition there was a very large number of deities, or spirits, of purely local significance, whose influence was scarcely ever carried much beyond the cult centres: Sequana, the divinity of the river Seine, possessed a large sanctuary near the source of that river, and it would seem that the source of the river Thames was similarly venerated. Indeed any form of water, either a spring, a pond, a lake, a river or even a bog, seems to have provided a focus for some sort of spirit which represented the power and movement of the water, and which was often endowed with healing properties. The sanctuary of the Three Gauls at Lyon may well have been devoted to a spirit representing the confluence of the rivers, as in Spain (see above, p. 184), before its complete submersion by the introduction of the classical cult of Rome and Augustus. The hot springs at Bath, dedicated initially to Sulis, were more fortunate in surviving, despite the link with Minerva. Coventina's well at Carrawburgh on Hadrian's Wall attracted considerable attention where the spring was housed in a small shrine and presided over by the nymph and her attendants.

Mother-goddesses of all sorts were widely venerated in Celtic religion, and it has been argued that they originated in Pannonia. More often than not they are represented in triplicate, utilising the mystical power of three which is common to many religions, including Christianity. When so represented, they are frequently associated with children, or fruit and bread. One variant of the cult equates them with the *Suleviae*, of which a number have been identified in Britain and which may also have been associated with the Suleae of Spain (see above, p. 187). Bonn has produced another local variation in dedications to the *Matronae Aufaniae*, one at least made by a lady in high society and including some odd iconographical connections. Closely related are the nursing mothers (*nutrices*) usually occurring as terracotta figurines and shown suckling a baby or, more rarely, twins. Very similar to some of the representations of the *Deae Matres* are the little hooded figures, which rejoice in the name of *genii cucullati*. These, though, are sometimes illustrated in such a way that it is almost impossible to assign a particular sex to them; but the all-enveloping cloaks not only disguise their sex but also add something of an air of mystery. Epona, the great mare, was a well-loved deity in parts of Gaul, particularly in the north-east and between the Saône and the Seine, where the Iron Age, and later Roman, settlements at Alésia appear to have been the centre for the cult. It was also popular in parts of Germany and along the frontiers there. A temple at Wroxeter in Britain would seem to be associated with the goddess, since it was furnished with 'horsy' equipment and possessed what might be interpreted as a race-track to the rear of the temple enclosure. Here, though, the cult had become sufficiently romanised for the temple to be of classical proportions, and for a winged *phallus*, a purely Roman charm to avert the evil eye, to be included among the votive objects.

In some representations where the goddess is shown mounted on a horse, she carries baskets of food, which would seem to suggest a connection with the Matres; as with them, there are also examples of Epona being depicted in triplicate. In Germany there are numerous examples of Celtic deities, some of which travelled to Gaul and Britain. One particularly interesting one is Nehalennia, who possessed a shrine at the mouth of the old Rhine. Long since swept into the sea, the site has yielded a harvest of nearly fifty altars from the sea-bed dedicated to the goddess by a wide spectrum of people. Another which appears in a series of different guises right across the Celtic world was Nemetona, goddess of the sacred grove. Vitiris, Vitris or Huitris – the 'old' god – seems also to have originated in Germany but became diffused through much of the north-western Empire, probably through the transfer of army units from one frontier zone to another. In the Danube provinces, the manifestations are not all that different. One of the commonest and widely distributed was a Rider God, most popular in the third century, which is not to be confused with a very similar, but theologically separate, rider-hunter in Thrace; both appear to be nameless.

The temples and shrines of all these Celtic cults differed considerably from the normal classical, or pseudo-classical, temples of Italy and the provinces. The commonest form, usually called the Romano-Celtic temple, consisted of a square within a square, although architectural embellishments might be added by way of projecting wings. Occasionally circular and polygonal forms are found. The inner square represented the *cella*, the repository of the cult statues, while the outer formed a colonnade or arcade about it. It was usually raised and steps would lead up to the portico. Altars and other votive offerings would be housed in the surrounding colonnade, and the whole would be enclosed within a *temenos* or sanctuary. From the often unsymmetrical position of the temple in the sanctuary, it is usually inferred that some sacred totem, like a tree, occupied the central position. Although many north-western urban settlements possessed temples of this kind, they are also to be found on many country sites. One of the largest collections of Romano-Celtic temples in an urban setting occurs at Trier in Germany, in the so-called 'Tempelbezirk', where are gathered over twenty temples of this or variant character, although not all are dedicated to Celtic deities. A similar, but much smaller, collection can be seen in Britain at Silchester, while another is known at Linz, in Noricum, which contained at least one temple to Epona.

In the countryside numerous sanctuaries also grew around the temples of local cults, some reaching a huge size. The sacred deity of Noricum was venerated in a number of rural sanctuaries such as those at Ulrichsberg and Hohenstein. In Gaul some of the largest of all rural shrines are to be found, such as those at Champlieu, Ribemont-sur-Ancre and Sanxay. In addition to the main temple there were usually many subsidiary buildings, which served perhaps as guest-houses for the worshippers, a theatre or amphitheatre often capable of accommodating several thousand spectators and where religious or semi-religious performances could be staged, a bath-house, and often shops and workshops, since such large crowds would be a lucrative source of income to local traders, as indeed they are today in renowned places of pilgrimage, such as Lourdes. In Britain at least three similar sites are known: at Gosbecks Farm a few miles south-west of Colchester, where there was also a theatre as well as the sanctuary, at Woodeaton near Oxford, where numerous small bronze votive objects have been found, and at Lydney in Gloucestershire, where the temple is linked with a guest-house and bath-house.

It must not be forgotten, though, that in the 'Celtic' provinces of the Empire, few of the local deities survived in an isolated form; most were coupled with classical or other deities as happened in the rest of the Empire, sometimes with surprising results and not always consistently. Thus Noreia was coupled with Isis at Frauenberg in Noricum. Mars appears as Mars Lenus and Mars Ocelus in both Germany and Britain and also as Mars Rigonemetos in the latter province. Moreover, in a Celtic context he tends to abandon his warlike attributes and take on others, such as healing. Jupiter is sometimes equated with Taranis, who can in turn sometimes be decked out as Hercules; in Gaul he is actually attested by an inscription as Jupiter Tarannarus. Mercury dominated the tribal territory of the Arverni from his temple on the top of the Puy-de-Dôme, where he was known as Mercurius Dumias but elsewhere as Mercurius Arvenorix. In this guise he is far removed from being simply the messenger of Olympus.

Needless to say, these many religious manifestations of the Empire required a veritable army of priests and priestesses to minister to the cults. Arising out of republican origins, there was in Rome a college of *pontifices*, apparently at first three in number, later sixteen; they were considered an advisory body for the state religion on matters of a sacred nature, especially with regard to the elaborate ceremonies which religions increasingly demanded. In imperial times, from Augustus to Gratian, the emperor invariably held the title of *pontifex maximus*, head of the sacred college. But even as a body they had no legal power except over their own members and those attached to them, which included most of the major priesthoods, the *flamines*, as well as the Vestal Virgins. The most important of the *flamines* were those attached to the major state cults: *dialis* for Jupiter, *martialis* for Mars, *quirinalis* for Quirinus. There were also numerous minor priests and others with religious duties, such as those who were associated with the less important cults, and the augurs. The latter had their own college and their duties were concerned with the divination of events by the observation of the behaviour of natural phenomena, such as the behaviour of birds, from which they were supposed to say whether the gods approved or disapproved of a particular course of action. It is wrong, though, to consider them as fortune-tellers. Many priests, like teachers, were also exempted from some taxes and the performance of liturgies.

The situation with regard to priesthoods and associated positions in Rome was, of course, endlessly repeated in the provinces; all cults, no matter how minor or local, were served by their priests. In the larger and more important sanctuaries it is to be suspected that some accumulated considerable wealth. The major exception, since it probably required a greater degree of organis- ation – and wealth – was the management of the provincial and local centres of the imperial cult. Starting first in the Italian towns and spreading out through the provinces, boards of six men, *seviri Augustales*, were created for this precise purpose. It was a post open to freedmen, who were otherwise debarred from holding municipal magistracies, and, since the post often required the expenditure of large sums of money for the ceremonies and ritual observances, it became a coveted post for rich, manumitted merchants. Also all major cities and towns in the Empire possessed their temples to the imperial cult, administered by the *seviri*, while additionally provincial centres usually existed. These were not always placed in the provincial capital. In Cyrenaica, there is a suggestion that the provincial cult centre lay at Ptolemais and not in the metropolis at Cyrene, while in Britain it is unlikely that Colchester, with its huge temple of Claudius, would have yielded up the

189

coveted position of provincial cult centre to the administrative capital in London.

Among the many priests in the Celtic provinces of the north-west were the druids, although some authorities are of the opinion that they were not truly priests, but had wider responsibilities in the Celtic social order. Wise men they certainly were, perhaps more akin to the witch-doctor or even the guru. They were probably the repositories of tribal lore and the fount of religious ceremonies. From the evidence of the Coligny calender from Gaul – fragments of a great bronze plate on which were recorded no less than sixty-two consecutive lunar months – they were clearly capable of computing the relative movements of sun, moon and earth. They also seem to have had educational responsibilities and must have wielded considerable political power. It was probably the latter which brought them into direct conflict with Rome, for they must have foreseen that their power would be severely restricted under Roman rule. That they indulged in particularly barbarous forms of human sacrifice is also often cited as the reason for their suppression by the Romans. The real reason was probably a mixture of both, and a succession of edicts, each more harsh than the previous one, was issued against them. Augustus prohibited Roman citizens from participating in their ceremonies; under Tiberius a decree of the Senate banned druidism in Gaul, while Claudius is credited with the complete abolition of the cult in both Gaul and Britain, where he took energetic measures to stamp it out. What is perhaps surprising is that, after the reduction of their stronghold on Anglesey, no more is heard of druidism from either literary or archaeological sources. It is strange that, if it was as powerful as is sometimes made out, it disappeared so suddenly, almost overnight. It seems more probable that it was driven underground, especially into the remote, rural areas, where, perhaps accommodating itself to the new conditions, it continued quietly to flourish unmolested.

The last great religion of the Empire to be considered is Christianity. The event which the Bible describes as taking place in Bethlehem in Judaea was essentially a Jewish phenomenon, and still carries, even today, marks of its origin. Christianity was, with Judaism, monotheistic, although with the birth of Christ and the embodiment of the Holy Spirit, it contrived to relate to the Holy Trinity and the mystical power of three, which, as recorded above, is found in many pagan religions. Its association with Judaism, which was noted in the Empire for its often extreme turbulence – it was the cause of numerous rebellions and civil wars even after the *diaspora* – was perhaps one of the reasons why it soon came into conflict with Rome; just another troublesome sect of a generally troublesome people, often noted for its extremism. The last stand of the Jewish zealots in the siege of Masada in AD 73 was typical of some, resulting in the suicidal death of the entire besieged band when the fortress was captured by the Romans. Indeed it was Judaism which attracted most Roman hostility for a considerable period of time, while, except for odd occasions like the extraordinary persecution of the early Christians by Nero, little official notice seems to have been taken of them; neither must it be forgotten that there was little love lost between Jews and Christians, especially in Asia, where strong communities of both existed in many cities. Some of the stories relating to St Paul's journeys provide vivid accounts of the clashes between Jews, Christians and pagans.

Judaea was incorporated with some neighbouring areas as a procuratorial province in AD 6; legislation had been especially sponsored by Augustus to protect the Jewish religion. The ineptness and inefficiency of a series of procurators, including Pontius Pilate, led to a growing resentment, which culminated in open Jewish revolt in AD 66. It was crushed by Vespasian and Titus in 70, the Temple was destroyed, together with much of the city of Jerusalem. Further revolts, both in Judaea and among the dispersed Jews of the eastern and African provinces, occurred in 115 and again in 132, when it was led by Bar Cochba, following Hadrian's attempt to refound Jerusalem as the *colonia Aelia Capitolina*, from which all Jews were excluded. Loss of life in these revolts was often heavy, amounting to nearly a million on occasions. Subsequent history was punctuated by further uprisings of varying degrees of seriousness all of which led in some places to strong anti-Semitic demonstrations, in which the early Christians may have been unwittingly involved.

The early Christians were undoubtedly affected by the apocalyptic atmosphere engendered by the idea of the Second Coming, which tended to encourage martyrdom. Apart from the Neronian persecutions referred to above, there appears to have been yet another, mainly in Asia, under Domitian in which the Jews allied themselves with the pagans against the Christians. Pliny, when governor of Bithynia, asked Trajan's advice on how to deal with them, and it is clear from the emperor's reply that Christianity was treated as an illegal doctrine, although it is not at all evident why this should have been so; many scholars have argued the case without forming any significant conclusions. Equally, it is true that no Christians appear to have been prosecuted for belonging to an illegal *collegium;* equally too, many who were Roman citizens refused to take the oath of loyalty to the emperor, demanded by the imperial cult, when pressed to do so; this in itself constituted a treasonable act. But this reason alone is still not really adequate to account for the differing treatment of Christians by successive emperors. Under the later emperors of the second and early third centuries pressure on them seems to have been relaxed, although Severus decreed a ban on conversion to either Christianity or Judaism which resulted in a number of well-known martyrdoms such as those of St Alban in Britain and St Perpetua in Carthage. Caracalla's granting of citizenship to most freeborn members of the Empire would also have brought more within the class who were expected to make

191

obeisance to the official religion, hence bringing more within the risk of persecution.

But during the first and second centuries, and particularly under the more benign regimes of the latter, the Church had grown in strength and numbers, and had probably reached out to most provinces. Unfortunately, since it was a proscribed religion, references to it are few and far between. Cryptograms of the word-square:

ROTAS
OPERA
TENET
AREPO
SATOR

which is reputed to contain a hidden reference to Christianity in the rearrangement of the letters into the form:

A
P
A
T
E
R
APATERNOSTERO
O
S
T
E
R
O

are known from Pompeii where they must precede the eruption of Vesuvius in AD 79. They have also been found at Dura-Europus, dating to the third century, and at Cirencester and Manchester in Britain. The earliest buildings attributable to Christian worship date to the beginning of the third century in Dura-Europus and in places in Cappadocia. But the growing strength of the new religion attracted what would now be called a 'bad press'. All manner of evil customs were attributed to it, such as incest and cannibalism, while its active proselytising brought it into disrepute with loyal citizens. Consequently Christians were seen as a disruptive element in society and, when the convulsions in the third century began, they proved a convenient scapegoat for much of the Empire's ills. But even then the treatment was uneven. Under Maximinus, bishops were exiled or martyred, but under his immediate successors there was a reversion to tolerance. It did not last. From Decius Trajan to Diocletian and Galerius, apart from short intermissions, the Empire declared war on the Church, with a degree of ferocity probably only equalled by Nero's earlier persecution; it was no longer just a scapegoat but the defined origin of all that had gone wrong with the Roman state. Yet despite this, the Church had grown strong enough to withstand the onslaught, and even Galerius in the east had to call a halt to the persecutions in 311.

This long period of persecution was followed almost immediately by one of the most remarkable conversions to the Christian faith. Emperor Constantine I, who had already secured the western Empire for himself, is reputed to have had a dream or a vision which led to his own conversion and the issue of the Edict of Milan in 313, by which Christianity was recognised as a permitted religion. In 325, following the Council of the Church at Nicaea, it became the official religion of the Empire. Some attempts were subsequently made to revive paganism, notably under the Emperor Julian, but without much success. Under Theodosius, victory for the Church became final, although it is sad to record that by then it was showing, in some places, the same degree of barbarity and intolerance towards pagans that they themselves had once suffered.

Once freed from proscription, monuments and other articles relating to Christianity proliferated. Some of the greatest churches were begun by Constantine himself, notably the forerunner of Justinian's Haghia Sofia in Constantinople, and St John Lateran in Rome. Objects of a personal nature, such as rings, brooches or pendants, were sanctified with the ☧ monogram, representing the first two letters of the Greek name *Christos*. This monogram and other works of an iconographical nature were incorporated into wall decorations and mosaic floors, and also appear on silverware and ceramics; the latter are often seen as church plate for communion. Lead water-tanks marked with the symbol are also known and usually interpreted as baptismal fonts, while some emperors used the device on coins.

Unfortunately, the early Church, having achieved its aim and official recognition in the Empire, was at war within itself. Several heresies emerged, causing some serious schisms; Pelagianism, propounded by a man, born in Britain, who gave his name to his own particular brand of Christianity, was one which proved serious in the west.

Yet, despite the rise of Christianity and its more despotic developments in the later fourth century, there still lingered in some remote areas traces of paganism, often associated with places of antiquity, such as some of the hill-forts of Britain and Gaul (whatever happened to the druids?). In some places too there were curious conjunctions of Christianity with pagan mythology, which are not easy to explain, especially given the intolerance of the state and Church administration of the time.

Lastly there remains to be considered the attitude of the people of the Roman Empire to their dead, the way in which they disposed of them and thereafter

193

cared for them. Obviously much of the ritual observed and many of the beliefs were closely bound to their superstitions and religious thoughts. Many of the burial customs were inherited from the varied ethnic communities of which the Empire was composed. In most parts some sort of existence after death was envisaged and traditionally the customs connected with the disposal of the body were designed to expedite and help the departed to achieve that existence. Thereafter, offerings of food, oil and drink usually made at funerary feasts partaken at the graveside were intended to keep the dead 'alive'. Some burials were specially equipped with a pipe arising from the remains of the dead person to the surface into which libations could be more conveniently poured. It is clear also from the construction of some sepulchral monuments that they were sometimes considered as the actual residences of the dead. So on burial the person was frequently provided with many useful or decorative objects that had been possessed in life.

The quality and quantity of these grave goods can sometimes be taken as an indicator of the social standing of the dead person. Perhaps one of the most remarkable simulations of these conditions is a stone sarcophagus from Simpelveld in Holland, where the interior is sculpted to represent a lady's bedroom, complete with sleeping couch, washstand, linen closets and numerous little bottles and jars used to contain perfumes and cosmetics. But the greatest care must be taken in viewing such handsomely appointed burials, for most of them represented only a small proportion of Roman society. By far and away the largest part of that society was buried in undistinguished circumstances, with but scanty grave goods, if, indeed, any at all, and often with one interment interfering with earlier ones. Although some ceremony may have been attached to the actual burial, there must, in these cases, remain a strong suspicion that it was carried out for hygienic rather than for other reasons. But at least one burial ground near York in Britain, and probably many others elsewhere, used by poorer members of the community must have presented a distinctly unhygienic look with part-decomposed and dismembered limbs and bodies lying around on the surface where they had been disturbed by later burials.

The burial rites of the Roman Empire were divided between inhumation and cremation. Some contemporary authorities record that inhumation was the custom in earliest Rome, although by the fifth century BC both rites were being carried on side-by-side, as indicated by one of the earliest statutes, the Law of the Twelve Tables; among other matters relating to the dead, these Laws also forbad burial within the boundaries of town or fort. By the late Republic, embalming had been added to the list, possibly brought in from certain eastern provinces like Egypt where a long tradition had existed; curiously, it must have given rise to a somewhat similar custom in the later Empire which appears to have originated in the western parts of Africa and thence spread northwards, even as far as Britain, of encasing the body in liquid gypsum – plaster of Paris – inside a coffin (see below, p. 198).

The actual rite of cremation could be carried out in one of two ways. The body could be burnt on a special site set aside for the purpose – an *ustrinum* – from which the ashes and remaining bone fragments would be collected in some sort of container, which could vary from a piece of cloth, a cooking-pot, a special funerary urn, sometimes with a crudely applied face, a glass bottle, or lead casket, to an elaborate and costly vessel of marble or precious metal; again the status of the dead person's position in society is indicated by the material used. This container would then be interred in one of a number of ways in a cemetery usually set alongside a main road leading out of a city, town or fort. Grave goods would often be included, together with food and drink for the journey to the underworld. Sometimes the neck of the cinerary urn was left showing above the ground, to make easier the provision of subsequent libations; in this case the mouth of the vessel would be covered by a piece of flat stone or brick. Others, as indicated above (p. 195), had a pipe communicating with the urn from the ground surface. Some might be enclosed within a cyst of stone or brick. In many cases a vertical grave-stone was erected at the spot, on which was recorded the name, rank in society, or the army, and the origin and heirs of the person commemorated. Occasionally a few lines of appropriate poetry would be added, or some other suitable epitaph. In many cases also a pictorial representation was added, either depicting the dead person in a suitable pose – a cavalryman was almost always depicted riding down a fallen enemy – or in a family group, or, in the case of traders and artificers, illustrating the work that they had practised.

The iconographical study of such tombstones is a very important source of evidence for the people of the Empire. But if a tombstone could not be afforded, a simple wooden post might be used to mark the spot. As an alternative to burial below ground the urn could be placed in a niche in a family mausoleum, or in one maintained by the many burial clubs which existed throughout the empire. These clubs formed one type of association among private persons which were invariably classed as legal, and the members made annual contributions to ensure themselves a decent burial. The other type of cremation – a *bustum* grave – took place on the intended site of a burial, usually over a pit dug to receive the ashes. But in all other ways they were treated the same.

Although cremation became the principal rite of burial during the early Empire, inhumation never entirely died out, either in Rome or the provinces. Indeed by the early third century inhumation was more than regaining its popularity. Cremation had always been abhorred by the Jews and by Christians, and it is sometimes argued that the rise of Christianity was the cause for the reversal of the trend. But, by and large, the change had begun to

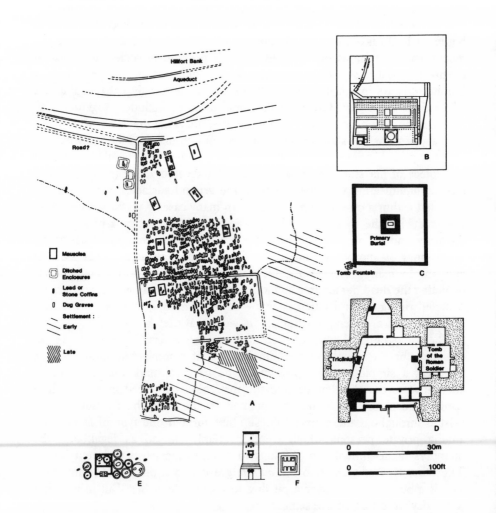

Hillfort Bank

Aqueduct

Road?

Mausolea

Ditched
Enclosures

Lead or
Stone Coffins

Dug Graves

Settlement :
Early

Late

A

B

Primary
Burial

Tomb Fountain   C

Triclinium

Tomb
of the
Roman
Soldier

D

E

F

0   30m

0   100ft

196

occur some considerable time before Christianity reached its ascendency, and it is best accounted for simply by a change in fashion, as has happened in Britain today, where cremation has become far more popular than it used to be in the early part of the century. Inhumation burials in the Roman world were attended by the equivalent ceremony accorded to cremation. In richer graves the body was usually dressed in the everyday manner – shrouds were seldom used – and enclosed in a wood, lead or stone coffin; sometimes more than one material would be used, so that lead or wood containers were often placed in stone sarcophagi. These were frequently sumptuously carved with scenes from the person's life, or of scenes of the actual funeral procession. Most displayed appropriate inscriptions, similar to those on upright grave-stones. It seems clear that such sarcophagi were not intended for burial, but remained on the surface; consequently also, it is not surprising that many were reused over the years and it is often found that the inscription does not apply for the later occupants. Many elaborate and very large family mausolea were also constructed, some even in the family garden, such as that belonging to Claudia Peloris and Tiberius Claudius Eutychus, which is recorded in plan on a marble slab now in Perugia Museum.

Multiple graveyards also existed in the Christian catacombs of Rome and Italy and in the *hypogea* of some eastern provinces, such as those at Dura-Europus. In the north-west provinces, the custom of constructing *tumuli* survived from the Iron Age. A very large number are known in Belgium and around Trier.

Some of the most remarkable mausolea and memorials occur on outlying sites on the edge of the desert in Tripolitania. The most imposing is that at Gasr Doga, three stories high on a rectangular platform and built using the Corinthian order of architecture. Others adopted an obelisk form and now usually stand isolated and a little forlorn surrounded by the encroaching desert. Another noted memorial is the Igel monument near Trier in Germany which records the productive activities of the Secundinii family and contains an interesting series of scenes depicting rural and commercial activities.

Most of the cemeteries centred on cities and towns of the Empire were very large and probably once contained many thousands of burials, especially in communal or family tombs of the type described above. But estimates of civilian populations from these figures are notoriously difficult to achieve and the figures quoted should be treated with great caution. In some cemeteries it is found that all the graves, especially when inhumed, are orientated east-west and the assumption is usually made that they were of Christian origin. In this context it is worth noting the use of gypsum to preserve the dead, as noted above (p. 196). The custom seems to have originated in north Africa and probably dates back to the first century BC, occurring principally at Carthage. There can be no doubt of the pagan origin of the method, yet by the fourth and fifth centuries AD the custom seems to have spread to Gaul, Germany and Britain, where it is sometimes associated with Christian burial. But it should not be overlooked that the later manifestations may have been of completely independent origin and used by some wealthier Christians to preserve the body in a fitter state for the resurrection. A more certain way of identifying Christian tombs, apart from their orientation, is the general lack of grave goods, which were deemed unnecessary (fig. 27).

So, in life, the religions of the people of the Roman Empire represented a remarkable spectrum of beliefs and superstitions coloured by local native traditions, and only reaching a degree of unification with the arrival of Christianity. In contrast, in death, for all were to die, a much greater degree of uniformity can be detected, in which some belief in a life beyond the grave is normally accepted.

X

THE EASTERN PROVINCES

As already indicated in earlier chapters, the provinces of the Empire were accumulated in a piecemeal fashion, beginning under the Republic. Much territory was gained from successful wars which were engendered by conflicting trade interests with other Mediterranean or eastern powers, such as the Etruscans, Carthage and Macedonia; other areas were bequeathed by allied or client native rulers. Each province therefore tended to reflect its origins, which often survived to a greater or lesser degree even under Roman rule. Thus in Asia Minor and the east there was a combined strain, not only of eastern, but also of Greek and Hellenistic culture which had spread through much of the region; yet in the middle of the former was a remarkable survival of a Celtic culture inherited from earlier immigrants from Europe. In Egypt, the later Ptolemies had tried thoroughly to hellenise the country, although an impenetrable substratum of dynastic custom, administration and religion continued to pervade the province. Much of north Africa, west of Cyrenaica, had come under Carthaginian influence, as had parts of Spain and some of the major Mediterranean islands, such as Sicily. This contrasted with the generally Celtic background of much of the Iberian peninsula and the north and north-western provinces. When in the late-third or early-fourth century the Empire was divided in two, the break naturally fell between east and west, with the east containing mostly those provinces with a Greek or Hellenistic background, while the west, apart from Africa, embraced those with a Celtic origin; all were neatly classified in the *Notitia Dignitatum*, that vital compendium of information on the late Roman Empire. Consequently, it is most convenient to take this break between east and west in considering the individual provinces. But it should be noted that, as in most matters to do with Roman provincial administration, the situation was often complex and not immutable, and provincial boundaries and methods of government were

199

not infrequently changed. A number of provinces also began as client or allied states, only being reduced to provincial status as the need arose.

The Eastern Empire

This included Moesia, Thracia, Macedonia, Epirus and Achaea on the European mainland. The sometime province of Dacia, north of the Danube, had been abandoned before the later division of the Empire had taken place; although it would probably have been included in the eastern half, it is better to consider it as part of the west, in view of the nature of its cultural affinities with other Danubian provinces. In modern Turkey, there were the provinces of Asia, Lycia and Pamphylia, Bithynia and Pontus, Galatia, Cilicia and Cappadocia, with the short-lived additions further east of Armenia Major and Mesopotamia. To the south of these were placed Syria and its adjunct Judaea (later Palaestina), together with the later-constituted Arabia Petraea. Egypt and Cyrenaica complete the list together with the two islands of Crete and Cyprus; the former being administered in what must have been a somewhat cumbersome manner with Cyrenaica. In the treatment of the individual provinces which follows, they are considered in the order of their acquisition by Rome (figs 35–38).

Macedonia

Macedonia was the first of the eastern provinces to fall to Rome, and probably at first included Thessaly, Epirus and Achaea. Before that the area had been united as a kingdom by the combined but successive efforts of Philip II and Alexander I. It emerged as a major military power under their rule, which also introduced a measure of hellenisation into the northern Balkans. But it was this strength which ultimately caused its failure as a united kingdom and led it into conflict with expanding Rome. In 167 BC Rome carved it into four autonomous republics, only to reunite them and incorporate the whole area as a province about twenty years later (146 BC). Augustus, in 27 BC, separated Epirus and Achaea, and Macedonia became a senatorial province. This arrangement lasted until Tiberius, who, in his attempts to strengthen the Danube frontier in AD 15, reunited Macedonia with Achaea and added Moesia, placing the whole area under an imperial legate, C. Poppaeus Sabinus, who achieved the extraordinary distinction, with twenty-four years in office, of being one of the longest, continuous serving governors ever to hold such a post in the Empire. Claudius reversed Tiberius' decision in AD 44 and restored the joint provinces of Macedonia and Achaea to senatorial control. Nero went a step further and, as the result of the Greeks' cordial reception, not to say abject flattery, of his artistic abilities, 'freed' Achaea from dependence on the governor of Macedonia. As a result it gained the privilege, as did many other Greek cities, of not paying taxes.

The governor's residence in Macedonia was situated at Thessalonika at the top of the Gulf of Therme; the city also lay on an important trade route connecting Greece with central Europe. It did not, however, receive colonial status until the middle of the third century AD. It would appear to have been laid out on a grid-iron pattern similar to many other Hellenistic cities in the east, but little is known of its early period. Cicero spent part of his exile here and recorded the existence of a *quaestorium* and a citadel. The city seems chiefly to be noted for the amount of building which went on during the second half of the second century and early third century AD, to which period can be attributed a two-insula *agora* and a small *odeum;* it also possessed a hippodrome with a track length in excess of 400 m (430 yd). New fortifications replaced those of the Hellenistic period in the third century as the result of Gothic threats to the province. Under the Tetrarchy the city was further dignified by the construction of a large palace complex on its eastern side, possibly connected with the eastern emperor, Galerius.

Several other cities in the province appear to have been given colonial status, of which perhaps the most interesting is Pella, the ancient capital of the Macedonian kingdom and reputed birthplace of Alexander. Livy described the city at the time of its capture by the Romans, but its origins have been shown by excavation to go back to the Neolithic period. Colonial status was also conferred on Philippi, so named after its capture by Philip II of Macedon. Its nearby gold-mines were important in its early economy, although it is likely that they, like the province's other mineral resources, had become nearly exhausted by the time of the principate. The Philippian defensive wall still survives, largely because it was reused in the Byzantine period. The known buildings of the forum are dated by inscriptions to Marcus Aurelius. As with Thessalonika, the city lay on the Via Egnatia, which served as the *decumanus maximus* and which connected it to the markets of the Danube and central Europe and so provided a degree of prosperity.

Apart from the mineral resources mentioned above, other economically important goods produced in the province were wine, timber and textiles, which were woven from the fleeces of its numerous sheep and goats.

Asia

The province of Asia was bequeathed to Rome by King Attulus III of Pergamum in 133 BC and therefore it largely coincided with the boundaries of his kingdom; it also became Rome's first possession on the Asian continent. It was first composed of the regions of Mysia, Lydia, Caria, Phrygia and Pisidia, and most of the coastal islands, although it was not until Vespasian that Rhodes was added. Under Augustus the province was delegated to senatorial control, with a proconsul as governor, whose post was the most sought-after among provincial governorships; he was assigned three legates and a quaestor to assist him. Although the seat of the governor was probably at Pergamum, that of the imperial procurator and the provincial treasury was established at Ephesus, so that a degree of rivalry arose between the two cities. This rivalry to some degree encapsulates what was going on elsewhere in those provinces where control was largely divided between a multitude of cities with their territories, most of which had been autonomous before the arrival of Rome; some retained these rights, others did not.

Although a provincial council was formed in Asia by representatives of these cities as a token of unity, its functions were much impaired by the jealous rivalries between them. For the administration of justice the province was divided into at least nine *conventus*. At first the province enjoyed enormous prosperity which was reflected in the growth of its cities, although it is worth noting that most of them were situated in the coastal region and there is little doubt that the interior was more impoverished. The coastal prosperity, though, was largely generated by the east-west trade routes aiming for Greece and later Rome. When the capital of the eastern Empire shifted to Constantinople much of this trade swung away northwards, so passing them by.

The principal city was Pergamum in the Mysian region and its buildings and ruins are well known. At its core lay a steep-sided mountain on which the acropolis was planted. The early, Hellenistic city descended down the south side by a series of terraces, but under the principate it was also extended across the plain to the west. Several different circuits of fortification have been identified, the latest being that of the third century AD, which follows for the most part the line of the wall constructed in the third century BC. The city possessed two agoras, one on the hill-top, the other at the bottom of the south face. The hillside also provided a natural slope against which the *cavea* of a theatre was built. The gymnasium terraced on three levels, was the other great building complex in this area. In the lower city much construction was carried out during the second century AD, under both Trajan and Hadrian. The so-called 'Red Courtyard', built of brick rather than stone (hence its name), has been identified as a religious complex dedicated to a triad of Egyptian deities. Also visible are the remains of another theatre and an amphitheatre. The upper city was supplied with water by a pressurised aqueduct; other aqueducts brought water from as far as 40 km (25 miles) away.

The other major city of Asia was Ephesus, famous for containing one of the seven wonders of the ancient world: the temple of Diana. Other notable buildings included the harbour baths, a theatre capable of holding 24,000 people, and the library of Celsus; it is interesting to compare the huge temple of Domitian, rededicated to Vespasian after the former's *damnatio memoriae*, and the small but more graceful temple of Hadrian. Among the many other cities, Aphrodisias in Caria and Apameia in Phrygia are worth mentioning. The latter was a *conventus* centre while the former was noted for its long history and great temple of Aphrodite, from which deity it took its name; recent excavations in the south-west quarter have produced a large number of inscribed fragments of Diocletian's Edict of Prices, which had probably been displayed on the walls of the nearby basilica.

The province of Asia was rich in natural products, including various types of marble which were exported to many other places, while wine, fruit and fine woollen cloth were renowned for their quality.

Cilicia

This district in south-eastern Asia Minor had a chequered history until Vespasian constituted it as an imperial province under the command of a praetorian legate in AD 72. Before that the eastern part had been occupied by Rome as early as 102 BC as a military necessity against numerous pirates who infested this area of the Mediterranean. But this suppression was not effectively completed until Pompey's campaigns in 67 BC. For a time it included Phrygia and Pisidia until these were returned to the province of Asia as part of the original Pergamene kingdom. Cicero was one of the governors of the province and defined it, probably incorrectly, as composed of Lycia, Pamphylia, Pisidia and Phrygia. Over a number of years a large part in the north was relegated to a client king, but under Augustus the province was reduced to the eastern part only, under a procurator, who was responsible to the legate of the neighbouring province of Syria; the western rump appears to have been attached to Galatia. Yet another part was ruled by a succession of client kings of Galatia, Cappadocia and Commagene. Eventually, as noted above, Vespasian reconstituted the province and suppressed the remaining client rulers. Although the western part was mountainous, the east contained extremely fertile land and produced flax, fruit, olives, wine and wheat in abundance; excellent timber was produced in the west. The province was also strategically and economically important as it lay across the main trade route between Asia and Syria.

The principal town was Tarsus, a seat of learning in the east, whose best-known son was St Paul. It was also visited by Cleopatra when she travelled north to meet Antony. Although the site has been identified, little is known about it, since it lies deep beneath the modern city, while its once famous, land-locked harbour is now a swamp.

Bithynia and Pontus

As with Asia, the province of Bithynia, amalgamated with neighbouring Pontus, was bequeathed to Rome by a client king, Nicomedes IV. In the provincial organisation first established by Pompey, the region was divided up among the cities for administrative convenience. In the early Empire it was a senatorial province and governed by a proconsul. Gradually, however, its strategic importance, at the mouth of the Black Sea, led to an increasing interest on the part of the emperors. First the imperial procurators were given greater powers, then special legates were appointed by Trajan and Hadrian – Pliny was one – until Marcus Aurelius completed the conversion to an imperial province.

It suffered similarly to Asia in the rivalries which grew between its many cities, leading often to extravagant waste, which it was partly the duty of the special legates, like Pliny, to check. Hadrian established the headquarters of the legate at Nicomedia, a city which in some ways matched Pergamum in its position, lying across the northern, east-west trade route between Europe and Asia Minor, and, with the advantage in the late Empire, of being far closer to Constantinople; indeed, under Diocletian it was for a short time the capital of the eastern Empire, where he built himself a palace. Pliny often wrote to Trajan about the city, drawing the emperor's attention even to quite minor matters. One subject he mentioned was the enormous cost of two aqueducts, both abandoned unfinished because they failed to provide a general supply for the whole city; another concerned the connection, by means of a canal, of an inland lake with the sea, so as to improve the trade route. The city also possessed a garrison and was the headquarters of the Black Sea fleet in the late Empire.

Not far distant to the south lay Nicomedia's chief rival, Nicaea, which contended even for the seat of the provincial governor. Several emperors took personal interest in its development; Constantine held a council of the Church there in 325, while Justinian built himself a palace. Its position on the shore of lake Ascania rendered it particularly fortunate, since it was surrounded by fertile ground, very similar to the main valleys of the province, which was otherwise somewhat mountainous. Another major city, which lay on the main road from Nicomedia to Amasra in Pontus, was Prusa. Others, founded as Greek towns, received colonial rights, while there were also some new foundations under the principate. The province, as a whole, was prosperous, deriving most of its wealth from the agricultural production of the coastal plains and river valleys, but it also produced some fine marbles and timber.

Cyrenaica and Crete

Cyrenaica was a small, fertile territory situated on the African coast to the east side of the Gulf of Sydra. It was separated from its neighbouring provinces – Egypt to the east and Africa to the west – by long distances of arid desert; further deserts and a range of hills to the south cut it off from the interior. It was formed from the territories of the original five Greek colonies usually referred to as the Pentapolis – Cyrene, Apollonia, Ptolemais, Arsinoë and Berenice – and its isolated position from the rest of Africa made the area northward-looking towards Crete and Greece. For a time the area was under Egyptian control, until assigned by Rome to a Ptolemaic dynast as a separate kingdom. After a short return to Egypt it was bequeathed to Rome in 96 BC; the royal lands were sequestered, but the cities were allowed to remain free. Disorders followed and the area was constituted as a province in 74 BC, to which Crete was added seven years later, after its conquest from pirates. Augustus finally established it, together with Crete, as a regular senatorial province. The city of Cyrene is itself noted for having produced an inscription containing five edicts of Augustus, of which four apply to the province.

Cyrene was situated some kilometres inland from the coast and Apollonia was founded as an independent city to act as its port. Much is known from excavations and inscriptions about this principal city of the province, whose original prosperity relied on the agricultural produce of corn, wool, oil and horses, together with a medicinal plant called silphium; bad management, though, caused this plant to become virtually extinct by the time Pliny was writing his *Natural History*. The city and the whole region suffered badly in the Jewish rebellions of the late first and early second century and Hadrian had not only to bring in new colonists but also to restore many buildings; it was probably he who conferred colonial status on Cyrene and also on Arsinoë, and established the new foundation of Hadrianopolis.

Crete was the less prosperous area of the joint province, with the principal town at Knossos, once the great Minoan capital. Much of the building during the principate appears not to have been undertaken until the second century. Large estates in the country had been granted by Augustus to Campanian families.

Syria

Syria was once the domain of the Seleucid dynasty, extending almost from the Black Sea in the north to the Red Sea in the south, but by the middle of the first century BC it was being attacked by Arabs, Parthians, Egyptians and Jews; several local rulers carved out kingdoms for themselves. Finally Pompey forced its surrender and constituted a Roman province in 64 BC, although a number of client states were allowed to survive and some Greek cities remained free. Under the principate Syria became the most important military command in the east with at first four legions under a proconsular legate facing the powerful Parthian empire across the Euphrates. The Jewish kingdom of Judaea was for a short time administered by a procurator responsible to the governor of Syria, but following the revolt of the Jews and the sack of Jerusalem in AD 70 it was given its own provincial structure and legionary garrison under a praetorian legate. Later, Hadrian, apart from rebuilding the city of Jerusalem as a *colonia*, added another legion and the rank of the governor was raised to that of a consular legate; the province was then renamed Syria Palaestina. Other kingdoms were gradually incorporated into the main province, notably Commagene in AD 72 and Ituraea finally in 93. Trajan split off the southern end bordering the Red Sea as the new province of Arabia Petraea under a praetorian legate.

Cities on the whole were few and much of the rural areas was administered from villages. In consequence, owing to their distance apart, some of the cities grew to great size, enjoying much prosperity from the trade routes which crossed the Arabian desert from the east. Such entrepots as Antioch, Palmyra with its major oasis, and Damascus grew from this trade and from the agricultural produce – cedar-wood, wine, dates, plums, nuts, linen and wool – of the rural areas. The most fertile parts were the coastal plain and the river valleys which bisected the mountainous north-south spine of the country and which, in turn, kept the desert at bay. Two major industries were glass-making and the production of the famous Tyrian purple dye.

The principal and greatest city in the province was Antioch, which lay on the river Orontes some 40 km (25 miles) from the Mediterranean coast and on a main trade route from the east to Asia Minor. It was, long before the arrival of the Romans, laid out on a Hippodamian grid and expanded in a succession of building phases; at its greatest extent it occupied an area over 3 km by 1.5 km (2 by 1 miles) in size. Both the history and the structure of the city are well known from documentary sources, notably those recorded by Libanius. In the second century AD the main street, which was the city's axis, was 27 m (30 yd) wide, and flanked by colonnades. Tiberius was responsible for fortifying the expanded city, although these defences were rebuilt by Justinian; Diocletian rebuilt the imperial palace, and many other public buildings and monuments are mentioned in the texts, but it is unlikely that all will ever be located, since they lie deeply buried beneath the modern city. Yet it suffered one major drawback. It lay in an area often shaken by earthquakes and several times it was badly damaged or destroyed, each time, fortunately, to be rescued by an emperor.

Palmyra was another of the great cities of the province and its impressive ruins lie today out in the great Syrian desert. Its fine oasis was the prime cause for its original development, serving as a watering place for the trans-desert caravans on the roads to Damascus, Sura and Antioch; the tariff of customs dues charged on each kind of merchandise has survived. It became extremely rich and ruled a vast area, and during the crisis of the Empire in the third century, threw up its own royal dynasty which managed for a time to protect the eastern frontier where Rome had failed. But its power became too strong and threatened the Empire itself; consequently it had to be reduced and Aurelian destroyed the city, an act from which it never fully recovered.

Cyprus

The island of Cyprus was annexed by Rome from the Ptolemaic dynasty of Egypt in 58 BC, and attached to the mainland province of Cilicia for administrative purposes. Temporarily returned to Cleopatra by Caesar, it was regained after the battle of Actium and was eventually turned into a minor senatorial province by Augustus. The principal city and seat of the proconsular governor was Paphos until the fourth century AD, after which it reverted to Salamis, possibly as the result of damage to the former site by an earthquake. The fortifications of Paphos, which can still be traced, enclosed an area of approximately 100 ha (250 acres). Under the Ptolemies, the province had been noted for its skill in ship-building, but its chief source of economic prosperity lay in the rich copper mines which it possessed, even though there is reason to believe that they were nearly exhausted by the time of the principate.

Egypt

Under the Ptolemies, attempts were made to hellenise Egypt, but they were never truly successful, except in major cities like Alexandria. Although Greek became the official language, the inhabitants of the rural areas continued to speak Egyptian, worship Egyptian deities and were administered according to Egyptian principles.

The way in which Egypt fell to Rome and became a central issue in the civil wars between Pompey and Caesar and later between Octavius (Augustus) and Antony is well known. Once Augustus had gained control, the entire province, for reasons which are not entirely clear, was reduced virtually to the status of an imperial estate and governed by a prefect; this position was deemed to be the peak of an equestrian career. He commanded, somewhat exceptionally, a force, at first of three legions under Augustus, of two under Tiberius and of one in the second century; there were also a considerable number of auxiliary regiments deployed in the Nile valley and at other places in the interior, where their duties embraced both military and civil administration. Significantly, Augustus forbad senators to visit the province without his permission, a rule continued by his successors. The southern boundary of the province extended as far as the first cataract on the Nile, but otherwise it virtually consisted almost entirely of the narrow, fertile belt irrigated annually by the river and its delta. In addition a number of oases, notably the Fayum, west of the river were developed, while the arid hills which lay between the Red Sea and the Nile contained important mineral resources, including decorative building stones such as red porphyry. Huge exports of wheat were delivered to Rome, while other vegetables, papyrus and linen were also produced.

The province was organised like no other in the Empire, retaining much of the old Ptolemaic system which was both extensively centralised and bureaucratic; the job of the officials attached to the administration was to maximise the taxes paid to the emperor. The chief city was Alexandria, near which were stationed the main legionary forces. Although the city was accorded formal autonomy, it is doubtful whether much existed in practice, and it is known that no city council existed in the early days under Roman rule. It then possessed a prefect who was in charge of public order, a very necessary requirement in view of the cosmopolitan nature of the populace, consisting of Greeks, Romans, Egyptians and Jews, who were often at one another's throats. However, some of these communities, such as the Jews, possessed their own independent organisations. Yet in other ways it continued to function as a city, appointing magistrates, making dedications and honorary decrees. It possessed a magnificent harbour guarded by two *pharoi* and capable of accommodating some of the largest merchant ships in the Empire. But apart from Alexandria, Greek cities were few, there being only Naucratis, Paraetonium and Ptolemais, and it was not until Hadrian's principate that a fifth was founded at Antinoöpolis, halfway between the delta and the southern frontier; it was given a constitution modelled on that of Naucratis. Gradually, though, the municipalisation of Egypt took place, and the restoration of the city council to Alexandria by Severus marks the beginning of the change, which was completed by the fourth century when most of the nomes with their villages had been converted into city territories. But even then little romanisation occurred and retired soldiers and officials who settled in the province were rapidly swallowed in the mass of the people and went 'native'.

Achaea

This province covered the southern part of the Greek peninsula and included many of the ancient Greek city states. From 146 BC the region was attached to the province of Macedonia (see above, p. 201) following a revolt. Within it, though, the cities were treated differently according to the way in which they had behaved in the revolt. Athens and Sparta became federate states; some were freed from paying tolls and taxes; Corinth, Thebes and Chalcis were destroyed, and the whole area was generally disarmed and fortifications removed. After Actium, Augustus detached it from Macedonia and united it with Aetolia, Thessaly, part of Epirus and Acarnania to form a new senatorial province, with the governor's seat at Corinth, which had been re-established as a Roman colony by Julius Caesar in 44 BC. Tiberius, though, again temporarily joined Achaea to Macedonia as an imperial province governed by the legate of Moesia. So it remained until Claudius restored it once again to senatorial control. Nero's pleasure in his reception there led to its being given formal freedom, which was later revoked by Vespasian. Under Antoninus Pius at the latest, Epirus was detached as a separate province, while Thessaly was united with Macedonia. During Hadrian's principate in particular the cities flourished within a newly-formed Panhellenic League, and he was responsible for initiating much new building work, in which the provincial capital of Corinth was provided with a huge new bath complex.

As the provincial capital, Corinth was favoured in many ways. After the foundation of the Caesarian colony, a great building programme seems to have been begun in the early first century AD. Greek structures which had been damaged in the sack of the city were, when sufficient survived, reconstructed; hence the temple of Apollo, the theatre and Asklepieion came into being again. An arch, probably to commemorate the colony's foundation, was built on one of the main roads leading to the forum. At least three basilicas were constructed around its piazza, one of which possessed a horse-shoe-shaped council chamber. Temples of Venus, Herakles, and later Commodus, were grouped in this complex. The Greek theatre was rebuilt in the Roman manner and later altered so that the orchestra could serve as an arena which could even provide aquatic displays. A small *odeum* was constructed nearby. Extra market places were also provided, surrounded by colonnades, and they attest the commercial wealth of the city. It was equally well provided with water through an accident of geology; a porous limestone bed on top of a layer of impervious clay allowed the water which penetrated the rock to flow out along the rock/clay interface where it was trapped in large cisterns; there were also more traditional aqueducts.

Private houses demonstrate the wealth of many of the inhabitants and also show the influence of Italian architects. Yet despite these displays of municipal success, in which several other cities were given colonial rights, and others like Athens continued to flourish, trade declined and with it both the population and its wealth. Great estates were formed by a few rich landowners which eclipsed the poorer cities; some rural areas may have retained a modest prosperity, but never again at the level of ancient Greece.

Galatia

This province enclosed a heterogeneous collection of peoples situated in central Asia Minor. It contained a large Celtic nucleus derived from the immigrants that had originally crossed from Europe in 278 BC. The Roman province which was constituted in 25 BC from the kingdom of a client ruler also contained parts of Phrygia, Pisidia, Lycaonia, and probably Pamphylia; later, areas of Pontus and Paphlagonia were attached. The governor was, at first, a praetorian legate, but when Vespasian added Cappadocia and Armenia Minor, his status was raised to consular rank. These arrangements lasted only a short time. When Trajan began his eastern campaigns, the Pontic districts, together with Armenia Minor, Lycaonia and Cappadocia were placed under a separate praetorian legate and Galatia was reduced considerably in size; a further reduction seems to have been undertaken late in Hadrian's principate.

The province contained few cities, but some, such as Antioch in Pisidia, received colonial status under Augustus. The capital and seat of the governor was at Ancyra (modern Ankara), chiefly famous for its copy, inscribed on stone slabs, of the *Res Gestae* of Augustus, in both Latin and Greek versions, which were fixed to the walls of the temple and its precinct dedicated to Rome and Augustus. Much of the ancient site lies buried under the modern city, although a huge bath-house, attributed to the principate of Caracalla, has been excavated; it is notable for the very large number of hot rooms which it contained, made desirable perhaps by the severity of the winters in central Asia Minor. The city flourished throughout both the Roman and Byzantine periods, when it was strongly fortified to withstand eastern invasions.

Of considerable interest is the survival under Roman rule of the tribal entities of the early Celtic immigrants, in very much the same manner as happened later in Gaul and Britain (see below, p. 223). They were organised administratively into three territories: Tolistobogii, Tectosages and Trocmi. Ankara was originally the tribal capital of the Tectosages. As in Gaul, the tribes possessed a central council which met at Drynemetum, and which seems to have had greater power than the *Concilium Galliarum*, since it could try cases of capital crime. When St Jerome visited the province in the late fourth century, he found that the Celtic language was still commonly spoken.

Pamphylia

Pamphylia was a coastal region in south-west Asia Minor, to the east of the province of Asia. It was first ceded to Rome in 189 BC by the Seleucid king Antiochus III. From 102 BC to 44 BC it seems to have become part of the province of Cilicia, only to be transferred to Asia in the latter year. Temporarily given to the client ruler Amyntas, it became part of the province of Galatia on his death, under the arrangements made by Augustus. Claudius revised these arrangements and formed the new province of Lycia-Pamphylia, only for Galba to reverse the situation when he freed the Lycians. Finally Vespasian re-formed the Claudian imperial province, although Pamphylia retained its own council separate from the Lycians. Hadrian exchanged the joint province with the senate, in return for Bithynia, after which it came under senatorial control.

The chief city of Lycia was probably Xanthus, situated on a river bearing the same name and some 12 km (7½ miles) from the coast, while Side, Perge or Aspendus may have served similarly for Pamphylia. The area probably possessed one of the most densely packed distributions of cities in the Empire; Pliny quotes thirty-six for Lycia alone. Some remained free under the principate, while others were deprived of their freedom and had to pay taxes. Even that, though, did not cause the league of cities to be dissolved and all retained their votes, as well as continuing to mint and issue their own coinage. One of the best-known city sites in the province is Aspendus, which lay some 13 km (8 miles) inland on the Eurymedon river. It possesses one of the best-preserved Roman theatres in the Empire, which was constructed in the second century AD by a local architect, Zeno. Other buildings, including the agora and a huge, flanking basilica, have been identified, as well as a stadium and a market hall. An interesting aquedect, given to the community by Ti. Claudius Italicus, employed pressure pipes, made by boring holes through solid stone blocks, and a syphon system, to raise water to the hill-top city.

Cappadocia

The area in western Asia Minor which became the province of Cappadocia was rugged and generally inhospitable, although parts provided excellent grazing for horses, mules and sheep. The severity of the winters, though, restricted crops to hardy cereals and fruits. Urbanisation made only slow progress. Before the arrival of the Romans, most natives lived in villages under a system resembling that of feudal estates. Pompey restored the region to its ruler after the Mithridatic war and it remained a client state until AD 17, when, successive kings having proved unreliable in a crisis, it was annexed by Tiberius, because of its strategic importance on the eastern frontier. At first a procuratorial province with no troops, it was joined with Galatia by Vespasian (see above, p. 210) under a consular legate, until Trajan constituted Cappadocia a separate province with Pontus. Its internal administration remained much as it had been as a client kingdom, under which it had been divided into eleven districts, each with its own *strategus*. Its eastern border, along the Euphrates for much of its length, formed the eastern frontier of the Empire and was always a politically sensitive area. But the transfer of large bodies of troops to the border and the construction of strategic roads opened up the interior greatly to the benefit of the native population. As a result, some communities gained municipal or colonial status, but for the remainder of the countryside an ever-increasing number of imperial estates were formed, which cannot have been entirely beneficial to the resident populations.

The provincial capital was situated at Caesarea Cappadociae, the old city of Mazaca, which had been rebuilt by Pompey. Little is known of it. Another important site lay on the Black Sea coast at the foot of the Pontic mountains: Trapezus. At first an open roadstead, it lay at the northern end of a trade route leading over the Zirgana Pass from the Euphrates. It therefore developed not only as a trading post, but also as a supply port for the eastern frontier and the prime base of the *classis Pontica*. Hadrian enclosed the harbour with twin moles, while in the late Empire it became a legionary fortress. On the frontier further south, several other existing cities became the sites of permanent fortresses, such as that at Melitene, the ancient city which gained colonial status under Trajan.

Thrace

Despite its nearness to Rome, Thrace was only incorporated as a province into the Empire comparatively late. Before that it had undergone a number of vicissitudes under several client kings, in which regicide was the most commonly occurring event. The murder of the last king by his wife in AD 46 gave Claudius the excuse to form a province under a procurator. Trajan downgraded the status of the governor to that of a praetorian legate, although only few troops were quartered in the province, and indeed defence was provided by the governor of Moesia. As in Cappadocia, there were few cities and administratively the province was treated in much the same way; a central bureaucracy with divisions managed by *strategi*. Some new colonial foundations were made by Claudius or Nero and by Vespasian, Trajan and Hadrian. The provincial capital was Perinthus, which lay on the northern shore of the Sea of Marmara, not far from Byzantium. A coastwise and riverine trade existed in wine, timber and textiles, but the most significant 'import' into the early Empire was cavalrymen, and a number of auxiliary cohorts and *alae* of Thracians existed in the Roman army.

Arabia Petraea

This province was not formally constituted until AD 105 under Trajan, in order to protect caravans on their way from the east to Syria; its governor was a praetorian legate with a single legion. It had been part of the original Nabataean kingdom, a region which had been fostered and developed by the careful husbanding of its limited water resources. Augustus mounted an expedition southwards which reached Aden and opened the Red Sea to merchants from India and the east; spices, gold, gemstones and incense were among the most valuable materials traded, which was facilitated by the great road which Trajan constructed from Aqaba on the Red Sea, by way of Petra and Bostra to Damascus.

The two chief cities were Bostra and Petra, the former becoming the provincial capital and acting as the legionary base. It was a city remarkable for its appearance, being constructed almost entirely of black basalt. Although the modern town lies over it, a certain amount of information has been recovered from surviving remains. They include a theatre and a huge 'palace' complex which may have served as the governor's residence. The city was ultimately raised to colonial status. Petra was the old Nabataean capital and is remarkable for its situation in a basin surrounded by sandstone cliffs and is only approachable through a narrow gorge in the rock, 2 km (1¼ miles) long. It is chiefly known for the colour of the rock from which its elaborate, architecturally created tombs were cut in the cliffs in and around the gorge. Large and small theatres are known, as well as possible markets and temples.

Armenia Major

This kingdom to the north-east of Cappadocia and beyond the Euphrates was long contested between Rome and Parthia. Rome was normally content, as long as one of her own nominees sat upon the throne, to leave the area unmolested. After Pompey's campaigns, the kingdom became a Roman protectorate; Augustus and his successors aimed to continue the arrangement but it was not always successful and tended to develop into a critical tug-of-war between the major contestants. Trajan temporarily solved the Roman problem by creating a province of the kingdom in AD 114 with a legate and a procurator, but only three years later Hadrian surrendered the kingdom and returned it to the original status quo.

Mesopotamia

This area, basically between the rivers Tigris and Euphrates as far down as the head of the Persian Gulf, was annexed by Trajan in his Parthian wars, although, as with Armenia, his Provincia Mesopotamia was abandoned by Hadrian shortly after its constitution. It was reconquered by Lucius Verus in 162–165 while Septimius Severus, in his campaigns against a weakening Parthia, consolidated Verus' gains in the north-western part and created a province, which was only yielded in the later third century to the new and more vigorous Sasanid dynasty of Persia. Nevertheless, a number of new cities were founded as veteran colonies, notably Carrhae under Severus or Caracalla. Others at Singara and Edessa are worth noting; Edessa was once capital of the dynasty which ruled the district of Osrhoene. But the area, as with Armenia, always remained a buffer between the then primary powers of Europe and western Asia.

XI

THE WESTERN PROVINCES

As with the eastern provinces, the order of acquisition by Rome has been taken as the basis for individual descriptions of western provinces (figs 29–35).

The Western Empire

Sicily

Sicily was the first land outside Italy to fall to Rome. Before Roman intervention, there had been both Greek and Phoenician settlements, rule by tyrants, and also Carthaginian interference. It was the conflict of the Carthaginians with Rome which led to their ultimate defeat in Sicily and, after the capture of Syracuse in 211 BC, the whole island became a Roman province. At first the provincial administration was in the hands of a praetor, later a propraetor and finally a proconsul, with two quaestors to assist him. As in other newly conquered provinces at later dates, the cities were treated differently: some, such as Taormina, received federate status, others, such as Segesta, remained free of taxes, while the remainder paid dues or rents – sometimes both. Much of the land was declared public and initially used for the production of cereals for Roman consumption. A parallel development was the growth of huge, slave-run *latifundia* as the result of individual Romans investing in the new province. But for three years, 73–71 BC, the province suffered from the notorious, not to say infamous, governor C. Verres, whose name became a byword for all manner of extortions and corruptions; eventually on his return to Rome he was indicted for his crimes before the Senate and prosecuted by Cicero, who in his account of the trial provides some significant insights into provincial administration. Caesar gave the citizens Latin rights, but Augustus revoked the general grant and restricted it to some cities, though a few of these were promoted to full Roman citizenship. As a

214

result, a mixture of free Roman *coloniae* and *municipia*, and their tax-paying equivalents with Latin rights grew up together. Augustus also founded six new veteran colonies, of which Syracuse, Taormina and Catania were probably the most important.

Syracuse was probably the premier city and the seat of the governor in the Roman period, but it was already old when Augustus grafted his colony on to the existing city. The new colonists undoubtedly had a rejuvenating effect, since its importance had been declining. Only vestiges of its buildings have been discovered, since much is still covered by the modern city. One of the oldest buildings to be excavated was the sixth century BC temple of Apollo, originally erected by the Greek colonists and adapted to later needs in ensuing years. There was also a smaller temple dedicated to Jupiter. The *cavea* of the theatre, almost certainly of Greek origin, also survives, since it was cut out of the rock-face of that part of the city which also contained the agora. The amphitheatre was similarly constructed not far away, probably in the third century AD: it is one of the largest in the Empire, measuring 199 m (218 yd) by 140 m (153 yd). Syracuse is also noted for its well-preserved defensive circuits, the major length of which was 27 km (16¾ miles); much of it dates to the fifth century BC, and it was constructed on a singularly massive scale, although alterations continued down to the Byzantine period. Perhaps most important, though, were the city's two natural harbours, which had once served as a base for the Athenian and, later, the Carthaginian fleets. Of the other main cities on the island, Taormina is chiefly famous for its second century AD theatre cut into the rock-face of one of the city's hills. From its auditorium is gained a superb view of the Mediterranean coast climbing inland to the peak of Mount Etna, which acts as a most effective back-drop to the stage buildings.

Sardinia and Corsica

These two islands were first captured by Rome from the Carthaginians and were constituted as a single province under a praetor in 227 BC. It was allowed few concessions and under the Republic there were no free cities. Instead, and not unlike what happened in Sicily, Sardinia in particular was used to provide grain and taxes for Rome. Corsica, more rugged and less fertile, produced good timber for ship-building, as well as cattle. But both islands contained violent and almost uncontrollable native populations. Sardinia was reft by revolts for a good century after its capture; even when these were finally suppressed, the population turned to brigandage. Only the east coast of Corsica, with its good harbours, came fully under Roman control; the mountainous west was virtually abandoned. Under the Empire, Augustus first placed the islands under the senatorial control of a praetorian consul, but by AD 6 they had reverted to imperial control under a procurator. Nero exchanged the islands with the senate in return for the liberation of Achaea. Under Vespasian they once more became imperial, finally being traded back to the senate for Baetica in southern Spain, by Marcus Aurelius. During this time a small measure of prosperity was achieved, the iron and silver mines of Sardinia providing an economic base in addition to its crops. At some later date during the principate the islands were made into separate provinces.

Caralis, modern Cagliari, was the principal city in Sardinia, becoming a *municipium* under Sulla and being given full Roman rights by Caesar. But little is known of it. An aqueduct still functions to bring water to the modern city; remains of a bath-house and amphitheatre have been identified; perhaps most interesting of all, owing to their rareness, are substantial traces of a fuller's shop, probably of the republican period to judge by a mosaic in one of the rooms. Two other *coloniae* were promoted on the island. In contrast, Corsica was given two veteran colonies, both situated on the east coast: Aleria and Mariana. The former was founded by Caesar and enlarged by Augustus; it became the administrative capital of the island when it received its own provincial status. Parts of the fortifications are still visible, including a main gate. The forum has been identified, and it possibly contained a temple dedicated to Augustus and Rome, erected during Hadrian's principate. A *mansio* with its own bath-house is known to have existed near the harbour, which for a time sheltered a detachment of the fleet primarily based at Misenum.

Spain

Although the Iberian peninsula eventually became three provinces, it is most convenient to consider them under a common heading, which reflects the way in which Rome came to possess them and subsequently to organise them.

Phoenicians, Greeks and Carthaginians had all in turn founded colonies in Spain, mainly on or near the south and east coasts. When Rome became involved with Carthage in the Punic Wars, the coastal strip, in Italy leading north from Rome, and then along the southern and eastern coasts of Gaul and Spain respectively, was one of the main routes by which Carthage attacked Rome and eventually by which Rome reciprocated. As the area grew in strategic importance it therefore had to be conquered and guarded, and Carthage was first ejected from its European strongholds in 206 BC. As a result Rome held this narrow coastal strip from the Pyrenees to Gibraltar and divided it first into two parts under the separate command of two praetors. These provinces gradually expanded inland as the result of wars against the native tribes of the interior and, by the time of Caesar, covered some two-thirds of the peninsula.

Augustus interested himself early in Spain and after a succession of campaigns, finally reduced the remaining districts and reorganised the whole peninsula into the three provinces of Baetica, Lusitania and Tarraconensis. He returned Baetica to the Senate in 27 BC but retained the others under his own control; Tarraconensis then possessed three legions, mustered in the more hostile north-west of the province, but this number was reduced to one under Vespasian. Roman control was also bolstered by the creation first by Caesar and then by Augustus of a total of twenty-one *coloniae* and a number of Roman and Latin *municipia;* between them these cities controlled much of Spanish territory, which was formed, again by Augustus, into several *conventus*. Vespasian extended Latin rights to all those inhabitants not by then franchised.

All three provinces had a sound economic base on which their prosperity rested. Perhaps most important of all, though, was the fact that Spain was about the only large area in the Empire where the problems of a frontier did not arise until late; surrounded by the sea on three sides and the Pyrenees in the north, the provinces could evolve peacefully in the absence of any external threat. Fertile plains, hill-slopes and river valleys supported all manner of crops: vines, olive-trees, cereals, fruit and nuts. Pastures provided food for large herds of cattle and sheep. The sea-coasts provided abundant fish. Where the agriculturally productive land ceased and ran into the more rugged hills and mountains, they were found to be rich in minerals of which gold, silver, lead, tin, iron, copper, and mercury all occurred. Indeed, the provinces of Spain supplied the Empire with almost its entire requirements of precious and other metals for most of the principate; annual production of gold was as much as 20,000 lb and of silver eight tons by the end of the first century AD. Only towards the end of the Empire were these resources nearing exhaustion.

The three provincial capitals were Corduba (Baetica), Tarraco (Tarraconensis) and Merida (Lusitania), but as mentioned above many other cities rivalled them on terms almost of equality both in size and importance. Historically, four are important since fragments of their charters of constitution have come to light, yielding much information on the way in which cities were administered in the Western Empire.

Ancient Corduba lies beneath not only the modern city, but also below the remains of the Moslem period; as sometimes happens, though, the modern street system closely reflects that of the Roman city, which was divided in four quarters by the *cardo* and *decumanus* and arranged according to the points of the compass. The sixteen-arched bridge which crossed the river Guadelquivir outside the city boundary is still in use, although heavily restored. A building at the centre has provisionally been identified as the forum, although it is so closely connected with a large and opulent bath-house that this attribution may be mistaken. A large temple has also been identified, and it has been claimed that the city was the most thoroughly romanised of any in the peninsula. Best known is the series of cemeteries which lay along the roads leading out of the city.

The city of Tarraco had been the centre of the local Iberian tribe, and possibly also an Etruscan colony. It became the base for Scipio's wars against Carthage, and later Caesar conferred colonial rank upon it. Augustus convalesced here during his campaigns in Spain, and created it the capital of the erstwhile province of Hispania Citerior. Hence it was the natural choice of capital when this province expanded into Tarraconensis. Its chief building seems to have been a temple constructed on the city's highest point and dedicated to Augustus. Although its remains are now beneath the cathedral, the façade was recorded on contemporary coins. Inscriptions record the existence of an amphitheatre, baths and a forum with basilica; a theatre and a circus are known from other sources.

The third provincial capital of Merida lies close to the border between Lusitania and Baetica, and began as a veteran colony founded under Augustus in 25 BC. In plan it is not dissimilar to Corduba, and its street grid can be traced from those of the modern city. Among the surviving remains are a theatre probably built by Marcus Agrippa, an amphitheatre and a circus, and a monumental arch dedicated to Trajan. The water supply is also well attested, with aqueducts and reservoirs of large capacity.

Illyricum (Dalmatia)

This area, roughly equivalent to modern Yugoslavia, first attracted Roman attention when pirates based on the numerous coastal islands began to attack shipping in the Adriatic. Intermittent Roman intervention followed until the area was allotted to Caesar when he was governing Cisalpine Gaul. A number of coastal settlements, populated by Roman citizens, backed Caesar against Pompey, even though the Illyrians as a whole declared against him. Octavian took limited action against the tribes of the interior, and, after he became Augustus, constituted a senatorial province. But in the succeeding years, which were punctuated by severe wars and rebellions, particularly in the part known as Pannonia, it was placed under imperial control *c.* 11 BC. Further wars resulted in its division, *c.* AD 9; soon after and certainly before the Flavian period these two new provinces had become Dalmatia and Pannonia (see below, p. 228).

Dalmatia was governed as an imperial province by a consular legate whose capital was at Salona; at first he possessed two legions stationed at Burnum and Tilurium and a number of auxiliary units. One legion, though, was moved to Moesia sometime around the middle of the first century AD, to be followed, *c.* AD 86, by the second; thereafter, except for temporary garrisons during the Marcomannic wars, no further legions served in Dalmatia, and the area was demilitarised, even though it remained under imperial control. The provincial capital at Salona was an ancient foundation, colonised by Roman citizen traders and settlers from Italy in the first century BC. It became a *colonia* probably under Caesar, but possibly not until Augustus' principate. It presents an unusual appearance containing two separate, but linked, walled enclosures, usually referred to as the *urbs vetus* and the *urbs nova;* the former lies to the west, and its walls were already in existence when its territory was centuriated, the west wall forming the axis of the *cardo*. Equally, the amphitheatre at the north-west corner, itself dated to *c.* 170, ought to predate these defences since it became incorporated in them, although admittedly this could be as the result of a much later alteration. Intercommunication between the enclosures was provided by a massive gate, dating to the time of Augustus. Within the old quarter a theatre and temple have been identified, together with a structure which may be part of a forum; both are situated near the south-eastern corner. In the new city, some substantial private houses and a large bath building have been identified. The extensive harbour could only be approached from the landward side through a gate in the sourthern circuit of the new city.

Not far from Salona and separated from it by a peninsula lay the great palace which Diocletian built for himself at Split in anticipation of his retirement. Born in the region, he returned to die there, after he had severed all his connections with imperial control; in the interval between his retirement and death he was here able to give full attention to his hobby of gardening.

Africa

The original Roman province of Africa was formed after the defeat of Carthage, but instead of including the entire conquered territory in the new province, it was confined to the north-eastern area of modern Tunis, while the remainder was handed back to the local dynastic rulers; the boundary of the new province was marked by the *fossa regia*. After Caesar won the battle of Thapsus in 46 BC he added to the original province – then called Africa Vetus – a large portion of the neighbouring westerly kingdom of Numidia, to be called Africa Nova; he also founded several colonies, and planned to include Carthage in the number, but this move was not achieved until Octavian became emperor. He, as Augustus, also reorganised the Caesarian arrangements and extended the new province, renamed Africa Proconsularis, as far as the Cyrenaican border to the east and to the Numidian border to the west; he returned some of the territory taken by Caesar from the latter kingdom to the reigning dynasty. But with the creation of thirteen new colonies on the coastal strip of Mauretania, west of Numidia, and the transfer of the Numidian king to rule the hinterland behind it, the original kingdom of Numidia seems once again to have been incorporated within the African province; it was senatorial and administered by a proconsul, whose prestige was deemed to be virtually the equal of the governor of Asia. His capital was moved from Utica to the rebuilt Carthage under Augustus. The governor was in an almost unique position during the first part of the principate for having under his command the only legion in Africa outside Egypt. Gaius stepped in to remedy what he clearly saw as an anomaly in the system and detached the legion, under its legate, from the governor's control, giving it charge of Numidia and the more sensitive frontier districts; it was stationed successively at Ammaedara, Tebessa and Lambaesis, the last two places being in Numidian territory. Numidia was finally separated from Africa and constituted as a separate province by Severus (see below, p. 235).

The capital of Africa Proconsularis became Carthage, a city founded by Phoenicians from Tyre. It had rapidly become the centre of the expanding Carthaginian empire, which was largely based on naval power and the seafaring abilities of its inhabitants. Recent excavations have established the positions of the great sheds alongside the harbour which were used for ship-building and also the outlines of the harbours themselves. Although the street plan of the city has been recovered, most of the buildings have been pillaged for stone. Still surviving, though, is the huge bath-house, almost the largest in the Empire, attributed to Antoninus Pius. Other large cities existed along the coast as well as inland; they included those on the coast of Tripolitania which, taken together, form one of the most complete records of city life and its structure in the Empire. Much land was attributed to them and there are numerous examples of centuriation. Imperial and private estates also flourished and the province was exceedingly prosperous, producing very large quantities of olive oil, cereals, fruit and textiles. There was also a good deal of trade with the nomadic tribes of the interior, who may well have been allowed also to practise controlled transhumance into the Roman provinces, especially into the pastures of Numidia.

Gallia Narbonensis

Rome's initial interest in the area, at first called Transalpine Gaul, was focussed on the need to maintain overland communications with Spain. In this she was aided by the Greek colony at Marseilles, an old ally. It was threats to this colony by the local tribes that caused Rome, in 121 BC, to annex the territory inland from the sea port, while further threats from the Helvetii provided Caesar with a political expedient for his campaigns, which eventually resulted in the Roman conquest of all Gaul. Under Augustus the earlier acquired territory was constituted as a senatorial province with its capital at Narbo, from which the provincial name was taken. Some veteran colonies had been established by Caesar, of which Narbo was one, grafted on to an earlier city; he also promoted some native centres, such as Nîmes, to municipal status with Latin rights, although under Augustus the city was advanced to a *colonia* with full Roman rights.

The provincial capital at Narbo was already a prosperous city when Caesar established his colony, and remained so for the first two centuries AD. It lay on the main road from Italy to Spain at the point where another major road crossed it. Although it was some distance from the sea it had good navigable access by way of the river Aude and a thriving port developed. At its zenith it covered an area of 100 ha (250 acres). Unfortunately little is known about the city's buildings, except for some literary accounts. The position of the forum is known, together with the neighbouring *capitolium;* the forum contained an altar which set out the calendar for the festivals celebrated for *Divus Augustus*. Beneath the forum were a series of subterranean chambers which may have been granaries. The amphitheatre is situated beyond the eastern suburbs and was part of a complex of buildings, attributed to the Flavian period, which is thought to have contained the provincial centre for the imperial cult. An inscription found nearby sets out the duties and privileges of the chief priest of the province.

Apart from Narbo, more is perhaps known about the province's other main cities, which, especially Nîmes, came into greater prominence after a serious fire in the mid-second century destroyed much of Narbo, so precipitating its decline. Arles, Orange, Vienne and Vaison are also much better known and have more extant, surviving structures.

The province was economically prosperous, producing olive oil and wine in quantity, as well as cereals, for which the multiple water-mills at Barbegal, near Arles, were presumably designed. For a time it also exported large quantities of good-quality pottery. The river Rhône and its tributary the Saône provided important communication links with other parts of Gaul which, at an early date, were nearly extended by the construction of a canal to link the Saône with the Moselle; but the scheme never came to fruition.

Tres Galliae

That part of Gaul outside Narbonensis which was conquered by Caesar was at first named Gallia Comata; Caesar planted its first veteran colony at Nyon in the territory of the Helvetii; other *coloniae* were founded at Augst and Lyon. In 44 BC he separated it from Narbonensis and divided the area into two unequal halves, each with its own legate. At this stage and for some time to come the legate of Belgica was also responsible for administering the land right up to the Rhine. Augustus extended the reorganisation and three provinces emerged: Aquitania with its probable capital at Bordeaux, Lugdunenis with its capital at Lyon, and Belgica with its capital at Rheims. Each now was governed by a legate, while Narbonensis was returned to senatorial control (see above, p. 221). Lyon was early selected to be of special importance. It was founded as a colony in 43 BC and Drusus established there the *Ara Romae et Augusti* at Condate in the angle formed by the junction of the two rivers. It was intended to be the religious centre of the imperial cult for the Three Gauls and the federal seat of the provincial council to which all the 60 or so *civitates* of imperial Gaul sent representatives. Many are recorded on inscriptions. Later under Tiberius the site was further dignified by the construction of a great amphitheatre and temple dedicated in the same manner as the altar. Nearby were found the massive bronze plates, on which was inscribed the speech of Claudius to the Roman senate, proposing that Gauls should be adlected to that body.

It was not, however, until the Flavian period, in *c.* AD 90, that Domitian finally separated Germany from Gaul by the creation of two provinces along the Rhine, each with its own consular legate. But even then, for tax purposes, the people of Germany still came within the jurisdiction of the procurator of Gallia Belgica.

As already indicated above, the three provinces which had once comprised Gallia Comata were probably far more backward than any other areas of the Empire which had so far been acquired. There was little urban development of a kind that Rome could recognise, and consequently the local adminis-tration was based on the Iron Age tribal units which were constituted as *civitates*. A parallel was the earlier treatment of Galatia (see above, p. 211). Nevertheless each *civitas* required an administrative centre and a series of towns grew up to serve this need, often becoming large and prosperous, although few reached chartered status. As indicated above, Augst and Cologne – although later part of Lower Germany – were created *coloniae* at a compara-tively early date: Augst, planned by Caesar but dedicated to Augustus, and Cologne under Claudius. A small number of civitas capitals were later promoted, such as Trier in Belgica which became very important in the late Empire, and Avenches which seems to have had a veteran settlement grafted on to the existing town under Vespasian.

The premier city was undoubtedly Lyon. It possessed an imperial mint, to guard which it was given an urban cohort, one of only two cities outside Rome to possess such a unit. The first city here was established on the top and slopes of the hill which lies west of the river junction. In its heyday it possessed a large forum and capitol on the hill-top and two theatres – the only other city in Gaul, apart from Vienne, to possess two; the larger was the oldest in Gaul, the other smaller, but set close beside it, was an *odeum*. A second forum was built in the mid-second century and appears to have contained a temple dedicated to Jupiter. The early city ultimately expanded over both rivers to link with the federal site of Condate and on to the one-time island in the Rhône. Considerable industries grew in these newly developed areas and Lyon became noted as a centre for the manufacture of fine pottery, glass and metalwork. The city was served by four aqueducts, one of which, built under Hadrian, used pressurised pipes to supply the higher parts.

Other towns in Gallia Lugdunensis which show a marked degree of romanisation and development were Autun, capital of the Aedui, Paris, capital of the Parisii, and Alésia, capital of the Mandubii, and site of the defeat of Vercingetorix by Caesar, whose siege works around the *oppidum* have been investigated.

The provincial capital of Gallia Belgica was Rheims, although Trier grew and prospered to such an extent as to be a serious rival; indeed, with its promotion to colonial status, it attracted central government and contained the office of the procurator of Belgica and Germany, while in the early fourth century it not only received an imperial palace, but also became the seat of the praetorian prefect of Gaul.

Rheims, though, was the centre of provincial administration and contained the governor's residence, as well as acting as the civitas capital of the Remi. Unfortunately, although four monumental arches mark the limits of the inner quarter along the two main streets, not a great deal is known of the rest of the plan. A cryptoporticus near the central cross-roads suggests the position of the forum, and an orthogonal street plan is indicated. As with many Gaulish cities and towns, it suffered during the disastrous invasions of the third century, and in consequence was much reduced in size when the fortifications were built. Other main towns in Belgica, apart from Rheims and Trier, were Bavay, capital of the Nervii, and Amiens, capital of the Ambiani. The province was also remarkable for its rural development in the Somme and Moselle valleys, which are thickly clustered with villas, sometimes of great size and splendour.

It is usually argued that Bordeaux was the provincial capital of Aquitania, although two other candidates for the position are possible: Poitiers and Saintes. Bordeaux probably had greater commercial viability than its rivals, since it was the major port of south-west Gaul, situated on the river Garonne. It was also the civitas capital of the Bituriges Vivisci, and it is likely that it was given municipal status by Vespasian. Unfortunately little is known of its plan or internal buildings. As with Rheims, it suffered in the third century invasions and, when rebuilt, its original 125 ha (310 acres) were compressed inside a wall which enclosed only 31 ha (77 acres). An amphitheatre is known to lie outside these walls and apparently dates to the Severan period, while sections of the massively built quays in the port have been uncovered. Ausonius, the poet and high imperial official of the late Empire, retired to Bordeaux in his old age and wrote about the wines of the region and also of the fine oysters from the river estuary, although Saintes appears to have been the main trading centre for the latter. Other major towns in the province were Bourges, capital of the Bituriges Cubi, Clermont Ferrand, capital of the Arverni and centre for a major pottery industry, and Périgueux, capital of the Petrocorii.

The financial affairs of Aquitania were dealt with jointly with Lugdunensis by a procurator, who was based at Lyon.

Noricum

Noricum, derived from its chief Celtic tribe of the Norici, started as a federal state, minting its own coinage. It became an independent kingdom which supported Caesar in the civil war, and was peacefully absorbed as a province *c.* 16 BC. For a time it may have been left under a *praefectus*, or even a *princeps*, *civitatum*, but eventaully it came to be governed by a *procurator*, who had only auxiliary troops at his disposal and whose residence was at Virunum. During the Marcomannic wars, its garrison was increased by a newly recruited legion, stationed first at Albing, later at Lorch, and the legionary legate became the provincial governor; the provincial capital was then moved to Ovilava, but the financial procurator remained at Virunum.

Virunum lay at an important road junction, with direct connections to the Danube frontier and to Aquileia in north Italy. It replaced the important native political and industrial centre on the Magdalensberg, and it became, together with a small handful of other towns in Noricum, a *municipium* under Claudius, but was never promoted higher. The plan is characteristic of most newly-planned urban settlements under the early principate, although the forum and capitol were east of centre and separated from each other by the *cardo*. The forum was apparently flanked on one side by a basilica which contained only one aisle, not unlike some British examples. A bath-house has been identified, together with a theatre; the baths were noted for their large number of classical marble statues. Indeed, it seems likely that in the second century AD the city possessed a flourishing school of local sculptors. It was apparently never fortified and its people migrated to defended hill-tops nearby during the unsettled period at the end of the western Empire.

Ovilava also received municipal status, but not until Hadrian's principate, although it was more fortunate than Virunum, being promoted to a *colonia* by Caracalla, who may also have been responsible for its fortifications. Unfortunately few of the main buildings have been identified, although it is known to have had an aqueduct, which in the second century AD consisted of wooden pipes; this was rebuilt as a vaulted channel in the third century.

The chief importance of the province of Noricum lay in its rich iron ore mines and the near-steel which they produced, to the extent that coins were issued referring to this metallurgical factor (see above, p. 162).

Raetia

Raetia, the western neighbour of Noricum, was conquered by Drusus and Tiberius in 15 BC together with the celtic Vindelici, and was placed under the control of the legate of Gallia Belgica, who appointed in AD 16–17 a *praefectus civitatum* to look after the region. Later the province was reconstituted under an equestrian procurator, as in neighbouring Noricum, who resided at Augsburg and who controlled only auxiliary regiments; under Trajan these consisted of four *alae* and eleven cohorts, the senior of which was the *Ala II Flavia milliaria* stationed at Heidenheim and later at Aalen. During the Marcomannic wars, the province was upgraded by the placing of a legion at Regensberg, whose legate then became the provincial governor.

The principal town of the province was Augsburg, which at first may have been no more than the civitas capital of the Vindelici. Under Hadrian, if not before, Augsburg acquired the status of a *municipium*, but never seems to have been promoted to a *colonia*. Although the site of the Augustan legionary camp has been established there is little evidence for the city; no public buildings are known other than a large bath-house; the fortifications are thought to date from the time of Hadrian.

Alpes

In 14 BC Augustus reduced the area of the western Alps, which separated France from Italy, to a province: Alpes Maritimae; it was at first governed by a *praefectus*, later by a procurator. Further north the district that came to be known as the Alpes Cottiae was annexed by Nero, having previously been left under the control of Cottius, an ally of Rome. The two major towns were Nicaea, originally a Greek colony of Marseilles, and Segusium. The latter became a *municipium* under Nero, who conferred Latin rights. Unlike the planned cities of the region, it shows a degree of spontaneous formation with the main streets radiating from an early nucleus. The forum has been identified at the intersection of two major roads in the centre, and an arch dedicated to Augustus still stands. The only other public building of which remains survive is the amphitheatre. The fortifications were probably not built before the later third century AD, in the face of invasions from Germany.

Moesia

The Moesi were a nation in the lower regions south of the Danube. Their earliest contacts with Rome are marked by confusion. They were defeated, together with the Dacians, by M. Licinius Crassus, proconsul of Macedonia, in 29 BC and informally attached to either Macedonia or Illyricum. For the next nearly fifty years, at which time the first legate is recorded in Moesia in AD 6, little is known of the historical events, although the area was inextricably mixed with the Pannonian wars and revolts of the period. It was not until the principate of Tiberius that Moesia emerged as a defined province under an imperial legate, who during the years AD 15–44 also had oversight of Macedonia and Greece and, from the principates of Claudius to Trajan, Thrace as well (see above, p. 213). Under Domitian, when the Dacians were threatening from across the Danube, the province was divided into two unequal halves, the larger western part being given the title of Superior, that to the east Inferior; each had its own consular legate, and for a short time, as a temporary expedient, part of Pannonia was attached to Superior in order to unite under one command the Roman forces facing Dacia.

Although the area was well endowed with legionary and auxiliary garrisons, and with some urban coastal sites of Greek origin on the Black Sea, the growth of urbanisation was slow, being confined almost entirely to the promotion of civil settlements established outside the main fortresses and forts: Belgrade, Koštolac, Arčer, Niš, Silistra, Troesmis and Oescus. Most of these eventually became *municipia* or *coloniae*. The earliest was established near modern Skopje in the Flavian period, probably on or near the site of an abandoned legionary fortress. Some domestic houses have been investigated, as well as the theatre, but a disastrous earthquake in AD 518, which destroyed most of the city, has made research difficult. Under Trajan another new colony was established at Arčer, which, as with Skopje, may also have been a fortress. Yet another important centre was Niš, which may even have received its colonial status at an earlier date; it flourished especially in the early fourth century, when it enjoyed the patronage of Constantine I who had been born there. Of the other cities which developed, most did so along the line of the Danube where the chief military bases lay. Among this group, Koštolac (Viminacium) became the seat of provincial administration at first for all Moesia, later for Superior. The town was advanced to municipal status under Hadrian and given colonial rank in the third century. Little is known about the ancient city. In Moesia Inferior, the senior and, for a long time, the only city was Gigen (Oescus) on the Danube, which became a *colonia* under Trajan, after the transfer of its legion to a new base. It has been presumed that it occupied the site of the fortress and would almost certainly have contained the residence of the governor. Recent excavations have established that the city was irregular in outline and defended by a wall and ditch. One of the main streets has been identified, as also two aqueducts which brought water to the city.

The province profited from its position along the river and by its connections across the Black Sea, especially with the Greek colonies along the northern shore. Although not rich in mineral resources, the region was fertile along the Danube and produced quantities of cereals and other fruit and vegetables.

Pannonia

This province lay in the angle formed by the major southward dog-leg of the Danube. First Roman contact was made as early as 119 BC, although it was not until 35 BC that Octavian captured Siszek and there established a garrison. The next decades were turbulent with several wars and insurrections, of which that during the years 16–12 BC resulted in the Roman advance under Tiberius to the Danube. Further disturbances occurred down to 8 BC, with another major rebellion in AD 6–9, after which the area ceased to be part of Illyricum and became a separate province under the jurisdiction of a consular legate. Under Trajan this new province was divided in two: Pannonia Superior was the larger and lay to the west with its capital at Carnuntum, while Inferior was smaller and lay to the east with its capital at Budapest. The former was governed by a consular legate, the latter by a praetorian, until Caracalla changed the boundaries so as to enlarge Inferior, when its governor was promoted to consular rank.

Although there were some early urban foundations in the interior of the province, notably Siszek and Szombathely – the latter founded as a colony under Claudius – it was not until the Flavian period that, along with the systematic development of the frontier, a more vigorous policy of urbanisation was instituted. Nevertheless, the two provincial capitals still had to wait until the principate of Hadrian for their promotion to *municipia*. The correct identification of the actual sites of these cities has not been easy, since recent research has shown that most legionary fortresses on the Rhine and Danube frontiers possessed not one but two civil settlements. At Carnuntum, the legionary fortress lies close to the south bank of the Danube and is surrounded by its own *canabae*, in which were also situated the legionary *ludus*, a bath-house and numerous other buildings, including a large porticoed market place; since the last contained several wells, it has been suggested that it was a cattle market, for cattle formed one of the principal trades of the area. The *municipium* was situated a little distance south-west of the fortress and possessed its own, much larger, amphitheatre, capable of accommodating an estimated crowd of 13,000. The centre, with its forum and basilica, has not been identified. The most important building so far to be investigated is the so-called palace, or *praetorium* of the governor, situated on the bank of the Danube, along which an impressive architectural façade was created. It was supposedly from this building that Marcus Aurelius conducted his war against the Marcomanni, and it was from here that Septimius Severus, while governor of Pannonia Superior, embarked on his campaigns in the civil war of AD 193 which were to lead him ultimately to Rome as emperor. Apart from its strategic military value, the site at Carnuntum was also important as it lay on the 'amber' route from the south Baltic to north Italy at the point where it crossed the Danube; this no doubt increased its prosperity.

Aquincum (Budapest), like Carnuntum, became a legionary fortress under the Flavians, with the *municipium*, promoted by Hadrian, lying a short distance north of it, on the west bank of the river; the fortress, as at Carnuntum, also possessed its own *canabae*. Of the fortress and the *canabae*, little remains to be seen, except the bath-house below some modern buildings and the amphitheatre and some private houses in the *canabae*. As at Carnuntum, the legate's palace has been partly excavated, revealing a huge and elaborate building with internal courtyards and gardens, a bath suite and an imposing frontal architectural façade, situated on a sometime island in the Danube, between the fortress and the river. The main dining-room was situated in the centre of the riverside wing, so enjoying excellent views over the river. It is also known that the two principal streets of the *municipium* were lined with colonnades, while the forum, basilica, a bath-house and a market hall have been identified. The fortifications separate the city from its own, smaller amphitheatre, while the remains of the shrine, which stood over the source of the aqueduct supplying the city with water, have been preserved. The city was advanced to colonial rank under Severus. Perhaps, though, the most interesting relics to come from the site are the bronze parts of a portable water organ.

Germania

The Rhine was reached by Caesar in his Gallic campaigns and became, for a time, the limit of Roman conquest. Augustus entertained the idea of advancing the frontier to the river Elbe, with a corresponding expansion northwards from the Danube, although, after the Varus disaster in AD 9, he abandoned the scheme, and a strip of territory west of the Rhine was organised as a military zone containing eight legions under the command of two legates, one in Lower, the other in Upper Germany. Civilian administration was, however, left in the hands of the governor of Gallia Belgica. Under Vespasian and Domitian the frontier of Upper Germany was pushed beyond the river to include the Taunus and the so-called Agri Decumates, supposedly to shorten lines of communication between the Rhine and Danube, and to cut off the awkward, funnel-shaped re-entrant between the headwaters of the two rivers. Domitian, *c.* AD 90, organised the two areas formally into separate provinces, each under its own consular legate, although their financial affairs continued to be handled by the procurator of Belgica. Trajan reduced overall the number of legions in the two provinces to two; Hadrian marked the frontier of Upper Germany by a large palisade; Antoninus Pius advanced the Hadrianic frontier along the length leading southwards from the river Main. But after the invasions of *c.* 263, all land east of the Rhine was evacuated, and the river once more became the empire's boundary.

The capitals, respectively, of Germania Superior and Germania Inferior were Mainz and Cologne. Mainz was first used by Augustus as a double-legion camp, which in the early first century AD became a permanent fortress for the same number of legions. Only after the Civilis revolt was its size reduced to accommodate one. A civil settlement began to develop during the first century in the area between the fortress and the Rhine; it became the seat of the provincial governor. Although it did not receive municipal status until the middle of the fourth century, when it was also fortified, it developed, as far as it is known, along the normal lines for a town in the north-western empire. The only major public building to have been excavated is the amphitheatre, which was one of the largest in Gaul and Germany; remnants of the military aqueduct serving the fortress have also survived. Some form of triumphal monument must also have existed, probably to commemorate Domitian's successful campaigns, since fragments of it have been found.

As at Mainz, so at Cologne, the earliest Roman presence was marked by a double-legionary camp. It also became the capital of the Ubii, a friendly tribe who were transported westwards across the Rhine by Agrippa for their own protection. Here was also built an altar dedicated to *ara Romae et Augusti*, perhaps intended, as at Lyon, to become the centre of emperor worship for Germany. The legionary fortress was evacuated towards the end of the principate of Tiberius, although the *classis Germanica* remained in garrison nearby. Under Claudius the settlement was granted a colonial charter and received fortifications. It became the seat of the governor of Germania Inferior under Domitian. The street system of the ancient city coincides well with that of the modern, especially the principal north-south axis which, until comparatively recently, ran out through the Roman north gate. A number of major buildings have been excavated and include a bath-house, a Mithraeum, a shrine to the Matrones and a temple of Mercury and Augustus, as well as private houses. The legate's palace, as at Carnuntum, occupied a central position in the city's river frontage, once again presenting an imposing architectural façade and providing views over the river for the occupants. It was probably no accident that these great buildings were placed in such positions as would impress unconquered 'barbarians' across the frontier with the might and splendour of Rome. Parts of the aqueduct which served the city have also been investigated. Cologne eventually established a considerable reputation for its industries, which included glass and pottery-making, jewellery in precious metals, and, more specialised, carving in British jet, which must have been imported for the purpose. The products of these industries were traded widely over the western Empire, by way of the Rhine, which like its nearby sister river the Danube acted as a major artery in the system of communications on the European mainland. In the third century Cologne became the capital of the short-lived Gallic Empire.

Mauretania

This was the area of north Africa which stretched westwards from Numidia to the Atlantic coast. Much of it was mountainous and, indeed, communications between the western and eastern parts were never satisfactory or reliable, resulting in Tingitana's tighter bonds with Spain. Caesar campaigned briefly in the region, while Augustus established Roman control over much of the coastal strip, founding some *coloniae* along it. But much of the inland area was at first entrusted to a sequence of client kings, most notably Juba II, who became a Roman citizen and married into the reigning Egyptian dynasty. His son and successor was murdered by Gaius, after which the area became an imperial province in AD 40. Even then it was not fully pacified until after a Roman campaign in AD 41–42 had taken place. Thereupon Claudius on his accession split it in two: Mauretania Caesariensis to the east, Mauretania Tingitana to the west. Both were administered by procurators, with their capitals at Cherchel and Tangiers respectively; neither contained legions. The physical separation between the two provinces became most pronounced in the late Empire, when, under Diocletian, Tingitana was attached to the Spanish diocese.

The capital of Caesariensis at Cherchel was first fully developed on a Graeco-Roman model by Juba II; it received colonial status under Claudius. It possessed an excellent harbour, partly protected by an off-shore island, on which a lighthouse was erected, and it contained the full range of public buildings to be expected in such a city, although they are mostly inadequately recorded: amphitheatre, theatre, temples, baths, aqueducts. The theatre appears to have been adjacent to the forum. Recent small-scale excavations, though, have at least established something of the sequence of development, which showed its origins in a small Punic town.

The Roman city of Tangiers, capital of Tingitana, was also founded on an ancient site, reputed to have dated from a Phoenician settlement. In the civil war, its inhabitants had supported Octavian, subsequently receiving Roman citizenship for their services. Then the city was attached to Spain for administrative purposes. With the reorganisation of this part of north Africa by Claudius, it was given the rank of a *colonia* and became the capital of the newly created province. Little is known about the ancient site, since it is completely covered by existing buildings, although its limits can be gauged by the circle of cemeteries which surrounded it.

Other provincial cities are better recorded than these two capitals of Mauretania, and a number developed and prospered during the Roman period. Not far east of Cherchel, in Caesariensis, was Tipasa, which gained some Latin rights under Claudius, and was promoted to *colonia* by Hadrian. An inscription dates its fortifications to the mid-second century; they were erected as a protection against an impending Moorish attack. The forum, basilica and capitol, as well as some sumptuous private houses have been excavated. Together with its harbour, it made a highly attractive site in its Mediterranean setting. Among the other cities of Tingitana, the inland site of Volubilis is perhaps best preserved and recorded. Again a settlement with possible Phoenician, and certainly Carthaginian, origins, it seems from the first to have developed as a planned city. It received municipal rights and citizenship under Claudius. Most of the major public buildings have been identified, the earliest forum dating to the time of Nero, but the site is probably better known for its domestic dwellings of high quality, mostly constructed in an adapted-Italian manner with peristyles, mosaics, frescoes and statuary. A major bronze-working industry seems to have grown up, for which the city achieved a degree of fame. It was fortified during the Antonine period, which was also its time of greatest prosperity.

Although neither province contained large areas of cultivated land, good pastures existed for flocks and herds, while olives were grown everywhere. Wine, fish – and fish sauce – fruit, some cereals, and some good-quality marbles provided both provinces with an economic base.

Britain

Caesar mounted two campaigns in Britain in consecutive years as a side-show to his Gallic Wars, but permanent occupation only came under Claudius in AD 43, although both Augustus and Gaius toyed with the idea of invasion. Nevertheless, it took the Roman army some forty years to push its conquests to a logical conclusion, after which the province was roughly divided between military and civil zones. Much of the south-east, East Anglia and the Midlands was demilitarised and provided with a system of local administration resembling that of Gaul, where Iron Age tribes were organised into *civitates*, with a series of towns acting as centres. Although it has often been argued, probably incorrectly, that Colchester was intended to be the capital of the province, there is clear evidence to show that this function had devolved upon London by the end of the first century AD; nevertheless, the centre for the imperial cult remained at Colchester, where the huge temple dedicated to Claudius, founder of the province, was the focus. A vigorous policy of excavations in London over the last three decades has revealed much of the capital's street system and some public buildings, including the forum and basilica, part of a large bath-house, a Mithraeum, domestic housing and, perhaps most interesting of all, a succession of quays along the north bank of the Thames, together with the bridge-head for the earliest London Bridge; a suburb on the south bank is also known. The governor's residence, as with those on the Rhine, Danube and Euphrates, was likewise situated near the centre of the city's southern boundary along the river front; it contained several monumental features. Unusually, also, for a major civilian city in the west, a large fort was built on the outskirts under Hadrian, which probably accommodated troops connected with the provincial administration.

Apart from London, thought to have been at least a *municipium*, Britain contained four other *coloniae* and one probable *municipium*, of which Colchester was the premier city; the last, and the later first-century foundations of Gloucester and Lincoln were veteran colonies. York was promoted to colonial status in the early third century, and in many ways resembled some similar sites on the Rhine and Danube frontiers, where it existed in conjunction with the legionary fortress and its *canabae*, and was physically separated from them by the river Ouse. Verulamium was probably given municipal status in the first century, although the next largest town in the province to London developed at Cirencester.

But the most remarkable distinction in which Britain scored over all other provinces lay in its two northern frontier systems: Hadrian's Wall and the Antonine Wall. Although they were very different from each other, nothing quite like either was ever built anywhere else. Its other distinction was less enviable: it contained the largest garrison for its size of any province in the Empire.

Abundant pasture and cultivated land, associated with a well-developed villa system, provided the province's main economic base, although there was not insignificant mineral wealth, of which silver was probably most valuable. Small quantities of gold were mined in Wales, while iron was ubiquitous, giving rise to a flourishing industry. The famous tin, which had given the islands their earliest name of Cassiterides, was only sought in the first and again in the fourth century, by which time the Spanish mines were nearing exhaustion.

In the early third century the province was divided in two: Superior with its capital at London, Inferior with a capital at York. The latter city is but imperfectly known, for, despite an intensive sequence of recent excavations, little of it has emerged. Severus made York his headquarters during his Scottish campaigns and parts of a building thought to be the imperial palace lie under the old railway station, while Constantine I was hailed emperor in the city or fortress.

Dacia

The area north of the Danube, roughly corresponding to modern Transylvania, was not united under a common monarchy until *c.* 60 BC, and then became a serious threat to Rome. Caesar contemplated action just before his death, while Augustus attempted diplomatic solutions in the light of the Dacians' then waning military power. But that power was soon restored by a new king, Decebalus, who twice defeated a Roman army, until brought to battle by Domitian. Domitian's success, after which Decebalus ruled as a client, was not permanent and Trajan had again to take the field against him, in a series of campaigns which are depicted on his famous column in Rome. After these wars the area was finally reduced to the status of a province and provided with a garrison. Hadrian twice made administrative divisions, first into Superior and Inferior, and then between Superior and Porolissensis. Later, in the middle of the second century, all three provinces were placed under one governor.

Although some areas of the province obviously remained under military jurisdiction, notably the *limes Porolissensis*, a number of cities were promoted of which Sarmizegetusa, the ancient Dacian capital, was given colonial status and became the provincial capital. It was colonised by Roman citizens, and an inscription has been discovered which recorded its foundation. It was early fortified by Trajan for protection against border raids. Some of its public buildings have been recognised, including the forum and basilica, an extramural amphitheatre, and a number of temples. The governor's palace has also been identified. In the third century when Dacia was invested by invaders, the amphitheatre was fortified as a useful citadel, more easily defended than the long length of city wall.

The other important city in Dacia was Apulum. Roman occupation began with a legionary fortress in conjunction with which *canabae* developed. Under Marcus Aurelius this settlement, on the south side of the fortress, was given municipal status and was advanced to colonial rank under Commodus. It would seem, though, that further *canabae* were constructed on the north and east sides of the fortress, which were awarded their own, separate municipal charter by Severus, eventually reaching full colonial status. This second city is better known and either the buildings themselves, or inscriptions, attest the full range of public structures. Numerous workshops have been revealed, some obviously run for the residential legion, while a further series of inscriptions refer to various *collegia* connected with these industries. When the original province was divided, Apulum contained the residence of the governor of Superior, and ultimately that of the governor of the three Dacias.

Dacia contained, next to Spain, some of the richest gold mines in the Empire, producing almost legendary wealth, and there are records of skilled miners migrating to the province. Silver and iron mines were also brought into production. But this was not enough to save the province and, after the disastrous invasions in the middle of the third century, it was abandoned by Aurelian; henceforth the frontier remained on the Danube, even though in the fourth century the name Dacia was given to two new provinces carved out of Moesia along the southern bank of the river, which received the refugees from the evacuated area.

Italy

The ultimate reduction of Italy to provincial status was a slow process, started by Augustus and completed under the Tetrarchy, when it lost its immunity from taxation. The process began when Augustus organised the peninsula into eleven administrative districts, which naturally excluded Rome. These ran from the natural boundary of the Alps in the north to the toe of the peninsula, but excluded the off-shore islands, and covered what in the north had once been called Gallia Cisalpina. Domitian next interfered with the so-called free cities in Italy, by creating imperial *curatores* to oversee financial matters. Hadrian advanced the system by introducing four consular *correctores* and also *iuridici*, while under Diocletian two *vicarii* governed northern and southern parts respectively; the latter then included Sicily, Sardinia and Corsica, and each region was administered by a *corrector*, who had the powers and duties of a regular governor.

Numidia

The last major province to be constituted in the west was Numidia, after Severus separated the old kingdom from the province of Africa Proconsularis. The chief city seems to have been Cirta (Constantine) on the coast, which appears to have been given colonial status at the time of Caesar. It became the administrative centre for a curious federation of four neighbouring *coloniae;* when that was dissolved it became under Diocletian capital of Numidia Cirtenses and finally capital of all Numidia. In the interim periods, Numidia was governed by the legate of *Legio III* stationed at Lambaesis, which became the provincial capital, the *canabae* being given municipal status by Severus. It grew to the east of the fortress and contained many fine buildings, among them an arch of Commodus, an amphitheatre and a meat market, a reminder, perhaps, of the area's dependence on grazing land for transhuming nomads. Under Rome, the province was also encouraged to plant olive trees, and few farms, and even some urban houses, were without their oil presses.

The foregoing accounts in this and the preceding chapter can only provide the bare bones of Roman provincial expansion. Neither must it be forgotten that the arrangements herein described were by no means static. The high imperial period saw some provinces sub-divided, a move which was to reach its zenith in the late Empire, when most provinces were so dealt with and when an entirely new system of provincial organisation was introduced. These later developments, often of a highly complicated nature, can sometimes only be traced in outline; even when better evidence survives, difficulties of interpretation still abound. These changes will be reviewed in Chapter XIII.

XII

THE EMPIRE DIVIDED: CIVIL WARS

One of the great weaknesses of both the Roman Republic and principate was the misfortune to have indulged, from time to time, in disastrous civil wars. As an occasional blood-letting operation it may have removed some internal stresses and strains, as when the principate was created around Augustus, but the long-term and cumulative effect was disastrously to weaken the Empire's ability to withstand external attack.

As outlined in Chapter I, the last days of the Roman Republic were punctuated by increasingly serious civil wars, as the contestants, virtually with their own private armies, sought supreme power. Two such contests mark most clearly the Republic's end: Caesar v. Pompey and Octavian v. Antony.

The first began when Pompey, with some hesitation, added his support to Caesar's enemies in the Roman senate; as a result Caesar was ordered to surrender his command in Gaul. He refused and in 49 BC took the final step which could only result in direct conflict: he crossed the river Rubicon with his army. The Rubicon was the southern provincial boundary of Gaul and by this action he was in immediate violation of the law which restricted the military operations of a governor to his province. Nevertheless he rapidly overran Italy, although Pompey escaped to Greece. For the time being he abandoned pursuit and retraced his steps before going on to Spain, where he completely defeated the Pompeian forces arrayed against him. The next year, having returned to Italy, Caesar crossed to Greece and, after some confused fighting in which his forces suffered some casualties, Pompey was brought to battle at Pharsalus, and was completely defeated. But Pompey again slipped away and fled to Egypt, where he was assassinated on landing. Caesar, in pursuit of him, instead became involved in a war with Pompey's Egyptian allies. Having defeated them and placed Cleopatra, his mistress and nomineee, on the Egyptian throne, he retired through Asia Minor, dealing with Pompeian

235

opposition as he went, before returning again to Rome. In 47 BC, he was forced to turn towards north Africa, where a Pompeian army under Scipio was still holding out; it was beaten at the battle of Thapsus, which strictly marked the end of this civil war. Nevertheless, two years later a resurgence of Pompeian supporters in Spain again required his presence and again he was successful. Having secured for himself by force of arms the highest military power in Rome, when he was made *dictator*, initially for a period, later for life, he was still not able equally to hold full political power.

Few great generals have ever made good politicians. The Duke of Wellington was a hopeless prime minsiter, while more recently Eisenhower, a reasonable president of the USA, had not shown well as the supreme commander of allied forces in north Africa and Europe. Neither was Caesar's generalship proof against his lack of political understanding, even though outwardly he attempted to placate his political opponents through his policy of 'clemency'. Although his commentaries on his wars contain some propaganda, he emerges as an essentially uncomplicated man, possibly even somewhat naive, to whom the most straightforward and simple solution usually appealed: a simple 'soldier-man'! Hence he seems to have remained unaware of the conspiracy mounting against him and fell to the assassins' knives in 44 BC.

Although, for a short time, Rome was quiet after Caesar's death, the divisions which the civil war had opened in the Roman leadership not only remained but also continued to widen, if at first only just perceptibly. A new face appeared, that of Caesar's great-nephew, Octavian. Scarcely twenty years old when Caesar was murdered, he found himself Caesar's heir and adopted son; he determined on revenge. Although he gained powerful allies in the Senate, including Cicero, he was not so popular with Antony, and was only awarded the consulship through the power of his army. A temporary compromise with Antony enabled him to secure a grip on an increasing number of western provinces, which was later followed by Antony's marriage to his sister. The re-emergence of Pompey the younger, on the side of Antony, from a Sicilian base, to which he had been outlawed after making a pact with Octavian, led to further hostilities along the old lines of loyalty: Caesar's successors against Pompey's. Both were inherited struggles, and carried with them something of later Italian vendettas. Octavian himself suffered some reverses, notably off Taormina, but his friends, Agrippa and Lepidus, were more successful and after a further battle S. Pompeius was forced to flee to Asia where he was put to death. The relationship between Antony and Octavian was then patched up and the triumvirate, which they shared with Lepidus, was renewed. But Lepidus was forced into retirement, leaving Antony and Octavian as the two central protagonists.

Octavian had meanwhile gained more and more support in Italy and from the Roman aristocracy to add to his already existing power base in the western provinces; this contrasted with Antony's reliance on the eastern provinces, more especially Egypt, against which war was declared by Rome. When the triumvirate was not renewed, it again became a question of two individuals, each with his own army, each facing the other in a contest, the result of which would leave the survivor master of Rome and all the provinces. The inevitable battle took place at sea off the promontory of Actium in north-western Greece in 31 BC; Octavian was triumphant. Thus a major civil war which saw the effective end of the true Roman Republic ushered in at the same time a new and invigorated era of Roman ascendency in the ancient world.

With the conferment of the title of Augustus upon Octavian and the establishment of the principate, Rome entered upon a period of peace and prosperity unseen for many decades. So long as the line of succession remained firmly in the hands of the Julio-Claudian dynasty all seemed well, despite the peculiarities of Tiberius, the paranoia and murder of Gaius and the physical disabilities of Claudius. Even Nero's principate set out well, although it rapidly degenerated until he was hated not only by all classes, but also by the army. By antagonising the army, Nero forfeited his power; moreover he had entirely failed to secure a dynastic successor. Rebellions against him were started by the governors of Spain, Africa and Lugdunensis. The defection of the Praetorian Guard caused Nero to flee from Rome and ultimately to commit suicide in AD 68, to be supplanted by Galba, governor of Tarraconensis, and so began one of the most disastrous civil wars of the principate, during the time usually referred to as the Year of the Four Emperors.

Backed by the Praetorians, Galba took the title of Caesar and, with his provincial garrison, marched on Rome, accompanied by Otho, his fellow governor of Lusitania. Galba rapidly lost the support of the army by his meanness and moreover insulted Otho by appointing another man as his successor; at least he realised the necessity for naming one, not that it did him a great deal of good. Otho, once again backed by the influential Praetorians, quietly murdered Galba and was hailed emperor in his place. But already another contestant was making his mark. Vitellius, commanding the garrison of Lower Germany, where he had been sent by Galba, had already been hailed emperor by his own troops and by those in Upper Germany, Spain, Raetia and Britain. Otho, in contrast, could depend on the loyalty of the legions on the rest of the Danube and Euphrates as well as Egypt and Africa, although the nearest of them were too slow in coming to his aid. Encamped on the line of the river Po, his forces were able to inflict a minor defeat on Vitellius' advance guard, but with the arrival of the main force from the Rhine, Otho was totally defeated at the battle of Bedriacum, near Cremona, in April 69; he committed suicide and so Vitellius became emperor.

237

Meanwhile in the east, Vespasian, the commander of the army in Syria and Judaea, who had been sent to suppress the Jewish rebellion, had decided at first to accept Galba. But on hearing of his murder, Vespasian and the governor of neighbouring Syria ostensibly transferred their allegiance to Otho, while at the same time planning a coup against him. This was accelerated when the two Egyptian legions openly hailed Vespasian as emperor, soon followed by their confederates in Judaea and Syria. Shortly afterwards the Danubian legions declared for Vespasian as well and, advancing on Italy, defeated the Vitellian forces at Cremona. After their victory, they reached Rome on the day following that on which Vitellius had been put to death. Vespasian, when he arrived in Rome, was immediately accepted as emperor by the Senate, and so began the Flavian dynasty.

There was, however, a less desirable side-effect of Vespasian's accession. His principal supporter on the Danube had invoked the support of G. Julius Civilis, a Roman citizen of Batavian origin, who had probably served in an auxiliary regiment. He was asked to create a diversion on the lower Rhine to prevent reinforcements being sent to aid Vitellius. Civilis used this request as a pretext for starting his own war against Rome, for apparently he had personal grievances against the government. With the help of some German tribes across the Rhine and some Gallic tribes, he destroyed the double legionary fortress at Xanten as well as a large number of auxiliary forts along the frontier; the legion at Neuss came out in his favour. But the arrival of Vespasian's general Petillius Cerealis, with fresh units, encompassed his defeat, thought not before the repercussions had affected Britain, to which province Cerealis had been assigned as governor. The situation in Britain had been one of uncertainty. Before the civil war had broken out, the legions had expelled the governor and were in a mutinous state. Vitellius had sent a replacement, whose loyalty to Vespasian was obviously in question. The delay in the arrival of Cerealis, due to the revolt of Civilis, brought about conditions in which a major Brigantian chief took direct action against his wife, Cartimandua, an ally of Rome. With an unreliable army and governor, it would appear that the aid of the client king, Cogidubnus, was invoked to hold the province until a reliable Vespasianic governor could take over.

The Year of the Four Emperors, therefore, had far-reaching effects, involving the eastern provinces, Egypt, the Danube, the Rhine, Gaul and Britain as well as Rome and Italy. In Rome the temple of Jupiter had been burnt, the city of Cremona had been twice fought over and sacked, most of the forts and fortresses of the lower German frontier had been burnt, Gallic tribes thought peaceful had revolted, Britain was in disarray, tribes beyond the German frontier had been encouraged to attack; only Africa west of Egypt appears to have been untouched. Yet when all was said and done and Vespasian had taken energetic measures to restore the damage, the overall effect on the Empire was probably good. The Julio-Claudian dynasty was exhausted; apart from Augustus, and perhaps Claudius, its members had not enjoyed exactly distinguished careers. The Empire needed a tonic to refresh it and the little-known Flavian family, although newly recruited from the equestrian to the senatorial order, provided it. If the cost was high, the Empire could at the time afford it, in terms of both money and manpower.

The Flavian dynasty, despite the 'reign of terror' imposed by Domitian, advanced the cause of Rome. But the murder of Domitian, without an acknowledged successor, could have started yet another civil war. Fortunately a short-term compromise was found in the person of Nerva, who, though acceptable to the Senate, had little support in the army. Fortunately also, Nerva had the foresight to adopt a serving soldier as his heir, for six months later he was dead.

From the time that Trajan was fully installed as emperor, until almost the end of the next century, Rome enjoyed its most prolonged period of internal peace, under a succession of enlightened and administratively efficient emperors. There were wars, but mainly on the frontiers, and some acquisitions of new territory occurred; indeed, under Trajan the Empire reached its maximum limits of expansion. There were also internal rebellions, such as a major uprising of the Jews, which caused a high loss of life. But they were contained and, since they did not greatly affect Italy, did not upset the stability of the state. It was not until the accession of Commodus, son of the emperor Marcus Aurelius, in 180, that this internal peace was once more seriously threatened.

Largely thanks to his father's protracted frontier campaigns, Commodus inherited an Empire which was mainly at peace and free from external threat. But he became again an emperor for whom absolute power corrupted absolutely; although not in any way related, he imitated the weaker members of the Julio-Claudian family and fell a victim to all the vices to which they had succumbed. As in the case of Nero, he also failed to secure his succession, so that, on his assassination in 192, the control of the Empire was once more open for bids from the strongest contestants. The first was Pertinax, who had made his mark as a soldier in Raetia and Britain and who was elevated by the Praetorian Guard. He was, though, a strict disciplinarian, which did not endear him to his supporters; they disposed of him in three months, and then 'auctioned off' the Empire to Didius Julianus. He proved equally unpopular, especially with the provincial garrisons, and within a short time the Danubian legions put up their own choice, Septimius Severus, governor of Upper Pannonia, which was matched by the army of Syria, who proposed their own governor, Pescennius Niger. As though three claimants were not sufficient, Clodius Albinus, governor of Britain, entered the lists, supported by his own army. Of the four, Severus undoubtedly wielded the greatest power, which was augmented when the fickle Praetorian Guard disposed of Didius Julianus, and declared their loyalty to him. Severus clearly saw Niger as the greatest threat to his aims, so Albinus was pacified by the award of the title Caesar, while Severus turned his attention to the east, having first secured Rome behind him. Three times he defeated the forces placed against him by Niger in Thrace and Asia Minor until finally they were overwhelmed near Antioch; fleeing eastwards Niger was caught and killed, and his main base, Syria, divided in two, in order to prevent a recurrence, whereby a powerful governor, with a large legionary backing, could threaten Rome and the emperor. Severus, having disposed of Niger, was then able to return westwards to face Albinus.

Albinus must have found himself in a difficult position. His army was nowhere as large as that of Severus, even though he could count on assistance from Spain. If he stayed in Britain, he would probably be safe from attack, but unable to further his ambition to become emperor, even though he had been recently hailed Augustus by his legions. He prepared, therefore, to cross to Gaul with his army, hoping to gain the loyalty of the German garrisons. They failed him and he was forced to accept battle with Severus, outside Lyon, in February, 197. His army was defeated and he himself appears to have been killed in the battle, so leaving Severus in undisputed control of the Empire. The immediate effect of this part of the civil war was the nearly complete destruction of the city of Lyon, which never fully recovered its prestige, yielding precedence in Gaul to Trier. Britain, like Syria, was also divided in two.

But this civil war did far more damage than the Year of the Four Emperors, since Severus appears to have carried on a vindictive campaign against the supporters of his sometime adversaries, even going to war with Parthia, because they had supported Niger. In both Spain and Britain, as well as in the east, many of them had their land sequestrated, which in some respects was sufficient to upset the economic viability of these provinces; what happened to the landowners can only be guessed, but the overall effect must have been to liquidate a large proportion of the land-owning class, so inevitably weakening the stock from which the natural leaders such as magistrates, decurions and other local and provincial officials were drawn; it could well have affected the quality of recruits to the army. Severus also disbanded the Praetorian Guard as untrustworthy and capricious – which they had been – and replaced them with a new guard recruited from all the legions. He also reduced the importance of the senate by supporting instead members of the equestrian order for a whole new series of administrative posts which he introduced, in his eagerness to exert more influence over affairs of state. A further effect was caused by the numerous battle casualties of the civil war which weakened the army, especially the legions, at a time when manpower resources were beginning to become critical. This led directly to an increase in the non-Roman elements of the army, and a consequent reduction in the power of the legions, a change which was to be accelerated during the ensuing century. If the civil war after Nero's death can be said on balance to have brought long-term benefits to Rome, the same is not true of this one. Indeed it can be argued that it was the watershed which separated the full-grown power and might of Rome from its ultimate end, over two centuries later.

If it can be said that Severus lived and prospered by the sword, he escaped the normal fate attributed to those who do, dying in York of sickness and exhaustion following his Scottish campaigns; he was the last emperor to die in his bed for a long time. But his sons reaped the reward which justly should have been their father's. Geta was murdered (no. 1)* by his elder brother, Caracalla, who was himself assassinated (no. 2) in 217 by Macrinus, subsequently hailed emperor by his army.

Macrinus was the first emperor of Rome not to have been a senator, and may be said to have initiated the long period of near-anarchy which the Empire suffered in the third century; his reign lasted scarcely a year, when he was murdered (no. 3) in turn in favour of Elagabalus, an off-shoot of the Severan dynasty, who was dominated by his mother. Both mother and son (no. 4) fell to the Praetorians four years later, when Severus Alexander, having been earlier adopted as heir, succeeded to the throne. Again overshadowed by his mother, who was one of the formidable series of women connected to the Severan dynasty, both met their deaths (no. 5), after his comparatively lengthy reign – for the times – of thirteen years, at the hands of the German garrisons for adopting a peaceful approach towards some local tribes. This mutiny in 235 threw up Maximinus as emperor, a man who had begun life as a Thracian peasant, and who had been rapidly promoted to the equestrian order. But the Senate refused to recognise him and opted instead for the aged Gordian I (governor of Africa Proconsularis) and his son as joint emperors, after a rebellion in Africa had elevated them. Even though Maximinus invaded Italy, he made little progress and a change of heart in his own army resulted in his murder (no. 6). But the governor of Numidia remained loyal to Maximinus and succeeded in killing Gordian's son in battle (no. 7), after which Gordian himself (no. 8) committed suicide in 238, having reigned twenty-two days.

The Senate's next choice fell on Balbinus and Pupienus, who among others had been appointed to defend Italy against Maximinus. They took as a junior confederate Gordian III, grandson of Gordian I, who was given the title of Caesar. Once more the Praetorians struck, declining to accept the Senate's

---

* The numbers in parentheses in the following paragraphs refer to the emperors who died mostly violent deaths.

nominees, and mutinied, killing both Augusti (nos 9 and 10). But they spared the thirteen-year-old Gordian III and hailed him as Augustus, with the praetorian prefect acting as regent. A successful campaign in the east against the Persians resulted in the prefect's death, and Gordian appointed Philip, of Arabic origin, in his place. It was an unwise step, since Philip rapidly developed ambitions for imperial power; on a pretext, approved by Philip, Gordian who was still only a boy was murdered (no. 11) in 244. Philip, however, was acceptable to the Senate, and scored some military successes on the Danube, after which his son was also raised to the rank of Augustus. But the Goths had begun to raid the Empire and Philip appointed the City prefect, Decius, to the command of the army on the lower Danube facing their invasion; this same army forced Decius to become emperor, despite the intervention of three other very minor usurpers (nos 12, 13 and 14), and Philip and his son were killed (nos 15 and 16).

By now external threat was being added to internal dissent in the Empire, although whether the former was caused by the latter is difficult to judge. What was more marked, though, was the increasing inability of the Empire to cope with its frontier problems in its present state. Even in the high imperial period, a major threat on more than one frontier at once was not easy to contain because of the lack of a central reserve. Now, with the waxing Persia replacing the weakened and defunct Parthia in the east and the arrival of the Goths on the Danube, the position changed dramatically for the worse. Decius himself was defeated and finally killed by the Goths (no. 17) in 251. Despite Decius' recognised claim, no less than five other claimants received a greater or lesser degree of recognition in the years 250–253; the last, Aemilianus, reigned for only three months after he had been elevated by his own army in Moesia, having just repelled a Gothic invasion. To show how deeply divided opinion was on the promotion of an emperor, Aemilianus, governor of the province, was put forward in opposition to the candidature of one of his own legates, Trebonianus Gallus, whose claim had been staked after Decius' death in battle. But however they were appointed, the end was for all the same: all died suddenly and brutally, often at the hands of those who had first promoted them (nos 18, 19, 20, 21 and 22).

Their place was taken by Valerian, a well-known senator, who was engaged in military operations in Raetia under Gallus, when he heard of Aemilianus' claim. Setting out to support Gallus' cause, he was hailed emperor himself when news of Gallus' death arrived, an action which caused the murder of Aemilianus by his own soldiers, and the universal acceptance of Valerian and his son Gallienus. Together or separately, they reigned for fifteen years, an incredibly long time in the circumstances, although their reign did not go entirely unchallenged. But their lengthy survival was the only remarkable aspect of their principate, since during it the Empire reached the nadir of its fortunes and ended almost on the point of collapse. It was beset by external invasions, notably of the Goths who penetrated both Bithynia and Asia, and the Persians who even reached and captured Antioch. Valerian himself set out to deal with the Persian invasion and after several years ineffective campaigning was captured by them in 259–260. His ultimate fate is unknown (no. 23), but what was left of the central Empire came to be ruled by his son for another eight years.

While Valerian lived, Gallienus had ruled in the west, where he had carried out some quite successful campaigns on the Rhine, on one occasion turning back an Alamannic invasion of Italy. On his father's death he left the eastern defences in the hands of local officers, to which the growing strength of Palmyra was added. In Pannonia, he defeated two usurpers, Ingenuus and Regalianus (nos 24,25). But the revolt of Postumus in 260 was more serious, since Gallienus completely lost control of Gaul and other western provinces in a bid which created a separate Gallic Empire, and which was ultimately recognised by Gallienus. Africa was also in a state of unrest, while the east threw up yet another usurper, Macrianus, who was nevertheless quickly defeated (no. 26) by Aureolus. In 267, further Gothic raids penetrated as far as Athens, which was sacked. In the meantime Aureolus (no. 27) had been hailed emperor by his troops, but he was quickly defeated in battle by Gallienus; the latter was then murdered by his officers (no. 28), who proclaimed Claudius II in his place. The principate of Gallienus was also noted for the appalling inflation which was added to the Empire's extreme difficulties; the currency depreciated to a point where it was virtually worthless and the repercussions were felt even in those provinces which had hitherto avoided the violence of the period.

Claudius II was a professional soldier of senior rank and he was able to stem the tide of Gothic progress in the Balkans, defeating them twice and breaking up their armies. But he was less successful in the east, where the power of Palmyra, under its self-proclaimed queen, Zenobia, had expanded as far as Egypt in the south and Bithynia in the north. His chief claim to fame, perhaps, is that he was the first of twenty-nine 'emperors' to die (no. 29) from a cause other than assassination, by disease in 270, having reigned for less than two years.

During a brief interlude Quintillus (no. 30) ruled, then Aurelian, commander of the cavalry under Claudius II, was elevated by his troops. He had already been successfully campaigning against the Goths, after which he was faced by other invasions on the Danube, the Vandals in Pannonia and the Juthungi in Italy. A visit to Rome saw the start of the great Aurelian Wall, for which he is chiefly famous, as a defence against barbarian attack. His next concern was to restore the Empire's unity, against which the most serious threat was then Palmyra. But before his campaign against Zenobia, he withdrew all troops from Dacia, together with a sizable band of refugees, who were settled on the south bank of the Danube in a new province of the same name; the old province was abandoned to the Goths. In the east he defeated the Palmyrene forces and their supporters and captured Zenobia; Palmyra was eventually deprived of its civic status. Turning westwards, he destroyed the Gallic Empire and captured its emperor, Tetricus, so reuniting all the Roman Empire under one central ruler. While engaged in all these campaigns, he had also dealt with three provincial usurpers (nos 31, 32 and 33). Finally, after setting out on a renewed campaign against Persia, he was killed by his own officers near Byzantium in 275.

The Gallic Empire, which Aurelian eliminated, had begun as a breakaway movement by Postumus against Gallienus in 260. The Empire included all Gaul and Germany as well as Britain and Spain. Although Postumus was successful in repelling invaders from across the Rhine, his Empire suffered from the same defect as that from which he broke away: assassination. In meeting the revolt of Laelianus at Mainz (no. 34), he was murdered by his own troops (no. 35) and replaced by Victorinus, whose reign lasted three years (no. 36). The latter was succeeded by Tetricus I, governor of Aquitania, who, with the assistance of his son, Tetricus II, survived uneasily until 274, when he appealed to Aurelian for assistance, deserting his army in the final battle. Although he featured – together with Zenobia – in Aurelian's great Roman triumph, he survived to be given a minor official post in Italy, together with his son (nos 37 and 38). So ended the Gallic Empire.

After Aurelian's death, the Senate's choice fell on one of its elder members, Tacitus, who was once more the victim of his own troops (no. 39), of whom his successor Florian was praetorian prefect. Claiming brotherhood, Florian grabbed the Empire, but was immediately challenged by Probus, a candidate of the Egyptian and Syrian armies. Florian was disposed of in the usual manner – by his own troops (no. 40).

Although Probus was faced by the usual quota of usurpers, among whom was Saturninus, a serious threat from the east (no. 41), he was able to contain them and also pursue the unfinished programme of Aurelian to strengthen the Empire. He repulsed the raids which penetrated deep into Gaul from across the Rhine, and started to repair and reorganise the river frontier; he defeated Vandals on the Danube and his forces dealt with an invasion of Egypt from the south. He also continued the earlier policy of settling barbarian peoples in deserted lands inside the Empire, notably in Thrace, although he was not so successful in his selection of barbarians. It is probably untrue to claim, as some have done, that there was more serious discontent in the army under Probus than before; the sequence of nearly forty emperors, mostly murdered by their *own* troops, indicates grave dissatisfaction going back over fifty years. Certainly a breakdown in discipline, coupled with the recruitment of more and more non-Romans, who owed very little loyalty to the Roman way of life, must have made a major contribution to the anarchic state of the army. Poor leadership, perhaps in combination with a watering down of the old 'officer' class – senators were no longer given commands, so that the experience gained by young officers passing through the *cursus honorum* was wasted by no longer appointing them to higher office – and by increased promotion through the ranks must equally have had some effect, although it is difficult to gauge how much. The falling value of the pay packet, given the rate of inflation, cannot have helped. Whether or not the fortunes of the Empire touched bottom under Probus, it made no difference to his final fate. The troops in Raetia proclaimed Carus, the praetorian prefect, emperor, whereupon Probus, like so many before him, was killed by his own men in 282 (no. 42).

Carus survived little more than a year. He marched from Raetia, leaving his son Carinus in charge of the west as Caesar, in order to take on the Persians. At first he was successful, capturing Ctesiphon, but, venturing further, was killed either by the Persians or by his own army (no. 43). Carinus, now Augustus, joined forces with his brother Numerian, who had been with Carus in the east. Numerian, having little stomach for continuing the Persian campaign, withdrew and was apparently murdered by his father-in-law and praetorian prefect at Nicomedia in 284 (no. 44). He was replaced by Diocletian. Carinus meanwhile had crushed the usurper, Julian (no. 45), only to be faced with a challenge from Diocletian, which he lost in 285 (no. 46).

With the advent of Diocletian, the fortunes of the Empire underwent a major recovery, but it must not be forgotten that both Aurelian and Probus had previously contributed to it; without their action on the frontiers and on imperial defence, Diocletian's task would have been that much greater. Although a Dalmatian of humble origin, Diocletian rose through the ranks to become commander of Numerian's bodyguard. He had shown himself not only to be a competent soldier but also a good organiser; he seems in addition to have had the gift of choosing loyal, reliable and efficient colleagues, unlike some of his predecessors. One of his first acts was to appoint an old comrade, Maximian, as Caesar in the west, promoting him to Augustus in the following year. Secondly he turned his attention, together with Maximian, to the serious problems of frontier defence, which they both addressed with energy and some success. But even now, the end to civil war had not been achieved. In Britain, Carausius proclaimed his own empire in 286–7, which survived until just after his murder (no. 47) by Allectus; the latter was defeated (no.48) finally by an invasion force mounted by the new western Caesar, Constantius Chlorus in 296. Finally, Diocletian himself put down a rebellion in Egypt, and for the first time in over sixty years the Empire knew peace from internal strife; in the meantime, excluding Diocletian and his colleagues, no less than

245

forty-eight people (the numbers above set in brackets) had aspired to be or had become emperor. Of those, one had died of disease, two had survived to take up a more peaceful existence; the remainder had met death in a violent form. Such was the toll taken of the Empire's resources. It is hardly surprising that the army which entered the third century scarcely resembled that which emerged at the century's end.

It was not to last. The Tetrarchy which Diocletian established to circumvent the difficulties of ensuring a peaceful succession worked well in the first instance, both Diocletian and Maximian retiring in favour of their respective Caesars, who replaced them as Augusti, on 1 May 305. But the following year Constantius died in York, and his son Constantine was hailed as Augustus by the British garrison in direct conflict with the claim of Severus, who had been Caesar to Constantius. Galerius, then Augustus in the east, reluctantly accepted Constantine as Caesar, but refused to disagree with Severus' claim to be Augustus. The position was then made more complicated by the rebellion of Maxentius, son of Maximian, who, having been passed over by his father, was promoted Augustus by the city of Rome; this enabled Maximian to end his retirement in order to support his son. When Severus advanced against them into Italy, he was defeated and forced to surrender, while Galerius, who had refused to recognise Maxentius, was a short time later similarly forced to retreat. At this point, Diocletian was recalled from retirement in order to help create a new settlement for the Empire, and, at Carnuntum in 308 Licinius was appointed an Augustus in place of Severus, Maximian was again forced to resign and Maxentius was outlawed.

Unfortunately neither of the two legitimate Caesars, Constantine and Maximinus Daia, was prepared to accept the titles offered, and both were hailed Augusti. In the meantime Maximian had tried to oust his son and had also successfully reclaimed Constantine's allegiance. Despite this, in 310 he eventually rebelled against Constantine and was forced to commit suicide. Galerius died in 311, and Constantine, professing himself an ally of Licinius, defeated Maxentius in the following year at Milvian Bridge. Finally, Licinius removed Maximinus Daia, the last surviving rival, and married Constantine's sister, by which act the Empire might have regained its internal peace, with Constantine ruling in the west and Licinius in the east, but with all traces of the Tetrarchy having been swept away by the intervening civil wars.

But again it was not to be. War broke out between them and Constantine made inroads into the domain of Licinius. In 323, Constantine had to take action against a Gothic invasion, which resulted in war once more being declared between the rival emperors. Constantine's great victories, at first at Adrianople and lastly at the Hellespont, forced Licinius' abdication and ultimate execution, leaving Constantine as sole ruler of the Empire; he survived until 337 and restored much of the Empire's fortunes in a period of comparative external peace, free from internal strife.

Although Constantine was forced to execute his eldest son, he gave the other three, Constantine II, Constantius II and Constans, each the title of Caesar, in the hope that they would enable a peaceful succession to take place on his death. His hopes proved false, and the Roman Empire was never again to know complete respite from internal warfare. Constantine II, who had inherited Britain, Gaul and Spain, rashly invaded Italy only three years after the death of his father in order to wrest Rome from his brother Constans. He was defeated and killed, and Constans was able to claim the whole western Empire as his own. But a usurper, Magnentius, was proclaimed emperor at Autun; he successfully defeated Constans, whom he murdered. His success, though, was short-lived. In making an attempt on the whole Empire, he was himself defeated by Constantius II and committed suicide two years later in 353.

Constantius II now ruled the entire Empire, and to assist him he first appointed Gallus, whom he executed, and then, Julian as Caesar: the latter to take charge of the western provinces. Julian rebelled against his authority, and Constantius II died, apparently a natural death, on his way to put down the revolt. Julian, therefore, became sole emperor in 361. At the time, war with Persia was anticipated and Julian, after initial successes, was killed in action, and one of his officers, Jovian, hailed emperor in his place. Jovian lasted but a year, and on his death the army picked Valentinian I to succeed him. He shared his rule with his brother Valens, who, having been allocated the east, was killed in 378 in battle with the Visigoths at Adrianople, some three years after the death of Valentinian. Meanwhile Valentinian's son Gratian had succeeded him to the throne, having been made joint Augustus in 367. Unfortunately for a peaceful accession, Gratian's brother Valentinian II was also declared emperor by his troops on his father's death, without the approval of either Valens or Gratian. Nevertheless, in an act of undoubted generosity for the age in which they lived, Italy, Africa and Illyricum were handed over to the new Augustus. Valens' death in action, therefore, left Gratian and Valentinian II as joint emperors, although they were joined by Theodosius I in the following year.

In 383 another serious rebellion threatened the Empire's stability, this time from Britain, where the commander of the garrison, Magnus Maximus, was hailed emperor. At once crossing to Gaul, he defeated Gratian, who was murdered in Lyon, and then expelled Valentinian II from Italy. Theodosius I recognised him as a colleague, until the time for dealing with him ripened, and allocated Britain, Gaul and Spain to his jurisdiction. Eventually brought to battle by Theodosius I, and resoundingly defeated, he was finally executed, while Valentinian II was restored to rule Gaul. By then Theodosius, emerging as the 'strong man' of the Empire, proclaimed as Augustus his elder son Arcadius and in the following year repeated the process with his younger son Honorius, whom he had taken with him to the west, leaving Arcadius to rule the east. His visit to the west was no accident of travel, for Eugenius had emerged as a usurper in 392, following the murder of Valentinian II. Theodosius not only refused him recognition, but also, having taken the field against him, defeated him without difficulty. But six months later, Theodosius himself was dead, leaving the Empire in the hands of his two sons. Unlike their father, both were weak and ineffectual; in the east Arcadius' ministers, Rufinus and Eutropius, were for a space in executive command, while in the west the great Vandal general, Stilicho, wielded the power; unfortunately Honorius ordered his execution in 408, thus destroying the one man who might have controlled future disasters.

After Stilicho had been removed, Honorius, safely ensconced at Ravenna, presided over the beginning of the final break-up of the western Empire. Rome was sacked, Britain was abandoned, and in consequence threw up three usurpers one after the other; Spain and much of Gaul were occupied by Vandals and other barbarians, who eventually overflowed into north Africa. Honorius died in 423 without nominating a successor, leaving the western Empire in tatters, a state from which it never fully recovered. He was, in fact, succeeded by Valentinian III, the son of Constantius III, a sometime colleague of Honorius, but as before, effective control – insofar as it could be effective – was in the hands, first of his mother, then of Aetius, until the latter was murdered by Valentinian's own hands; he was killed in turn, in 455, by two of Aetius' retainers. There followed a series of short-lived successors, of whom Anthemius was the most successful in staying alive, surviving for five years until he was beheaded, but to all other intents the western Empire was dead.

In the east, a more fortunate line of succession ensured survival until the advent of the House of Justin set the Byzantine Empire firmly on its future path.

It can be seen from the foregoing accounts that the effects of civil war on the Empire were manifold. To begin with, that which brought Augustus to power was beneficial, since it disposed of outmoded people and concepts and released Rome from the bonds that were preventing her from realising her full potential; at that stage Rome still had much to give the ancient world. Although it has been frequently disputed, even as recently as the Second World War, it is probably true to say that an Empire, a war or simply a battle cannot be effectively directed by a committee, even when all its members are in agreement, and the Senate and consuls of republican Rome seldom were. But the dividing line between a benevolent dictatorship, giving recognition to the needs of a democratic constitution, and a regime headed by one person who tramples rough-shod over all other institutions, has ever been a fine one; all shades of this spectrum can be seen in the succession of Roman emperors. Augustus probably came as near as any of them in getting the balance right; others like Trajan, Hadrian and Antoninus Pius were not far removed from it. But the reverse could be seen operating under Gaius, Nero, Domitian and Commodus. Even with them, it was fortunately the democratic functions which survived, not the man, since they found expression in the murder of the tyrant, even if, simultaneously, the Empire was plunged into a costly civil war.

However, the chances of conflict were in effect greatly increased as soon as more than one person was involved in running the Empire. This was indeed shown in the second century when Marcus Aurelius was the first emperor to have shared control with Lucius Verus, his adoptive brother. As he was a weak and vacillating man, Verus' death was probably a benefit rather than a loss, since his weakness could have permitted a stronger man, by climbing over Verus and using his troops, to challenge Aurelius. Fortunately on this occasion it did not happen. The next time power was split came with Severus and his two sons and ended disastrously for the Empire in the murder of Geta and the ultimate assassination of Caracalla, and might be said to have set in train the violent events of the third century. Even the Tetrarchy of Diocletian, aimed at better control of the Empire, could be argued with the benefit of hindsight to have been doomed from its outset, since it simultaneously allowed four men to have almost equal power and military strength. Sooner or later, it was bound to give way in internecine strife, which is precisely what happened in the first decade of the fourth century.

Only when the Empire was once more reunited under Constantine I was calm restored to internal affairs. Consequently it is possible to anticipate, again with the benefit of hindsight, what would happen on the death of Constantine, when, from then on, multiple rulers became the norm. Only with the demise of the western Empire and the unification of the east under a single ruler were the chances of survival of this rump enhanced. Had matters turned out differently in the west, and had it been blessed at the critical moment with a stronger ruler than Honorius, it is possible to postulate its separate survival in parallel with the east. But two rulers of equal strength, even if at first working together in a combined empire, could only mean the ultimate separation into two independent empires; it is not possible to say whether or not they would have remained in peaceful coexistence. But the march of history dictated otherwise and only one survived.

Many contributory factors played their part in the fall of the Roman Empire, and much argument has taken place as to which were the most important. Undoubtedly, though, as can be seen from the events described in this chapter, it would be unwise to under-estimate the effects which duplication, triplication – or more – of the internal command structures of the Empire had in promoting rivalry, dissent and, in the end, civil war, causing the gradual wastage of the Empire's resources until they were exhausted.

XIII

THE TETRARCHY AND AFTER

The anarchy produced in the third century has been considered in the preceding chapter. It may be said to have ended with the advent of Diocletian as emperor in 284. Although much of what follows below has already been anticipated in outline in Chapters III and IV, it can now be seen in greater detail and in a better context.

Diocletian was probably the first emperor who not only realised what lay behind the series of crises of the third century, but who also initiated remedial actions. One critical factor was the inability of reigning emperors to ensure a peaceful succession to a predetermined heir. The other was that Diocletian now deemed the Empire to be too large and too complex for one man to control adequately; one wonders what a Trajan of a Hadrian would have made of this decision! The solution which he first proposed to solve both factors involved the appointment of an old army friend, Maximianus, as Caesar with military responsibilities in the west; a year later Maximian was raised to the constitutionally equal position of Augustus, although Diocletian claimed superior authority as the senior of the pair. But even this was not sufficient to cope with the continuing serious problems besetting the Empire and in 293 a Caesar was appointed to each Augustus: Constantius Chlorus in the west and Galerius in the east. So was instituted the Tetrarchy, whereby, in addition to each of the four members being allocated territorial rights, each Caesar acted as an understudy and heir to his Augustus, with the latter intended to reign for only twenty years before retiring. A weakness in the system was thus inbuilt; with territory to be ruled and an army at his beck and call, each Caesar could challenge his own, or the other, Augustus, as was to happen some years later.

This new arrangement, moreover, became the peak of a new and elaborate hierarchical system of control which was set up to administer Italy and the

251

provinces. The next lower step below Caesar contained the praetorian prefects, who, under Diocletian, achieved powerful positions as chief staff officers to the Augusti and Caesars, executing both judicial and financial functions. Below them again, as devised by Diocletian, was interposed a new level of administration which was intended to link the emperors with the greatly increased number of provincial governors, over whom they could no longer hope to exercise a close control. Consequently the Empire was divided into twelve dioceses, most of which were supervised by an equestrian *vicarius*, who was, in effect, a deputy of the praetorian prefects. The dioceses were: Britanniae, Galliae, Viennensis, Hispaniae, Africa, Italia, Pannonia, Moesiae, Thracia, Asiana, Pontica and Oriens. There were, however, exceptions to this model which are indicated by conflicting evidence. For instance in the Verona List, Africa Proconsularis becomes Proconsularis Zeugitana, under the charge, presumably, of the *vicarius Africae*; yet in the *Notitia Dignitatum* the province retains its old name and also its proconsular governor, who seems to be not only equal to, but also independent of the *vicarius*. A similar state of affairs apparently existed in Asia. The two Gallic dioceses of Galliae and Viennensis shared a *vicarius* but were independently managed for financial matters, while Egypt remained under its prefect. In the *Notitia*, the diocese of Oriens is placed under the *comes Orientis*, although its actual composition was not stable, and it seems clear that, as with Egypt, it was subject to later changes. The diocese of Italiae not only had its own *vicarius*, but also the *vicarius urbis Romae*, who was responsible for most of the southern part of the peninsula as well as the City.

This reorganisation made the provinces more remote from the emperors by inserting this new level of administration into the old regime, under which a provincial governor had been directly responsible to his emperor or to the Senate. It was largely caused by the division in two of almost all the provinces then in being, in addition to those divisions which had earlier been made mainly under Septimius Severus. Thus in Britain, the two Severan provinces of Inferior and Superior became four: Britannia I, Britannia II, Maxima Caesariensis and Flavia Caesariensis, with a fifth, Valentia, probably being added at a later date. The three original provinces of Spain became respectively Baetica, Lusitania, Carthaginiensis, Tarraconensis and Callaecia, to which was added Mauretania Tingitana in north Africa, as well as Insulae Balaerum, according to the *Notitia Dignitatum*. In general, though, most provinces were divided only in two, such as Lugdunensis I and II, but later III, Narbonensis I and II and Mauretania Caesariensis and Sitifensis. Others, however, were divided more, such as Asia, which ended up as seven provinces.

With an ultimate total of some 119 provinces there was a corresponding increase in administrators. Admittedly many of the new provinces were governed by *praesides*, lower-ranking officers from the equestrian class, whose *officia* probably contained no more than 100 or so officials; but some consular governors remained with larger staffs. Among the latter were Maxima Caesariensis, in Britain, and the two Germanies. In Italy, now divided into several provinces, the old title of *corrector* was retained. The general policy seems to have been aimed at a tightening of control by the central government, working through the governors, who, although they had smaller areas to administer, were required to run a much more complex bureaucratic system. It has been claimed that an estimated total of some 30,000 civil servants, required to administer so vast an empire, is but a modest figure. But there is a danger that this is only seen to be modest when viewed against modern bureaucratic government machines. Some time ago it was shown that more and more dockyard workers and officials were required to service a much declining Royal Navy. But when compared with the way in which the Roman Empire was most effectively run during the first and second centuries AD, 30,000 civil servants seems monstrous, and well deserved the jibe that receivers of public money seemed to outnumber the payers. As stressed earlier, the most economical form of administration is government by consent and not by litigation.

These increases naturally began at the top in the emperor's court and secretariat with the officials and attendants of the imperial household, while the emperors themselves became hedged around with ritual, precedent and protocol after the manner of absolute monarchs. At the head of the court was the praetorian prefect, who remained the principal financial controller with responsibility for supplying the army and civil service. Second in importance was the Master of the Offices, a sort of court chamberlain, created as a separate office under Constantine, and responsible for control of the secretariat with its multitude of duties. The fact that many taxes were now collected in kind as well as in bullion gave rise to two further subsidiary financial controllers, whose officers largely replaced the old-styled provincial procurators, although Egypt remained an exception. The *comes sacrarum largitionum* was responsible for the collection of taxes levied in gold and silver and also, quite logically, had charge of the metals' production and use in the mines and mints; these taxes, when distributed as payments, were essential for maintaining the loyalty and morale of the army and civil service. The other officer, the *comes rei privatae*, was responsible for all the emperor's estates and property, and collected rents and forfeited land and goods – usually forfeited through treasonable actions on the part of their erstwhile owners. The fourth of the great officers of state was the *quaestor*, who was directly responsible for the secretarial departments, processed the many petitions and appeals to the emperor and drafted imperial constitutions. In addition to these civil officers there were the corresponding military officers, commanding the palace guards and the elements of the field army which were attached to the emperor, and which came to be known as *palatini*.

Diocesan vicars acted as deputies to the praetorian prefects, and the two principal financial offices were also represented at diocesan level, from where they could communicate directly with the governors over the collection of taxes. At all these levels of the administration there was a tripartite division of the services between judicial, financial and clerical, which really only became combined in one person's hands at gubernatorial level and below. By now little power remained in the hands of local magistrates and almost all cases, both civil and criminal, ended up in the governors' courts. Consequently access to the courts, or to a governor, became slower and probably more expensive, since a governor would be required to travel from assize centre to assize centre all round his, albeit smaller, province. The removal of much power from local magistrates also meant that the governor had much more work to do in the actual administration of urban centres. When the burdens of tax collection – both in cash and in kind – were added to these duties of a governor, it can be seen that he might become quite overworked, despite his large force of civil servants.

It must not be thought, though, that the governor could only rely on his paid civil servants, for many of the older, voluntary holders of offices, which had originated in the principate, still continued active, although they were shorn of much real power. One less-desirable aspect was the enforcement of a hereditary element in such voluntary offices; once a man was a decurion, so was his son and grandson after him. Consequently, if promotion to a higher social class did not provide relief, a man's family could be condemned to carry out painful and costly liturgies from one generation to the next. Neither did bankruptcy relieve them of their obligations. Moreover, despite their importance, decurions generally ranked only with the lowest of the professional civil servants. However, they had one benefit. Although receiving no pay, they still belonged to the privileged class, like all the professional administrators, of *honestiores*, which guaranteed their immunity from the more brutal punishments and from interrogation under torture, a fate which was normal for the lower caste of *humiliores*.

All the civil service was organized on lines similar to the army, since it was from the army that it had originated. Consequently, as with soldiers, its members were paid both in cash – usually gold – and in materials such as food or fodder. Imperial freedmen for a time still played their part in the imperial secretariat, although there was an increasing tendency to recruit replacements from the equestrian order. Many of the senior men in the hierarchy were also able to supplement their somewhat meagre salaries many times over with fees obtained from the general public, whose cause they may have assisted; the system became, in effect, a great running sore of legalised bribery and extortion with official scales of fees often being laid down for services rendered. Even tax collectors were paid fees, for the 'service' they rendered to the tax payers!

Probably the largest and most complex operation carried out by the administration at all levels was the collection of taxes, without which there would have been no civil service – or army. In many ways, it was entirely unlike the *ad hoc* processes of the principate and much more akin to modern practices. First of all an annual budget was prepared in the office of the praetorian prefect from estimates submitted by all military and civil departments. From this budget were calculated the requirements of each area of the Empire, ranging from food to clothing and footwear. The levels of tax required to meet these requirements were then calculated first on a diocesan, then on a provincial, level and finally the burden was distributed amongst the cities and other units of local government. Decurions bore the final responsibility for making good any deficits that might occur, possibly from their own resources, and they also had the burden of transporting the goods levied for tax to the collection centres, which might be several hundred miles away.

The Roman Empire lacked a bureaucratic tradition. Many office holders in the late Empire also had no tradition of community public service to guide them, and most were out only to advance their own careers and for personal gain. In addition, with the graded hierarchy of control, the administrative and legal machine moved only with a ponderous slowness, in which law suits might take years, and cost a small fortune, to settle. One factor, which compounded the delays, was that a lack of adequate supervision allowed civil servants to absent themselves from official duties for long periods of time; even when discovered, the normal punishment was only loss of seniority, although absence for four years might lead to dismissal!

It is interesting to compare the elaborate command structure of this period with that of the principate, when, more often than not, single men were expected to command armies as well as to carry out the administration of provinces, including presiding over the provincial law courts and local assizes and dispensing justice, often according to both Roman and native law. Moreover, in some procuratorial provinces financial management was also added to the burdens of office. It has been argued that the system, whereby far more was expected from an individual man than might be thought humanly possible, tended to weed out the weak and the ordinary, leaving only those with an extraordinary and varied capacity to reach the highest offices; the whole *cursus honorum* was so designed to do just that. It is not surprising, therefore, that it has been claimed that Roman provincial governors in the principate were either resounding successes or abysmal failures. With the increase in bureaucratic power in the fourth century, and with the greater interference by the state in everyday affairs, it may well have been that the

Empire simply could not produce men of the required calibre. Alternatively, a more sinister explanation might be advanced, in that the blood-letting of the late second and third centuries had effectively extinguished, or seriously weakened, the social class which had, hitherto, provided the Empire's natural, born leaders. Revolutions, civil wars and major foreign wars tend to have that effect, as has sometimes been argued for France after the revolution.

Another court officer was the *primacerius notariorum*, who became a person of some consequence and whose task it was to keep up-to-date all military and civil records; from his office came the document now known to scholars as the *Notitia Dignitatum*. This is an illustrated list of all military commanders and their staffs, and army units and stations, as well as the principal officers and staffs of the civil service. It is divided into two main parts which represented the separation of the Empire into east and west. Unfortunately it is a difficult document to interpret, since there are several internal inconsistencies which imply varying dates for the compilation of different sections. Much argument has taken place, and will no doubt continue to do so, over the dates of the various parts. It is generally thought to have been compiled towards the close of the fourth or early fifth century, although one section at least, referring to Britain, represents military dispositions at the end of the third century, while another records units which could never have served in this province. Nevertheless, it is an invaluable document when dealing with the late Empire, and, in particular, clearly records the separation of the imperial service into military and civil arms.

This separation, although it began under Diocletian, was not fully completed until Constantine I; even then some further changes took place after his reign. Under this reorganisation, which included the disbanding of the old Praetorian Guard, probably because it had sided with Maxentius against Constantine, most governors were stripped of their military commands, as were, eventually, the praetorian prefects and *vicarii*. Constantine was probably the first of the late Roman emperors to realise the Empire's need for a central, mobile striking force, the *comitatenses*, which in some ways carried with them an echo of the earlier Augustan arrangements in the border lands before static frontiers came into being. These field armies were commanded by two officers attached to the emperor's court, the *magister peditum* (infantry) and the *magister equitum* (cavalry). These armies and their constituent regiments now became the military élite, replacing the old corps of legions of the principate, and they received pay and privileges commensurate with their prestige, which was higher than that received by the static frontier forces, now called *ripenses* or *limitanei*. But the division between the static and mobile was not immutable and some *limitanei* were promoted to field armies, bearing the cumbersome title of *pseudocomitatenses*; they did not receive the same levels of pay and prestige as did their fully accepted brethren.

The *comitatenses* were eventually organized in regional groups which often overran provincial and even some diocesan boundaries. The larger of these groups, such as those in Gaul, or along the Danube, eventually came to be commanded by their own *magistri*, while the smaller were commanded by *comites*. The units which composed these armies were not assigned to any particular forts, but were mostly billeted in towns when not on active service. A number of imperial edicts refer to the billeting of troops in this way, since friction sometimes occurred with the civilian populations. The units themselves were largely derived from the frontier forces, and included some old legions now reduced in strength and made subordinate to the crack cavalry regiments, possibly the vestigial remains of the cavalry army formed by Gallienus in the third century. But Diocletian almost doubled the number of legions from those existing at the time of Severus, even though none was probably stronger than 1000 men each, and most of the mobile infantry units probably numbered between 500 to 1000 men; the vexillations of cavalry, though, were much smaller, and often well below 500. Many new and sometimes fancy names were introduced for regiments, sometimes reflecting the old garrison forts that they had once occupied; while other names such as *superventores*, *exploratores*, *constantes* or *petulantes* appear to be purely decorative and seldom have any specific military significance. A new type of weapon also appears on the scene for equipping certain detachments: the *martiobarbulus*, a small lead-weighted javelin for throwing by hand.

The frontier garrisons, *limitanei* or *ripenses*, were, in contrast to the *comitatenses*, entirely static and were not expected to fight any great distance away from their permanent stations. Old-style legions (probably reduced in strength), *alae*, cohorts, *cunei* and *numeri* still figure in these armies, although they are joined by units, probably newly recruited, named simply *equites* and *milites*, according to whether they were respectively cavalry or infantry. As with units of the *comitatenses*, they often took as part of their title the name of the fort where they were stationed. These frontier armies were normally commanded by *duces* and, as with the *comitatenses*, a single command might embrace more than one province or diocese. Africa, though, was different, and there frontier sectors were allocated to a series of *praepositi*, backed up by a field army and with overall command in the hands of its *comes*. It often used to be thought that many of these garrisons, such as those on the late *limes Tripolitanus*, were primarily farmers who lived in the forts with their wives and families, until a time arrived when they had to play at being soldiers. Modern thinking, though, now sees them as elements of the genuine late Roman army, which, owing to their static nature, became increasingly integrated with the local communities that, in earlier, less troublesome times, had lived in the *vici* attached to the forts.

Many fort commanders in the *limitanei* found themselves acting, in some ways, like the district commissioners of British colonial days. They often had to deploy men to keep the peace between quarrelsome inhabitants and to adjudicate in their disputes, besides carrying out all manner of other administrative duties, such as providing escorts for tax-collectors. Information on these multifarious activities is derived from the surviving letters and records of Flavius Abinnaeus, who commanded the fort of Dionysias in the Fayum region of Egypt. Care must be taken, though, to extrapolate this information not too far away from Egypt, which, as has been seen in previous chapters, was always something of an exceptional province, even in the fourth century. Nevertheless, the records enable us to see some of the possible extra-mural duties that a fort commander may well have been required to undertake.

Many of the units in the *limitanei* were, as with those of the *comitatenses*, named after their stations, and some also carried the same kind of fanciful names, such as the unit commanded by Abinnaeus, whose full name was *ala V Praelectorum, Dionisiada*. Many regiments of *limitanei* were much smaller than the old *alae* and *cohortes* of the principate, falling sometimes to a strength as low as 116, which was the total muster of a cavalry *ala* serving in Diocletianic Egypt.

In addition to the army units allotted to the frontier forces, there are naval units listed in the *Notitia Dignitatum* at appropriate places along the Rhine and Danube, and other major rivers and important coast-lines; one such was the *classis Histrica*, probably based at Carnuntum, and listed in the forces commanded by the *Dux Pannoniae Primae*. It is clear also that when some of these naval units were transferred to other stations they took with them the names they had already gained, in the same way as regiments of the *comitatenses*. For instance a *classis Anderetianorum* is listed at Paris on the Seine, although its name would imply that it had been stationed for a time at Pevensey (Anderida) on the south coast of Britain.

Other marked changes from earlier concepts affected the military architecture of the late Empire. Although external towers, projecting from town and fort walls, were not unknown in the early Empire, they became the norm in the fourth century, in many cases either being added to the curtain walls where they did not already exist, or being constructed as integral parts of new circuits. They ranged in shape from rectangular or multi-angular to semicircular or horseshoe-shaped, while some unusual fan-shaped examples are known, mostly in the lower Danube region. Gates tended to be made smaller and fewer in number, so as to restrict access; in some instances one of the portals in an earlier double gate might well be blocked. In a few cases a return was made to the plan of the old-fashioned claviculate gates to be seen in early campaign camps; this was done by building an external tower astride the portal with the point of exit being made through the side of the tower. At Pevensey, a late Saxon shore fort in Britain, a peculiar S-shaped

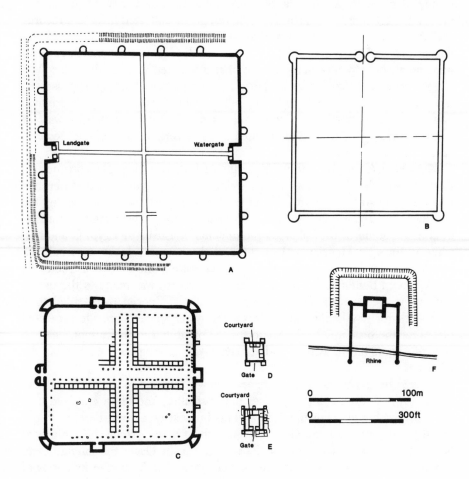

opening probably served the same purpose. Curtain walls often became much thicker and were less seldom revetted by an earth bank against the inside face.

The whole tendency behind the changes in fortifications in the fourth century was towards a greater defensive capacity. A fort was no longer a protected place from which a garrison could emerge to engage an enemy; instead it was intended to provide a safe refuge for collected taxes and records and other material supplies, while the defenders, safely inside with food and flocks and with the gates tightly shut, acted as a permanent threat and impediment to any advancing enemy that attempted to pass them by. The Roman army was also secure in the knowledge that few barbarians possessed heavy equipment, or the logistic capabilities, to mount a siege. It is possible now to detect the first steps in the development of a form of defensive warfare which ultimately led to the complicated multiple fortifications of the medieval castle.

Many changes in the internal planning of forts also took place in the late Empire, with the buildings often being more irregularly or differently disposed. Constantinian Drobeta, on the Danube, with the roads dividing the fort into four equal quadrants, is a notable example. The legionary fortress built about some of the religious monuments of Luxor in Egypt is another, while in forts on Hadrian's Wall some of the barrack blocks were split up into little individual dwellings and granaries were sometimes constructed in headquarters buildings. In many instances, a return was made to the use of timber for the construction of internal buildings. Special three-sided forts were built for naval units left open on the water side, to provide protected places for the beaching of ships and for the off-duty crews. Examples can be seen at Engers on the Rhine, and at Caer Gybi, on Anglesey overlooking the Irish Sea.

Among the towns and cities, the areas newly fortified in the late third and fourth centuries were in many cases much smaller, and often enclosed only the essential buildings at the centre. This is most notable at Périgueux and the new enceinte incorporated the amphitheatre in part of the circuit, as happened also at Trier, while at Sarmizegetusa in Dacia the amphitheatre actually became a type of fortified citadel against the barbarian invasions of the late third century, presumably since it required fewer defendants.

Another altered feature of the late Roman army was the reliance that was placed on the recruitment of barbarians often from beyond the frontiers. Recruitment of non-Romans into the *auxilia* had been traditional for a very long time, but it now reached its peak and even the most senior officers in the army often had barbarian origins. The most famous of them was perhaps Stilicho, a Vandal by birth, who became a *magister militum* under Theodosius and guardian of his son, Honorius; so great was his influence that he virtually ruled the western Empire on behalf of the latter and successfully defeated several large bands of invaders, twice including Attila and his Huns. Had he not been disgraced and beheaded, he might well have later saved Rome from sack. The culmination of this recruiting policy came with the introduction of whole nations and tribes into the Empire as *laeti* and *gentiles*, who owed little or nothing to the traditions either of the Roman army or even of the Empire. Ill-disciplined, poorly equipped and badly led, they were no real replacement for the old-style regular troops; but worse was to come with the introduction of *foederati*, an even lower grade of barbarian soldier, on which much of the western Empire had to rely in the fifth century.

The final breakdown of the Roman army and administration in the west came about through a multitude of causes. Chief among them, though, was the non-arrival of the regular pay-chests. With no pay to keep them serving and loyal, soldiers of the regular units simply faded into the background, presumably joining whatever community was nearest. Since the officers received no pay as well, there was no incentive for them to maintain discipline or prevent desertion; indeed they probably disappeared too! A graphic account has been left of the breakdown in frontier defence in Eugippius' *Life of Saint Severinus*, describing how the saint visited a part of Noricum bordering on the upper Danube. He found a regular detachment still guarding the fort at Passau; having received no pay for some time, they decided to send some men to Italy to see if any was forthcoming, but the emissaries were murdered and their bodies floated down the river. We hear no more of the regiment; presumably they melted away into the background and the only remaining troops in the area were some very low-quality *foederati*, whose subsequent performance can have done little to cheer the people they were supposedly protecting, despite the leadership and inspiration given by the saint.

Another factor which was of prime concern in the dissolution of the army of the west was the loss of territory off which it could feed and obtain other necessary supplies. Moreover, such territory usually contained taxpayers and the loss of their contributions to the state eventually deprived the army and civil service of its remaining logistical base.

The military strategy initiated by Diocletian and followed by Constantine was largely vindicated by events. The combination of static frontier defences with mobile units in the rear was well conceived, for, as already stressed, a fixed frontier is only as good as its garrison and even then a determined large-scale attack can soon punch a hole in the line, pour reinforcements through the gap so created and deploy without hindrance outwards into the hinterland. The German offensive in the low countries in 1940 did just that. But a good mobile fighting force situated to the rear should be able to contain the secondary deployment, especially when coupled with a series of closely-spaced, fortified, strong points as every city, town and village became in the

261

western Empire; even a mobile fighting force requires totally secure bases in which food and fodder, fresh horses and equipment can be guarded. We can only conclude that the apparatus, as devised ultimately by Constantine and refurbished by Valentinian, was present and in good working order when the western Empire finally failed. What destroyed it at the end must have been the declining numbers and quality of its troops, and a total breakdown in their logistical support system.

XIV

THE EMPIRE AND THE BARBARIANS

Barbarians were not unknown to the Republic. The Celtic invasions of Italy in the late fifth century BC showed what they could do. The early principate was well aware of their strength after the Varus disaster. Hadrian designed linear frontiers to separate them from the Empire and to keep them out. Marcus Aurelius had his fill of them on the Danube. But the third century AD saw them erupting again with all the force, and success, of the earliest invasion. But these were barbarian races that still lived beyond the frontiers. It must not be forgotten that many of the people inside the Empire also had barbarian origins, whether they were Gauls or Britons, Moors or Arabs, and yet had been more or less absorbed into it.

The principal barbarians outside the Empire in the principate can be briefly summarised. North and east of the Danube and Rhine lay the numerous tribes of Germany, like the Chatti, Cherusci and Suebi. Facing the frontiers of northern Britain were the tribes of Caledonia and the short-lived Maeatae, with the later emergence of the Picts, Scots and Attecoti; the last two came from over the Irish Sea. In north Africa there were the tribes to the south of the Atlas Mountains such as the Moors, the Garamantes facing Tripolitania and those abutting the southern and western borders of Egypt, including the notorious Trogodytes. Arab bedouins from Central Arabia and the Jordanian and Syrian deserts faced the eastern frontiers, while southern Russia was for a time the homeland of the Sarmatae. Many of these tribes, notably the Sarmatae, were nomadic pastoralists and famed for their horsemanship.

But later large-scale migrations eventually affected most of the static tribes along the frontiers. This was particularly so in central Europe, and to a lesser extent in the east where movements of the Alans through the Caucasus set up pressures. As in prehistory, most of these movements tended to be from the north and east, with tribes in central Asia putting increasing pressure on those in eastern Europe, with a knock-on effect that only ceased when the Atlantic was reached in Gaul or Spain or Britain. The cause was probably due to population explosions, following several 'good' years, which led to land-hunger and starvation when 'lean' years overtook the people. Thus the Sarmatae were forced westwards from southern Russia to the area north of the Danube, where they eventually came into direct conflict with the Roman Empire. Loose confederations of German tribes, such as the Franks in the middle and lower Rhine, the Alamanni, who had possibly been pushed into south-western Germany from the east, the Goths and Vandals originating in southern Scandinavia, the Alans, like the Sarmatians, from southern Russia, were all to play their part in the collapse of the western Empire. The Gothic migrations to the lands north of the Black Sea were ultimately frustrated by the westward movement of the Huns from central Asia, whose own migrations forced them and many barbarian peoples into the Roman Empire.

From the foregoing introductory paragraphs it can be seen that movements of peoples into and out of central Europe had been, and continued to be during the Roman period, an almost continuous process. But Roman conquests in north-west Europe had created a barrier to these natural movements. To begin with, the boundaries were permeable, so allowing seepage, such as the transfer of the friendly Ubii westwards across the Rhine, but the creation of static frontiers restricted this flow, which, in consequence, caused pressure to build up against them. With the benefit of hindsight, we can see precisely what was bound to happen once Hadrian and Antoninus Pius had created fixed barriers. In Gaul the movements had been going on long before Caesar arrived there, and he was one of the first Romans to encounter them. In the first century BC, the Suebi moved south-westwards from the Elbe region, causing the Helvetii to ask permission to enter Gaul and occupy new lands. Caesar refused, and what happened was only to be expected, although ultimately the tribe were settled peacefully within the Empire.

The Suebi were not the only people to move. Under Augustus the large tribe of the Marcomanni also migrated westwards, occupying what is now part of Czechoslovakia and imposing themselves on the indigenous Celts. Other movements had taken place somewhat earlier, seemingly from Scandinavia, with Goths, Burgundians, Vandals and Rugii all colonising parts of modern east Germany or Poland. Admittedly the professed origin of these tribes in Scandinavia is largely a matter of ancient tradition coupled with modern speculation, which may well be suspect.

The campaigns of Augustus into Germany brought the Roman Empire into even closer contact with the barbarians, most notably the Cherusci, under their leader Arminius, who not only inflicted a most decisive defeat on the army of Quinctilius Varus in AD 9, but also showed thereby that the Roman army was not invincible, even against barbarians, especially when it could not choose its own battleground. It was a lesson learnt with some difficulty and was perhaps a foretaste of things to come. Under Augustus' immediate successors, most of the Empire's boundaries facing the barbarians were little disturbed, with a stable alliance being made with the Quadi, and a very large number of barbarians, probably Sarmatians, actually being settled in Moesia during Nero's principate. Domitian, though, had to wage a war against the Chatti on the Rhineland and succeeded in neutralising their power. But during the Flavian period the rise of the Dacians under Decebalus, especially when they were joined by their neighbours the Roxolani, again showed what strength these people could muster. Indeed the Dacians were one of the very few barbarian nations that had been able to establish a reasonably stable state, which required considerable Roman force to overthrow, and it was not until both Domitian and Trajan had successively campaigned against Dacia that they were brought to heel. Trajan's war also involved the supposedly friendly buffer state of Sarmatian Iazyges, wedged between Roman and Dacian along the Danube; they failed to send help to Trajan and were punished accordingly.

The next major barbarian engagement occurred under Marcus Aurelius, when, between 166 and 178, he not only had to deal first with the Marcomanni and then with the Sarmatians, but also with a Moorish incursion across the Straits of Gibraltar into southern Spain. The abandonment of the Antonine Wall in Scotland due to Brigantian and Caledonian pressure appears slight in comparison when seen against this backdrop of major convulsions, although it was in a way the precursor to the much more serious invasion of northern Britain by the confederacy known as the Maeatae at the end of the second century. But for the time being, if Britain is excluded, the Empire's frontiers stood firm against these onslaughts.

The composition of the Maeatic confederacy has never been properly established, nor has its geographical region been identified. It was probably partly composed of Caledonians, against whom Agricola had fought at Mons Graupius, and it may in part have represented the people who, in the fourth century, came to be known as the Picts. The confederacy is only mentioned once in the literature in connection with this late-second century invasion of Britain. But the fact that barbarian tribes could ally themselves into confederacies was an alarming innovation and again heralded what was to come in the third century in Germany. Much of the weakness which had made barbarians so ineffectual when fighting Rome was due to their inability to form stable alliances. The new tendency augured ill for the Empire.

The confederacy that was to cause most trouble in the third century was that which welded the tribes of south-west Germany into the Alamanni, probably partly as the result of the absorption of westward migrations into this region from further east. Their initial attacks on Rhine and Danube frontiers, during the principate of Severus Alexander, may have been partly caused by the removal of vexillations from these areas to bolster the east against attacks by the resurgent Persia, consequently weakening the frontier defences. At first only minor damage was inflicted, in which some forts, including perhaps Pfünz, were destroyed and, for a time the Alamanni were held off by Maximinus, despite two mutinies in his army: but not for long. The next barbarian onslaught was by the Goths across the lower Danube into the Balkans in the middle 240s, while the middle Danube was being threatened by the Marcomanni, Quadi and Sarmatae. In the ensuing decade, all of them continued to attack, killing the emperor Decius, until finally checked by Gallienus. But far more serious was the invasion of Gaul across the lower Rhine by yet another confederacy, the Franks, coupled with renewed attacks on the upper Rhine and Raetian frontiers by the Alamanni. On this occasion the Franks overran Gaul and Spain and even crossed to the coast of Mauretania, while the Alamanni broke into northern Italy. Fortunately, as so often happened with barbarian raids, it was plunder not settlement that they required, and their ejection by Postumus, although not easy, was finally accomplished. The damage, though, was enormous, and many towns and cities, which up till then had remained unfortified, felt the effect, as well as country villas, causing possibly the flight of both people and capital from Gaul and Germany to Britain.

The Goths, moreover, continued to raid unchecked into the Balkan provinces, on one occasion reaching as far south as Athens. Gallienus managed to inflict a severe defeat on them, but they were not entirely quelled, for they were back again in 268, only being finally ejected by Claudius II, who took the name Gothicus in honour of his victories over them at Doberus and Naissus. In so doing he absorbed many of their defeated soldiers into the Roman army, while others were settled on derelict land in the Balkan provinces. But even then there was to be no lasting peace in Europe, for about 275 another invasion by the Alamanni took place in Gaul. Although not as widespread or disastrous as the first, it was serious enough until repulsed by Probus, who then strengthened the relevant lengths of the Rhine and Danube frontiers against them, and probably added the urban fortifications of Gaul and Germany. But the barbarians scored two notable permament successes against Rome in the Agri Decumates and Dacia, both of which were abandoned.

Renewed attacks by the Alamanni and the Franks continued throughout much of the reigns of Diocletian and his co-Augustus, Maximianus. The latter, having however defeated the Franks, induced them to become allies of Rome under a client king, so that they were able to act as a buffer between the frontier and the other tribes of free Germany. Diocletian inflicted a defeat on the Sarmatians across the Danube, but Galerius had to take further action against them and also the Marcomanni, while in Gaul yet another invasion of Alamanni had to be repulsed by Constantius. Even Africa was not immune and Galerius had to take hurried action to repel a Moorish invasion of Numidia.

A change in the direction of the barbarian attacks took place soon after Constantine became sole emperor. The Goths, instead of striking as they had previously done against the Balkans and Asia Minor, deflected their attacks towards the middle Danube, pushing the Sarmatians before them. It is not at all clear though if this was due to pressure being put on them by other tribes, such as the Huns from central Russia. At first the Goths were defeated and they even undertook to supply recruits for the Roman army; but it was only an intermission. Moreover, another significant change was beginning to take place. Whereas before most invading barbarians sought only loot, they were now more often looking for land and permanent settlement, as had to some extent happened earlier under Marcus Aurelius.

By the middle of the fourth century, the tide of barbarian invasions was rising still further under pressures from the east. A rebellion in Gaul may have caused the Alamannic and Frankish reactions, as the result of which Franks came to be settled in Gaul, while on the middle Danube the Sarmatians and their neighbours had once more to be repulsed.

From about 365 the northern and African frontiers came under almost continuous pressure. The Alamanni remained troublesome on the Rhine, while the Goths were pressing again on the lower Danube. Moorish tribes were raiding into Tripolitania and Africa Proconsularis, while Britain was for a time invested by yet another barbarian conspiracy between Scots, Attecoti, Picts and Saxons. The former came from across the Irish Sea into Galloway, the Picts seem to have been the direct descendants of the Maeatae, while the Saxons came from southern Jutland and northern Germany. A field army had to be sent to quell and disperse the invaders, and to restore the province. Slightly later the Sarmatians and Quadi were again on the march and the emperor Valentinian died during the campaign mounted to expel them. His younger brother Valens, who succeeded him, next faced one of the most serious crises yet experienced when the Visigoths, under pressure from Huns and Alans, asked to be admitted to deserted lands in Thrace, in return for agreeing to supply an almost unlimited supply of recruits to the Roman army. As a result, thousands of refugees crossed the Danube, causing severe administrative problems, which led to chaos. The Goths revolted and vanquished an army sent against them. Flushed with success, they then allied themselves with their sometime enemies, the Huns and Alans, and marched on Constantinople, where fortunately a force of cavalry beat them back before they could attack the city.

Pressure from the Huns was by now also being felt among the tribes of western Germany, who in turn threatened the Rhine frontier. Although

Theodosius liberated Thrace and Macedonia from the Goths and Huns, the Goths retaliated by invading Pannonia and were only removed by means of a large cash pay-off. Increasingly also, the massive barbarian recruitment into the Roman army was causing a weakening of morale and slackening of discipline, while the new settlers on derelict land, although ostensibly allies of Rome, could no longer be relied on to defend the frontiers; nor were there enough Roman officers to go round. From such settlers emerged men like Alaric, Visigothic king in Thrace, who for a time was given imperial command. But in 401 he invaded Italy, although he was at first forced to withdraw, since his army suffered jointly from disease and desertion. He was followed into Italy by a confederacy of German tribes who were defeated by Stilicho employing Goths, Alans and Huns. It was becoming increasingly difficult to distinguish friend from foe or ally from enemy. In 406–407 Gaul was invaded by Vandals and Alans with repercussions both in Britain and Italy. Pushing through Gaul they penetrated into Spain where they began to settle, with the Vandals finally crossing the Straits of Gibraltar and carrying their kingdom into north Africa. In Europe they were followed by Visigothic settlement in southern Gaul and Spain. Finally Alaric, dissatisfied with the offers made to him, captured and sacked Rome, and established a kingdom in northern Italy.

Meanwhile pressure from the Huns, feared by the Romans as the ultimate in ferocious and uncivilised barbarians, was growing in the east and in the Balkans. By about 430 they were invading Italy and slightly later Attila crossed the Danube into the eastern Empire; by 450 Attila was invading Gaul. Strangely, in the end, the Huns' strength turned in upon itself following the death of Attila, and they became a power no longer to be reckoned with.

The final state of the western Empire saw an Ostrogothic kingdom in Italy, Vandals in much of the Balkans and north Africa, a Visigothic kingdom in south Gaul and Spain, Burgundians and Franks in the remainder of Gaul and Germany, and Saxons, Frisians and Angles in Britain.

Perhaps one of the strangest aspects of these movements of hundreds of thousands of people – many largely nomadic in origin – which have been catalogued above is their transience. The Burgundians in Germania Prima and the Alamanni, who had settled permanently in Alsace and north Switzerland, were both overrun and conquered by Franks. The Goths were also driven from Gaul into Spain by the Franks, where they survived until they were defeated by the Moslem invasion in 711. The Alans were absorbed by the Vandals in Spain, who were in turn forced by the Goths into north Africa, where they took Carthage. Subsequently the Vandals launched a fleet which attacked and successfully captured Rome, and which also allowed them to hold out against the eastern Empire until 533. As with the Goths, no survivors outlived the Moslem conquests of north Africa. Only the Franks successfully beat off attacks from Rome when their king, Clovis, finally defeated Syagrius about 486 to establish the Merovinginian royal house, and to occupy the whole of the area how equivalent to modern France.

Yet in their day, these same transient peoples had brought the mighty Roman Empire to its knees. Perhaps the confederacies of which they were once part ceased to matter when they were permanently settled in their new lands, and they split up again into their constituent tribes, so ultimately melting into history like the Empire they had vanquished.

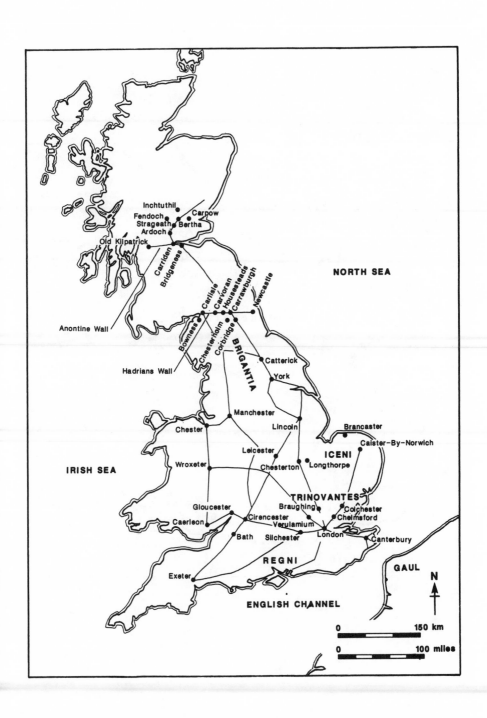

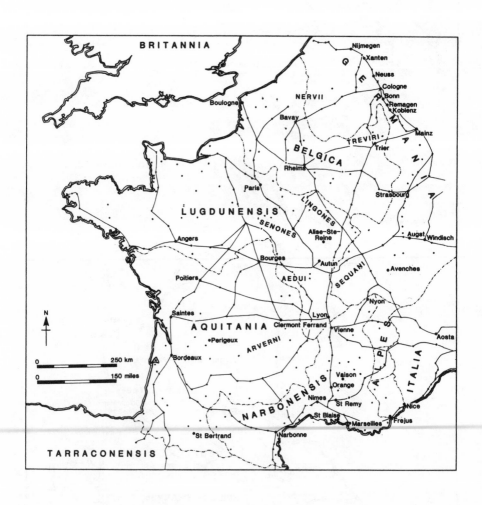

BRITANNIA

TARRACONENSIS

Nijmegen
Xanten
Neuss
Cologne
Bonn
Remagen
Koblenz
Mainz
Trier
Strasbourg
Augst Windisch
Avenches
Nyon
Aosta

NERVII
Boulogne
Bavay
BELGICA
TREVIRI
Rheims
Paris
LUGDUNENSIS
LINGONES
SENONES
Alise-Ste-Reine
Angers
Bourges
Autun
Poitiers
AEDUI
SEQUANI
Saintes
Lyon
AQUITANIA
Clermont Ferrand
Vienne
Perigeux
ARVERNI
Bordeaux
Vaison
Orange
Nimes
St Remy
NARBONENSIS
St Blaise
Marseilles
Frejus
Nice
St Bertrand
Narbonne
ITALIA

N

0   250 km
0   150 miles

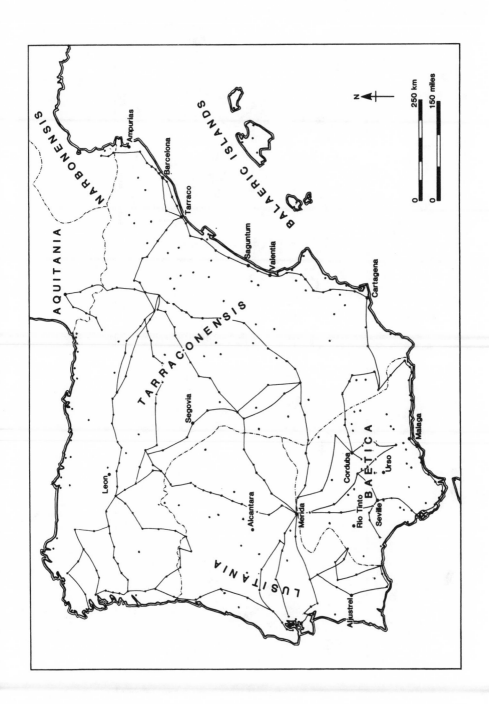

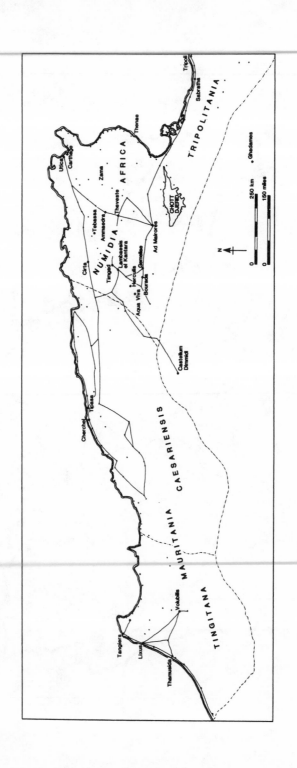

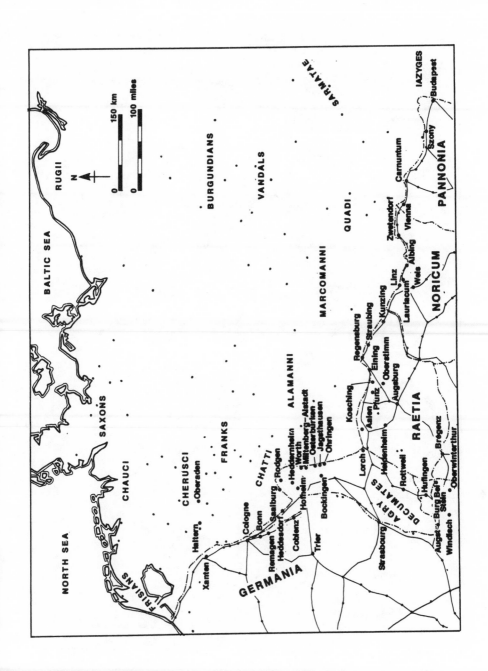

SARMATAE

HUNS

GOTHS

ROXOLANI

•Budapest

•Tac

IAZYGES

•Tchau

•Boldga   DACIA

•Potaissa

•Vetel   •Alba Julia
COSTOBOCCI
•Aquae • • •
Tapae•   •Sarmizegetusa

PANNONIA

Sirmium

•Belgrade

Golubac   •Turnu Severin
Kostolac•
Cezava   Donji Milanovac.

Arcer•

Troesmis•

Adamklissi•

Silistra•

DALMATIA

Nis•

Oescus•   Novae•

MOESIA

SUPERIOR

BLACK SEA

Skopije•

THRACE •

MACEDONIA • •

•Philippi.

Perinthus•   •Constantinople

Pella•
Thessalonika•

EPIRUS

•Pharsalia

AEGEAN
SEA

•Pergamum

•Actium
Panopeus•

Calcis•

•Smyrna

Thebes•
•Athens
Corinth•

ACHAEA

•Ephesus

•Miletus

•Sparta

N
↑

0   150 km

0   100 miles

Knossos•

CRETE

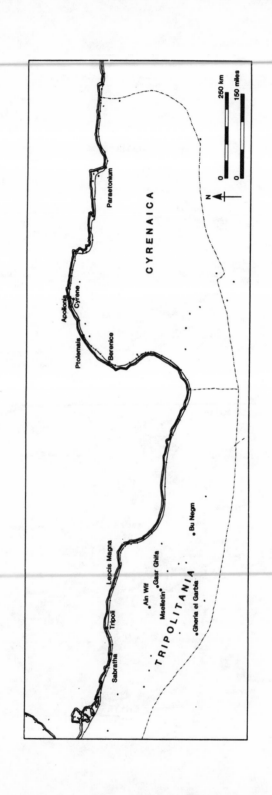

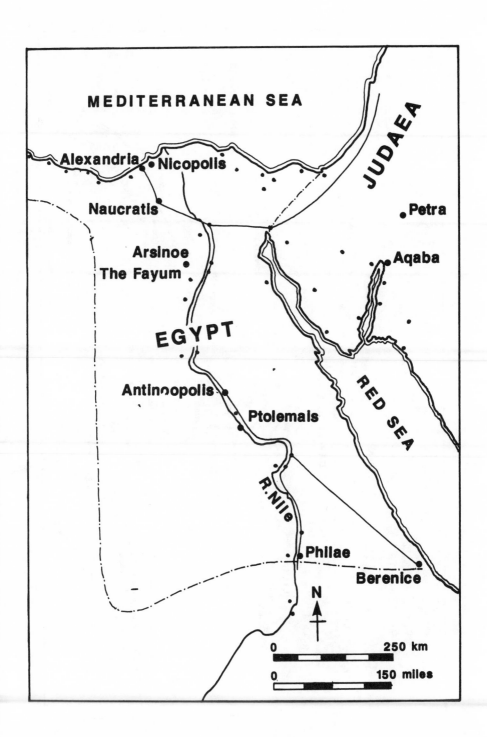

MEDITERRANEAN SEA

JUDAEA

Alexandria • Nicopolis

Naucratis

• Petra

Arsinoe
The Fayum •

• Aqaba

EGYPT

RED SEA

Antinoopolis •

Ptolemais

R. Nile

• Philae

Berenice

N

| 0 | | | 250 km |

| 0 | | | 150 miles |

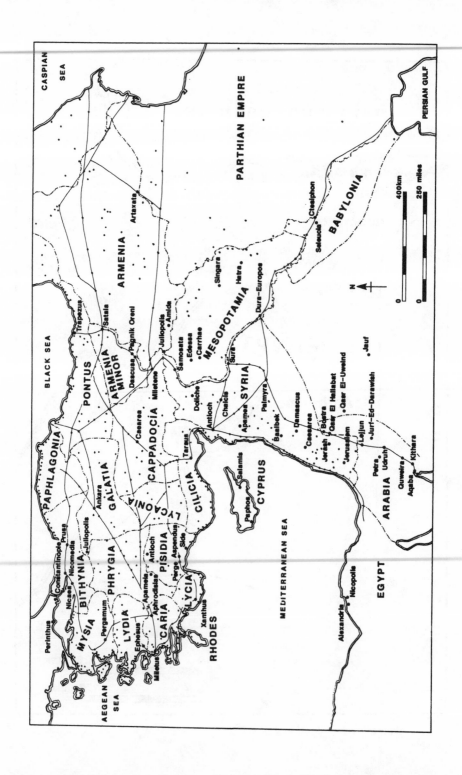

CHRONOLOGICAL CHART

Timeline (BC → AD): 55 · 50 · 45 · 40 · 35 · 30 · 25 · 20 · 15 · 10 · 5 · BC | AD · 5 · 10 · 15 · 20

AUGUSTUS (from 27) — **TIBERIUS** (from AD 14)

ITALY and AFRICA
- 49 CAESAR CROSSES RUBICON
- 48 CAESAR IN EGYPT
- 46 BATTLE OF THAPSUS
- 44 CAESAR ASSASSINATED
- 33 JUBA I IN NUMIDIA
- 30 DEATH OF ANTONY
- 29 CAMPAIGN AGAINST ETHIOPIA
- 27 OCTAVIAN BECOMES AUGUSTUS — REORGANIZATION OF THE PROVINCES
- 12 DEATH OF AGRIPPA
- 23 DEATH OF DRUSUS
- 17 TACFARINAS REBELS IN MAURETANIA

GREECE, BALKANS and MIDDLE DANUBE
- 49 POMPEY IN GREECE
- 48 BATTLE OF PHARSALUS — DEATH OF POMPEY
- 42 BATTLE OF PHILIPPI
- 31 BATTLE OF ACTIUM
- 29 LOWER DANUBE REACHED
- 12 PANNONIAN REVOLT SUPPRESSED BY TIBERIUS
- 6 PANNONIAN REVOLT
- 9 REVOLT SUPPRESSED
- 14 MUTINY IN PANNONIA
- 18 GERMANICUS IN GREECE

GAUL and GERMANY
- 52 VERCINGETORIX DEFEATED AT ALESIA
- 49 MASSILIA FALLS TO CAESAR
- 38 AGRIPPA SUPPRESSES AQUITANIAN REVOLT
- 16 – 13 AUGUSTUS IN GAUL
- 12 – 9 DRUSUS CAMPAIGNS ON THE RHINE
- 8 TIBERIUS CAMPAIGNS IN GERMANY
- 5 TIBERIUS CAMPAIGNS TO R. ELBE
- 9 VARUS DISASTER
- 15 GERMANICUS IN GERMANY
- 21 REVOLT OF FLORUS

THE EAST
- 53 DISASTER AT CARRHAE
- 24 AELIUS GALLUS IN ADEN
- 20 CLIENCY IN ARMENIA — REDUCTION OF CLIENT KINGDOMS
- 18 GERMANICUS IN THE EAST
- 19 DEATH OF GERMANICUS

SPAIN
- 46 CAESAR IN SPAIN
- 45 BATTLE OF MUNDA
- 27 PROVINCIAL REORGANIZATION
- 26 AUGUSTUS CAMPAIGNS AGAINST CANTABRI
- 19 AGRIPPA SUBDUES CANTABRI

BRITAIN
- 51 FLIGHT OF COMMIUS TO BRITAIN
- GROWING STRENGTH OF CATUVELLAUNI (TASCIOVANUS)
- c. 10 CUNOBELIN, KING OF CATUVELLAUNI
- DUBNOVELLAUNUS AND TINCOMMIUS FLEE TO ROME.

| 25 | 30 | 35 | 40 | 45 | 50 | 55 | 60 | 65 | 70 | 75 | 80 | 85 | 90 | 95 | 96 | 98 |

Emperors: 37 GAIUS — 41 CLAUDIUS — 54 NERO — 69 VESPASIAN — 79/81 TITUS — DOMITIAN — 96 NERVA — 98

ITALY and AFRICA
- 24 TACFARINAS KILLED
- 42 MAURETANIA MADE TWO PROVINCES
- JEWISH REVOLTS IN AFRICA
- 64 ROME BURNT
- 69 CIVIL WAR: YEAR OF THE FOUR EMPERORS: GALBA, OTHO, VITELLIUS, VESPASIAN
- BATTLE OF CREMONA
- 79 ERUPTION OF VESUVIUS

GREECE, BALKANS and MIDDLE DANUBE
- 46 THRACE ANNEXED
- 66 NERO IN GREECE
- 73 FRONTIER ON THE DANUBE
- 69 ROXOLANI INVADE
- 85 MOESIA DIVIDED
- 86 DACIAN WAR AGAINST DECEBALUS
- 88 BATTLE OF TAPAE I
- 92 PANNONIA INVADED
- 98 TRAJAN ON THE DANUBE

GAUL and GERMANY
- 47 CORBULO IN GERMANY
- 48 GRANT OF IUS HONORUM TO GAUL
- 50 INVASION OF CHATTI
- 68 REVOLT OF VINDEX
- 69 REVOLT OF CIVILIS
- 74 CREATION OF AGRI DECUMATES
- 82 CHATTAN WAR — LIMES IN UPPER GERMANY BEGUN
- 88 REVOLT OF SATURNINUS

THE EAST
- 34 PARTHIAN WAR
- SUPPRESSION OF CLIENT KINGDOMS
- 55 CORBULO IN THE EAST
- 66 VESPASIAN IN THE EAST: JEWISH REVOLT
- 70 FALL OF JERUSALEM — THE DIASPORA

SPAIN
- 74 GRANT OF IUS LATIUM TO ALL SPAIN

BRITAIN
- 40 FLIGHT OF ADMINIUS — DEATH OF CUNOBELIN
- 43 INVASION BY CLAUDIUS
- 47 PAUSE IN ADVANCE
- 60 BOUDICAN REBELLION
- 71 CEREALIS CAMPAIGNS IN BRIGANTIA
- 74 FRONTINUS IN WALES
- 78 AGRICOLA
- BATTLE OF MONS GRAUPIUS

283

	100	105	110	115	120	125	130	135	140	145	150	155	160	165	170	175

Emperors: TRAJAN — 117 HADRIAN — 138 ANTONINUS PIUS — 161 MARCUS AUPELIUS

ITALY and AFRICA
- 115 JEWISH/MOORISH REVOLTS
- 122 WAR IN MAURETANIA
- 128 HADRIAN IN AFRICA ? LIMES IN NUMIDIA
- 130 HADRIAN IN EGYPT
- 167 EPIDEMIC IN ITALY
- N. ITALY THREATENED BY INVASION
- 173 WAR WITH MAURI

GREECE, BALKANS and MIDDLE DANUBE
- 101 DACIAN WAR
- BATTLE OF TAPAE II
- 105 SECOND DACIAN WAR
- DEATH OF DECEBALUS
- 118 ROXOLANI THREATEN
- 124 HADRIAN IN GREECE
- 128 HADRIAN IN GREECE
- 167 MARCOMANNIC WARS
- 172 BARBARIAN SETTLEMENTS ON DANUBE
- 174 SARMATIAN WAR

GAUL and GERMANY
- 121 HADRIAN IN GAUL AND GERMANY: CONSTRUCTION OF PALISADE IN UPPER GERMANY AND RAETIA
- 140 ADVANCE OF UPPER GERMAN AND RAETIAN LIMES

THE EAST
- 106 ARABIA ANNEXED
- 115 PARTHIAN WAR BEGINS
- 116 JEWISH REVOLTS
- 117 TRAJAN'S CONQUESTS ABANDONED
- 123 HADRIAN IN THE EAST
- 128 HADRIAN IN THE EAST
- 132 JEWISH REVOLT
- HADRIAN RETURNS
- 162 ARMENIA INVADED BY PARTHIA
- ANTIOCH THREATENED. 166 WAR ENDED BY EPIDEMIC

SPAIN
- 122 HADRIAN IN SPAIN
- 173 INVASION BY MAURI IN BAETICA

BRITAIN
- 105 WITHDRAWAL FROM SCOTLAND
- 117 REVOLT IN THE NORTH
- 121 HADRIAN IN BRITAIN
- 122 HADRIAN'S WALL
- 143 ANTONINE WALL REOCCUPATION OF SCOTLAND
- 154? BRIGANTIAN REBELLION
- ?163 ANTONINE WALL ABANDONED

	180	185	190	195	200	205	210	215	220	225	230	235	240	245
	180 COMMODUS		192/193 PERTINAX		SEPT.SEVERUS		211 CARACALLA	217 CARACALLA ELEGABALUS	222		SEVERUS ALEXANDER 235			
			CIVIL WAR				211 CONSTITUTIO ANTONINIANA 212 GETA MURDERED				FIFTEEN EMPERORS IN A PERIOD			
ITALY and AFRICA					LIMES IN AFRICA STRENGTHENED MUNICIPAL AUTONOMY GRANTED IN EGYPT								238 REVOLTS IN AFRICA LEG III AUG CASHIERED	
GREECE, BALKANS and MIDDLE DANUBE			PEACE MADE WITH SARMATIANS		193 SEVERUS PROCLAIMED EMPEROR IN PANNONIA						DANUBE CAMPAIGNS		245 INVASIONS ACROSS DANUBE 248 REBELLION: GOTHS INVADE	
GAUL and GERMANY				DISTURBANCE CAUSED BY MATERNUS		196 ALBINUS DEFEATED IN GAUL AT LYON	'PFAHLGRABEN' AND ? RAETIAN WALL				233 ATTACKS BY ALAMANNI ARMY MUTINY			
THE EAST				194 SEVERUS DEFEATS NIGER	197 SEVERUS IN THE EAST MESOPOTAMIA A PROVINCE	SYRIA TWO PROVINCES		215 CARACALLA IN THE EAST		225 RISE OF PERSIA	230 MESOPOTAMIA OVER-RUN AND RECOVERED ARMY MUTINY		242 WAR WITH PERSIA PRETENDERS IN THE EAST	
SPAIN					TARRACONENSIS SIDES WITH ALBINUS DISTURBANCE CAUSED BY MATERNUS						TARRAGONA SACKED BY FRANKS			
BRITAIN NORTH	181 REVOLT IN NORTH		193 ALBINUS AS CAESAR ARMY MUTINY			208 SEVERUS RESTORES BRITAIN BRITAIN TWO PROVINCES								

Years: 250 255 260 265 270 275 280 285 290 295 300 305 310 315 320

EMPERORS

BETWEEN 235–270 OF ANARCHY · 270 AURELIAN · 275 PROBUS · 284 DIOCLETIAN · 293 CONSTANTIUS I · 305 CONSTANTIUS I 306 · FOUR WESTERN AUGUSTI · CONSTANTINE I · 312 BATTLE OF MILVIAN BRIDGE · CONSTANTINE CONVERTED TO CHRISTIANITY · CIVIL WARS 313 EDICT OF MILAN · 324 FOUNDATION OF CONSTANTINOPLE

ITALY and AFRICA

258 ITALY INVADED · 274 EMPIRE REUNITED ROME WALLED · BEGINNING OF REFORMS IN THE ARMY · REVOLTS IN EGYPT · THE TETRARCHY · DIOCLETIAN REFORMS · THE EMPIRE: SUBDIVISION OF PROVINCES

GREECE, BALKANS and MIDDLE DANUBE

GOTHIC INVASIONS · 251 DECIUS DEFEATED AND KILLED · 258 GALLIENUS CHECKS BARBARIANS · 269 CLAUDIUS II PACIFIES DANUBE FRONTIER · DACIA ABANDONED · PANNONIA INVADED · 289 DIOCLETIAN DEFEATS SARMATIANS · 322 SARMATIAN INVASION

GAUL and GERMANY

253 ALAMANNIC INVASIONS · 260 GALLIC EMPIRE OF POSTUMUS · 276 ALAMANNIC INVASIONS · 274 REJOINED TO EMPIRE · AGRI DECUMATES ABANDONED · FIGHTING ON THE RHINE · 314 COUNCIL OF ARLES · ALAMANNIC INVASIONS

THE EAST

250 MESOPOTAMIA FALLS TO PERSIANS · EPIDEMIC DISEASE · 260 VALERIAN AND ARMY CAPTURED BY PERSIANS · 267 KINGDOM OF PALMYRA · 273 AURELIAN RECOVERS EASTERN PROVINCES · 296 GALERIUS DEFEATS PERSIA · TWO EASTERN AUGUSTI · 314 LICINIUS EMPEROR IN THE EAST

SPAIN

260 PART OF GALLIC EMPIRE · 258 FRANKISH INVASIONS · 274 REJOINED TO EMPIRE

BRITAIN

260 PART OF GALLIC EMPIRE · 274 REJOINED TO EMPIRE · 285 CARAUSIUS DEFECTS · 294 MURDERED BY ALLECTUS · 296 ALLECTUS DEFEATED. PROVINCES REUNITED WITH EMPIRE NORTHERN FRONTIER OVER-RUN

Timeline (years): 325 330 335 340 345 350 355 360 365 370 375 380 385 390 395 400

337 CONSTANS / CONSTANTIUS II — CONSTANS 350 — 361 JULIAN — 363 VALENTINIAN I 375 — 367 GRATIAN 373 — VALENTINIAN II 392 — THEODOSIUS I 395

333

SUCCESSION OF PALACE REVOLUTIONS

ITALY and AFRICA
MOORISH REVOLT IN AFRICA

GREECE, BALKANS and
324 BATTLE OF ADRIANOPLE, CONSTANTINE SOLE EMPEROR
VISIGOTHS SETTLED IN THRACE

MIDDLE DANUBE
378 BATTLE OF ADRIANOPLE
398 VISIGOTHS SETTLED IN EPIRUS

GAUL and GERMANY
354 ALAMANNIC INVASIONS
357 VALENTINIAN AT TRIER
FRANKS SETTLE IN GAUL

THE EAST
338–350 SUCCESSIVE SIEGES OF NSIBIS
360 AMIDA CAPTURED
363 JULIAN IN THE EAST
PROVINCES SURRENDERED
368 FURTHER WAR

SPAIN

BRITAIN
CONSTANS VISITS BRITAIN
367 BARBARIAN CONSPIRACY
369 THEODOSIUS RESTORES BRITAIN
383 REVOLT OF MAGNUS MAXIMUS
395 STILICHO IN BRITAIN

Region	400	405	410	415	420	425	430	435	440	445	450	455	460	465	470	475
HONORIUS (West) / ARCADIUS (East) 408	HONORIUS (West)				423 VALENTINIAN III THEODOSIUS II (East)						450	455 VARIOUS (East and West)				476 DEPOSITION OF LAST WESTERN EMPEROR ROMULUS AUGUSTULUS
ITALY and AFRICA	402 VISIGOTHS INVADE ITALY	405 GERMANS INVADE ITALY	410 ALARIC TAKES ROME			VANDALS SETTLE IN AFRICA		HUNS INVADE ITALY	VANDAL KINGDOM			455 VANDALS SACK ROME			VANDAL KINGDOM RECOGNIZED	
GREECE, BALKANS and MIDDLE								438 THEODOSIAN CODE		ATTILA CROSSES THE DANUBE	HUNS IN EASTERN EMPIRE		VANDALS RAVAGE ILLYRICUM			
GAUL and GERMANY		406 MARCOMANNI, QUADI ALANS AND VANDALS INVADE GAUL	410 VISIGOTHS SETTLE IN S. GAUL								451 ATTILA INVADES GAUL		VISIGOTHIC KINGDOM IN S. GAUL			
THE EAST									440 PERSIA INVADES ARMENIA							
SPAIN		409 ALANS, VANDALS IN SPAIN		417 VISIGOTHS IN SPAIN						VISIGOTHIC KINGDOM						
BRITAIN		405 MARCUS GRATIAN CONSTANTINE III	410 RESCRIPT OF HONORIUS			429 VISIT OF ST. GERMANUS			JUTES, ANGLES AND SAXONS	'THE GROANS OF THE BRITONS'						

SELECT BIBLIOGRAPHY

General

Cambridge Ancient History, Vols. VII – XII

Frank, Tenney (ed.) (1938–41), *An Economic Survey of Ancient Rome, I–V*, Baltimore

Hammond, N. G. L. and Scullard, H. H. (eds) (1970), *The Oxford Classical Dictionary*, 2nd edition, Oxford

Hartley, B. and Wacher, J. (1983), *Rome and her Northern Provinces*, Gloucester

Hoddinott, R. F. (1975), *Bulgaria in Antiquity*, London

Lewis, N. and Rheinhold, M. (1966), *Roman Civilization, Sourcebook I: The Republic; Sourcebook II: The Empire*, New York

MacKendrick, P. (1980), *The North African Stones Speak*, North Carolina

Rostovtzeff, M. I. (1963), *A Social and Economic History of the Roman Empire*, Oxford

Stillwell, R. *et al.* (eds) (1976), *The Princeton Encyclopedia of Classical Sites*, Princeton

Temporini, H. and Haase, W. (1972–), *Aufstieg und Niedergang der römischen Welt*, Berlin

Wacher, J. (1987), *The Roman World, I–II*, London

Chapter I

Badian, E. (1970), *Sulla the Deadly Reformer*, Sydney

Badian, E. (1972), 'Tiberius Gracchus and the beginning of the Roman revolution' in Temporini, A. (ed.), *Aufstieg und Niedergang der römischen Welt*, I, 1, 668–731

Barrow, R. H. (1949), *The Romans*, Harmondsworth

Brunt, P. A. (1971), *Italian Manpower, 225 BC – AD 14*, Oxford

Gabba, E. (1976), *Republican Rome, the Army and the Allies*, Oxford

Gelzer, M. (1968), *Caesar: politician and statesman*, Oxford
Harris, W. H. (1979), *War and Imperialism in Republican Rome, 327–70 BC*, Cambridge
Salmon, E. T. (1982), *The Making of Roman Italy*, London
Scullard, H. H. (1959), *From the Gracchi to Nero*, London
Scullard, H. H. (1980), *A History of the Roman World 753 to 146 BC*, London
Syme, R. (1939), *The Roman Revolution*, Oxford

Chapter II

Braund, D. C. (1984), *Rome and the Friendly King*, London
Brunt, P. A. and Moore, J. M. (1967), *Res Gestae Divi Augusti*, Oxford
Cheeseman, G. L. (1914), *The Auxilia of the Roman Imperial Army*, Oxford
Collis, J. R. (1984), *The European Iron Age*, London
Holder, P. A. (1980), *The Auxilia from Augustus to Trajan*, Oxford
Jones, A. H. M. (1970), *Augustus*, London
Lepper, F. A. (1948), *Trajan's Parthian Campaigns*, Oxford
Luttwark, E. N. (1976), *The Grand Strategy of the Roman Empire*, Baltimore
Millar, F. (1977), *The Emperor in the Roman World*, London
Parker, H. M. D. (1928), *The Roman Legions*, Oxford
Salmon, E. T. (1968), *A History of the Roman World, 30 BC to AD 138*, London
Starr, C. G. (1960), *The Roman Imperial Navy*, Cambridge
Watson, G. R. (1969), *The Roman Soldier*, London
Webster, G. (1969), *The Roman Imperial Army*, London
Wells, C. (1972), *The German Policy of Augustus*, Oxford

Chapter III

Bell, H. I. *et al.* (1962), *The Abinnaeus Archive*, Oxford
Berchem, D. van (1952), *L'Armée de Dioclétien et la réforme Constantinienne*, Paris
Goodburn, R. and Bartholemew, P. (eds) (1976), *Aspects of the Notitia Dignitatum*, Oxford
Johnson, S. (1983), *Late Roman Fortifications*, London
Jones, A. H. M. (1964), *The Later Roman Empire, 284–602*, Cambridge
King, A. and Henig, M. (eds) (1981), *The Roman West in the Third Century*, Oxford
MacMullen, R. (1963), *Soldier and Civilian in the Later Roman Empire*, Harvard
Parker, H. M. D. (1961), *A History of the Roman World from AD 138 to 337*, London
Seeck, O. (ed.) (1962), *Notitia Dignitatum*, Frankfurt

Chapter IV

Baatz, D. (1974), *Der Römische Limes*, Berlin

Baradez. J. (1949), *Fossatum Africae*, Paris

Berciu, D. (1967), *Romania*, London

Birley, A. R. (1974), 'Roman frontiers and Roman frontier policy: some reflections on Roman Imperialism', *Trans. of the Archaeological and Architectural Society of Durham and Northumberland*, 3, 13–25

Birley, E. (1956), 'Hadrianic Frontier Policy' in *Limes Congress*, 2, 25–33, Köln

Bogaers, J. E. and Rüger, C. B. (1974), *Der Niedergermanische Limes*, Köln

Bogdan Cătănicui, I. (1981), *Evolution of the System of Defence Works in Roman Dacia*, Oxford

Bowersock, G. W. (1983), *Roman Arabia*, Cambridge, Mass.

Breeze, D. J. (1982), *The Northern Frontiers of Roman Britain*, London

Breeze, D. J. (ed.) (forthcoming), *The Frontiers of the Roman Empire*, London

Crow, J. and French, D. (1980), 'New Research on the Euphrates frontier in Turkey', *Limes Congress*, 12, 903–12

Euzennat, M. (1967), 'Les Limes de Volubilis', *Limes Congress*, 6, 194–9

Hanson, W. and Maxwell, G. (1983), *Rome's North-West Frontier*, Edinburgh

Jones, G. D. B. (1978), 'Concept and development in Roman Frontiers', *Bulletin of the John Rylands Library of Manchester*, 61, No. 1 (Autumn), 114–44

Limes Congress (1952–), *The Proceedings of the International Congresses of Roman Frontier Studies* as follows:

1. Durham, 1949, Eric Birley (ed.), Durham, 1952.

2. Carnuntum, 1955, Eric Swoboda (ed.), Graz-Köln, 1956.

3. Basle, 1957, R. Laur-Belart (ed.), Basel, 1959.

4. Durham, 1959, unpublished.

5. Yugoslavia, 1963, Grga Novak (ed.), Zagreb, 1964.

6. Süddeutschland, 1964, H. Schönberger (ed.), Köln, Graz, 1967.

7. Tel Aviv, 1967, S. Appelbaum (ed.), Tel Aviv, 1971.

8. Cardiff, 1969, Eric Birley, Brian Dobson and Michael Jarrett (eds), Cardiff, 1974

9. Mamaia, 1972, D. M. Pippidi (ed.), Bucarest, 1974.

10. Lower Germany, 1974, Dorothea Haupt and Heinz Günther Horn (eds), Köln, 1977.

11. Székesfehévár, 1976, J. Fitz (ed.), Budapest, 1977.

12. Stirling, 1979, W. S. Hanson and L. J. F. Keppie (eds), Oxford, 1980.

13. Aalen, 1983, D. Planck and C. Unz (eds), Stuttgart, (forthcoming).

Mann, J. C. (1974), 'The Frontiers of the Principate', Temporini, H. (ed.), *Aufstieg und Niedergang der römischen Welt*, II, 1, 508–33

Mitchell, S. (ed.) (1983), *Armies and Frontiers in Roman and Byzantine Anatolia*, Oxford

Nash Williams, V. E. (ed. Jarrett, M. G. 1969), *The Roman Frontier in Wales*, second edition, Cardiff

Poidebard, A. (1934), *La Trace de Rome dans le désert de Syrie*, Paris

Reynolds, J. M. (ed.) (1976), *Libyan Studies: select papers of the late R. G. Goodchild*, London

Schönberger, H. (1969), 'The Roman frontier in Germany: an archaeological survey', *Journal of Roman Studies*, 59, 144–97

Chapter V

Abbott, F. F. and Johnson, A. C. (1926), *Municipal Administration in the Roman Empire*, New York

Brunt, P. A. (1981), 'The revenues of Rome', *Journal of Roman Studies*, 71, 161 ff

Burton, G. P. (1975), 'Proconsuls, assizes and the administration of justice under the Empire', *Journal of Roman Studies*, 65, 92 ff

Garnsey, P. D. (1970), *Social Status and Legal Privilege in the Roman Empire*, Oxford

Hardy, E. G. (1912), *Five Roman Laws* (Oxford)

Honoré, A. M. (1981), *Emperors and Lawyers*, London

Jones, A. H. M. (1960), *Studies in Roman Government and Law*, Oxford

Kunkel, W. (1966), *An Introduction to Roman Legal and Constitutional History*, Oxford

Mackie, N. (1983), *Local Administration in Roman Spain AD 14–212*, Oxford

Schulz, F. (1951), *Classical Roman Law* (Oxford)

Sherwin-White, A. N. (1963), *Roman Society and Roman Law in the New Testament*, Oxford

Sherwin-White, A. N. (1973), *The Roman Citizenship*, Oxford

Stevenson, G. H. (1949), *Roman Provincial Administration*, Oxford

Chapter VI

Boethius, A. and Ward-Perkins, J. B. (1970), *Etruscan and Roman Architecture*, Harmondsworth

Broughton, T. R. S. (1968), *The Romanisation of Africa Proconsularis*, New York

Clavel, M. and Lévéque, P. (1971), *Villes et Structures Urbaines dans l'Occident Romain*, Paris

Duval, P.–M. and Frezouls, E. (1971), *Thèmes de recherche sur les villes antiques de l'Occident*, Paris

Fevrier, P.–A., Fixot, M., Goudineau, C. and Kruta, V. (1980), *Histoire de la France urbaine: la ville antique*, Paris
Hobley, B. (ed.) (1985), *Romano-British Urban Topography*, London
Jones, A. H. M. (1940), *The Greek City*, Oxford
Jones, A. H. M. (1971), *The Cities of the Eastern Roman Provinces*, Oxford
Lepelley, C. (1979), *Les Cités de l'Afrique romaine*, 1, Paris
Levick, B. M. (1967), *Roman Colonies in Southern Asia Minor*, Oxford
Mazzolini, L. S. (1970, *The Idea of the City in Roman Thought*, London
Meiggs, R. (1960), *Roman Ostia*, Oxford
Salway, P. (1967), *The Frontier People of Roman Britain*, Cambridge
Wacher, J. S. (1975), *The Towns of Roman Britain*, London
Ward-Perkins, J. B. (1974), *Cities of Ancient Greece and Italy: planning in classical antiquity*, London
Wightman, E. M. (1970), *Roman Trier and the Treveri*, London

Chapter VII

Agache, R. (1978), *La Somme pré-romaine et romaine*, Amiens
Bokonyi, A. (1974), *A History of Domestic Mammals in Central and Eastern Europe*, Budapest
Brunt, P. A. (ed.) (1974), *The Roman Economy*, Oxford
Dimbleby, G. (1967), *Plants and Archaeology*, London
Fernandez Castro, M. C. (1982), *Villas Romanas en España*, Madrid
Jashemski, W. F. (1979), *The Gardens of Pompeii*, New York
Jones, M. and Dimbleby, G. (eds) (1981), *The Environment of Man: the Iron Age to the Anglo-Saxon Period*, Oxford
Luff, R.–M. (1982), *A Zooarchaeological Study of the Roman North-West Provinces*, Oxford
Percival, J. (1982), *The Roman Villa*, London
Rees, S. (1979), *Agricultural Implements in Prehistoric and Roman Britain*, Oxford
Rossiter, J. J. (1978), *Roman Farm Buildings in Italy*, Oxford
Thomas, E. B. (1964), *Römische Villen in Pannonien*, Budapest
Todd, M. (ed.) (1978), *Studies in the Romano-British Villa*, Leicester
White, K. D. (1967), *Agricultural Implements of the Roman World*, Cambridge
White, K. D. (1970), *Roman Farming*, London
White, K. D. (1975), *Farm Equipment of the Roman World*, Cambridge
White, K. D. (1984), *Greek and Roman Technology*, London
Zeuner, F. E. (1963), *A History of Domesticated Animals*, London

Chapter VIII

Callender, M. H. (1965), *Roman Amphorae*, Oxford

Casey, P. J. and Reece, R. (eds) (1974), *Coins and the Archaeologist*, Oxford
Casson, L. (1970), *Ships and Seamanship in the Ancient World*, Princeton
Chevallier, R. (1976), *Roman Roads*, London
Cleere, H. F., and Taylor, J. du Plat (eds) (1978), *Roman Shipping and Trade*, London
D'Arms, J. H. (1981), *Commerce and Social Standing in Ancient Rome*, Cambridge, Mass.
Davies, O. (1935), *Roman Mines in Europe*, Oxford
Duncan-Jones, R. (1974), *The Economy of the Roman Empire*, Cambridge
Finley, M. I. (1973), *The Ancient Economy*, London
Garnsey, P. D. A., Hopkins, K. and Whittaker, C. R. (1983), *Trade in the Ancient Economy*, London
Healey, J. F. (1978), *Mining and Metallurgy in the Greek and Roman World*, London
Jones, A. H. M. (1974), *The Roman Economy*, Oxford
Kent, J. P. C. (1978), *Roman Coins*, London
Landels, J. G. (1978), *Engineering in the Ancient World*, London
Loane, H. (1938), *Industry and Commerce of the City of Rome*, Baltimore
McWhirr, A. D. (1979), *Roman Brick and Tile: studies in manufacture and distribution in the Western Empire*, Oxford
Meiggs, R. (1982), *Trees and Timber in the Ancient Mediterranean World*, Oxford
Millar, F. (1967), *The Roman Empire and its Neighbours*, London
Milne, G. and Hobley, B. (eds) (1981), *Waterfront Archaeology in Britain and Northern Europe*, London
Peacock, D. P. S. (1977), *Pottery and Early Commerce*, London
Strong, D. E. and Brown, P. D. C. (eds) (1976), *Roman Crafts*, London
Sutherland, C. H. V. (1937), *Coinage and Currency in Roman Britain*, Oxford

Chapter IX

Chadwick, H. (1967), *The Early Church*, London
Ferguson, J. (1970), *The Religions of the Roman Empire*, London
Ferguson, J. (1980), *Greek and Roman Religion: A Source-Book*, Park Ridge
Grant, R. M. (1978), *Early Christianity and Society*, London
Green, M. J. (1983), *The Gods of Roman Britain*, Aylesbury
Jones, R. F. J. (forthcoming), *Burial and Society in the Roman West*, London
McMullen, R. (1981), *Paganism in the Roman Empire*, Yale
Ogilvie, R. M. (1969), *The Romans and their Gods*, London
Palmer, R. E. A. (1954), *Roman Religion and Roman Empire*, Philadelphia
Reece, R. (ed.) (1977), *Burial in the Roman World*, London
Ross, A. (1967), *Pagan Celtic Britain*, London
Sweet, L. M. (1919), *Roman Emperor Worship*, Boston
Toynbee, J. M. C. (1971), *Death and Burial in the Roman World*, London

Chapter X

Casson, S. (1926), *Macedonia, Thrace and Illyria*, Oxford
Casson, S. (1937), *Ancient Cyprus*, London
Jones, A. H. M. (1971), *The Cities of the Eastern Roman Provinces*, Oxford
Larsen, J. A. O. (1968), *Greek Federal States*, Oxford
Lesquier, J. (1918), *L'Armée romaine d'Égypt d'Auguste à Dioclétien*, Cairo
Levick, B. (1969), *Roman Colonies in Southern Asia Minor*, Oxford
Magie, D. (1950), *Roman Rule in Asia Minor*, Princeton
Miller, J. I. (1969), *The Spice Trade of the Roman Empire, 29 BC to AD 641*, Oxford
Milne, J. G. (1924), *History of Egypt under Roman Rule*, London
Sherk, R. K. (1951), *The Legates of Galatia*, Baltimore
Stark, F. (1966), *Rome on the Euphrates: the story of a frontier*, London

Chapter XI

Alföldy, G. (1974), *Noricum*, London
Brogan, O. (1953), *Roman Gaul*, London
Broughton, T. R. S. (1929), *The Romanisation of Africa Proconsularis*, Baltimore
Carcopino, J. (1947), *Le Maroc antique*, Paris
Casson, S. (1926), *Macedonia, Thrace and Illyria*, Oxford
Daicoviciu, C. (1938), *La Transylvanie dans l'antiquité*, Bucharest
Drinkwater, J. F. (1983), *Roman Gaul*, London
Fentress, E. W. B. (1979), *Numidia and the Roman Army*, Oxford
Finley, M. I. (1968), *Ancient Sicily*, London
Freeman, E. A. (1890–4), *History of Sicily, I–IV*, Oxford
Frere, S. S. (1978), *Britannia*, London
Guido, M. (1963), *Sardinia*, London
Hatt, J. J. (1967), *Histoire de la Gaule romaine*, Paris
MacKendrick, P. (1975), *The Dacian Stones Speak*, North Carolina
Mócsy, A. (1974), *Pannonia and Upper Moesia*, London
Picard, G. C. (1959), *La civilization de l'Afrique romaine*, Paris
Rüger, C. B. (1968), *Germania Inferior*, Köln
Salmon, E. T. (1982), *The Making of Roman Italy*, London
Salway, P. (1981), *Roman Britain*, Oxford
Stähelin, F. (1948), *Die Schweiz in römischer Zeit*, Basel
Stein, E. (1932), *Deutschland unter dem Prinzipat*, Vienna
Sutherland, C. H. V. (1939), *The Romans in Spain, 217 BC – AD 117*, London
Thomsen, R. (1947), *The Italic Regions from Augustus to the Lombard Invasions*, Copenhagen
Wacher, J. S. (1986), *Roman Britain*, London

Wightman, E. M. (1970), *Roman Trier and the Treveri*, London
Wightman, E. M. (1985), *Gallia Belgica*, London
Wilkes, J. J. (1969), *Dalmatia*, London
Wiseman, F. J. (1956), *Roman Spain*, London

Chapters XII – XIII

See bibliographies for Chapters II – IV.

Chapter XIV

Bury, J. B. (1928), *The Invasion of Europe by the Barbarians*, London
Cunliffe, B. W. (1975), *Rome and the Barbarians*, London
Thompson, E. A. (1948), *A History of Attila and the Huns*, Oxford
Thompson, E. A. (1965), *The Early Germans*, Oxford
Thompson, E. A. (1966), *The Visigoths in the time of Ulfila*, Oxford
Thompson, E. A. (1969), *The Goths in Spain*, Oxford
Todd, M. (1972), *Everyday life of the Barbarians: Goths, Franks and Vandals*, London
Todd, M. (1975), *The Northern Barbarians, 100 BC – AD 300*, London

INDEX

Aalen, 74, 225
Acarnania, 208
Achaea, 200, 208–9, 216
Achaemenids, 41
Actium, battle of, 12, 17, 207–8, 237
Adamklissi (Tropaeum Traiani), 30
Aden, 19, 212
Ad Maiores, 70, 124
Adrianople, 46, 49, 246–7
Aebutius Faustus, L., 101
Aedui, 23, 25, 92, 94, 223
Aelius Gallus, 19
Aemilianus, 242
Aemilius Lepidus, M., 1, 12, 236
Aequi, 4–5
Aethiopia see Ethiopia
Aetius, 248
Aetolia, 208
Africa, 219–20
  Africa Nova, 219
  Africa Proconsularis, 140–1,
    219–20, 234, 241, 252, 267
  Africa Vetus, 219
  agriculture & villas, 127–9, 132,
    137–8, 140–2, 147, 149–50
  cities & towns, 107, 119
  civil wars, role in, 237, 241, 243, 247
  defence & frontiers, 18–19, 22–4,

32, 41, 43, 47, 57, 59, 65, 70–2,
  77, 80, 257, 267–8
  diocese of, 252
  government of, 85, 88
  industry & trade, 155–6, 161, 164,
    166, 173, 175
  Proconsularis Zeugitana, 252
  religion & burial, 185–6, 194, 197
  republican period, 8–9, 11
African continent, trade with, 174–5
Agricola see Julius Agricola
Agri Decumates, 28, 44, 228, 266
Agrippa see Vipsanius Agrippa
Aïn Wif (Thenadassa), 125
alae:
  1 dromedarii milliaria, 149
  II Flavia, 74, 225
  V Praelectorum, Dionisiada, 258
Alamanni, 40, 42–3, 45–6, 48–9,
  77–8, 243, 264–8
Alans, 49, 51, 124, 263–4, 267–8
Alaric, 51–2, 174, 268
Albing, 76, 224
Alcantara, 155
Aldwinkle, 155
Aleria, 216
Alésia, 187, 223
Alexander the Great, 103, 200–1

297